Skånska spår – arkeologi längs Västkustbanan

# Making place *in the* landscape

Early and Middle Neolithic societies in two west Scanian valleys

Magnus Andersson

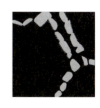

National Heritage Board, Sweden

**National Heritage Board**
**Archaeological Excavations Department**
UV Syd
Åkergränden 8, 226 60 Lund, Sweden
Phone        +46-46-32 95 00
Fax           +46-46-32 95 39
Internet      www.raa.se
E-mail        uvsyd@raa.se


Skånska spår – arkeologi längs Västkustbanan
Making place in the landscape

Translation    Alan Crozier
Design         Staffan Hyll, Anna Åström
Layout         Anna Åström
Maps           Magnus Andersson
Paper          Inside   Eurobulk 115 g
               Cover   Elektra Butten
Print          Elanders Berlings, Malmö, Sweden, 2004
Copyright      © 2004 Riksantikvarieämbetet
               1:1
ISSN           1650-2787
ISBN           91-7209-328-5

Making place *in the* landscape

THE ARCHAEOLOGICAL EXCAVATIONS preceding the expansion of the West Coast railway line in Skåne were on a very large scale. The line between Landskrona and Kävlinge mainly ran through the valleys of the Saxån and Välabäcken. The railway thus cut through an area that has known human settlement since ancient times, with countless archaeological remains, particularly from the Neolithic: the excavations uncovered dwelling sites, graves, votive sites, and a central place. Some of the results have previously been presented in Swedish in the book I det Neolitiska rummet, which is part of the series "Skånska spår - arkeologi längs Västkustbanan". The present volume is the second of three books dealing with the excavations in the part of the project known as "Neolithic Space".

However interesting an individual excavation may seem, a site only acquires meaning when it is considered in a broader spatial and chronological perspective. This is perfectly clear from this book, where Magnus Andersson examines the Early and Middle Neolithic societies around the rivers Löddeån/Kävlingeån and Saxån/Välabäcken. This small piece of land is one of the richest Neolithic areas in Sweden. Earlier research in the area has only looked at individual types of antiquities and categories of finds. Magnus Andersson's work, in contrast, means that this core area is regarded for the first time from a holistic perspective, combining modern theories with a meticulous empirical approach. The detailed studies of dwelling sites, votive sites, graves, and places of assembly give us a significant new factual base and – not least of all – an increased understanding of how a Neolithic local community emerged, how it was organized, and how it changed. The results of the excavations of the large and complex Neolithic remains by the West Coast Line Project are the cornerstones of this synthesis, which will probably be significant for Neolithic research in other parts of northern Europe as well.

Lund, October 2003
Mac Svensson
National Heritage Board,
Southern Excavations Department

THE CONSTRUCTION OF THE WEST COAST LINE, from Helsingborg via Landskrona to Kävlinge, has been a successful project. The new line will function as a quick and safe route between Scandinavia and the European continent.

The project has had a distinctive dimension in the shape of the many archaeological excavations carried out in collaboration with the National Heritage Board. We have stood with one foot in the future and the other in the distant past. By means of exhibitions of the archaeological finds, we have been able to give the local people a chance to find out more about their history, while we have simultaneously used advanced technological expertise to built environment-friendly means of transport for the future.

Today's railway navvies have laid their rails over the ancestors in this district. Yet they have done so with respect for the knowledge of the past that the National Heritage Board staff have been able to communicate to us through excavations and archaeological finds.

This is something that gives us at the National Rail Administration both pride and pleasure. We hope that we shall meet the future with greater respect and more knowledge about our shared history.

Caroline Ullman Hammer
Manager, Southern Rail Region
National Rail Administration

# Contents

*The pillars of Nature's temple are alive*

*and sometimes yield perplexing messages:*

*forests of symbols between us and the shrine*

*remark our passage with accustomed eyes.*

C. Baudelaire 1857

# Introduction

This archaeological study attempts to understand the emergence, organization, and transformation of Neolithic societies in the river valleys of western Skåne in southernmost Sweden. Several excavations and surveys have shown that the area has extensive remains of Neolithic activities – in the form of settlements, graves, wetland deposits, and special assembly places – ranging in time from the earliest to the latest phase of the Funnel Beaker culture and the Battle Axe culture. These categories are parts of a greater whole which, taken together, elucidates the social, economic, and spiritual conceptions of the local Neolithic communities.

For south-west Skåne (Scania), the new millennium has seen large-scale expansion in construction activity. The building of railways, bridges, and roads, together with the construction of new housing and industrial estates, has changed the face of the landscape at an increasing speed. In the area south of Malmö where I spent my childhood, the landscape has been transformed almost beyond recognition in less than a decade. Landmarks large and small have changed a once familiar setting into something new and, for me, alien. My old school, with all its new buildings, is now spread over the arable fields and the marl pit that used to be the scene of secret meetings; on the countless vacant plots that were once the very best playgrounds, luxurious villas have been built; and what for us was then the "eternally wild" neck of clay called Lernacken has been transformed into a bridge abutment which once again, in a physical sense, links Skåne in Sweden with Sjælland in Denmark. The changeable landscape in my immediate surroundings, and the absence of familiar monuments and symbols from my childhood, has made me palpably aware of the significance of the social landscape. Personal memories are closely connected to the landscape, and well-known places are linked to bygone events and relations. When these frequently visited places were transformed, part of my childhood history ceased to exist.

In recent years, archaeological studies of man and his surroundings have increasingly focused on the idea that the landscape should be regarded as a social and semantic construction and that its meaning changes over time and place. It has been noticed that landscapes are shaped by the work of earlier generations, and the way people perceive their surroundings is therefore dependent in large measure on the special conditions prevailing at a certain point of time in a particular area. Today's Scanian landscape does not have very much in common with the landscape that existed just 200 years ago – and even less with what existed 5,000 years ago. There are few areas today that are not cultivated or built on; mechanized agriculture has levelled out small bumps in the terrain, and the majority of the former wetlands have been drained. Not least important is the dramatic change in the soundscape since the triumph of industrialism. Few places are not affected by the noises of modern society. Silence is rare in our world. The accelerating metamorphosis of the world around us has not just affected our perception of space; technological development also means that concepts of time have taken on a different meaning.

The intention behind the infrastructure investments of recent decades has been to improve communications, with a well-functioning network of roads and railways offering a free choice of types of transport. The investments in western Skåne, with the West Coast Line, the Outer Ring around Malmö, and the Öresund Fixed Link, are an important part of the national and international communication network. Regions are linked together and the physical distance between people is reduced. The aim is that we should be able to move as quickly as possible between two places. At the same time, our perception of the landscape is reduced to blurred images flashing past us without giving us time to register any details. We lose the sense of the road, that is, the social and physical connections between places, which can give us an understanding of the localization of various phenomena. Distances that in pre-industrial society could take weeks to cover with the means of transport available then, can today be travelled in just a few hours. The relationship between great distance in space and great distance in time is no longer self-evident. This is accentuated even more by the emergence

N

Häljarp
Teckomatorp
Marieholm
Saxån
Dösjebro
Välabäcken
Kävlinge
Kävlingeån
Måre bäck
Löddeköpinge
Furulund
Igelösa
Barsebäck
Lödde å
Flädie

0 1 2 3 4 5 6 7 8 9 10 kilometres

of the IT society, with information about events on the other side of the globe reaching us virtually instantaneously. The effects of this globalization are scarcely possible for us to survey today. In the modern world that emerged during the nineteenth century there were clear divisions between different spheres of society, with distinctly demarcated political, economic and social spheres. This was also the period when the social sciences were split up. The most distinctive feature of the society of which we see the contours today is instead the dissolution of boundaries between countries, cultures, economies, and political systems. In this respect we may soon be reaching a stage where – perhaps as in prehistoric times – there is no clear distinction between economic, social, and religious categories.

Recent years' interventions in the landscape have simultaneously given us archaeologists the opportunity to document formerly unknown parts of our prehistory. The Southern Excavations Department (UV-Syd) of the National Heritage Board (Riksantikvarieämbetet, RAÄ) was given the task of managing the excavations in connection with the construction of the new West Coast Line by the National Rail Administration. In several cases the railway line was given a completely new course, which involved a change in the immediate environment for many people in western Skåne. There was sometimes heated debate about the most suitable route for the new line. Regard had to be paid not only to cultural history and the natural environment but also to purely personal interests. In accordance with the provisions of the Act concerning Ancient Monuments and Finds, the overall aim is to preserve ancient remains. Only if they constitute an obstacle or a nuisance that is not in reasonable proportion to the importance of the remains may they be removed. In connection with the expansion of the West Coast Line it was considered necessary to remove the archaeological remains, and excavations were therefore ordered. I was attached to the

project in connection with the preliminary archaeological inquiries started in autumn 1995, and I was given responsibility for the part of the line just north and south of Glumslöv. It was this in this magnificent hummocky landscape that my interest in the relationship between man and his landscape seriously began. The visible antiquities that set their stamp on this landscape today, in the form of burial mounds and megalithic tombs, were supplemented during our investigations with formerly concealed remains of dwelling sites and special ceremonial places such as the area of hearths north of Glumslöv (Andersson, M. 1996). Here I gained a glimpse of the link between different places that must have existed for prehistoric people, and how, through more or less conscious choices, and based on their experiences, they organized and divided up the landscape, with each activity being given its specific place. This impression followed me over the subsequent years when I had the opportunity to take part in the large-scale excavations of various Stone Age sites in the valleys of the Saxån and Välabäcken. Several of the places covered by our investigations were unusually well preserved – by comparison with the diffuse remains that often characterize Stone Age dwelling sites – and of varying character. Along the planned course of the railway line through the valleys, we excavated sites that can be said to correspond to different aspects of Neolithic society, such as settlements, graves, a palisaded enclosure, and finds in wetland contexts. As a participant in the subproject "Neolithic Space", I had the opportunity to conduct a study of the organization of Early and Middle Neolithic settlement and society in these valleys, based on the archaeological material from the West Coast Line excavations. Earlier studies have shown that there is a concentration of megalithic tombs, Neolithic settlement remains, and wetland deposits in the area around the valleys of the Saxån and Välabäcken and in the valley to the south with the rivers Lödde Å and Kävlingeån (Hårdh 1982, 1990b; Karsten 1994). It therefore felt natural to let the study comprise that valley as well (fig. 1).

13

◀ Fig. 1. Map of the investigation area.

One of the purposes of the investigations should of course have been to recreate prehistoric settings. The view stated above that man's relationship to the changing landscape is specific to each time and place should make us aware of the difficulty of this task. How people act in each particular situation depends on the prevailing culture-historical context. Our way of life and our perception of the west Scanian landscape thus differ significantly from how people in the Neolithic perceived and moved in the same area. Just as what is interpreted was once part of a specific context of meaning, we who make the interpretations are also shaped by the values of our own times. Although it cannot be regarded as a deliberate strategy, every interpretation is steered by the underlying norms that constitute the foundation for our perception of man and society. The past and the present are mutually related to each other. Contemporary values steer the questions we ask about the past, our choice of study object, and the process of interpretation, but the finds we turn up can in certain cases be used to criticize, challenge, or legitimate the prevailing conditions, and – of course – stimulate us to formulate new problems.

What, then, can we say about prehistory? Although we are steered in our interpretation by our various backgrounds, it is our life experiences as humans that enables us to understand other people's life experiences – even if they happened in prehistoric times. The material remains in the valley landscape of the rivers Saxån-Välabäcken and Lödde Å-Kävlingeån exist in time and place in a relationship to other archaeological remains. Through a study focusing on the local and specific culture-historical context, where the different mutual relationships of the remains are made clear, I believe that one can come closer to an understanding of prehistoric activities. It should be a crucial advantage that I spent a long time in this landscape in connection with the excavations and thereby developed a feeling for it. The results that can be achieved are of course not absolute truth,

just interpretations, and it is therefore important to state one's premisses. A scholarly interpretation of the historical and social contexts requires a presentation of the scholar's source material and scientific outlook. In this way the interpretation process can be followed and it can be permitted to put forward alternative explanations of the same material. This means that there can in fact be several competing pasts which are dependent on contemporary social and ideological values. Probably one of the most important tasks of the humanistic disciplines is to study past cultures and thereby perhaps contribute to an increased understanding of the distinctive features of our own culture. The fact that our different backgrounds and varied source material lead to a large number of suggested interpretations illuminates the importance of understanding cultural diversity. Several diverging theories about our prehistory are a confirmation of divergent conceptions in our own time – and in bygone times. Objective long-term studies of man and his conceptual world are valuable precisely for the aim of understanding the different expressions that human activity can take.

## Aim and outline

The overall aim of my work is to study the emergence, organization, and change of the Early and Middle Neolithic societies in the valleys of the Saxån-Välabäcken and Lödde Å-Kävlingeån in western Skåne. Several excavations and surveys have shown that the area has extensive remains of Neolithic activities – in the form of settlements, graves, wetland deposits, and special assembly places – ranging in time from the earliest to the latest phase of the Funnel Beaker culture and the Battle Axe culture. These categories are parts of a greater whole which, taken together, elucidates the social, economic, and spiritual conceptions of the local Neolithic communities.

The investigation will be conducted on three different spatial levels:

- How did the people organize their activities in the different places?
- How were the different categories of place related to each other? Can man's perception and use of the landscape be understood through the function and meaning of the places and through their topographical location and spatial relations? By studying the arrangements at different Neolithic places in the investigation area and their distribution in the landscape, the aim is to understand the form of social organization. Previous ethnographical research has often drawn attention to the ordering of spatial patterns in settlement and in the landscape according to rules that reflect the social organization (Whittle 1996). How and why did spatial perception change over time, and how can this be related to the organization of society?
- What similarities and differences can be discerned in the organization of settlement and society *vis-à-vis* other well-investigated Scanian and Danish areas?

In my study I have been greatly assisted by the work of my colleagues on the West Coast Line Project "Neolithic Space". Their results concerning Neolithic houses, pottery, and votive finds, which have been published in a special collection of articles (Svensson 2003), have been important contributions to my conclusions.

A survey of research history with the focus on Skåne and Denmark is presented in chapter 2. I have considered it important to describe the background on which Neolithic research rests. Since my own argumentation is naturally based on previously presented results and hypotheses about Neolithic social organization, the reader should be offered the necessary basis on which to follow the reasoning. Here I also give a closer presentation of the topography and geography of the investigation area and previous archaeological research on the region. In chapter 3 there comes an account of the theoretical stances that I advocate in my endeavour to understand parts of our prehistory. The emphasis is on people's relationship to the landscape. A source-critical discussion of the representativeness of the archaeological material in the investigation area follows in the next chapter. It should be stressed that the intensity of investigation varies between different areas. The excavated sites with material and features that can be dated to the Early and Middle Neolithic in the investigation area is presented after this discussion. The major part of the book is chapter 5, in which I present my interpretation of the Early and Middle Neolithic societies around the Saxån–Välabäcken and Lödde Å-Kävlingeån on the basis of the archaeological evidence and my basic stance on theory of science. Since these societies are in no way isolated units, the region is placed in a broader geographical perspective in chapter 6. Finally, the threads are tied together and the findings are summed up. ▮▮

15

# History of research

*How people act in each particular situation depends on the prevailing culture-historical context. Our way of life and our perception of the west Scanian landscape thus differ significantly from how people in the Neolithic perceived and moved in the same area. Just as what is interpreted was once part of a specific context of meaning, we who make the interpretations are also shaped by the values of our own times. Although it cannot be regarded as a deliberate strategy, every interpretation is steered by the underlying norms that constitute the foundation for our perception of man and society. This means that there can in fact be several competing pasts which are dependent on contemporary social and ideological values.*

A study of Neolithic social organization presupposes insight into the history of research and a grasp of the various approaches and theories that have dominated research. The present account of Early and Middle Neolithic archaeology does not claim to be comprehensive, aiming only to describe the most important trends – mainly in the Danish and Scanian sphere. In the different chapters of the book I go into greater depth in connection with discussions of specific themes.

The great significance of the Funnel Beaker and Battle Axe cultures in north-west Europe is obvious from their extent in time and place. Material that can be linked to the Funnel Beaker culture has been found in large amounts from today's Netherlands in the west to Poland in the east, and from southern Scandinavia in the north to Bohemia and Moravia in the south (Midgley 1992:32). The Battle Axe culture or the Corded Ware culture are frequently used umbrella terms for the groups with related features that peopled a very large part of Europe, from its westernmost areas to the Black Sea region (Malmer 1962). Because of the large distribution area, the different research fields and interests, and the varied material, the cultures have rarely been studied as a unit. It is instead special regions or themes, such as megalithic tombs, pottery, or flint objects, that have been in focus.

During the Middle Neolithic there were three partly different material cultures in Skåne. Besides the Funnel Beaker culture and the Battle Axe culture, there is the Pitted Ware culture. Recent years' research has shown that these were presumably partly contemporaneous (Larsson, L. 1989b, 1992a). The Battle Axe culture occurs over virtually the whole of Skåne, with the centre of gravity in the core areas of the Funnel Beaker culture (Malmer 1962). The Pitted Ware culture is certainly represented in north-east Skåne.

Whether the north-west Scanian dwelling sites around Jonstorp should be regarded as belonging to the Pitted Ware culture, however, is problematic since they show similarities to material from the Funnel Beaker culture (Carlie 1986). In the investigation area flint craft showing features of Pitted Ware culture has been found at Stävie and elsewhere, together with pottery whose closest parallels are with MNA V/Valby in Denmark, which is traditionally regarded as belonging to the closing phase of the Funnel Beaker culture (Becker 1955; Davidsen 1978:10; Larsson, L. 1982).

Up to the mid-1970s, Neolithic research was dominated by two questions: the Neolithization process and Neolithic chronology. These problems are still being considered, but as a result of new theoretical approaches in archaeology in recent decades, other questions have also been raised.

## Typology and chronology

The earliest Neolithic research aimed, broadly speaking, at ordering the material, specifying the general features of development, and ascertaining the relationship between different cultures. Archaeology applied traditional empirical presentations of material, and the interpretations were dominated by attempts at objective observations rather than theoretical aspects. From the end of the nineteenth century onwards, researchers and museum workers built up increasingly detailed chronological networks. Evolutionistic links between ancient artefacts and chronologies were put forward, often with art-historical argumentation about the chronological development of stylistic groups. This approach assumed that a style arose and evolved towards perfection, which was then followed by retardation, after which the style ceased to exist. Typological series were worked out, in accordance with theories of stylistic evolution in art history, which was also considered to be chronological (Petersson 1999).

The scholar who polished the methodology of compiling types and combinations of objects, Oscar Montelius, also studied megalithic tombs and arranged them typologically. He divided the Neolithic into four periods – the pre-dolmen era, the dolmen era, the passage grave era, and the dagger or stone cist era (Montelius 1905). Sophus Müller was the one who made the first serious classification of the pottery from megalithic tombs. He divided Funnel Beaker pottery into nine styles and constructed a chronology on this basis. By the term "style" he meant a combination of ornamental techniques, patterns, and vessel forms. Müller's styles correspond to special stages in the development of a culture. He saw the emergence, flourishing, and decline of megalithic culture reflected in the development of pottery (Müller 1918). Müller's classification of ceramic styles was slightly revised by John Elof Forssander in connection with his publication of the material from the passage grave at Västra Hoby in western Skåne (Forssander 1936). A number of large settlement sites and passage graves were excavated from the mid-1920s until the mid-1940s, resulting in the elaboration of a Middle Neolithic chronology for the Funnel Beaker culture. The five large Danish settlement sites, Troldebjerg, Blandebjerg, Trelleborg, Bundsø, and Lindø, were considered to represent a chronological sequence (Mathiassen 1944). Therkel Mathiassen believed that his chronology was preferable to the old system which sought to date the often mixed finds in the megalithic tombs. In contrast, he thought that the settlement sites were homogeneous finds from relatively short occupations. The sites are all on the Danish islands, that is to say, in a relatively limited geographical area. Mathiassen was not sure whether the system was applicable to the whole of Denmark (Mathiassen 1944:97). The division of the Middle Neolithic into five phases on the basis of settlement site pottery is still the foundation for the chrono-

logical system that applies today, although it has been adjusted on various occasions. Carl Johan Becker argued that Blandebjerg and Trelleborg should belong to the same phase (Becker 1947). Axel Bagge and Lili Kaelas reached the same conclusion in their studies of material from Scanian megalithic tombs (Bagge & Kaelas 1950). The phases came to be numbered MNI (Troldebjerg), MNII (Blandebjerg/Trelleborg), MNIII (Bundsø), and MNIV (Lindø). The Klintebakke style was added to the system by Hakon Berg in 1951. He thought that the Klintebakke material represented an independent phase between Troldebjerg and Blandebjerg, calling the period MNIb. Berg suggested that the Klintebakke style coincided with the construction of the first passage graves and that the Troldebjerg phase went together with the earlier mortuary practice of dolmens (Berg 1951:16ff). In 1955 Becker supplemented the system with a fifth phase, MNV (Store Valby) (Becker 1955). To distinguish the Middle Neolithic cultures, the Funnel Beaker culture has been given the designation MNA and the Battle Axe culture MNB (Nielsen, P. O. 1979). This division is not without problems, however, since material which has traditionally been placed in MNB also occurs, in certain contexts, in the late Funnel Beaker culture. In addition, the Pitted Ware culture seems to exist during both the late MNA and MNB. It is above all the thick-butted flint axes of types A and B that are found in the same context. Type A has traditionally been assigned to the late Funnel Beaker culture, while type B seems to belong to the Battle Axe culture and the Pitted Ware culture (cf. Nielsen, P. O. 1979; Svensson 1986; Larsson, L. 1992a).

At the end of the 1940s there was a change to an approach that was to last until some time into the 1960s. A detailed study of the material on a firm empirical basis prevailed. Finer and more detailed typological classifications of earlier scholars' division into culture groups were developed. These were then used to create accurate chronologies. Archaeologists continued with their comprehensive and careful presentations of finds placed in their cultural context (Petersson 1999:31).

Becker's work, which was published in 1947, meant a breach with categorization on artistic grounds. According to Becker, chronologies could only be established on the basis of a homogeneous body of material in which chronological changes could be distinguished. Efforts to build chronologies through the morphology of the graves were far too crude, in his opinion, and the flint tools were only suitable for regional division. A true chronology could only be established through analyses of pottery. The view that increased stylistic variation was synonymous with chronological development survived in his division of the Early Neolithic. With the aid of pots found in bogs, Becker divided the Funnel Beaker culture into five phases, A–E. The first three phases (A, B, and C) correspond to the Early Neolithic while D and E represent two phases of the Middle Neolithic. Settlement sites and graves containing these types of pottery were also considered so that an all-embracing chronology could be achieved (Becker 1947).

In the 1970s several works were published in Denmark, chiefly by Karsten Davidsen and Klaus Ebbesen, which dealt with Middle Neolithic chronology based on ceramic analyses (Davidsen 1975, 1978; Ebbesen 1975, 1978, 1979). Davidsen based his studies on dwelling site pottery. He drew up a chronology (1975) for the clay discs of the Funnel Beaker culture, based on their ornamentation. In a later work (1978) he concentrated on pottery from the last phase of the Funnel Beaker culture (MNA V). Ebbesen worked with Middle Neolithic pottery from megalithic tombs. He presented a list of ornamental details in an endeavour to define styles and develop chronological systems. Both Davidsen and Ebbesen followed, by and large, Mathiassen's chronological schema, and [14]C dating was not used to any great extent.

Interest in landscape archaeology grew during the 1970s. One aim was to gain a broad view of the development of Neolithic society. The new studies also resulted in the elaboration of several new ceramic chronologies (Koch 1998). The following decade thus saw changes in Becker's Early Neolithic ceramic classification from 1947. This should be viewed as a revision of the existing classification rather than a new chronology. Since new studies show that the ceramic material consists of two types, the Early Neolithic has been divided for the sake of simplicity into two periods by means of [14]C datings: EN I (5100–4800 BP) and EN II (4800–4650 BP) (Larsson, M. 1988b; Liversage 1992). These have been divided into several regional groups, mainly through studies of ceramic decoration on rims. The Oxie group is an east Danish/Scanian group which is dated to Becker's period A or EN I. The Svaleklint group also has an eastern distribution and is compared with Becker's period B and EN I. A distinct western spread to Jutland is seen in the Volling group, which seems to have existed over a fairly long time. This group is compared with Becker's periods B and C and thus seems to occur in both EN I and II. Virum and Fuchsberg are later groups which are placed in EN II, with Fuchsberg being found chiefly in Jutland, whereas Virum has a broader distribution (Ebbesen & Mahler 1980; Andersen & Madsen 1978; Madsen & Petersen 1984). Mats Larsson's studies of the Early Neolithic in south and south-west Skåne have resulted in the distinction of four groups here: the Oxie, Svenstorp, Mossby, and Bellevue groups. The first three are considered partly contemporary and dated to EN I. The Mossby group is regarded as a south and east Danish local group with parallels on the island of Bornholm. The Bellevue group is later, placed in EN II. The Svenstorp group parallels the Svaleklint group in Sjælland. The Bellevue group is comparable with the Virum group in Sjælland and the Fuchsberg and Volling groups in Jutland (Larsson, M. 1984, 1992; Kihlstedt et al. 1997). The new classifications elaborated during the 1980s should possibly be regarded as locally or regionally distinctive groups which have been named after certain type sites. The view that style and material culture were expressions of social affiliation meant that the Early Neolithic became socially diverse. Some of the groups are more clearly geographically demarcated than others, and some of the styles lasted longer than others. In the investigation area, however, there are ceramic styles which can be placed in both the Oxie and the Svenstorp group on the same sites. Obviously, the two ceramic groups here cannot be considered to represent different population groups; instead the differences in ornamentation and vessel forms should perhaps be attributed to different functions and meanings of the pots (Lagergren-Olsson 2003).

19

The chronological divisions of the Early and the Middle Neolithic have their defects. They reduce the material at our disposal far too much. The chronology of the Middle Neolithic Funnel Beaker culture is inadequately defined. Only its latest phase, MNA V, has been studied thoroughly (Davidsen 1978; Larsson, L. 1982, 1985). The other phases of the Middle Neolithic have not been subject to any comparable modern revision. Despite the extensive typological studies in the twentieth century, then, there are still question marks. The Danish Middle Neolithic chronology, for example, cannot automatically be transferred to Skåne (Svensson 1998). It should also be stressed that the dividing line between the Early and Middle Neolithic is an artificial construction which cuts through a continuous development in the pottery and other material culture of the Funnel Beaker culture. The division is based on Montelius's early classification of grave forms. In a recent work, published in 1998, Eva Koch divides the Funnel Beaker culture into four phases: (1) a short transition period, (2) EN I, (3) EN II–MNA II, and (4) MNA III–V. Her typology is based on the shape and decoration of pots found in bogs. It differs in part from previous classifications, for example, in that the later part of the Early Neolithic is grouped together with the early part of the Middle Neolithic (Koch 1998).

One of the earlier general works dealing with the Battle Axe culture was published in 1933 by Forssander. Here he presented the first proper classification of the Swedish boat axes. Forssander based his studies on 160 Swedish graves, including secondary burials in megalithic tombs (Forssander 1933). In 1952 Andreas Oldeberg presented a refinement of Forssander's classification of battle axes (Oldeberg 1952). The present chronological division of the Swedish-Norwegian Battle Axe culture is largely based on Mats Malmer's works (1962, 1975). His analyses of the pottery resulted in a division into 14 groups and a total of 29 variants. His material came from 244 graves in Sweden, Norway, and Bornholm. Based on the pottery, he di-

vided the culture into six periods. Each of them begins with the introduction of pottery of types A, B, G, H, J, and C in Skåne-Blekinge. In a study of the Scanian Battle Axe culture, Christopher Tilley presents a classification of the pottery in which the form and decoration of the vessels serve as a foundation for a slightly different division from Malmer's. Tilley argues that Malmer's different ceramic groups overlap and that it is difficult to draw clear dividing lines between them. Using above all the position of the decorative elements on the pots, he claims that only a division into three periods is possible, as follows: (1) A, B, and D pots; (2) G and H pots; (3) J, K, L, O, and C pots (Tilley 1982a).

In Denmark the culture is called the Single Grave culture because of the mortuary practice. Scattered over Jutland, especially in the middle and western parts of the peninsula, there are hundreds of small barrows from this period. Müller investigated several of these barrows in the late nineteenth century. He noted that they contain inhumations and that they were used over a long period. The oldest burials were found lowest down, under the original ground level, known as under-graves. The slightly later graves were placed at a higher level, known as bottom graves. The latest graves were those placed in the filling of the grave, known as over-graves (Müller 1898). Later works have shown that there are great regional differences in Denmark. By dividing the archaeological source material into four categories of finds – grave finds, settlement site finds, hoards/votive finds, and unsystematic finds – Ebbesen concludes that three different areas with different traditions crystallized during the early Single Grave culture: (1) north-east Jutland and the northernmost parts of the islands where the influence of the Pitted Ware culture made itself felt; (2) north Jutland, east Jutland, and the islands, where dolmens and passage graves were used to a large extent during the Single Grave culture as well, and where flint axes dominate as grave goods; (3) the classical areas of the Single Grave culture in central and western Jutland, where low barrows dominate, with battle axes and amber beads as the most common grave goods (Ebbesen 1986).

The Pitted Ware chronology is largely based on Becker's works. In western and southern Sweden the culture has mostly been defined on the basis of special key artefacts, which include the cylindrical blade core and blade arrowheads of types A, B, and C. The A-arrowhead has been considered to belong to the earliest part of the culture, while B and C belong to the later phases (Becker 1951, 1954, 1980; Malmer 1973).

# The organization of society

Explanatory models for the origin of the Funnel Beaker culture and the introduction of agriculture to southern Sweden were initially dominated by evolutionist and diffusionist perspectives. An evolutionist attitude was expressed in discussions concerning matters in the Funnel Beaker culture and its relation to the earlier Mesolithic cultures. The tendency was to describe the development from a "lower" (Mesolithic) to a "higher" (Neolithic) stage.

Few questions in archaeological research have seen such intensive debate as the problem of Neolithization in southern Scandinavia. Two fundamentally different opinions dominated the discussion during the 1950s and 1960s. Becker claimed that the farming population were immigrants from the south. The immigrants who introduced the A-beaker came from the east while those who brought the B-beaker with them arrived from the west. The bearers of the C-beaker were divided into a megalithic and a non-megalithic population group. The immigrants gradually replaced the Ertebølle population (Becker 1947). Jørgen Troels-Smith argued an opposite view. He believed that Neolithization arose locally through a change within the Ertebølle culture (Troels-Smith 1954).

Although some large settlement sites were excavated, it was mainly typological and chronological issued that were discussed. A change in archaeological research was nevertheless noticeable during the 1970s. The growing amount of chronological data and cultural complexity opened the way for new discussions. Under the influence of the "New Archaeology", whose supporters claimed that changes in society are chiefly the result of external influence, questions such as economy, population pressure, ecological adaptation, site-catchment analysis, and social organization became relevant. This affected the discussion about the transitions between the Mesolithic and the Neolithic and about societal development in the Early and Middle Neolithic.

The idea that it was immigrants who introduced agriculture was relegated to the background. Instead the focus was on changes in the environment inhabited by the Ertebølle population. Carsten Paludan-Møller (1978) believed that increased sedentism in the Ertebølle together with a plentiful supply of resources led to population growth. Marginal areas, less rich in resources, were now claimed, which forced an adaptation to agriculture. Marek Zvelebil and Peter Rowley-Conwy argued that the introduction of agriculture was the result of changes in climate (Rowley-Conwy 1983, 1984, 1985; Zvelebil & Rowley-Conwy 1984).

In the Late Mesolithic a decrease in the marine salt content is said to have had a negative effect on marine resources. The consequence was that the inhabitants were forced to change their subsistence strategies, and cultivation gradually became the predominant economic activity.

The new interest in economic and to some extent social processes in the 1970s and 1980 is noticeable in some of the major works dealing with the pattern of settlement and subsistence in different parts of southern Scandinavia. Influences were also derived from anthropological studies of historically known "primitive" societies. Discussions of social organization have tended to see a development from simpler to more complex societies (e.g. Service 1958, 1962; Sahlins 1968, 1972). The theories were applied to prehistoric societies, suggesting that population growth led to increased specialization and a more complex social structure.

Two regions in Skåne have been the subject of intensive studies, the areas around Malmö and Ystad. Mats Larsson (1984) applied site-catchment analysis to understand changes in the pattern of settlement during the Early Neolithic in south-west Skåne. The earliest Neolithic settlements (the Oxie and Svenstorp groups) were small, located on sandy heights in the hummocky landscape. The ecological variation there meant that different resources could be used. In the later part of the Early Neolithic (the Bellevue group), when the population is assumed to have increased, these areas were abandoned. Settlements became denser and more permanent, and they were concentrated in areas of till soils around Malmö. This may have meant that more permanent units arose, with the megalithic tombs marking territories. The dwelling sites were still relatively small, however.

The Ystad Project, which was an interdisciplinary venture, sought to study the cultural landscape in southern Skåne over 6,000 years. The aim was to investigate the relationship between man and the environment. The studies conducted in the Ystad area in

21

the 1980s paint a picture that agrees in large measure with conditions in the Malmö area, with small dwelling sites located on light, sandy soils. The dwelling sites are of family size, centred around the fixed institutions of the society – the megalithic tombs (Larsson, M. 1992; Larsson, L. 1992a). The studies conducted by the Hagestad Project in south-east Skåne likewise suggest that settlements, at least in the Early Neolithic, were small (Strömberg 1988a, 1988b, 1988c).

Development during the Middle Neolithic follows on that of the Early Neolithic, at least up to MNA III, when a structural change in seen in the Malmö area, with a seeming concentration of dwelling sites in a large, strategically located site in the Hindby area (Svensson 1986, 1993).

The results of studies conducted in various regions of Denmark partly resemble what has been found in Skåne. In Torsten Madsen's landscape-archaeological investigations in central Jutland he describes three phases in the development of the Funnel Beaker culture. The first phase (Volling) is characterized by small dwelling sites with seasonal hunting stations. The middle phase (Fuchsberg, MNA I and MNA II) saw the construction of the megalithic tombs (as territorial markers) and the enclosed central places. Dwelling sites, which were surrounded by temporary hunting stations, were slightly larger and more permanent than in the preceding phase. During this phase there was an increase in ceramic production, and pottery was an important component of ritual activities such as offerings at megalithic tombs and central places. The last phase (MNA III–V) consists of large and permanent dwelling sites where several different activities – hunting, fishing, cultivation – were combined (Madsen 1982, 1988). The opinion that the EN II/MNA I transition was a time of extensive ritual activity agrees with the findings of Ebbesen (1975). He believes that the large deposits of axes can be associated with the period when the megalithic tombs were built. The Middle Neolithic Funnel Beaker society, according to Ebbesen, was organized in a complex way. There were long-distance trading connections, with amber, pottery, and copper being important commodities. The society included specialized groups such as craftsmen and merchants. In his comprehensive study of Neolithic votive finds in Skåne, Per Karsten (1994) shows that the period EN II–MNA II was characterized by a higher frequency of votive deposits than the preceding period and the subsequent period. One explanation for the noticeable growth in votive finds could of course be a change in votive practices. The objects selected for sacrifice in other periods may have been of material which has not been preserved in the same way as flint. The votive finds from MNB are essentially a repetition of the votive practice of EN II–MNA II and thus seem to be based on similar beliefs (Karsten 1994). In the material from the islands south of Fyn, Jørgen Skaarup sees a distinct difference between EN and MN. The Early Neolithic is characterized by small dwelling sites. At the end of this period the megalithic tombs were built as territorial markers. At the transition to the Middle Neolithic the number of dwelling sites increases and they also become bigger. There are no longer any hunting stations. Fishing and hunting expeditions proceeded from the big dwelling sites. The hunting stations, however, return during MNA V (Skaarup 1985). Nils H. Andersen's excavations in the area around Sarup in south-west Fyn have shown a similar pattern. Several small settlements at the end of the Early Neolithic and the start of the Middle Neolithic seem to have been concentrated into a larger settlement on the Sarup peninsula in MNA II–IV. During MNA V there seem once again to be more settlements with specialized activities together with larger base settlements (Andersen 1997:116ff).

There have been few attempts to understand the internal organization of sites. Research has mainly been geared to describing the distribution of settlements in the landscape as elements of an overall economic system. One of few exceptions is Mac Svensson's study (1986) of the settlement at Hindby, where he can see in the material a division of the site into two parts.

In the problematization of how Neolithic society was organized, several scholars have taken the megalithic tombs as their starting point. Through the influence of New Archaeology and the processual tradition, general patterns and functional explanations prevailed for a long time. This made itself felt particularly in studies of the megalithic tombs, which were considered to reflect a special society. The interpretations put forward have mostly been connected with models of territory, power, and control of social relations (e.g. Fleming 1973; Renfrew 1973, 1976; Randsborg 1975; Hårdh 1982; Larsson, M. 1988b). Klavs Randsborg (1975) related the graves to population pressure. He believed that the areas where megalithic tombs occurred had a larger population, while the flat-earth grave was the predominant form of grave in more sparsely populated parts. The difference in mortuary practice was due to social relations and indicated a non-egalitarian society. Andrew Fleming (1973) argued that the grave had the function of confirming the leader's status in the following ways: (1) the grave was a forum for ceremonies emphasizing the social posi-

22

tion of a leader; (2) the grave marked a territory; (3) the grave had a position as an impressive monument. Colin Renfrew (1973, 1976) believed that the megalithic tombs, which were an expression of territorial consciousness, were built in a segmented and egalitarian society. This society was characterized by small groups consisting of not more than a few hundred people. The groups were of roughly the same size, and no group had supremacy over any other. They were not subordinate to any larger central power, instead functioning as independent economic and political units. In small-scale societies, belonging to a group is defined by kinship, which can nevertheless indicate a clear territorial behaviour. The spread of megalithic tombs as territorial markers, according to Renfrew, can be explained by social stress provoked by population growth.

The interpretations described above are valuable, but through the concentration on describing settlement site patterns and social conditions, scholars have sometimes overlooked the symbolic and ideological aspects of society. In the 1980s and 1990s, through the influence of the postprocessual school, there was a noticeable tendency to an increased interest in more ideological and critical social angles and a toning down of scientific problems. Archaeologists used a contextual approach to try to study all parts of the society in order to understand its structure and organization. Ian Hodder (1990) tried to integrate and elucidate both the practical and the symbolic function of the society in a new way. He argued that there was cultural continuity over a large area and for a longer time when the first Neolithic monuments were erected. Rather than being the result of diffusion, this is due to the principles behind the construction of houses, graves, and central places. Economic transformations are connected with, or preceded by, a social and symbolic change. For hunter-gatherers the home was a secure point in life. The home (*domus*) was the safe world in relation to the untamed and wild nature (*agrios*). The idea of the safe *domus* led to a desire to tame the wild *agrios*. The structural preconditions thus existed for domesticating and farming the soil. The surplus production thereby generated meant that larger units were formed, which meant that more labour- and time-consuming projects could be implemented. The control of the wild (*agrios*) led to control of the relationship between individuals in society, and certain dominant interest groups were favoured. To be able to maintain the symbolic power of the *domus* principle required more communal projects to be undertaken (Hodder 1990).

In a survey concerning the Early and the Middle Neolithic in southern Scandinavia, Christopher Tilley applies a post-processual approach. He makes no distinction between the functional on one hand and the symbolic and stylistic on the other hand. Animals and cereals are not primarily food and secondarily of symbolic meaning; they are both simultaneously. He supports those who believe that cultivation originated in social and ideological considerations (cf. Jennbert 1984a; Thomas 1991), with grain and domesticated animals being used for ritual ceremonies. A system of ownership emerged whereby grain and cattle were produced and exchanged. This led to greater competition between groups and the growth of social differentiation. Monuments, pottery, and axes were intimately associated in these strategies between rival groups. They were not just purposeful objects, but components in a symbolic system with a meaning beyond their functional value (Tilley 1996). In his dissertation Pär Nordquist deals with the problem of power structures and the emergence of social inequality from the perspective of historical materialism. He says that the earliest phase of the Early Neolithic in southern Sweden was characterized by a low degree of social integration, as is evident from the limited deposition of offerings and the absence of monumental graves. The coming of single farms may to a certain extent have meant the origin of private property. Some households achieved greater success in their economic production, which may have been associated with their being particularly favoured in the sacral sphere. A hereditary élite therefore grew up gradually, institutionalizing and marking its power visually through megalithic tombs. Nordquist further claims that the strategy of the social élite, to achieve a higher degree of real integration and economic control by their ideologically manifest megaliths, was partially unsuccessful in Skåne. The system of single farms during the Funnel Beaker culture shows, in his opinion, that an ideology of the autonomy of the household seems to have continued to be reproduced in the course of the megalithic

24

phase. This structural and ideological opposition, finally, led to the dissolution of the Funnel Beaker culture and the rise of the Battle Axe culture with its social system geared to prestige and competition without hereditary ranking (Nordquist 2001). Nordquist's reasoning falters slightly, since he ignores that, during MNA III in Skåne, there seem to have been larger settlements where several farm units may very well have coexisted, as at the Hindby site in Malmö and the Dagstorp settlement in the Välabäcken valley.

A controversial topic in south Scandinavian Neolithic archaeology is the relationship between the three material cultures: the Funnel Beaker culture, the Battle Axe culture, and the Pitted Ware culture. These relations have been interpreted in both chronological and economic and/or social terms. The earliest research was dominated by diffusionist interpretations concerning the origin of the Battle Axe culture. The new elements in Middle Neolithic material culture were explained as being solely a consequence of immigrations (e.g. Müller 1898; Almgren 1914, 1919; Rydbeck 1930; Forssander 1933; Glob 1944). Linguistic hypotheses formed a basis for theories about the expansion of the Indo-European peoples gradually penetrating southern Scandinavia. The new population was thought to have lived side by side with the old Funnel Beaker culture until the two populations gradually blended. $^{14}$C datings have shown, however, that the Battle Axe culture more likely followed the Funnel Beaker culture, perhaps with a brief period of coexistence (Tauber 1986).

The few and small dwelling sites have sometimes been interpreted as showing that the Battle Axe population consisted of nomadic herders. Malmer, however, says that the Battle Axe culture in Skåne had the same relationship to the good soils as the Funnel Beaker culture and believes that this indicates similar economic strategies. He claims that the rise of the Battle Axe culture should rather be viewed as changes in socio-economic organization rather than in ethnic terms (Malmer 1962, 1975). In recent years, studies of dis-

tribution maps have changed the picture for southern Skåne slightly. $^{14}$C datings indicate that the Funnel Beaker culture existed parallel to the earliest phase of the Battle Axe culture. Lars Larsson (1989b) sees the spread of the Battle Axe culture in the form of a missionary movement representing a new ideology with powerful religious overtones. He argues that the supporters of the Battle Axe culture were initially forced to occupy marginal areas and later expanded into the core areas of the Funnel Beaker culture. The immigration hypothesis was raised once again at the start of the 1990s by Kristian Kristiansen (1991). His argument in favour of migration was based in part on the claim that it was a seemingly "fully developed" Battle Axe culture that appeared in southern Scandinavia, and that there are no clear indications of contacts between Battle Axe and Funnel Beaker populations in Denmark.

Of the Middle Neolithic cultures, the Pitted Ware culture has been most difficult to describe and define since the source material varies greatly between different regions. This is above all reflected in the forms of artefacts and the ceramic tradition, but the environmental and hence the ecological conditions differ between the different regions where the culture is represented (Carlie 1986). Research into the Pitted Ware culture has mainly been concerned with its origin and relation to the contemporary Middle Neolithic cultures. Since the Pitted Ware material differs so much between different parts of Scandinavia, it is doubtful whether the Pitted Ware culture should really be regarded as a unit over the large area in which it occurs. Perceptions of how the varied material should be interpreted have also diverged. One theory has claimed that the Pitted Ware people are groups who stuck to the Mesolithic way of life. They carried on the traditions of Ertebølle, Nøstvedt, and Fosna and developed them into a common Pitted Ware culture but with regional differences (Malmer 1969). Others have asserted that the origin of the Pitted Ware culture in southern Sweden may have taken place simultaneously with a general deterioration in the climate during the Middle Neolithic. This had consequences for the Funnel Beaker populations, who had hitherto based their economy on simple agriculture. As a result of the fall in temperature, they were forced increasingly to switch to a hunting economy. This explains why blade arrowheads are not uncommon as finds on Funnel Beaker sites. From this point of view, Pitted Ware sites should be regarded as the hunting stations of the Funnel Beaker culture (Nielsen, S. 1979). In the same way, some scholars think that the Pitted Ware settlements are the hunting stations of the Battle Axe culture. Similarities between the two material cultures, above all the pottery, have been highlighted. In addition, the blade arrowhead also occurs in the Battle Axe culture (Malmros 1980). Bozena Werbart, on the other hand, has demonstrated similarities with the eastern Combed Ware culture (Werbart 1999). As a consequence of the great variation shown by the Pitted Ware culture over large geographical areas, several scholars have also suggested that one should define a number of local groups (Bagge & Kjellmark 1939; Bagge 1951; Welinder 1973; Wyszomirska 1975; Nielsen, S. 1979; Edenmo et al. 1997). Stig Welinder would see the different types of Pitted Ware sites as an adaptation to the differing resources of the regions. He questions whether they should be regarded as a common culture when the only real similarity is that they have an economy based on hunting and fishing (Welinder 1973).

## The investigation area

Defining an archaeological region is always arbitrary, mostly proceeding from purely geographical factors. Since cultural phenomena operate within spatial areas whose size varies through time, these "phenomena" cannot be simply placed in a special unit or region. The Early and Middle Neolithic remains in the two valleys, the Saxån-Välabäcken and Lödde Å-Kävlingeån, represent just a small geographical area within the northern European complex of the Funnel Beaker and Battle Axe cultures.

The distribution of settlements, votive sites, and megalithic tombs nevertheless suggests that the valley landscape of western Skåne can be regarded as a Neolithic region which is appropriate for study. A frequently used distribution map shows five areas of megalithic tombs in Skåne (fig. 2) (Strömberg 1980; Tilley 1999a, Andersson 2004), as follows:

1. The valley landscape around the Saxån–Välabäcken and Lödde Å–Kävlingeån;
2. The Råån valley just south of Helsingborg;
3. The Segeån valley outside Malmö;
4. The Österlen area;
5. The lake system around Hammarsjön and Ivösjön with the Vramsån in north-east Skåne.

Through archival studies, the second survey, in the years 1985–87, has supplemented this picture of distribution with data on removed megalithic tombs and shown that they were spread along virtually the whole coastal region (Holmgren & Tronde 1990; Sandén 1995). Clear concentrations are noticeable, however, in the five areas stated above. The accumulated votive sites likewise display a geographical distribution concentrated in the coastal zone with its areas of megalithic tombs, with only a few examples in the interior (Karsten 1994). The survey of ancient monuments, together with the excavations of recent decades, has demonstrated that the area around the Saxån-Välabäcken and Lödde Å-Kävlingeån moreover contains a large number of Neolithic sites besides the megalithic tombs and votive finds.

Archaeological distribution maps, however, always involve problems of source criticism. The areas most thoroughly affected today by agriculture and housing have the largest number of remains of settlements and votive finds. It is naturally within these areas that most archaeological excavations have been conducted in connection with building, and it is here that most stray finds have been discovered during work with the earth. The absence of remains in the inland is thus in large measure due to the shortage of archaeological excavations in combination with the museums' scant interest, from the 1930s onwards, in these inland areas. On the other hand, today's distribution of megalithic tombs in Skåne is regarded as giving a representative picture of the prehistoric situation. Since development has been heaviest in the coastal regions, the absence of megalithic tombs in the inland is probably not due to their having been ploughed away.

Although archaeological distribution maps naturally are not always a complete reflection of prehistoric conditions, it cannot be denied that they are at least a partial reflection of the prehistoric situation.

### Topography

The geographical area included in my study comprises 29 parishes with a total area of about 320 km². It is bounded on the west by the Öresund strait, and the area then follows the system of ridges just over 20 kilometres inland to the east, towards the small towns of Marieholm and Igelösa. In north–south direction the area extends almost 20 kilometres, from Teckomatorp in the north to Flädie in the south (fig. 1).

Virtually all parts of the landscape of western Skåne today are either cultivated or built on. Human action has thus reshaped nature. The expansion of agriculture in recent centuries, for example, has levelled the ground and removed small irregularities from the terrain. It is thus not possible to undertake a full reconstruction of the prehistoric landscape of the valleys. Although palaeobotanical studies allow a partial

25

26

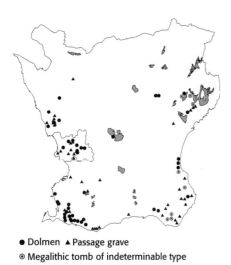

● Dolmen ▲ Passage grave
◉ Megalithic tomb of indeterminable type

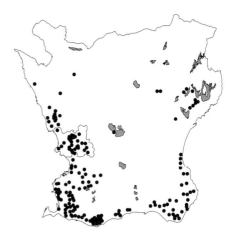

● Megalithic tomb (including possible megalithic tombs)
(Revised after Karsten 1994)

Fig. 2. The distribution of megalithic tombs and votive finds in Skåne.

reconstruction of vegetation, we cannot know exactly where trees and bushes stood in relation to the dwelling site. On the other hand, the rough outlines, such as cliffs, heights, valleys, and watercourses, are the same.

The powerful processes of the ice sheet have shaped the topography. The area, which is gently undulating, is broken up by only three major rises. In the north, between the Saxån and Välabäcken in Dagstorp parish, a section of elevated landscape extends from south-west to north-east, reaching a height of up to 65 m a.s.l. South of the Välabäcken are the hills of Karaby Backar, whose highest point is 50 m a.s.l. In the south-west of the investigation area, in Barsebäck parish, a hill rises steeply in the otherwise flat coastal landscape, reaching a height of 25 m a.s.l. The region can be described as framed by the areas of higher terrain to the far north-east and south-east (fig. 3).

In topographical terms the landscape is dominated by the valleys of the Saxån and Lödde Å-Kävlingeån. Between these larger rivers is a stream called the Välabäcken, which flows into the Saxån in its broad valley at Dösjebro. The course of the rivers has varied through the ages, and nutrient-rich alluvial deposits have grown at its banks. The Välabäcken today is a

stream measuring one or two metres across in a valley that is 200–300 metres wide. The Välabäcken valley is at a relatively high altitude in its eastern part, 25–30 m a.s.l., while it is about 10 m a.s.l. where it flows into the Saxån, which then falls evenly down towards the Öresund coast in the west. The Lödde Å-Kävlingeån runs east–west through the investigation area. The river is on average about 25 metres wide and the valley is roughly a kilometre wide. The valleys of the Välabäcken and Kävlingeån are linked by the broad, flat Dösjebro valley, which used to be a large, continuous area of wetland. Centrally located between the Kävlingeån and Välabäcken is a large plain which gives way in the west to Karaby Backar and is demarcated to the east by the Dösjebro valley. At Västra Hoby, just east of Kävlinge, there is a valley extending to the south, marking the course of a large river. Today only a small stream runs through the valley. After a kilometre or so, the valley swings towards the west-south-west and once again joins the Kävlingeån at Furulund (figs. 1 and 3).

Wetlands and watercourses had a much larger extent in prehistoric times than in today's modern cultural landscape. The reconnaissance map of Skåne, which

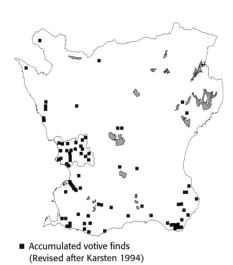

■ Accumulated votive finds
(Revised after Karsten 1994)

was drawn in 1812–1820 by the military field survey brigade with the aim of charting the terrain, probably gives a truer picture of the relations between firm ground and wetland during the Neolithic than the well-drained, fully tilled landscape that is Skåne today (fig. 4). This map shows that, in the last 200 years, almost 90% of all lakes, watercourses, and wetlands have been drained dry (Wolf 1956). We see from the map that extensive areas within the region were formerly wetlands. Studies in the area have shown that the sea level was two to three metres higher at the start of the Early Neolithic than it is today. At the end of the period the level rose further, and at the transition to the Middle Neolithic it reached a transgression maximum of almost five metres over today's level (Regnell, M., pers.com.).

## Soils

The investigation area is a mosaic of different soil types. Generally speaking, it may be observed that the land on the coastal strip mainly consists of sand or glaciofluvial sand, while the heavy clay soils tend to be further inland. The sandy soils, however, form wedges extending inland (fig. 5).

## Vegetation

Reconstructions of vegetation in the area are mainly based on pollen diagrams from the bog of Barsebäck Mosse (Digerfeldt 1975). The results there agree in large measure with analyses performed in other parts of Skåne. The general picture is that the proportion of elm pollen decreases at the start of the Subboreal. At the same time or slightly later, a tendency is observed for other stands of deciduous woods, such as oak, ash, and lime, to decline in favour of grass pollen. Many explanations have been suggested for the elm decline. Several scholars think that the most likely cause is changes in climate (Nilsson 1948; Iversen 1949; Göransson 1988; Whittle 1988). Others believe that the reduction in the stock of elm was due to human activity. The people in the farming communities supposedly cut off twigs and branches from elm trees to use the foliage as cattle fodder. This prevented the elms from flowering and producing pollen (Troels-Smith 1960). The most reasonable explanation, however, should be sought in elm disease. The chief support for this theory is that the elm decline took place at roughly the same time over a large geographical area. The increase in cereals and grass pollen can probably be attributed to human impact on the environment, which began in the Late Mesolithic (Friman 1996). In the final phase of the Early Neolithic and the start of the Middle Neolithic, the proportion of forest pollen in the diagrams increases once again; this is known as the regeneration phase (Berglund 1969, 1999). This need not necessarily reflect a reduction in the intensity of the agrarian economy; it could instead be the result of coppice woods growing up in the wake of forest clearance. Coppice woods are a type of vegetation that is suitable for animal husbandry, both as pasture and for harvesting foliage as fodder (Göransson 1996). In the latter part of the Middle Neolithic, the pollen diagrams once again suggest that larger areas than before were transformed into cultural landscape (Welinder 1998).

27

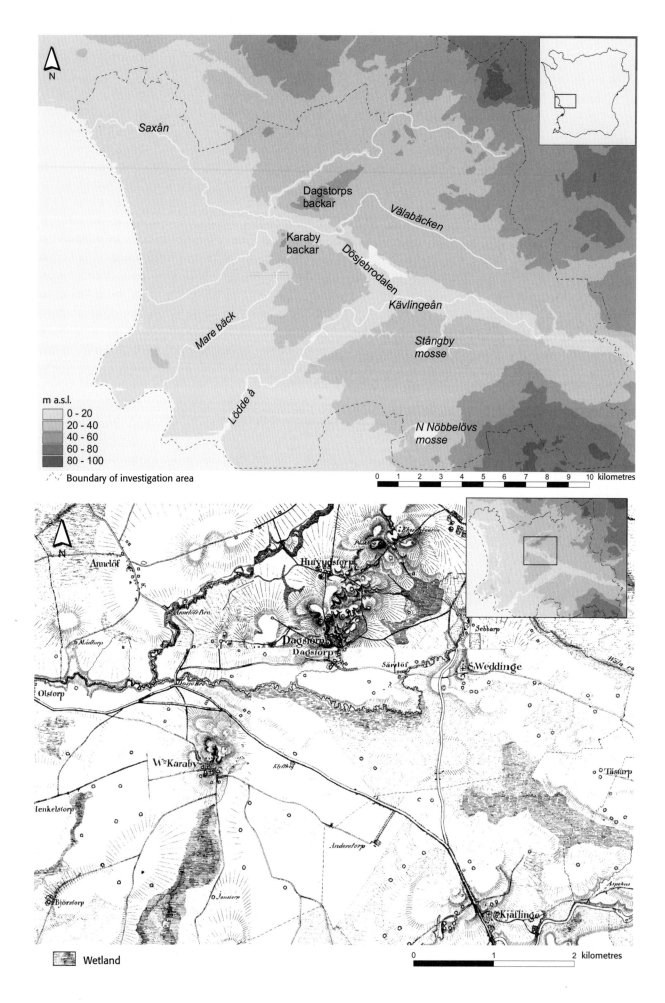

m a.s.l.

0 - 20
20 - 40
40 - 60
60 - 80
80 - 100

∕\/ Boundary of investigation area

Wetland

## History of research in the investigation area

A survey of previous research shows that the areas around the Saxån-Välabäcken and Lödde Å-Kävlingeån have seen several archaeological investigations. Knowledge of Neolithic settlement and its development here is still limited, however. There has been no synthesis of the region's Neolithic society comprising all the categories of remains, of the kind performed for the areas around Malmö, Ystad, and Hagestad in the south-west and south-east parts of the province (e.g. Strömberg 1971, 1988a, 1988b, 1988c, 1990; Larsson, M. 1984, 1985, 1992; Larsson, L. 1985, 1992a, 1998; Svensson 1986, 1991). One reason for this

could be that these valleys have not previously seen anything comparable to the large-scale rescue excavations conducted by Malmö Museums within their region in the last few decades. The results in south-west Skåne have since proved useful in research (Larsson, M. 1984, 1985). Nor has the area been the subject of any large interdisciplinary research projects like the Ystad Project which began at the start of the 1980s (Larsson, L. 1992a) or the Hagestad Project, which began back in the 1960s (Strömberg 1990). The work that has been done in the valleys of western Skåne has therefore been mainly geared to individual categories

29

◀ Fig. 3. Topographical map.
◀ Fig. 4. The Välabäcken valley according to the reconnaissance map of Skåne, 1812–1820.
▼Fig. 5. Soil map.

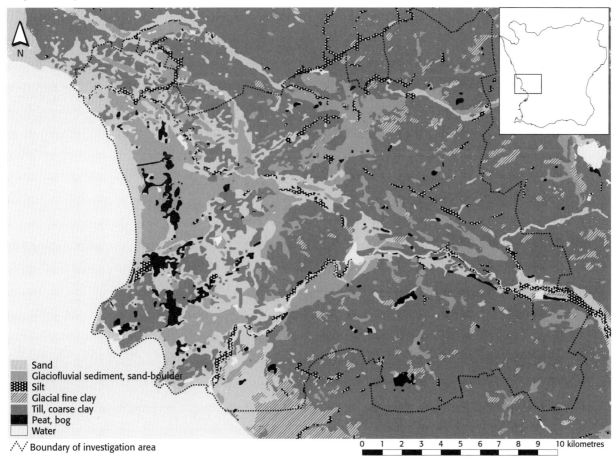

Sand
Glaciofluvial sediment, sand-boulder
Silt
Glacial fine clay
Till, coarse clay
Peat, bog
Water

Boundary of investigation area

0  1  2  3  4  5  6  7  8  9  10 kilometres

of remains; as a result there has never been any attempt at an all-round perspective.

Several of the megalithic tombs in the area have undergone excavation on various scales (Hansen 1919a, 1919b, 1923, 1926, 1930, 1931, 1932; Forssander 1930, 1936, 1937; Petré & Salomonsson 1967; Hårdh 1982, 1990a, 1990b). In some cases the amount of ceramic material from the excavated megalithic tombs is extensive. In the passage grave at Västra Hoby an estimated 50,000 potsherds were documented, and 30,000 sherds at Hög (Hansen 1932; Forssander 1936; Petré & Salomonsson 1967). It is the megalithic tombs and the material retrieved from them that have been the main focus of archaeological research in the area.

In the 1930s Forssander, as we have already seen, used the ceramic material at Västra Hoby to set up a typological sequence. He used the sherds found in the layers in front of the passage grave, where he was able to distinguish a horizontal stratigraphy. He thought that the layers with pottery could be the result of repeated clearances of the chamber. Based on this material, he discerned four different styles which combined several of Müller's previously defined ceramic styles. In the layer closest to the grave he observed earlier pottery with line and whipped cord decoration, while the later pottery, in the outer part of the area, was dominated by tooth-stamped decoration (Forssander 1936).

Based on the megalithic tombs, Birgitta Hårdh has studied the organization of society in the Middle Neolithic in the Lödde Å-Kävlingeån and Saxån-Välabäcken region. To ascertain contacts within the area and contacts with other regions in Skåne, she investigated the extensive corpus of pottery from excavations of megalithic tombs. Hårdh believes that the relatively free choice of patterns on the pottery, despite a certain fundamental norm, indicates that there was no central pottery manufacture; instead, production was locally based. The pottery deposited at the graves shows that they were used over a long time and that they served as a place of assembly for a small area. An examination of the size of the territories around each grave and a study of the natural environment provide the background to the pattern of contacts that can be discerned in the pottery. By dividing the area into territories, she shows that the megalithic tombs are evenly spread and the hypothetical territories were of roughly equal size. A site-catchment analysis demonstrates that the graves were related to a resource landscape along watercourses and on soils suitable for "primitive" agriculture. Hårdh thinks that the graves as territorial markers must have been fully visible from the settlement and the resource area that they were set up to mark (Hårdh 1982, 1986, 1990a, 1990b). It is above all, in accordance with the theoretical perspective of the time, a physical and economic landscape that is used and stressed in the study, without any specific social and ideological functions.

Within the investigation area, a number of Neolithic settlements have been excavated (see chapter 4). In most cases these have been rescue excavations, conducted under the auspices of the National Heritage Board's Southern Excavations Department, resulting in technical reports. The discussion has rarely been continued with specially focused questions. Up until the start of the 1990s, the basic tasks of a rescue excavation were primarily defined as documentation and fact collection. It was not until the second half of the decade that the excavating institutions formulated a clear strategy both for the production of knowledge and for making this knowledge visible (Säfvestad & Ersgård 1999). Moreover, settlement site excavations in Skåne in the 1970s and 1980s, in some cases with large areas stripped by machine, were above all geared to studies of the more distinct remains of earlier periods. In most excavations, the often diffuse occupation layers and features that usually characterize Stone Age settlement were ignored or given low priority.

Fig. 6. Passage grave in Södervidinge during excavation in 1919 (photo F. Hansen).

One of the exceptions, however, is the material from the Löddesborg site on the coast of the Öresund. Based on the material from here, Kristina Jennbert discusses in her dissertation questions about the origin of agriculture and animal husbandry. She sees on the site a continuous transition from the Ertebølle culture to the Early Neolithic Funnel Beaker culture. She considers the produce of agriculture and animal husbandry to have been luxury commodities, the real significance of which was in the social rather than the economic sphere. The population on the Öresund coast lived in favourable ecological circumstances and probably had no economic need to change their mode of production. Instead, cereals and livestock were important constituents in the exchange of goods and thus in the maintenance of contacts between groups (Jennbert 1984a, 1999).

The frequency and distribution of votive sites in the region, several of which were used repeatedly over a very long time, have been surveyed by Karsten in his study of Scanian Neolithic votive finds. The results show a striking concentration of votive sites in the landscape around Lödde Å-Kävlingeån and Saxån-Välabäcken (Karsten 1994). ▮

# Space, time, and social interaction

*The historical landscape must be read, interpreted, and perceived not just in terms of different patterns in space but also in the form of the temporal perspective. What links goal-directed human behaviour is not just the presence of special natural conditions but the existing network of cultural traditions and social memories which together make up the context within which people act (Thomas 1996, 1999a). The landscape is thus not just multifunctional but also multiperiodic. The Early and Middle Neolithic comprise a period of about 1,500 years, during which time people's perceptions of different places and the landscape changed. By following the development of society over a long period, we have a greater chance of understanding the interaction between the different parts of society.*

A society contains a number of different fields of knowledge – everything from tool production and ceramic craft to familiarity with legends and origin myths. Despite this, in studies of prehistoric societies, as the above survey of research has shown, it is usually the individual phenomenon, such as parts of the material culture, the settlements, or the graves that have been studied. Since the Neolithic in much of northwest Europe is associated with the construction of large monuments in the form of megalithic tombs, research in many places has focused on this phenomenon. In actual fact, however, grave monuments are just one aspect of society. In the Neolithic landscape there were many places with differing meanings and functions – settlements, graves, votive sites, and places of assembly – each of which represents a part of social life, but which together give a more complete picture of people's daily, seasonal, and annual activities. The places are closely linked and cannot be separated without losing the whole. Burials are best understood through their contextual relationship to contemporary settlements and votive sites. I therefore believe that it is difficult to obtain any idea of the organization of society solely by examining a part of a culture. In the present work I try to maintain a holistic perspective by dealing with categories of Early and Middle Neolithic places from both synchronic and diachronic perspectives. The places are parts of a system that acquires its meaning through mutual relationships in a social and historical perspective.

Conditions in the valleys of the Saxån-Välabäcken and Lödde Å-Kävlingeån are favourable in the sense that there is continuity in the area from the earliest Funnel Beaker culture into the Battle Axe culture, with the various components of Neolithic society – settlement, graves, votive sites, and places of assembly – represented in the archaeological material. I believe that these categories make up parts of a whole which together reveals the society's social, economic, and spiritual composition. The study consequently deals with the Early and the Middle Neolithic within a limited geographical zone during a period of time comprising about 1,500 years.

The two valleys and the surrounding area were thus used intensively in the Neolithic. The adoption of agriculture did not mean that people lived a stationary life in one place throughout the year. Neither houses, cultivation, nor animal husbandry tied people to just one place. Hunting, fishing, and collection were probably significant in varying degrees throughout the Neolithic and required movement in the landscape. In addition, other special ritual or social activities were performed in places which were not always attached to the actual settlement. The remains in the landscape should be regarded as the traces of different activities of differing intensity, meaning, and duration. These different traces in different places in the landscape may be regarded as signs to be brought together and read by archaeologists in order to give meaning to prehistory. How these signs are to be interpreted depends in large measure on the view of the landscape within the prevailing social organization. The form of the settlement is associated with the character of the landscape with its special natural formations – watercourses, valleys, heights, rocks, and vegetation.

I intend to consider three aspects in my study: space, time, and social interaction. Neither time nor space are regarded in this study as passive objects; they are profoundly involved in the shaping of social behaviour.

## Landscape

The relation between man and the surrounding land-scape has for a long time interested archaeologists and anthropologists. Research has usually focused on the ecological conditions, and the changing vegetation, fauna, and climate of the landscape has been reconstructed in this way. These parameters have then been related to demography, technology, and territoriality in the prehistoric society. This view has meant an understanding of how the external circumstances have affected people and the organization of society. Actions and activities were, however, conceptually and physically separated from the landscape, which was considered to be universal, with a cross-cultural influence on individuals and society. The advantage of this method is the possibility to make comparative studies of artefacts, settlement sites, and so on, and to study the flow of information between different regions. Everything can be systematized in maps; distances can be measured and expressed according to the same quantitative scale. It may be questioned, however, whether it is relevant to separate different categories of studies such as "economic archaeology" or "environmental archaeology" since the understanding of why a society applies a special mode of production cannot solely be read out of the osteological or palaeobotanical material. Ecological factors are just one explanation of why a group of people chose to set up a dwelling site or a monument in a particular place. How people reacted to environmental circumstances and the form in which they chose to arrange their lives in accordance with these depended on more or less conscious social and cultural choices. It is in fact also necessary to understand the inner dynamics of a society (Hodder 1982, 1986; Thomas 1999b). Ecological conditions are significant in the analysis, but our knowledge of human capacity shows that this influence, both during the Neolithic and in later periods, should not be overestimated. In the past few decades, other perspectives than the purely functional and adaptive aspects of human relations to the landscape have been considered (e.g. Bradley 1993, 1998, 2000;

Ingold 1993; Tilley 1994; Nash 1997; Cooney 1999, 2000).

In an alternative outlook, the landscape is regarded as a medium for action. Rather than being a background to human activity, the landscape has a special meaning in every specific culture-historical context and hence also a dynamic, meaning-bearing role in interaction with the people who live in it. Alongside – and as part of – the ecological conditions, the landscape is filled with social memories and meanings created by the actions of former generations. I therefore support the idea that the landscape should be defined on the basis of how it is perceived by those who live in it. The meaning of the landscape thus depends on those who perceive and experience it, but the landscape is not substantial in itself, instead acquiring its meaning in the relations created between people and places. Cultural and personal identity are associated with different places which can be monuments, meeting places, camps, settlements, or special natural formations. However, people did not just move within settlements or at monuments; they occupied areas which acquired integrity, structure, and symbolic meaning (Hodder 1982; Tilley 1994). It is through the relationship of places to each other that I believe that separate "landscape spaces" existed in people's consciousness. Knowledge of geography starts with places, and other places are reached through space, and in this way – through human movement – landscape spaces are created. The area that is relevant for a group of people is therefore much larger than the site and what is archaeologically observable. The focus of studies should therefore not be confined to what happened at individual places, but also consider events within a larger space. In the valley landscapes of the Saxån-Välabäcken and Lödde Å-Kävlingeån we find a concentration of Neolithic settlements, megalithic tombs, votive sites, and places of assembly in relation to surrounding regions. These places with different meanings are associated with each other. To understand the social construction of the landscape, the dis-

34

tribution of the settlements must be related to the megalithic tombs and votive sites, and in this way I believe that different Early and Middle Neolithic landscape spaces can be discerned. The landscape spaces are socially constructed and culturally conditioned, and it is important to be aware that their mental and physical distribution and demarcation are vague and can vary over time.

In the Western world there is a special, historically constituted way of perceiving the world around us, and this impairs our understanding of how prehistoric people perceived their surroundings (Bender 1999). Since the same physical landscape can be perceived in different ways by different people, we cannot hope to view the landscape in the same way as prehistoric people did. On the other hand, we can reconstruct an image of the elements that made up a special landscape and then try to understand what the elements meant to the people who inhabited this landscape (Cooney 1999; Layton & Ucko 1999).

Even though the most important source for understanding a prehistoric society must be the remains of the material culture, this is not always sufficient. Correlations between material culture and human behaviour hint at what happened, but it is difficult to understand the causal connections. Explanations of human reactions to challenges from the environment, to pressures exerted by neighbouring peoples and tensions within the community must be partly sought in what the archaeologist knows about human logic and human decision making. Ethnographic comparisons of various kinds can thus be very rewarding (Dodgshon 1987). Although one cannot make direct comparisons and transfers between different objects of study, one can use ethnographical parallels to obtain new approaches to handling different questions and knowing what one ought to look for in the archaeological evidence. A large number of ethnographical studies of "small-scale" societies, both hunter-gatherers and farmers, have shown the mutual relationship between myths, rituals, and the landscape. Categories which

they use to describe their surroundings often reflect symbolic codes or beliefs (Descola 1994; Hviding 1996; Darvill 1997). The landscape is regarded as a room or a framework, which many small-scale societies divide into different zones such as dark–light, pure–impure, back–front. This clearly illustrates that the landscape is socially produced and different groups, individuals, and societies perceive the landscape in different ways (Tuan 1979; Ingold 1993; Tilley 1994).

The idea that the landscape is not "neutral" but instead ideologically constructed is therefore significant for an understanding of the social organization and structural changes of prehistoric societies.

## Long-term perspectives

From this standpoint, I believe that the long-term perspective is another important component to consider. Neither the geographical region nor the people who live there should be regarded as stable units. The landscape should not be viewed as an object; it is a living process in that places, regions, and identities are products of people operating within a network of power relations and exchange of knowledge, which in turn are historically constituted (Ingold 1993). Culture and cultural identity are both the result of this process and the medium through which it is passed on. An area of land has a long development, with many successive episodes leaving their traces. Earlier human activities are represented in the landscape in that different places – natural formations or artificial structures – are well-known and recall bygone events. The places and landscape places are inherited in the social and individual memory. In small-scale societies, geographical knowledge is based on the accumulated observations of generations. They constitute norms which guide people in the annual use of all the parts of the landscape (Allison 1999).

An illustrative example can be cited from the Aborigines in Australia, for whom land use and personal identity are closely associated with the landscape. As regards people's perception of the landscape in the Barunga region of Northern Australia, Claire Smith writes:

> "The socialised landscapes of the present have their genesis in the dreaming, the creation era during which ancestral beings travelled throughout the land, creating its topographic features through their actions. Thus, every facet of the landscape became imbued with ancestral associations ...
>
> In the Barunga region, social identity is constructed and reconstructed in relationship to place and ancestral associations, as people live in and move through their landscapes. An integral part of the process of growing up is that of each community member learning their unique complex of relationships to place. As people move through their lands, not only do they learn about relationships between place and their ancestors, they also learn about themselves and their particular rights and responsibilities in this land-based scheme of existence. As Rowley (1986:86) points out, the separation of land, kinship, inheritance and religion in Australian Aboriginal societies is simply a western intellectual exercise. Moreover, this sense of being bound to land is a major force behind the mobility of the Barunga population." (Smith 1999:193)

The historical landscape must therefore be read, interpreted, and perceived not just in terms of different patterns in space but also in the form of the temporal perspective. What links goal-directed human behaviour is not just the presence of special natural conditions but the existing network of cultural traditions and social memories which together make up the context within which people act (Thomas 1996, 1999a). The landscape is thus not just multifunctional but also multiperiodic. The Early and Middle Neolithic comprise a period of about 1,500 years, during which time people's perceptions of different places and the landscape changed. By following the development of society over a long period, we have a greater chance of understanding the interaction between the different parts of society.

## Social interaction

The community to which people belong is ordered and regulated by social norms. As we have seen, time and place are active in this process, with a series of underlying structures and arrangements which are forces in the shaping of the social organization. How people behave when they find themselves in a new place or visit a familiar place is closely associated with their earlier experiences. It is therefore a matter of finding evidence for the underlying structures as they are expressed in the material remains. Once these have been identified, a bridge has been created which gives access to the specific meaning that characterizes a prehistoric culture (Lévi-Strauss 1970). A distinction must be made between structures and social formations or organizations. I use the concepts in accordance with the belief that structures are used in the creation of social organizations but they do not constitute them. The actions of individuals and groups within the social organization are communicated and given meaning through the different structures. There cannot be structures that are common to all cultures; each structure is limited in both time and place. The social organization consists of the total relations between individuals and groups and their relationship to the natural and social order (cf. Tilley 1982b; Giddens 1984).

The problem of identifying the underlying structures and social organization of a society is that these are not determined by the natural environment. Several conceivable cultural systems and social relations can exist within the same ecological space, and none can be predicted as a whole or specifically on the basis of the ecological conditions (Hodder 1984, 1986). The construction of monuments or other significant transformations of the landscape can only be partly explained in terms of theories of adaptation. A complete view should therefore include a description of the significance of the action to be performed. People lived in different ways in different parts of southern Scandinavia. There were shared traditions and activities, but these could differ in appearance. The challenge is to understand the meaning of these different regional identities. In addition, we should be aware that this regional identity changes in the course of the Neolithic. We cannot expect the way of life to have been fixed for 1,500 years.

Even though a prehistoric world of ideas leaves only diffuse traces in the environment, I believe that social, ritual, and economic activities can all be read in the landscape. The performance of social actions which lead to or prevent change can manifest itself archaeologically in the form of material culture. Different customs leave traces in the landscape since the maintenance of the social order must be ensured through repeated actions and rites. The meaning is transferred from one generation to the next through social relations, house designs, and rituals (Bourdieu 1977; Lévi-Strauss 1977:210). When a persistent cultural tradition is handed on from generation to generation, patterns are formed which become sufficiently ingrained to be perceived by the archaeologist. If references to objects and places become visible as a recurrent custom, the distinctive aspect of prehistoric communication can still be clear (Miller & Tilley 1984; Fairclough 1999; Layton & Ucko 1999).

Social organization, however, is not fixed and unchanging. There is constant interaction between actions and the underlying structures or norms. Some structures seem to be constant over a long period while others change. Sociology and anthropology have developed theories of action which are useful instru-

ments for studies of societies in long-term perspective (e.g. Bourdieu 1977; Giddens 1979, 1981, 1984). Anthony Giddens and Pierre Bourdieu have both propounded theories dealing with the relationship between social actions and underlying structures. The crucial feature of Giddens's structuration theory is the structural dualism which attempts to explain the dialectic between action and structure. To the same extent that structures function as a series of rules and resources which steer, initiate, or prevent action, the structures are in turn a product of action: they are constantly created, reproduced, and changed by action. The actions of the individual are influenced by the underlying structures, which in turn are influenced by the individual's actions. The structures therefore do not function independently of the individual; they are both the medium and the result of his social actions (Giddens 1979, 1981, 1984). Through the routine of daily activities, the prevailing structures are reproduced and continuity is created in social life. Recurrent festivals or rituals, such as rites of passage in which individuals or groups are transferred from one stage to another within the social sphere, likewise have the character of routine and constitute the structures of society. In my work I wish to regard ritual as an action that reproduces the structures and constitution of society, and we may suppose that rituals involved tasks and actions at every level. The difference between ritual and non-ritual can therefore sometimes be insignificant and difficult to distinguish in the archaeological material. Ritual is often an action that exemplifies the ordinary and the everyday, and therefore cannot always be placed in a pigeonhole separate from other activities. The distinction between ritual and everyday activities could be that ritual is a stereotyped, formalized, and repeated action with a specific purpose (cf. Bell 1992; Rappaport 1999). At the same time, it cannot be ignored that that it is precisely the repetition and routine that characterize everyday activities and which therefore also reproduce the prevailing structures.

The inherent dynamic in the structuration process is the shape of social relations, which are the forces that steer people's actions and can thereby change the underlying structures. It is therefore important to analyse the construction of social relations and power structures in relation to the development of society. Giddens distinguishes two forms of exercise of power which he calls "allocative" and "authoritative" resources. The first refers to control of the material world while the other refers to control of the social and cultural world. The social actor is thus always involved in a power game (Giddens 1984:258f). Conflicts and antagonisms occur even in smaller types of society where the asymmetry is based on unequal relations between e.g. men and women, children and parents, old and young, or between social groups such as clans, kindreds, etc. Even in so-called classless societies there are of course interests in reproducing the prevailing social and political conditions, and it is ideology that is the foundation for social reproduction (Meillasoux 1972; Tilley 1984; Giddens 1984).

I have tried above to clarify how essential relations of time and place are in the analysis of all social interaction. People spend most of their time in places which are fundamental for establishing their personal and group identity. It is here that actions take place, and the meaning of place can be detected in the physical remains. Places are therefore important for defining the character of social relations and actions. It is well known from ethnographical sources that spatial patterns on the habitation site and in the landscape are often shaped in accordance with rules which reflect the social organization (Whittle 1996). Special attention must therefore be paid to spatial patterns which recur repeatedly in the archaeological record. Reconstructions of the surroundings and dwelling sites in time and place, as revealed by excavated archaeological and palaeobotanical material, in combination with investigations of soil, geology, and topography, must be supplemented with studies stressing the mutual influence of the physical surroundings and the people living in them, as individuals and groups (Barber 1997). One method for gaining some idea about the underlying ideas and structures in Neolithic society in the valley landscapes is, in my view, to examine each place separately. Detailed studies of, above all, the excavated sites, seek to understand the meaning of the individual place. An understanding of the organization of the place is dependent on an ability to identify the type and date of individual features and to ascertain their mutual spatial relations, to analyse the composition of the material, and to chart the topographical location of the place and its relation to contemporary surrounding remains. The aim is to distinguish separate processes on the site, such as dwelling areas, production, burials, and so on, and to distinguish continuity and discontinuity on the site. Can the function of the place be linked to a single occasion, or was it used over a long period, and if so, was the meaning of the place the same? Which elements vary and which are constant in each phase of the Early and the Middle Neolithic?

Unbroken continuity, in the sense that a place has been constantly occupied, cannot be verified in the archaeological material. In my study it is not necessary to prove any such unbroken continuity. It is sufficient to confirm that people returned to the same place and that in all probability they knew about the former use of the place. There is thus continuity even if there was an interruption in the use of the place for several hundred years, provided awareness of the place was kept alive through the oral tradition or via myths of origin and the cosmology. Discontinuity is what we have when those who inhabit a place are unaware of its earlier history. At the same time as there can be a continuous awareness of a place, however, there can be discontinuity in that the meaning of the place changes over time. Former main settlements, for example, can change to become sites associated only with seasonal activities.

# Local, regional, and interregional levels

To accomplish the study thus requires investigations at different levels: the local level (the place itself), the regional level, and the interregional level.

## The local level

Just as individuals and material objects obtain an identity over time, places have a narrative identity. A locality becomes a place as soon as we are aware of it and use it. When people change a place, something significant happens. When a building is erected, an interaction arises between people and the world around them. The act of building illustrates how people exist in the world in a special way. Architecture creates a relationship between person and place and simultaneously manifests the relationship. Building involves a change to the place, but mostly by strengthening its meaning rather than rejecting its previous meaning (Thomas 1996).

A strict division of different categories of archaeological remains, such as dwelling site, burial place, and so on, is – at least in part – irrelevant. We can expect that prehistoric people did not distinguish between different concepts such as economic, social, and spiritual. Setting up a camp or erecting a monument no doubt had what we define as social, economic, and spiritual meanings, but for prehistoric people these categories were probably indistinguishable. We also see in the same places traces of activities which we could consider to be of both sacred and profane nature. The occurrence of human bones both on dwelling sites and in votive settings, for example, indicates that the graves were not the only "storage places" for the dead. In the same way, votive deposits are found in habitation contexts. Places constitute a "specific landscape" with a series of socio-economic activities, a network of meanings and rituals, all interwoven. The categorization of the landscape can be constructed so that the arrangements are applied on several levels at the same time, in almost all the dimensions of life. For instance, patterns in the landscape can at the same time be reflected in decorative schemas in the material culture or in the ordering and distribution of activities on settlement sites.

The classification of places as dwelling, votive place, and so on, is thus arbitrary. The categories must nevertheless be considered useful when we try to give meaning to prehistory, and it is likely that a place could have had a primary function as, for example, a dwelling site or a votive place. In fact, it is a question of a network of human activities (e.g. cooking, dwelling, sacrifice, burial) which, depending on the circumstances, were at times performed in different places but sometimes also on the same spot.

**Settlement**   Our knowledge of the internal organization of Early and Middle Neolithic settlements is still limited in comparison with what we know about the megalithic tombs of Skåne and Denmark. Although several scholars have devised systems to describe settlement patterns, few attempts have been made to understand the activities performed in habitation areas. A study of the settlements can provide answers to questions concerning everyday activities such as exploitation of resources, land use, and tool manufacture. Broadly speaking, two different categories of settlement can be distinguished. The first is the main settlement where the habitation areas (the sites with the houses) are found, where everyday life goes on, with the elements required by this life, such as storehouses and various activity areas. Alongside the settlement there is a series of camps for special activities such as hunting, fishing, or manufacture. They can be seasonal and may be expected to leave fewer traces than the settlement. In addition, there are temporary camps used only for short stays, perhaps just overnight.

An important precondition is that the houses and dwelling sites are more than just a place for sleeping and eating. No dwelling site can be understood if we assume that all its elements have solely a practical function (Bradley 1998). The houses can tell us about the organization of the household, but they can simultaneously be reflections of cosmology and beliefs (Cooney 2000). In the account of the places in chapter 4 there are several examples of the polysemy of settlements. Like all human activity, the arrangements in the habitation area, tool manufacture, cooking, or waste handling followed structured, deep-rooted cultural norms. Building houses, clearing areas for cultivation and animal husbandry, or making a tool were transformative events, which were probably accompanied by special rituals. It is reasonable to imagine rituals on several social levels, from the collective, general ritual to the acts of the individual or the family group. It is therefore important that different features on the settlement site are studied on the basis of their context and that the analysis does not focus solely on their form and content (cf. Hill 1995:96ff; Chapman 2000).

39

these are the material traces of conscious ritual actions which to some extent reflect the prevailing world of ideas, they can give an – albeit fragmentary – understanding of the social and ideological meanings of the graves. Features adjacent to the graves can tell of various activities both before and after the construction and testify to the meaning of the monuments for the survivors in a longer temporal perspective.

Settlement sites, however, are only a part of the greater network of activities that also includes, for instance, graves and votive sites.

**Graves** The grave as we meet it in an excavation is an extremely fragmentary reflection of the multifaceted society. In large measure the construction of a grave monument is of course an action associated with people's beliefs. The sepulchral evidence should thus give us access to parts of the spiritual aspect of life. Even though the grave and the burial ritual are not necessarily a direct reflection of the beliefs of a society, there is often a close connection. One of the functions of ritual is to explain and confirm the mythology to the society and its members. It is a part of the celebration of a cult, in which people use symbolic or dramatic rites to repeat primeval happenings and thus renew and ratify the world order to which creation gave rise (Ringgren 1968:43; Lévi-Strauss 1977:210). In this way the social power structure was presumably also confirmed through the ritual. The graves and the rituals connected with them are therefore probably also an expression of secular purposes and may be seen as an instrument in the exercise of power and the maintenance of the prevailing social order. The graves should be regarded as the result of ideological values and beliefs in mutual interaction with economic and social patterns (cf. Thomas 1991; Bergh 1995:142).

In the graves there were various constructional details which are of course difficult to interpret. The conceptual world may have been asserted in a way that seems irrational to an outside observer, but which had an important role to play in the social context where it occurred. Each object taken separately is usually dumb, but when placed in their context, material remains can contribute significant clues in the process of interpretation. The question is whether it is possible to find in the graves patterns which we can interpret and understand today. One way to grasp the ideas behind monument building is to study burial methods and various constructional elements in the graves. Since

**Votive sites** The deposition of votive gifts, mainly in wetlands, occurred throughout Nordic prehistory. In Skåne we know of a large number of Neolithic votive finds, discovered above all during digging for peat. It is mostly single finds that are encountered at each place, and a limited number of artefact categories are represented, chiefly axes. At some places, however, objects were deposited on repeated occasions, resulting in what we call accumulated votive sites (Karsten 1994). Deliberate deposits of whole and fragmented objects occur in several different settings outside wetlands too – on dwelling sites, at graves, and beside large stones. It is reasonable to imagine that the different deposition contexts varied partly in function and meaning. I believe that what we consider to be votive deposits can, in many cases, be closely connected to everyday activities and be difficult to separate from these in the archaeological material. This may illustrate the prehistoric state of affairs, when there was no distinct boundary between what we perceive as secular and what we perceive as sacred. In my work I would emphasize the importance of trying to understand people's intentions when depositing objects in different contexts. To some extent we must ignore our own sharp distinction between deeds of a profane character and sacred acts and instead focus on the activity performed in prehistoric times in its specific context.

**Central places** A traditional society needs meeting places for several different reasons: economic, administrative, social, and spiritual. The form of these can vary and seems to have done so during the Early and Middle Neolithic. Well-known examples are the large Sarup enclosures (causewayed enclosures), which began to be built in southern Scandinavia at the end of the Early Neolithic, or the palisaded enclosures that occur at the transition from the Funnel Beaker to the Battle Axe culture (Andersen 1974, 1997; Svensson 1991, 2002; Andersson & Svensson 1999). Other monuments, such as megalithic tombs, may also have been a focal point for a society's activities on special occasions. Other places such as settlements or special natural formations in

40

the landscape may also have functioned as meeting places for people.

**Natural formations** Natural formations are not monuments since they were not constructed by human labour. However, it is not necessary for a place to be physically reshaped to become a place of cultural importance. A distinctive topographical feature, such as a rock, a valley, or a watercourse, can constitute such a place. A fundamental aspect of the daily occurrences in traditional societies is the physical perception of the landscape – earth, water, wood, stone, high and low hills, wind, rain, sunshine, stars, and sky. The rhythm of the landscape and the seasons corresponds to the rhythm of life. Natural formations acquired meaning through associations with social events of a mythological character. These places could be symbolic resources of great significance for prehistoric populations. Place-names, associations, and memories humanized and cultivated the landscape and linked topographical landmarks with human intentions (Tilley 1994; Bradley 2000).

It is one matter to recognize the concept of physically unspoiled places, but quite another matter to identify their localization and significance archaeologically. In several cases the meaning of a place has been manifested through depositions of sacrifices, for example, in wetlands or beside a large stone.

## The regional level

In the area around the Saxån-Välabäcken and Lödde Å-Kävlingeån there is a distinct grouping of Neolithic settlements, megalithic tombs, places of assembly, and votive sites which suggests a demarcated region. Taken together, these places make up a settlement organization which is the result of a complex relationship between economic, social, and spiritual factors. It is obvious that these factors operated during prehistoric times just as they do today.

In an interpretation of social organization, I do not believe that it is appropriate to concentrate solely on the individual parts such as settlements or graves. The relation between the antiquities must be clarified. It is necessary to determine which categories are dependent on each other and in what way, that is, how the parts function in the whole. Can we demonstrate, for example, that changes in mortuary ritual were synchronized with changes in other parts of society?

The identification of a place as a locality with one or more meanings demonstrates the relationship to other places. In the valley landscapes it is likely that such a study, seeking to establish the chronological

relationship and the spatial interaction between the places, can distinguish different local communities or societies. By a society I mean in this study a group of people and their places within a defined geographical area – a landscape space – within which the group's seasonal and annual activities were maintained. The people in a society felt that they had a common identity which made them different from surrounding societies. Even though we tend to regard the home and the grave as two isolated phenomena, we should bear in mind that for people who lived and died in the Neolithic they were probably part of the same life cycle. People shape a complex network of activities in the landscape, of varying intensity and duration. It can be expected that people were closely connected to the home/house, and beyond this there were places which were visited at certain points in time during the year or on special occasions. Through an understanding of the function of each place, knowledge can be obtained about the relationship between settlements, graves, and votive sites, and about how changes in these different aspects of social organization correspond to each other. In this valley landscape, where do we find different places and how are they linked?

To varying extents, the different groups or societies within the valley landscapes presumably maintained mutual contacts, which were necessary for their survival, and in this way formed a cohesive district or region.

## The interregional level

Naturally, the investigation area was not an isolated unit during the Neolithic. People never live in isolation; they always have contact with other regions. The supraregional social network is significant for an understanding of the spatial distribution of innovations. It is clear that ideas and commodities were exchanged between different regions within the same cultural sphere or with other culture complexes. Similarities in material culture appear over much of Europe during both the Funnel Beaker and Battle Axe cultures (Malmer 1962; Midgley 1992). In this work my comparative study will chiefly be concerned with nearby areas, that is, the rest of Skåne and Denmark. This largely shared Late Mesolithic background, in the form of the Ertebølle culture (Jennbert 1984a), provided the special social and economic conditions for a new ideology to establish itself. At the same time, each society has unique features, and a study of these surrounding regions can give perspectives on the situation in western Skåne.

# Neolithic settlement around the two valleys

*Some of the Early and middle Neolithic main settlements were much larger in area than previous archaeologists had found for Skåne. It seems in fact that both large and small sites existed in parallel. Both the excavations and the surface surveys in the investigation area show that some of the Early and middle Neolithic dwelling sites were rather large. This may be a sign that space was needed for different activities and that there was successive expansion. It is difficult to calculate how large a group lived on each site at the same time. It may nevertheless be assumed, on the basis of the varying activities and the extent of the settlement, that, at least at Dagstorp 19 and Saxtorp 23, the groups could have been bigger than a single family.*

# The picture of remains
# from the Early and Middle Neolithic

My intention here has been to bring together all known Early and Middle Neolithic remains within the investigation area. To arrive at an understanding of the function and meaning of places and to ascertain their relative chronological and chorological relations using the above approach requires the existence of carefully documented information about the features and finds from the sites. It is therefore of great significance whether the places were identified solely through surface surveys or were also excavated.

## Periodization

The absence of pottery, above all from places which have only been surface-surveyed, means that it is difficult to give exact datings for a large number of the sites. The assessment of the duration of use for each aceramic place must therefore be made according to a much cruder chronological division than where we have access to pottery. In the present work I have divided the Early and the Middle Neolithic into four periods, chiefly on the basis of different axe types: EN I, EN II–MNA II, MNA III–V, and MNB. It goes without saying that the transitions between these "periods" must be fluid. Some of the axe types and ceramic decorations can occur in more than one period. My intention, however, is not to prove whether the different classification systems work but – primarily – to study the region's Neolithic social organization and settlement patterns in a long-term perspective. With this approach there cannot be any sharp dividing lines; a certain overlap between two phases can be accepted. Where the find material permits, however, I intend to give closer datings for some of the excavated sites. Despite the problem of chronology, I shall henceforth follow Poul Otto Nielsen's division and connect MNA with the Funnel Beaker culture and MNB with the Battle Axe culture. The finds influenced by the Pitted

Ware culture which are documented on some sites, or the Stävie group as I shall call this variant of the Funnel Beaker culture below (cf. Larsson, L. 1989b), seem to occur both in the late MNA and at least in the first part of the MNB – there are no distinct boundaries. In my work it will also be clear that changes in social organization in different phases, above all at the end of the Funnel Beaker culture, could warrant a different periodization. For the sake of simplicity, however, I have chosen to divide the chapters according to chronological phases based on pottery and axe typologies. In this way I believe it will be easier for readers to orient themselves in time and to compare my results with other works dealing with the same period.

The division into the different phases follows Nielsen's periodization from 1993.

One problem is that there are great differences in time between uncalibrated and calibrated $^{14}$C datings. The discrepancies in the calibrated values correspond to a prolongation of the periods EN I, EN II–MNA II, MNA III–V, and MNB by about 33%, 25%, 33%, and 30% respectively. The length of the periods is relevant chiefly in the discussion of settlement intensity. In this study $^{14}$C datings will therefore be presented in both uncalibrated and calibrated values with one sigma. The calibrated values are shown in parentheses.

**EN I** The earliest phase, EN I, can be dated to 5100–4800 BP (3900–3500 cal. bc). Characteristic artefacts which date sites to this period are the pointed-butted flint axe and pointed-butted rock axe. Pottery which can be linked to the south or south-west Scanian groups of Oxie, Svenstorp, or Mossby also belong to this phase. The Oxie group is characterized by funnel beakers with a short neck and decoration above all with imprints, short strokes, and small pits concentrated around the rim. Cord decoration is a significant

Table I. Periodization.

| 5100 | 4800 | 4400 | 4250 | 3900 | Uncal. BP |
|---|---|---|---|---|---|
| EN I | EN II–MNA II | MNA III–V | | MNB | |

Funnel beaker culture

Battle axe culture

The Stävie group

| 3900 | 3500 | 3000 | 2800 | 2350 | Cal. BC |

element in the Svenstorp group, but we also find stick imprints and other stamped impressions. The decoration becomes more complicated than in the Oxie group and several vessel forms occur. The Mossby group can be regarded as a parallel to the Svenstorp group but with a greater presence of cord decoration (Larsson, M. 1984; Kihlstedt et al. 1997). The pointed butted flint axe occurs above all in Oxie group contexts but also in some cases together with pottery from the Svenstorp group (Hernek 1989; Karsten 1994; Kihlstedt et al. 1997). Nielsen has conducted an exhaustive analysis of the pointed-butted flint axe and defined three types. Type I is two-sided and has a pointed-oval cross-section, type II is three-sided with a round-oval cross-section, while type III is characterized by a square cross-section (Nielsen, P. O. 1977). Karsten's analysis of combined deposits shows that the pointed-butted axe of type III occurs in certain cases together with the thin-butted axe. In this work I therefore choose to associate only the pointed-butted axe of types I and II with the EN I. The flake axe of Havnelev type is also found in EN I contexts (Vang Petersen 1993).

Anna Lagergren-Olsson has analysed the extensive ceramic material from the Funnel Beaker culture found in connection with the West Coast Line excavations, mostly concentrated in the large Neolithic settlement of Dagstorp 19 north of the Välabäcken, and she has presented a division of the dwelling site pottery in terms of style and phase. "The period of small imprints" corresponds to what is traditionally described as EN I, characterized by sparsely decorated pots. The decoration is wholly dominated by two basic ornaments, small imprints under the edge of the rim and indentations on the edge of the rim. The majority of the pottery at Dagstorp 19 has parallels in the Oxie group, but the material also includes collared flasks and decorated lugged beakers, vessel forms that do not belong in the Svenstorp group. These vessels were not found in the occupation layers of the dwelling site but only in the pits. The occurrence of the ceramic groups

in different contexts within the Dagstorp settlement, according to Lagergren-Olsson, may suggest that the difference between the pottery that can be described as belonging to the Oxie group and the Svenstorp group is probably of a functional character and does not reflect two groups of people in the area (Lagergren-Olsson 2003).

**EN II–MNA II** Phase two, EN II–MNA II, comprises the period 4800–4400 BP (3500–3000 cal. bc). Artefacts which can be ascribed to this phase are above all the thin-butted axe, which Nielsen has divided into seven different types on the basis of the relative thickness of the butt, the location of the thickest part of the blade, the degree of convexity of the broad sides, the shape of the butt, and the polishing of the narrow sides (Nielsen, P. O. 1977). Apart from this type of artefact, halberds of flint and polygonal battle axes are linked to the late Early Neolithic and the start of the Middle Neolithic. The Bellevuegården group belongs to this phase, with pottery showing greater variation than the earlier groups of the Early Neolithic with their large proportion of whipped cord decoration. The belly decoration consists of vertical lines, covering the whole surface or in groups (Larsson, M. 1984). The earliest pottery of the Middle Neolithic is characterized by new vessel forms such as pedestalled bowls, clay ladles, and brim beakers. Line technique is the predominant method of decoration. Among the hatched patterns, cross-hatching dominates.

The ceramic style that corresponds to the period EN II–MNA I within the investigation area is called "the period of belly lines" by Lagergren-Olsson. Funnel beakers decorated with belly lines are a form of vessel found throughout the period. Larger parts of the pots are decorated than during the period of small imprints. Not just the belly but also the neck and shoulder are more often decorated. New ornamental elements such as angular lines, bands, angular bands, hatched fields, and pitted decoration are introduced during this period (Lagergren-Olsson 2003).

**MNA III–V** MNA III–V is estimated as the time between 4400 and 4250 BP (3000–2800 cal. bc). The characteristic object of the period is the thick-butted flint axe, which now replaces the thin-butted axe. The thick-butted axes have been studied by Nielsen, who divided them into two types, A and B. Type A is considered characteristic of the period MNA III–V while type B is usually placed in MNB. The criteria for type A are that the narrow-side angle is at least 8°, the narrow sides unpolished, the butt is straight, the shape is trapezoidal, and the axe is mostly thickest at the middle (Nielsen, P. O. 1979). With regard to the butt index, type A has been divided into three chronologically separate variants – Bundsø, Lindø, and Valby. The dating of the axes is complicated, however, by the fact that both types, A and B, have been found together, for instance, in hoard contexts. Nielsen believes that in such cases it is a question of a transition period between A and B (Nielsen, P. O. 1979). Further indications that the two axe types may overlap are finds of both A and B axes at Stävie (Larsson, L. 1992a), and the occurrence of B axes at Hindby Mosse. The settlement there has mainly been dated to the MNA III (Svensson 1986). The classification of the thick-butted flint axe is thus not entirely without problems. Since my aim is to study the organization of society in long-term perspective, however, it is sufficient to regard the B axe as a generally later variant, albeit with a certain overlap in time with the A axe.

MNA III also led to a distinct break in the ceramic tradition. The formerly so common and characteristic belly line decoration completely disappears. The pitted decoration reaches its zenith and occurs at least as often as other types of decoration. Tooth-stamp decoration becomes very common, and typical decorative elements are vertical bands, angular bands, chequerboard patterns, and angular lines. The stock of vessel shapes is more varied than in earlier periods. Apart from funnel beakers there are open bowls of different kinds and brim beakers.

In the late MNA (MNA IV–V) it is customary to distinguish between two traditions in Skåne. One is represented by sites like Karlsfält and Långåker and the other by the Stävie site (Larsson, L. 1992a:146). Ceramic decoration at Karlsfält is dominated by two techniques, lines and impressions. The most common patterns are pits of different sizes and tooth stamps. In several cases there are hanging triangles on both neck and belly. Flint objects have a composition agreeing well with that at other dwelling sites from the Funnel Beaker culture. Thick-butted axes of both Lindø and Valby type occur on the site, as do thin-bladed axes and chisels. Other tools are based on flakes. The clearly dominant ornamental variable at Stävie is finger impressions. Other types of ornamentation such as tooth stamps, oval and oblique impressions occur but to a lesser extent, as do hanging triangles or arches in line technique. Pottery in the Stävie group can be paralleled with the Valby phase in Denmark, MNA V. The flint artefacts give an impression of being influenced by the Pitted Ware culture in that several examples of cylindrical blade cores and blade arrowheads occur. A considerable number of blade scrapers in relation to flake scrapers also shows the importance of the blade technique among the tools. Among axes we find, as mentioned above, both the A and the B type of thick-butted axes (Larsson, L. 1982:103, 1986:151, 1992a:146, 1993). In the investigation area, no sites have yielded pottery traditionally associated with the Pitted Ware culture, but the Pitted Ware–influenced flint stock has been identified together with pottery which can be defined as belonging to the later Funnel Beaker culture and equated with the Valby phase.

Lagergren-Olsson see a clear difference, however, in vessel forms and decoration, between the ceramic material from Stävie and the pottery belonging to the "tooth-stamp period" in the Välabäcken valley. She therefore believe that the pottery in Stävie should not automatically be linked to the Funnel Beaker culture (Lagergren-Olsson 2003).

**MNB (Battle Axe culture)** The latest phase of the study, MNB, is dated to the period between 4250 and 3900 BP (2800–2350 cal. bc). The following types of artefacts are usually ascribed to the MNB and the Battle Axe culture: the thick-butted flint axe of type B, the thick-butted hollow-edged flint axe, the thick-butted thin-bladed flint axe polished on four sides, the thick-butted rock axe, and the battle axe of Malmer's groups A–E. The blade arrowhead of type D is usually assigned to the Battle Axe culture as well (Malmer 1975; Nielsen, P. O. 1979; Ebbesen 1984; Blomqvist 1989a; Vang Petersen 1993). Axes of type B should have a narrow-side angle of 8° at most, polished or unpolished narrow sides, a straight or oblique butt, usually a rectangular shape, and mostly with the greatest thickness close to the edge. The dating of the axes is complicated, however, by the fact that both types, A and B, are found together. The places where the only identified type of artefact is the B axe are henceforth marked in figures with a different symbol from sites with artefacts that can be securely placed in MNB. In the same way as the chronological relationship between the A and the B axe has not been completely clarified, not all hollow-edged flint axes can be automatically assigned to MNB. According to Nielsen, the pointed-butted hollow-edged flint axe is one of the key artefacts in the MNA IV–V in Denmark (Nielsen, P. O. 1979; Berg & Skaarup 1979). The type occurs rarely in Skåne, however (Karsten 1994:66), and has not been found in the investigation area. The thick-butted hollow-edged axe with a greatly flared edge, which is usually placed in the late MNB or the Late Neolithic (Vang Petersen 1993), is also missing from the investigation area. It is tricky to build a sustainable chronological division into later and earlier types based on the other thick-butted hollow-edged axe types. A periodization of the Battle Axe culture should therefore proceed from the pottery. Apart from isolated sherds, Battle Axe pottery has been found only in mortuary contexts or at the palisaded enclosure in Dösjebro, which makes it impossible to achieve a fine chronology of the Battle Axe culture settlements in the area.

The characteristic vessel during the Battle Axe culture is the small, rounded pot, which in its oldest form is given horizontal cord decoration solely along the edge of the rim. Later we find stamp-decorated garlands under these patterns, and there is sometimes decoration on the lower part of the pot as well. Surface-covering patterns of chevrons are common on the later pots (Malmer 1962, 1975).

## The relative representativeness of material from surface surveys and excavations

One problem with studies of prehistoric societies is the distorted distribution that arises because most excavations have taken place in the most intensively developed areas. Some areas are therefore relatively well excavated, while others are almost blank spots on the map of Neolithic excavations. Although south-west Skåne and the district around the river valleys are heavily developed and thus relatively well investigated by archaeologists, we must reckon that even within this region there are areas lacking excavation results. It is above all along the coast and the rivers that most excavations have taken place (fig. 7). An important complement is therefore the surveys which, at least in theory, have systematically charted the remains visible on the surface on all the economic maps sheets of Skåne.

**Excavated sites** Within the area there are 72 excavated sites which can be dated to the Early and/or Middle Neolithic (fig. 8). The majority of the excavations were performed by the National Heritage Board Southern Excavations Department in the last few decades. Some of the excavations, however, were conducted by Lund University Historical Museum (LUHM), partly in the form of seminar digs and research excavations.

The Neolithic element on the different sites varies in scale. In several cases it seems that later activities have destroyed any Neolithic structures, and Neolithic activities reveal themselves only through isolated finds discovered in later features. The excavated material is also of uneven scientific value. The excavations vary in quality and, in certain cases, have not been fully reported. The excavation methods used in older excavations did not record all the details required to understand the internal organization of a place. Mostly it

▶ Fig. 7. Areas excavated by the National Heritage Board, Southern Excavations Department.

▶ Fig. 8. Excavated sites within the investigation area dated to the Early and/or Middle Neolithic.

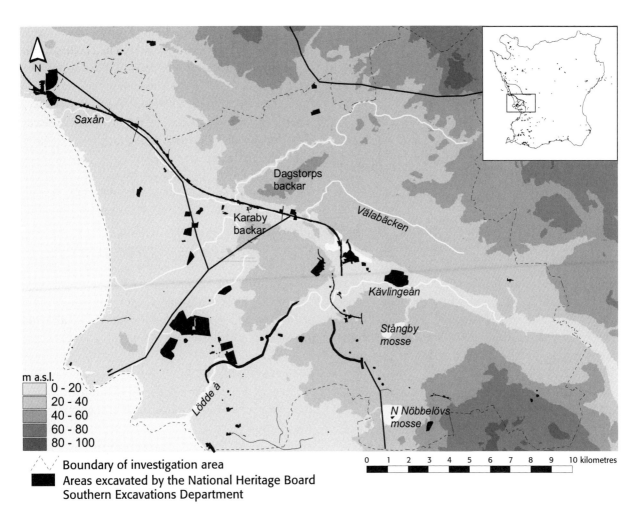

m a.s.l.
0 - 20
20 - 40
40 - 60
60 - 80
80 - 100

Boundary of investigation area

Areas excavated by the National Heritage Board
Southern Excavations Department

0  1  2  3  4  5  6  7  8  9  10 kilometres

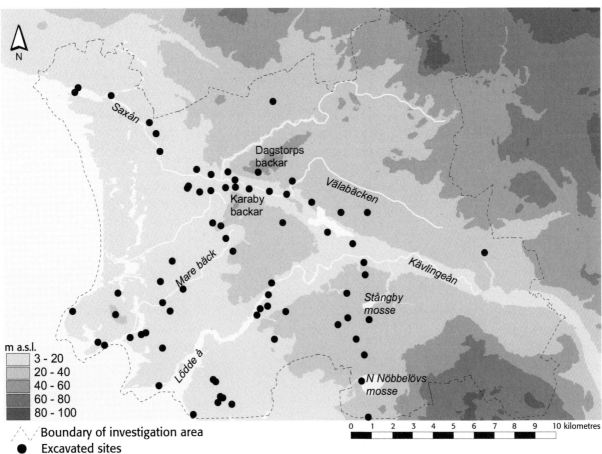

m a.s.l.
3 - 20
20 - 40
40 - 60
60 - 80
80 - 100

Boundary of investigation area

● Excavated sites

0  1  2  3  4  5  6  7  8  9  10 kilometres

48

was only small, limited areas that were excavated, which makes it difficult to interpret the function and meaning of sites. Understanding of the internal organization of a place requires larger areas so that more extensive remains of settlement will appear. It was not until recent decades that the method of machine stripping came into use, allowing the true features such as houses, fences, and pit systems to be properly documented and related to each other.

The variable quality of the excavations means that, in several cases, even on the excavated sites it is difficult to be sure of the function and duration of a dwelling site. In this work I nevertheless try to distinguish which places may have functioned as main settlements and which were activity sites. To be able to say with absolute certainty which of these different types of settlements is which would require a total excavation of each site, which is of course unrealistic. I nevertheless believe that a place can with good reason be called a main settlement if it satisfies certain requirements. By main settlement I mean a place where people lived for the major part of the year, or even the whole year, and from where special "work groups" proceeded. There may be several factors determining whether a place should be regarded as a main settlement: (1) the surrounding natural environment should be favourable for providing basic needs the whole year round, with opportunities for a varied diet; (2) the archaeological source material, in the form of features and finds, must show that a variety of activities took place on the site; (3) the area of the settlement should be big enough to show that different activities can have taken place there and that successive expansion can have occurred; (4) the presence of graves on or near the site is yet another sign of the significance of the place; (5) the place should have a demonstrable settlement continuity. The latter point indicates that there was probably an economic and social knowledge of the surrounding environment. The list of distinctive features which ought to characterize a main settlement could be made even longer, but at least three of the criteria should be

satisfied if a place is to be considered to be of stationary character. In most cases, remains of houses or huts should also have been documented, but since earlier excavations rarely noticed post-built buildings, this cannot be crucial for the assessment. My definition of houses and huts is that the latter differ from houses by not having a central row of roof-bearing posts (*mesula*), although there may sometimes be one or more roof-bearing posts. I am aware that there are probably main settlements within the investigation area which I have been unable to identify, but I believe that the places that I point out really were in all probability main settlements. Unlike the main settlements, the activity sites were only used briefly at specific times during the year and are therefore as a rule smaller and may be expected to have left fewer traces of structures in the ground. The sites that I have identified as activity sites or short-term settlements mostly show no more than two of the five points listed above. In cases where features have been found, they have been of a character indicating short-term occupation, for example, remains of small huts. Another important clue in the assessment of a place has been the relationship with other contemporary places, such as nearby settlements, graves, and votive sites. The relationship between different sites in time and place can clarify the meaning and function of a place.

In my calculation of the area of the sites I try to combine the horizontal spread of the artefacts with the occurrence and distribution of contemporary features (post-holes, pits, hearths, etc.). The earlier view has long been that the size of Early and Middle Neolithic base sites was limited to roughly 600–800 m² (e.g. Larsson, M. 1992). Recent years' excavations with machine stripping of large areas both in southern Sweden and in eastern central Sweden have shown, however, that main settlements can cover several thousand square metres and represent many different activities (e.g. Apel et al. 1997; Artursson 1997; Andersson, M. 1999; Lagergren-Olsson & Linderoth 2000). To a large extent the older view was based on limited excavation areas which gave a distorted picture of the real size of the settlements. There are also serious problems in comparing the composition and quantity of finds from different places since this depends on preservation conditions, on which parts of the site were excavated, and on the excavation method used. It is therefore not reasonable to assess the duration and function of a place solely on the basis of the amount of finds. On the other hand, a main settlement should have a varied composition of tools. Scrapers, knives, awls, arrowheads, and axe fragments should be represented in the toolkit, together with flint waste which shows that manufacture and repair took place on the site. I view pits with Early and/or Middle Neolithic material as a clear indication that the site was of a more permanent character. The deposition of objects in pits – whole or fragmented – is an action that shows a concern for the place. Efforts were expended on cleaning the ground or marking one's belonging to the place through the actual digging and depositing. I shall develop these ideas below.

Long barrows, dolmens, and passage graves are chiefly defined as burial places since remains of human bones show that they functioned as spaces for the dead (Strömberg 1968, 1971; Hårdh 1990b, Tilley 1996). It will be clear from my work, however, that traces of rituals adjacent to the monuments suggest that they also functioned as places of assembly for the surrounding communities. It is not uncommon that the deposition of special objects takes place right beside graves although the action cannot be linked to the actual burial of the dead. At megalithic tombs it is not uncommon to find hoards of flint axes or pottery in or outside the entrance, or by the kerbstones (Strömberg 1968, 1971; Ebbesen 1975; Hårdh 1990b; Tilley 1996). Identifying flat-earth graves, on the other hand, involves difficulties, since the preservation conditions for bone are usually limited in the sandy soils of the investigation area. The minimum criteria for regarding a feature as a flat-earth grave are that it must have a rectangular shape with clear, straight-dug edges and a flat bottom, and there should be traces of colouring left by a body or a coffin in the feature. The context of a site with adjacent flat-earth graves may also indicate that a feature with the form of a grave and presumed grave goods, but without clear colouring left by a body or skeleton, should be regarded as a flat-earth grave.

Deliberate deposits of artefacts, in the form of single finds or hoards of several artefacts, are phenomena which can occur either separately from what we normally regard as settlement site material and burials or in these specific contexts (Karsten 1994). The find circumstances can sometimes entail difficulties, above all in determining whether it is a single find/hoard or grave goods. Hoards, unlike grave goods, should not have anything to do with the actual burial. Objects which are considered to have been deposited together with the deceased are therefore not included in the term hoard (cf. Becker 1947; Stjernquist 1963; Nielsen, P. O. 1977; Ebbesen 1983; Karsten 1994). The many deposits of artefacts which occur in different wetland settings are presumably not ordinary graves. With finds on dry land it is trickier to determine whether they are linked to graves or not. Often the deposits are associated with large stones, which in theory could be part of a megalithic tomb (Karsten 1994). As a rule, however, the composition of objects in hoards differs from that of characteristic grave goods, besides which certain forms of Neolithic tools are unknown or very rare in grave contexts. Unpolished axes, preforms for tools, and so-called overdimensioned objects, for example, occur very seldom in grave contexts (Nielsen, P. O. 1977; Karsten 1994). Of course, it is difficult to determine whether the deliberate deposits are profane caches or sacred offerings. Karsten says that in the treatment of a large body of material, repetition as a reason for ritual interpretation of find material can be applied in both large and small perspectives: both when the finds occur as traces of repeated actions at a votive site, and when the category of find as a whole shares common features such as find spot, find circumstances, and the appearance of the objects. He moreover puts forward three arguments against the view that deliberate deposits of objects are treasure hoards or stockpiles. Firstly, it seems unreasonable that the majority of all the Neolithic people had a similar perception of what was to be concealed and how it was to be concealed. Secondly, it seems incredible that there was a need over such a long stretch of time to hide valuable objects in the earth. Thirdly, far too many caches were never dug up again (Karsten 1994). From this point of view, all closed

49

finds in wetlands should therefore be regarded as primarily deposits of a ritual character and thus constitute a votive site.

For a site to be regarded as a central place or an assembly place, there should be remains indicating that activities of a collective character took place there. These traces can consist of large buildings, deposits of artefacts, or traces of ceremonies and rituals adjacent to graves. In certain cases, then, not only burial places and votive sites but also settlements may have functioned as places of assembly.

As will be obvious, the different categories of place are closely connected to each other, and one place probably often had several functions. It is therefore important to focus on the meaning behind the action that was performed for each deposit, by putting it in its special context in time and place.

**Surface-surveyed places** The intensive agriculture within the investigation area has meant that traces from prehistoric times have to a large extent been gradually ploughed out or have disappeared. Today it is virtually only the surviving grave monuments that are still visible in the landscape, while the vast majority of the remains are unknown and completely concealed under ground level. At the same time, the intensive ploughing in the investigation area has unearthed hidden remains in the form of worked flint. There is probably no international counterpart

to the surveys of ancient monuments which have taken place in Sweden since the 1930s (Larsson, L. 2001:22). The National Heritage Board's revised survey of ancient monuments in Skåne 1985–1987 led to a tripling of the number of known antiquities (Olsson 1991). The reason for this was that this time the survey, unlike previous ones, also registered dwelling sites and remains of or information about burial mounds in a more systematic way. The dwelling sites that have been identified through the occurrence of knapped flint in the topsoil are registered as Stone Age dwelling sites, which raises some aspects of source criticism. Whether the sites represent permanent settlements or temporary camps for special purposes cannot be determined with certainty by surface surveys. In addition, excavations have shown that these places often contain remains from the Bronze Age and Iron Age. Important sources of error to bear in mind are the pressure of time on the person doing the survey and the conditions prevailing at the time. The National Heritage Board's survey of ancient monuments has often been defined as a quick survey because the surveyors were working under pressure. This means that they were forced to make priorities. Only in exceptional cases was it possible to make return visits to sites and to private farm collections. Surveys of ancient monuments depend on ocular inspection of the landscape. External factors such as the occurrence of crops or vegetation, the nature of the soil, how the earth has been worked, and the weather affect the degree of accessibility. The composition of the personnel is also significant for the results of the survey. The surveyors differ in their education, knowledge, and archaeological experience. It goes without saying that not all antiquities were discovered by the surveys. In the project "The Hidden Cultural Landscape", which was a collaborative venture involving the Department of Archaeology at Lund University, Malmö Museums, the National Heritage Board

Table II. Early and Middle Neolithic places and their assumed primary function.

| Periods | Main settlement | Main settlement with flat-earth grave | Dwelling/activity site | Flat-earth grave outside the settlement | Megalithic tomb (incl. long barrow) | Votive site | Axe-manufact-uring place | Central place |
|---|---|---|---|---|---|---|---|---|
| EN I | 6 | 3 | 18 | 1 | – | 5 | – | |
| EN II–MNA II | 12 | – | 76 | 1 | 21 | 50 | 1 | |
| MNA III–V | 6 | – | 45 | – | 9* | 8 | 1 | 2 |
| MNB | ?** | – | 42 | 4 | 6* | 27 | 3 | 2 |

*Megalithic tombs were constructed in the period EN II–MNA II but excavations show that all the passage graves at least were also in use during MNA III–V and some of them in MNB.
**The question mark illustrates that some of the settlements during the transition to the Late Neolithic were probably transformed into main settlements.

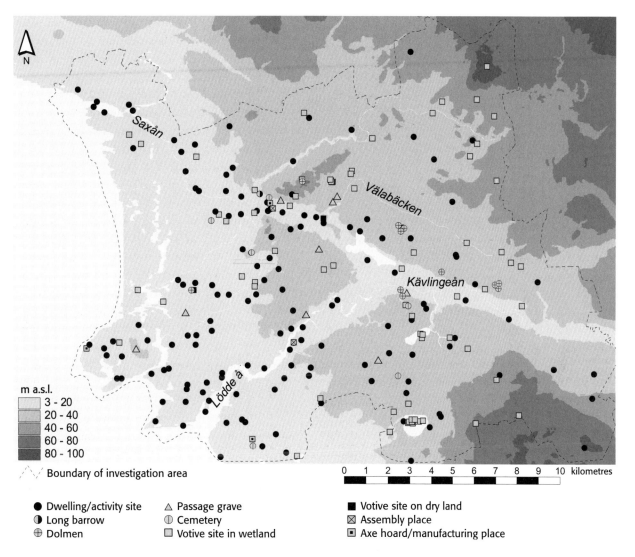

Fig. 9. Early and Middle Neolithic sites in the investigation area.

Southern Excavations Department, and the National Heritage Board Surface Survey Department in Karlskrona, conducted intensive surface surveys in specially selected parishes in the best conceivable external circumstances. One aim was to investigate the reliability of the revised survey of ancient monuments. A rough calculation based on the number of newly registered dwelling sites from this special survey shows that only about 3% of the total number

of dwelling sites were detected by the revised survey (Holmgren & Tronde 1990; Karsten 1990; Larsson, L. 2001:23).

The proportion of the total number of places in the investigation area whose type and age have been determined is nevertheless so large that they can be considered representative enough to allow an interpretation of the distribution, form, and content of settlement. Thanks to the National Heritage Board's survey of ancient monuments it has become possible to present a distribution map of all the known Stone Age dwelling sites in the investigation area. The survey was conducted by a limited number of people with long experience of surveying, and of the 29 parishes, almost 70% were surveyed by a single person. This means that the documentation from the survey of ancient monuments may be considered to be of good quality. On the basis of the collected material it is difficult to determine from a surface survey whether the finds represent a large settlement, a temporary camp, or a work site. However, the aim has been to use this material as a complement to the excavated sites to compile a chronological and chorological distribution map and as far as possible to ascertain the functions of the different places (fig. 9).

The difficulty lies in distinguishing dwelling sites from different phases within the Neolithic. In several cases there are no finds allowing a more exact dating, or the information on dating in the register of ancient monuments is inadequate: it was therefore necessary for me to go through the collected find material from the survey of ancient monuments. After this the number of places that could be dated to one of the four phases of the Early and Middle Neolithic stated above rose by almost 30%. For this purpose farm collections have been a significant addition. These naturally vary in scope and differ in value as source material. In several cases, however, it has been possible to link datable objects to individual fields and registered dwelling sites. They are therefore an important complement in studies of settlement development in the Early and Middle Neolithic. Apart from the source material mentioned above, museums and farm collections contain a large number of Neolithic finds with no more exact statement of find place than the parish. These objects have been removed from their original contexts, which makes it impossible to determine whether they come from dwelling sites, graves, or votive sites. Since the aim here is to investigate where in the landscape different things took

place and to understand the meaning of places, these objects have been left outside the analytical framework of the book. Only objects for which an exact find spot is stated can thus be considered in the study. Exceptions have been made for wetland finds, for which I have regarded it as sufficient that wetland and the property designation are stated. Within the investigation area, 247 places have been identified with material belonging to one or more of the periods EN I, EN II–MNA II, MNA III–V, and MNB, and 72 of these sites have been excavated.

A minimum requirement for a place to be designated a dwelling/activity site is the presence of knapped flint and at least one fragment of a tool. It is rare for potsherds to be discovered by surface survey, so this group of artefacts cannot be regarded as a requirement for being able to define a place as a dwelling/activity site. Stray finds of intact axes should not automatically be regarded as indicators of a dwelling site; they may come from graves or votive activities that took place away from the dwelling site. It must be possible to derive finds of whole axes from an exact find spot where they were found together with flint debitage if the site is to be regarded as a dwelling site. It is of course tricky to determine the size of a site. The distribution of flint objects at ground level must serve as a basis for assessing the size. The possibility of judging the character of places found by surface survey is however restricted compared with excavated sites, and in the present work they will therefore be assessed on the basis of other criteria. Occasional places – those where the flint discovered by surface survey shows several different categories of tools (scrapers, knives, awls) together with a rich amount of debitage/flakes, and where site continuity can be demonstrated – will be hypothetically regarded in the discussion as potential main settlements. Finds uncovered in wetland settings which suggest deliberate deposition are considered in this study as votive finds in accordance with the discussion above.

# The places

In the enumeration of the places I give a detailed description only of the places where there are distinct features that can be associated with the investigated period. Of course, the quantity of information and the details of the site descriptions vary depending on the quality of the excavation reports. Other places are included merely as dots on the map but are significant for an understanding of the spatial distribution of Neolithic societies, the mutual relation of the places in the system, and hence the relation of the people to the landscape. The places are presented first by their registration number, and in cases where there is no number, by the name of the parish and/or property. Important sites for my work are of course the Neolithic remains excavated in connection with the construction of the new West Coast Line. Since these places have previously been presented with an SU number (SU standing for *slutundersökning* or "final excavation") (Svensson 2003), this designation is also given in parentheses after the name of the place in the heading.

## EN I

**Settlement** Of the hitherto published Early Neolithic dwelling sites in Skåne, the majority are in the south-west and south-east of the province. The Hagestad and Ystad projects have dominated Neolithic research in south-east Skåne (Strömberg 1968, 1971, 1978, 1982a, 1982b, 1988a, 1988b, 1988c; Larsson & Larsson 1984, 1986; Larsson, L. 1985, 1989a; Larsson, M. 1987, 1988b, 1992), whereas for the Neolithic in the south-west of the province it is above all the intensive excavation work conducted by Malmö Museums in the last thirty years that has added to our knowledge (Salomonsson 1971; Svensson 1986; Björhem & Säfvestad 1989; Almquist & Svensson 1990; Billberg & Magnusson Staaf 1999; Sarnäs & Nord Paulsson 2001). The Early Neolithic dwelling site material in south-west Skåne has been published in a comprehensive study by Mats Larsson (1984). In both these areas one notices a change in settlement patterns during the Early Neolithic. The earlier preference for coastal sites is replaced by a more varied picture whereby more of the landscape is claimed in a completely new way, with both coastal and inland settlements. The settlements in both Skåne and Denmark have been described as consisting of small and scattered households which functioned for brief periods (Larsson, M. 1984, 1985, 1988a, 1991, 1992; Madsen & Jensen 1982; Eriksen & Madsen 1984).

In the innermost parts of the province, however, the lack of Early Neolithic settlements is striking. Occurrences of stray finds, above all in the form of pointed-butted axes of types I–II, nevertheless show that these areas were not unknown to the population at the time (fig. 10). It is presumably in large measure the lack of excavations in these regions that explains the absence of known settlements.

The distinctive features that can be identified in nearby regions such as Sjælland or in the Ystad and Malmö areas in Skåne cannot automatically be transferred to conditions in the areas around the Saxån-Välabäcken and Lödde Å-Kävlingeån. The introduction of agriculture in northern Europe is associated with the Funnel Beaker culture. This complex displays great similarities in its material culture over much of north-west Europe (Midgley 1992). At the same time, it should be noted that "the Neolithic way of life" was adopted in different ways and at different speeds in different regions. The transition from the Mesolithic to the Neolithic should be viewed as a protracted process rather than a sudden event. The Mesolithic background in each region created the basic conditions in time and place for the emergence of the local Neolithic societies.

There are relatively few well-documented settlements in the investigation area which have been dated to EN I. In most cases the Early Neolithic material is found together with later remains which have disturbed any Early Neolithic features and occupation layers. From this period there are 27 registered sites, 15 of which have been excavated (fig. 11).

**Main settlements on the coast**   In the initial phase of the Early Neolithic, the sea was about three metres higher than today's level (Regnell, M., pers.com.). The coastline was marked by bays and lagoons with long shallows extending out from the coastal strip (Christensen 1982, 1993). This means that bays cut like wedges into what are now the rivers Saxån and Lödde Å.

Along the bay of the sea which is today the river Saxån, four Early Neolithic places have been documented (fig. 11).

*Saxtorp 23 (SU10)*   On a height about 10 m a.s.l., which in prehistoric times was a promontory-like tongue of land between the Saxån to the south and the Kvärlövsån – now almost totally drained – to the north (fig. 11), there was in the Early Neolithic a large settlement with activities covering an area of several thousand square metres. During at least parts of the Early Neolithic, in connection with the transgression maximum, an offshoot of the bay reached all the way in to this place (Regnell, M., pers.com.). The remains, which were excavated by the National Heritage Board Southern Excavations Department in 1997–98 in connection with the expansion of the West Coast Line, are in a central location on the sandy part of the height. When investigated the tongue of land was cultivated, and according to the maps drawn for the *storskifte* enclosures, it has been used at least since the second half of the eighteenth century as arable, pasture, or meadow land. Different Early Neolithic activity areas have been distinguished (Andersson & Pihl 1997).

Small areas on the height tend to become peaty because areas with finer soils in the surrounding boulder clay bring the groundwater up to the surface. Within one such area two features (A2369 and A13939) and a find-bearing occupation layer were excavated (fig. 12). The two features were relatively small and shallow, about 1 m in diameter with a depth of roughly 0.4 m. The features were interpreted as wells since the

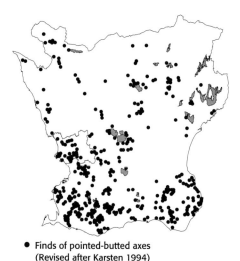

● Finds of pointed-butted axes
(Revised after Karsten 1994)

Fig. 10. Pointed-butted axes in Skåne.

groundwater could be reached by digging shallow pits. A $^{14}C$ dating taken from charcoal in one of the wells gave the result 4885±80 BP (3780–3540 cal. bc, Ua-8984), which corresponds to EN I. The finds from the wells included flake scrapers and pottery with small imprints under the edge of the rim. In addition, there was burnt clay and stone in large quantities. Of the osteological material, dental enamel from cattle could be identified. Analysis of the palaeobotanical material from the two wells shows that the forest vegetation consisted, among other things, of hazel, lime, oak, pine, alder, and birch. A large percentage of grass and herb pollen suggests, however, that the area was cleared in places and perhaps used as pasture or arable (Regnell, M., pers.com.). At least one of the features, which was documented in the preliminary investigation but later fell outside the area of the final excavation, may be yet another well (A3156). About 40% of the surrounding occupation layer (A103) was excavated. The flint material (2.3 kg) was dominated by flake scrapers. These tools are all made of relatively large flakes with a long convex scraping edge. The stratigraphical observations in the field indicated that the wells and the occupation layer are virtually contemporary. The area around the well was probably the scene

54

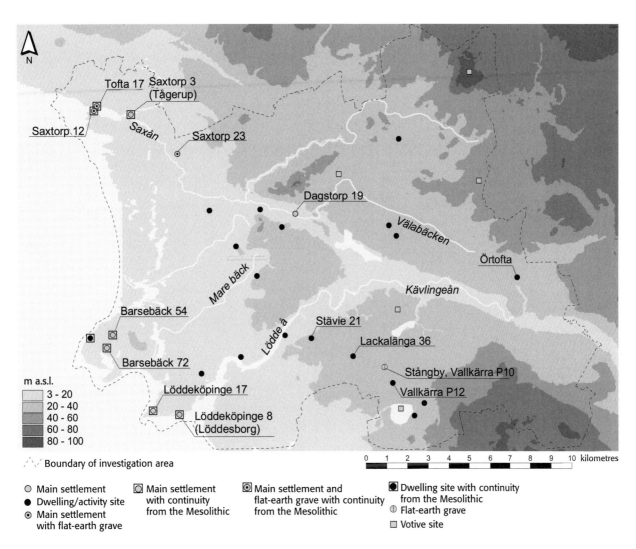

m a.s.l.

| | 3 - 20 |
| 20 - 40 |
| 40 - 60 |
| 60 - 80 |
| 80 - 100 |

/\/ Boundary of investigation area

0 1 2 3 4 5 6 7 8 9 10 kilometres

○ Main settlement
● Dwelling/activity site
◉ Main settlement
with flat-earth grave

◙ Main settlement
with continuity
from the Mesolithic

◙ Main settlement and
flat-earth grave with continuity
from the Mesolithic

● Dwelling site with continuity
from the Mesolithic
① Flat-earth grave
□ Votive site

Fig. 11. EN I sites in the investigation area.

of some specialized activity, with the flint scrapers used for working wood and skins. An asymmetric halberd, most likely of type A (Ebbesen 1994), was retrieved from the layer. These tools occur throughout the Early Neolithic. The pottery (0.4 kg) mainly consisted of small, unidentifiable sherds. One sherd showed traces of very vague decoration in the form of two parallel lines. The sherd cannot be dated any more precisely than to the Neolithic (Andersson & Pihl 1997; Andersson, M. 1999).

About 60 m east of the area with the wells, on a terrace in the gentle slope down towards the Kvärlövsån, the excavation documented a house adjacent to a find-bearing layer (fig. 12). The house was round-oval and was estimated to measure 4.5×7.5 m, oriented WNW–ESE. The wall structure consisted of two trenches and a total of eight post-holes, three of which were in the eastern trench. In the centre of the house were two post-holes which were interpreted as posts to hold up the roof. In the southern part of the

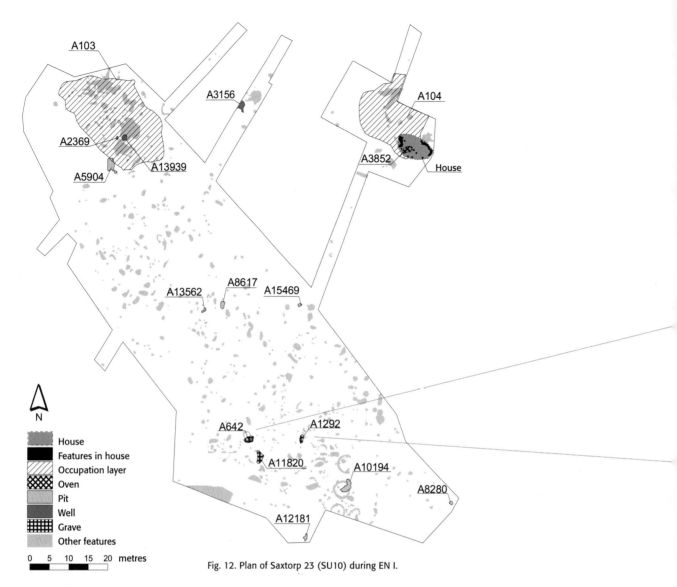

Fig. 12. Plan of Saxtorp 23 (SU10) during EN I.

structure between the trenches there was a black, sooty layer which was covered by a compact layer of burnt clay – perhaps the remains of a simple oven (A3852). The pottery in the sooty layer is undecorated but can be assigned to the Neolithic. A $^{14}$C dating from the sooty layer gave the value 4910±95 BP (3900–3540 cal. bc, Ua-8987), which corresponds to EN I. Since the area was not included in the final excavation, only 4% of the occupation layer (A104), or 400 m², was dug out. The stock of tools was dominated by flake scrapers, but also comprised a knife and two transverse arrowheads. The transverse arrowheads were made of flakes. Other flint material (4.2 kg) consisted of cores, flakes from axe manufacturing, retouched flints, along with debitage and debris. There was a concentration of flint within the layer; it included a core, several flakes from axe manufacturing and blades, but also a transverse arrowhead. The dense accumulation of flints (0.6 kg) and the occurrence of both debris and small and large flakes suggests a primary deposit. This material may

perhaps represent the waste amassed by tool production. The pottery (0.5 kg) is all coarse-tempered and mainly undecorated. A cord-decorated rim sherd was found, with decoration consisting of two horizontal lines placed under the edge of the rim. The rim is slightly everted with a small lip. On some of the sherds one could detect a distinct transition between the neck and the belly. All in all, the composition of the flint indicates that the material originated in EN I (Andersson & Pihl 1997; Andersson, M. 1999).

Higher up on the plateau, about 80 m south of the house and the wells, there were two features (A642 and A1292) which were presumed to be flat-earth graves (fig. 12). A642 ran from north-east to south-west and measured 2.32×0.79 m with a depth of 0.58 m. Two post-holes were found adjacent to the ends of the feature and may have been part of the structure. They could be the traces of some form of superstructure. Grey humus documented in the grave is probably the stain left by a body (fig. 13). No skeletal parts survived and it was not possible to determine how the

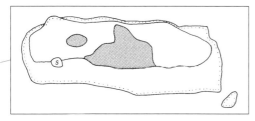

Fig. 13. Flat-earth grave (A642) at Saxtorp 23 (SU10). The grey hatching shows the colouring left by the body. Scale 1:40.

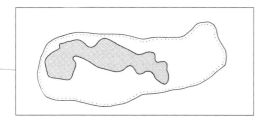

Fig. 14. Flat-earth grave (1292) at Saxtorp 23 (SU10). The grey hatching shows the colouring left by the body. Scale 1:40.

N

body had lain. On the same level as the body colouring there were eight stones of varying size at the north edge. Among the flint there were three flake scrapers and a fragment of a polished axe. The axe fragment shows parts of three polished sides and probably comes from a thin-butted or a pointed-butted axe of type 3 and can thus derive from either EN I or EN II (Ebbesen 1983:61). The pottery mainly consisted of undecorated sherds of general Neolithic character. Two small rim pieces, one of them with cord decoration, were found, however. A charcoal sample from the filling was $^{14}$C-dated, yielding the result 4885±85 BP (3780–3540 cal. bc, Ua-8986). This result falls within EN I and is thus contemporary with the house and the wells. Immediately to the south-west of the structure was an intact quern bedstone. Just over ten metres east of A642 was yet another grave-like feature (A1292) measuring 2.02×0.76 m; the depth was 0.63 m. The feature was oriented north–south. A grey colouring in the filling of the grave, about 1.3 m long, was interpreted as having been made by a body, show-

ing that the deceased was probably laid with the head towards the north (fig. 14). No skeletal parts or grave goods were found. A small amount of flint was retrieved from the filling. There was at least one more feature in the area (A11820) with a round-oval, grave-like shape, but no skeletal parts or body colouring could be documented (Andersson & Pihl 1997; Andersson, M. 1999).

Between these activity areas there were a number of pits with Early Neolithic material, some of them containing a fairly large number of finds. The composition – potsherds, flint flakes, axe fragments, flake cores, blades, awls, scrapers, and burnt bones – can be described as ordinary dwelling site material. The large quantity of burnt clay and clay daub found in the pits is remarkable. The clay occurred scattered in the features. No layers of soot or clay were documented, except in the remains of the house described above, where they could be the traces of an oven. One possible hypothesis is that it is clay daub deriving from other buildings on the site – outside the excavated area. The use of clay for Early Neolithic buildings has been documented from the nearby EN II settlement at Saxtorp (see Saxtorp 26). One of the pits, in the south of the area by the flat-earth graves, stood out by virtue of its distinctive appearance (A12181). The pit was about 2.3×1 m and just over 0.5 m deep. The sides of the pit bulged outwards and seemed to be lined with clay. The finds consisted of 2.5 kg of flint, including a number of flake scrapers, blade knives, and a core awl. Just over half a kilo of pottery was retrieved. The decorated sherds were dominated by small imprints, but whipped cord also occurred (Andersson & Pihl 1997; Andersson, M. 1999).

The place on the tongue of land was probably a main settlement. The various remains display a diverse picture, with a house, tool manufacture, wells, and specialized activities in the form of wood and skin processing. The flint is of the type associated with dwelling sites, with a large element of flake cores and flakes/debitage. The tools are dominated by flake scrapers, but knives, awls, and transverse arrowheads also occur in fairly large numbers. The palaeobotanical analyses indicate, moreover, that an area of forest was cleared, possibly for cultivation and/or animal husbandry. The area of the settlement is difficult to estimate since the whole site was not excavated, but the surface survey suggests an extent of roughly 25,000 m². This size reinforces the impression that the occupation was not short-term, and the presence of graves shows that the place had a function more than just as a settlement.

There were no remains on the site to suggest any Mesolithic activity. However, hut remains from the Middle Neolithic were identified, as well as hearths from the Late Bronze Age and Early Iron Age (Andersson & Pihl 1997; Andersson, M. 1999). It is noteworthy that 300–400 m south-east of the site a settlement from the Iron Age was excavated at the same time and one of the houses discovered there could be from EN I. It was a small house, about 7.5×5 metres, with two aisles. The typology led to its being interpreted as a building from the Roman Iron Age. A ¹⁴C analysis from one of the post-holes, however, gave a dating in EN I (Artursson et al. 2003). Nearby the preliminary investigation uncovered an occupation layer with finds from the Funnel Beaker culture. There was thus a possibility that this house could be Neolithic and be part of the Early Neolithic settlement complex on the tongue.

*Saxtorp 3 (Tågerup)*    Three kilometres to the northwest, on the shores of the same bay, was the Mesolithic dwelling site and burial place at Tågerup (fig. 11). The area is characterized by its proximity to the Saxån and Braån. The terrain beside the rivers today consists in large measure of marshy grazing meadows which are repeatedly flooded in winter and spring. The place comprises parts of a moraine plateau that slopes down towards the Braån to the west and towards the Saxån to the south. To the south-west there extends a large area of wetland running along the valley of the Saxån towards the village of Häljarp.

The archaeological excavations conducted by the National Heritage Board Southern Excavations Department in 1996–98 revealed comprehensive activities in the Late Mesolithic (Karsten & Knarrström 1999, 2003). An inventory of stray finds shows that the place was also visited during the Early Neolithic. The extent of these Neolithic activities is difficult to assess since the excavations covered only Mesolithic settlement layers along the former shoreline. The remains cover a large part of the foreland (over 100,000 m²), but according to the surface survey the Early and Middle Neolithic activities mainly took place higher up on the plateau. The composition of tools here, with scrapers, knives, awls, arrowheads, and axe fragments, indicates that the site probably functioned as a main settlement during much of the Neolithic as well.

*Tofta 17*    A little more than a kilometre and a half west of Tågerup, two sites (Tofta 17 and Saxtorp 12) with finds of Early Neolithic material were excavated, on either side of the Saxån bay (fig. 11).

Tofta 17, on the north side of the bay, was on a slight sandy rise. It was excavated by the National Heritage Board Southern Excavations Department in 1998 in connection with the construction of the West Coast Line. Within this area it has been possible to document a very long prehistory. Flint finds show that the first visit here came late in the Palaeolithic (Andersson & Knarrström 1999:60). The place was subsequently used for a long time as a burial ground. With certain interruptions, there are burials from the Late Mesolithic until the early part of the Iron Age. The long site continuity meant that stratigraphical interpretations were very difficult and that the older remains in several cases were disturbed by the later ones. In the north-west part of the area, above all, it was possible to document Early Neolithic activities (Cademar & Ericson 2000).

Parts of a house were identified, overlayered by a burial mound that has now been ploughed away (fig. 15). It has not been possible to arrive at an unambigu-

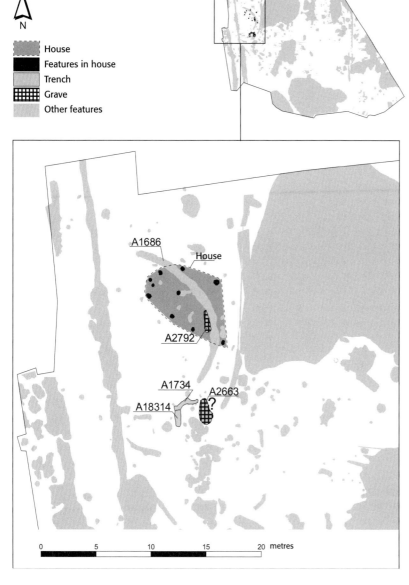

Fig. 15. Plan of Tofta 17 during EN I.

ous dating of the post structure, but the rounded gable in the western part of the building shows similarities to the two-aisled houses of Mossby type which are dated to the Early Neolithic (Larsson, M. 1992; Göthberg et al. 1995:100). Other central posts and wall posts in the eastern part of the house were probably destroyed in connection with the digging of the trench (A1686) around the edge of the barrow. This trench is dated to the earliest part of the Bronze Age, or possibly the Late Neolithic. It is likely that the barrow has preserved the post-holes in the western part of the structure (Cademar & Ericson 2000). In the area around the structure, Early Neolithic pottery was retrieved, along with a fragment of a pointed-butted flint axe. The dating of the house is of course uncertain since it has been disturbed by later activity. Any Early

Neolithic occupation layers that may have existed have also been destroyed by later activity. The form of the structure, the stratigraphical observations, and finds of Early Neolithic pottery in the area indicate a dating to EN I to be reasonable.

At least two of the flat-earth graves on the site may come from the Early Neolithic. In the south-east part of the house a feature measuring 2.01×0.8 m and 0.37 m deep (A2792) was excavated. It was oriented north–south and overlayered in the eastern part by the trench around the barrow. No skeletal colouring was identified, but there was a filling that was interpreted as the remains of a stain left by a coffin. The feature was therefore interpreted as a flat-earth grave. A charcoal sample from the filling gave a [14]C dating of 5105±75 BP (3980–3800 cal. bc, Ua-

8351). This corresponds to the transition between the Late Mesolithic and the Early Neolithic. Under two long barrows placed one on top of the other at Bygholm Nørremark in eastern Jutland, a grave was found inside a house. The long barrows have been dated to EN II (C) (Rønne 1979). Although the Bronze Age barrow overlayering the house and the grave in Tofta has preserved dug features such as post-holes and the grave, the construction of the barrow destroyed other remains of Early Neolithic activities. If a long barrow preceded the Bronze Age barrow, perhaps the traces of the traditional east façade of a long barrow, in the form of stains left by posts or pits and/or a stone packing, should nevertheless have been documented. None of these remains could be identified, which probably means that there never was a long barrow here. About five metres south of this grave, yet another grave-like feature (A2663) was excavated. This measured 2.33×1.04 m and was 0.4 m deep. The feature was oriented north–south. No bones or skeleton colouring could be observed, however. The finds in the filling included sherds of cord-decorated pottery, five flint blades, a butt fragment from a thin-butted flint axe, and almost 2 kg of flint flakes and debitage, of which 1.5 kg was burnt. A charcoal sample from the bottom filling gave the value 5540±70 BP (4460–4340 cal. bc, Ua-8352), corresponding to the middle Ertebølle culture. Both the function and the dating of the feature may thus be regarded as uncertain (Lindblad & Lund 1997). In two trenches (A1734 and A18314) immediately to the west of the feature there was cord-decorated pottery which can be dated to the Early Neolithic (Cademar & Ericson 2000). It cannot be ruled out that the graves are later and that the Early Neolithic material comes from an older occupation layer which has been dug up and is now ploughed away. Despite this, the Early Neolithic presence on the site is palpable, and it is particularly interesting in relation to the Late Mesolithic and Early Neolithic remains (Saxtorp 12) excavated on the other side of the Saxån.

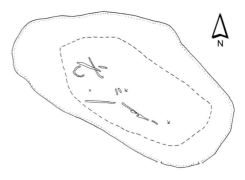

Fig. 16. Flat-earth grave at Saxtorp 12. Traces of colouring and skeletal parts are drawn in. Scale 1:40.

*Saxtorp 12*   This site, which was excavated by a seminar excavation in 1982 by the Department of Archaeology, Lund University, was located on what was once a sandy foreland south of the Saxån (fig. 11). The site had previously been dated to the Late Mesolithic and the Early Neolithic on the basis of the rich quantity of surface finds from the plough layer. In the south-west part of the excavated area, which was on a small plateau about 6 m a.s.l., an area of 30 m² of a dark-coloured occupation layer was dug out. The finds consisted of flint (3.3 kg) in the form of flakes, blades, cores, two blade scrapers, and three transverse arrowheads, and there were also small quantities of pottery (0.13 kg) of an Early Neolithic character; these included belly sherds with shallow parallel lines which can be categorized as ENC (EN II). Adjacent to the occupation layer was a grave measuring 2.10×1.20 m. Traces of colouring and skeletal remains could be distinguished (fig. 16). Towards the bottom the filling was denser and fattier, which could be interpreted as remains of a coffin. The grave was 0.70 m deep and oriented SSW–NNE. Finds of two potsherds, one of them decorated with shallow parallel lines, can be dated to ENC (EN II). About 50 m north-east of the grave, 26 m² of yet another occupation layer was excavated. Besides flint flakes and debitage, there were scrapers, knives, awls, polished axe fragments, transverse arrowheads, hammerstones, cores, and part of a quern. The large

Fig. 17. Dagstorp 19 (SU21) in the Välabäcken valley (photo L. Bygdemark).

amounts of flint (60 kg) and pottery (0.3 kg) here indicate dates in the Ertebølle culture and EN B–C (EN I–II) (Jennbert 1984b).

No clear boundaries to the settlement could be determined on the basis of the metre-square trenches that were dug. It is of course difficult from the excavation of a limited area to obtain a picture of the organization of the place. It is reasonable to assume that the grave is not a solitary phenomenon; there may well be more graves in the area. The composition of the flint suggests that the site was used for a long time during the Late Mesolithic/Early Neolithic and that it functioned, at least periodically, as a main settlement. Perhaps the place can be associated with the remains on the other side of the river. The two sites may very well have functioned partly simultaneously and constituted a larger settlement complex.

*Löddeköpinge 8 (Löddesborg)*   In the Early Neolithic there were also settlements along the bay that is now the Lödde Å (fig. 11). The only one that has been excavated is the Löddesborg site, Löddeköpinge 8.

The Löddesborg dwelling site was at an altitude of 4–5 m a.s.l. on the coast of the Öresund, roughly 1 km west of where the Lödde Å flows into the sound. The settlement was located on a raised beach on the south side of a small peninsula which was demarcated to the north by the former lagoon that is now the bog of Barsebäck Mosse. The site has been known since the start of the twentieth century, and excavations were conducted by LUHM during a total of six field seasons between 1964 and 1970. The total area excavated was 622 m², some 412 m² of this intensively, within an area measuring roughly 170×25 m (Jennbert 1984a).

Under the plough layer there were several occupation layers deposited by recurrent settlements. The total quantity of Late Mesolithic and Early Neolithic flint and pottery is very large. Several hundred kilos of knapped flint has been retrieved, and the pottery amounts to 130 kg. The latter is dominated by Ertebølle ware, but a large quantity of Early Neolithic ware was found, especially in the upper layers. Tools account for only about 1% of the flint (Jennbert 1984a).

In several of the occupation layers there were features in the form of hearths, post-holes, and a stone packing. Clay daub was identified in the upper occupation layer, which might suggest the remains of some kind of building in connection with an Early Neolithic settlement phase. The excavated areas are too small, however, to allow us to establish this for sure. Large

stones were found in the central parts of the site. Their size and finds of human bones do not exclude the possibility that there was once a dolmen here (Jennbert 1984a).

Jennbert thinks that the Löddesborg site is a settlement of "mixed character". The Ertebølle and Early Neolithic ceramic tradition can be distinguished in all the layers, with an increasing frequency of Early Neolithic sherds in the upper layers. Based on a [14]C dating from the lower occupation layer with the value 5260±80 BP (4230–3980 cal. bc, Lu-1842), the character of the stone finds, and the predominance of Ertebølle pottery in all the layers, all the occupation layers of the settlement have been dated to the Late Atlantic (Jennbert 1984a). Whether the absolute dating in the bottom layer also applies to the later horizons above it can of course be discussed. We cannot rule out a certain mixture of material between different stratigraphical horizons. In the upper layers in particular there is a significant element of material characteristic of the Early Neolithic.

Grain impressions in the pottery and remains of bones from domesticated animals, chiefly in the later settlement horizons (Jennbert 1984a), show that the settlement is a place where people probably pursued tillage and animal husbandry. This fact, together with the size of the place and the varied nature of the finds, is a powerful argument that there was a main settlement here.

Another six places with Early Neolithic material have been registered along the coast or in the bays. Since they have not been excavated, it is difficult to determine their function. At three of the places (Löddeköpinge 17 (Vikhög), Barsebäck 72, and Barsebäck 54) a large amount of flint has been collected, of both Late Mesolithic and Early Neolithic character. Since these sites also cover relatively large areas, it is reasonable to regard them as hypothetical main settlements.

**Main settlements in the interior**   Unlike the Late Mesolithic sites in the area, several of the registered Early Neolithic sites are in the interior. None of the settle-

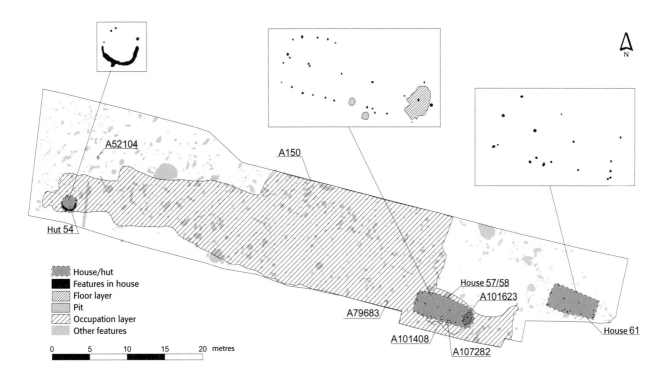

Fig. 18. Plan of Dagstorp 19 (SU21) during EN I.

ments in the area, however, is more than about 15 kilometres from the former coastline, which means that the sea was always within easy reach. Places within a few kilometres of the coast, from where the water can be reached in an hour or so, may be reckoned as coastal or near-coastal sites. When the distance to the coast is more than five kilometres, however, the sites should be regarded as inland sites since in these cases it was probably not the marine environment and its resources that dictated the choice of settlement location. Most of the inland sites, however, are close to watercourses or wetlands. It was above all the sandy soils that were claimed, but often in the zone where they border on the clay soils.

Most of the Early Neolithic inland settlements are relatively small, but one larger dwelling site in the interior has been documented beside the Välabäcken in the valley between the medieval church of Dagstorp and the hills of Västra Karaby (figs. 11 and 17).

*Dagstorp 19 (SU21)* Dagstorp 19 comprised remains of settlement from the Early and Middle Neolithic Funnel Beaker culture and the Late Iron Age, as well as occasional remains from the Battle Axe culture and the Late Bronze Age/Early Iron Age. On the site, which was excavated in connection with the construction of the West Coast Line in 1998, remains were found of about fifteen houses from the Early and the Middle Neolithic. The number of houses is the largest from this period in Sweden hitherto found on one site (Lagergren-Olsson & Linderoth 2000; Artursson et al. 2003).

The Välabäcken, the course of which has been straightened today, flows east–west, and the land on either side is used for tillage and pasture. The site is located on gentle slopes and tongues of land reaching out towards areas which in prehistoric time were wetlands beside the Välabäcken. In the northern part of the investigation area the terrain slopes gently down

64

towards a more waterlogged area. The subsoil closest to the water system consists of fine-grained sand, while the element of coarser stone becomes more noticeable on the higher parts of the ridge to the north. The remains are located on stretches of fine sand along the Välabäcken running for a distance of approximately 500 m. The dwelling sites make up a chronological sequence from EN I to MNA III (Lagergren-Olsson & Linderoth 2000).

In the western part of the site there were occupation layers (A150) with chronologically homogeneous find material, so the place here appears not to have been disturbed by later prehistoric activity (fig. 18 and 19). The area has not been subject to repeated deep ploughing, and there are well-preserved features both in and under the occupation layer. The layer comprised an area of about 3,700 m² and the boundary could be established wholly to the east and west and partially to the north and south. After an introductory surface survey of the whole occupation layer, 403 metre-square trenches were dug by hand. The remainder of the layer was investigated extensively by means of machine stripping. The pottery (16 kg) was of Funnel Beaker character and the total impression was of a dating to EN I (Becker 1947; Larsson, M. 1984; Lagergren-Olsson & Linderoth 2000). The decoration of the excavated material was done with stabbed dots around the rim. Fragments of at least one collared flask and a clay disc were retrieved. The clay disc had impressions on the edge, which was also thickened. Occasional elements of Middle Neolithic

Fig. 19. Layer 150 during excavation at Dagstorp 19 (SU21) (photo A. Lagergren-Olsson).

pottery consisted of sherds decorated with lines or tooth stamps. The layer also contained a concentration of pottery about 1.9×0.7 m (A79683) with about 160 sherds. Among the decorated pottery were large parts of a lugged beaker with decoration consisting of alternating vertical and horizontal fields of whipped cord on both belly and neck, and notches at the rim. There is also a rim sherd with impressions under the rim and there are remains of a clay disc. The flint in the layer (24 kg) was of Neolithic character; finds included several cores of polygonal and platform type, blades, and flakes from axe and flake manufacture. A fragment of a polished, probably thin-butted, flint axe and part of a polished halberd datable to EN–MN II (Ebbesen 1994:103) were found in the topsoil.

In and beside the occupation layer farthest to the west was a hut structure, designated hut 54. It was round with a diameter of 4.3 m, and with the opening towards the north-north-east. In the southern half the hut consisted of a trench with post-holes and in the northern half of post-holes. Charcoal taken from one of the post-holes gave a dating to EN I, 5040±75 BP (3950–3770 cal. bc, Ua-25730). Several Early Neolithic pits were found on the site. Pit A52104 northeast of the hut distinguished itself through the relatively large quantity of finds retrieved here. In the feature, which measured 0.98×0.7 m and was 0.3 m deep, there were flakes with polished surfaces, burnt flint, debitage from axe manufacture, parts of funnel beakers, and burnt bones. A fragment of a clay disc, with a raised edge and decorated with finger impressions along the rim, was also discovered. Clay discs of this type can be dated to EN I (cf. Nielsen, P. O. 1985). Two charcoal samples from the feature gave Early Neolithic datings, 4755±70 BP (3640–3380 cal. bc, Ua-8860) and 4800±70 BP (3660–3380 cal. bc, Ua-25059) (Lagergren-Olsson & Linderoth 2000).

Adjacent to the eastern part of the layer was a structure designated house 57/58. This was first regarded as two separate houses, but a reinterpretation has shown that it was probably a large building with no pairs of posts in the middle part of the long walls. What speaks in favour of this alternative is the occurrence of a distinct row of roof-bearing posts and the fact that there were similar contemporary finds. The weaknesses of the interpretation can be the exaggerated trapezoidal shape and the fact that the roof-bearing line was placed somewhat obliquely in the design. It is also uncertain what the interruptions in the long walls represent. The design was two-aisled and just over 20 m long, with a width varying between 7.7 and 5 m. Charcoal samples taken from one of the roof-bearing post-holes gave a date in EN I, 4915±85 BP (3800–3540 cal. bc, Ua-25726). In the eastern part beside the gable was a pit, A101623, which measured roughly 4.7×3.1 m and was 0.18 m deep. This feature can be interpreted as remains of a

sunken floor. In the middle of the house was a pit rich in finds, A101408 (1×0.7×0.2 m). Just outside the southern wall there was another find-bearing pit, A107282 (1.06×0.92×0.35 m). The pit in the central part of the house contained quite a lot of pottery and flint. The flint finds mostly consisted of flakes/debitage, but there were also tools in the form of four scrapers, a knife, a transverse arrowhead, and a polished axe fragment, as well as retouched flint and a microblade. Among the pottery there were parts of a lugged beaker with decoration consisting of alternating vertical and horizontal fields of whipped cord on both the belly and the neck. These sherds showed great similarities to the lugged beaker found in the layer, and they may come from the same vessel. The lugged beaker has decoration resembling what was found at Bellevuegården in Malmö, which has been dated to the late EN II (Larsson, M. 1984). Eva Koch, however, believes that this type of lugged beaker can be dated to EN I (Koch 1998:109ff). The pit also contained a piece of a clay disc and a sherd of a collared flask. In the sunken floor, A101623, there was flint, pottery, burnt bones, and the shell of a hazelnut. The flint mostly consisted of flakes/debitage, but there were also a couple of scrapers and some retouched pieces of flint. The pottery was not decorated. Pit A107282 contained a large quantity of pottery along with flint, burnt clay, burnt bones, and charcoal. Some rim sherds were decorated with notches on the edge. There were also two fragments of a clay disc with finger impressions on the edge. The finds of flint consisted of flakes/debitage, a flake core, debris, a couple of retouched flints, and a polished axe fragment. The pottery and the analysis of carbon samples, yielding the values 4925±70 BP (3780–3640 cal. bc, Ua-25719) and 4900±70 BP (3770–3630 cal. bc, Ua-25720), allow the pits to be dated to EN I (Artursson et al. 2003).

East of the layer there was yet another house structure, house 61, which according to the [14]C results from a charcoal sample taken from one of the wall post-holes can be dated to EN I, 4895±85 BP (3790–3540 cal. bc, Ua-25727). The house is a two-aisled structure, 16×7 m and oriented ESE–WNW, with a rectangular, possibly slightly trapezoidal form. Heavy ploughing in this part of the excavated area has removed any associated occupation layers. Occasional flint flakes were found in the features of the house. The dating, however, must be considered uncertain, since the $^{14}$C analysis points towards EN I, while the appearance of the house is more like that of houses dated to MNA I–III.

The total quantity of finds and the scope of the occupation layers and features at Dagstorp suggest that the site functioned as a main settlement.

### Dwelling/activity sites

*Stävie 21*  In the area around the Lödde Å and Kävlingeån valley, three small, similar Early Neolithic sites (Stävie 21, Lackalänga 36, and Örtofta) have been identified (fig. 11). They are relatively small and have a limited amount of finds.

The Stävie 21 site, which was excavated in 1990 by the National Heritage Board Southern Excavations Department in connection with the planned construction of new houses, was located on a moraine plateau just south of the Lödde Å. The natural environment is influenced by the meandering course of the river and the undulating terrain with sandy till ridges, interrupted by wetlands, now mostly drained. From the excavated plateau, with a view of the valley, the land slopes down to the west, at first gently and then steeply towards an area of wetland (Knarrström 1995).

The excavated area, which comprised about 4,500 m², contained two hut structures (fig. 20) which were rather difficult to interpret. Hut I was about 7.5×7.5 m, consisting of eighteen post-holes with an average depth of 0.15 m. The hut was badly damaged by recent drainage. No vestiges of occupation layers or floor levels were found in or beside the structure. One post-hole at the probable entrance in the south of the hut contained a small flint flake and an awl made from

frost-split moraine flint. Hut II measured 6.5×6.5 m with thirty-seven post-holes with an average depth of 0.09 m. No occupation layers or remains of floor levels were discovered. Flint flakes were found in two post-holes, one in the north wall, the other in the south wall. South-east of hut I was a pit almost 3 m in diameter and half a metre deep. Close on four kilos of pottery was retrieved from the pit. The combination of decoration, shape, tempering, and fabric quality indicates that about twenty different vessels were deposited in the pit (Knarrström 1995). The decorative and formal elements are comparable in typology and chronology to the Svenstorp group in ENB (EN I) (Larsson, M. 1984). A total of 95 scrapers were found in the pit, with a total weight of 3.7 kg, both worn-out and unused examples as well as preforms. Use-wear analysis showed that as many as 85% of the scrapers were used for working both wood and skins. In addition, a fragment of a thin- or pointed-butted flint axe was found and a large amount of flakes suitable for secondary knapping (Knarrström 1995, 2000a).

*Lackalänga 36*  A comparable hut structure was excavated only two kilometres west of Stävie 21 (fig. 20). The site, located on a flat terrace on a south-facing slope, was excavated by the National Heritage Board Southern Excavations Department in 1995 in connection with road construction. The excavated area comprised roughly 1,600 m². The district is dominated by light clay soils and has several areas of wetland. In prehistoric times the bogs were probably lakes and the hilly landscape was more wooded. A total of thirteen post-holes with an average depth of 0.15 m made up this round-oval hut-like structure. Charcoal from one of the post-holes gave the value 4790±80 BP (3651–3385 cal. bc, Ua-7402), corresponding to EN I–II. Other features on the site consisted of pits and hearths which could not be dated any more exactly than to prehistoric times. The few finds on the site were difficult to identify; however, a polished axe fragment was discovered (Andersson, A. 1997).

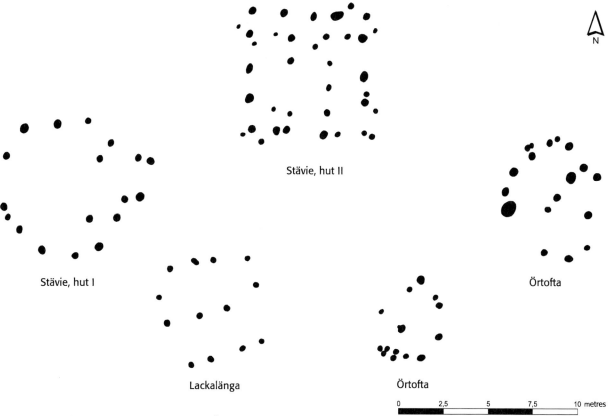

Stävie, hut II

Stävie, hut I

Lackalänga

Örtofta

Örtofta

0    2,5    5    7,5    10 metres

Fig. 20. Plan of the huts at Stävie, Lackalänga, and Örtofta.

*Örtofta*   Approximately 100 m east of the Braån in Örtofta parish, structures have been excavated (fig. 20) which show parallels to the structures from Stävie and Lackalänga described above. Areas totalling 16,200 m² were excavated here by the National Heritage Board Southern Excavations Department in 1992–1996 in connection with gravel extraction. The site is on a clayey plateau which slopes gently towards the south, down towards a small patch of wetland. The majority of the structures have been dated to the Bronze Age and Iron Age (Petersson & Hägerman 1997). There are, however, two post-built structures on the site which are slightly smaller than those in Stävie and Lackalänga but otherwise show a similar plan. They are round and about 5×5 m in size. Outside each structure was a pit containing Early Neolithic pottery. The pottery from one of the pits was highly fragmentary but it could be seen that it was decorated with oval impressions in least two rows under the rim. The other pit contained a large amount of pottery with a total weight of 1.4 kg. Among the sherds there were rim pieces decorated with cord and stick impressions grouped in several rows. The form and decoration of the sherds allow

the pottery to be assigned with some probability to EN I.

The large quantity of post-holes in the buildings, which are evidence of repair and post replacement, makes it hard to define the shape of the huts. The buildings on the three sites were probably round or round-oval. Of course, the structures may also have consisted of platforms supported on posts. No remains of occupation layers or finds normally associated with traditional settlement sites have been discovered beside these structures. One explanation for this could be that the sites have been exposed to protracted ploughing, and there was never any systematic surface survey before the excavation. The remains, which lack a central row of posts, have been interpreted as huts where repairs and new posts have made the form difficult to determine. The similar appearance of the buildings, the ¹⁴C dating from Lackalänga, and the Early Neolithic material in the pits from Stävie and Örtofta all mean that a dating to EN I seems reasonable. A comparable round structure was documented at the Late Mesolithic site at Tågerup. After careful investigation it was found that this building was used in two phases (Cronberg 2001).

*Vallkärra point 12*   In 1994 the National Heritage Board Southern Excavations Department excavated a number of places in connection with the construction of the West Coast Line between Lund and Kävlinge. Two of these places revealed remains which can be dated to the start of the Early Neolithic, although they are difficult to interpret.

The Early Neolithic activities at Vallkärra point 12 (fig. 11) were located on the crest of a plateau of sand and till which goes on to slope steeply to the south. The height above sea level varies between 25 and 30 m. At the lowest point in the excavated area was a thin, black layer of peat which indicates the occurrence of now-drained wetland.

The excavation covered an area of just over 5,000 m² and contained remains from several prehistoric periods. At the highest point on the crest of the plateau there was row of post-holes about eleven metres long. South of and parallel to the post-holes the archaeologists identified a small trench, about ten metres long and half a metre wide. North of the post-holes was a much bigger trench which could be followed for 25 m over the entire excavated area in a NNE–SSW direction (fig. 21). The trenches had diffuse boundaries and were up to 0.3 m deep. The filling of the post-holes, consisting of light brownish-grey sand, was only faintly visible against the sterile subsoil. A few unidentifiable pieces of flint flakes and debitage were retrieved from some of the post-holes. Roughly in the middle of the row of post-holes was a pit measuring 2×1.3 m with a depth of 0.8 m (A121). The pit contained remains of least ten different pots. The decoration consisted of horizontal rows of small imprints, rim bulges, and nail impressions, simple rows of nail impressions and tooth stamps. The ornamental elements and the vessel shapes correspond to a dating to EN I. The stratigraphical observations in the field showed that the pit preceded the making of the trenches and the row of post-holes. The impression of the excavators, however, was that the pit was an integral part of the system of trenches and post-holes. This picture is rein-

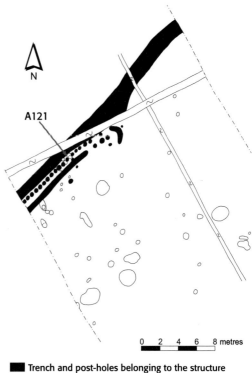

Fig. 21. Plan of Vallkärra point 12 during EN I.

forced by the fact that the pit is situated roughly between the two trenches and exactly under the row of post-holes. There was no datable material in the trenches or the post-holes, nor was there any charcoal for analysis. It is therefore difficult to ascertain whether the structures are contemporary. Based on the observations in the field, the remains could be regarded as parts of a ploughed-out long barrow. The pit may have been a votive pit or possibly a grave above which a long barrow was subsequently built (Knarrström, ms). The weakness of this interpretation is that there are no traces within the excavation trench, to either the north or the south, of any mark of the width of the long barrow. If the long barrow was more than 16 m wide, however, it is possible that the northern part of the structure lay outside the excavated area.

68

Finds from the peat layer included a dagger, a spoon scraper, ordinary scrapers, several rubber stones, and a rock whetstone. There was no material here which could be dated to the Early and Middle Neolithic. At least during the Late Neolithic/Early Bronze Age the wetland probably functioned as a votive site (Knarrström, ms).

## Burial place

*Stångby (Vallkärra) point 10*  About 2.5 kilometres north-west of Vallkärra and less than two kilometres north-west of point 12 (fig. 11) an area of roughly 1,700 m² was excavated. The site is located on clay soil about 30 m a.s.l., some 500 m east of the nearest large area of wetland. The dig unearthed a total of twenty-nine features (post-holes, pits, and hearths) which were deemed to be prehistoric. The only feature containing datable material was a pit measuring approximately 2.4×1.5 m and 0.27 m deep. The structure was surrounded by four post-holes. Small stones were found at the edge of the pit. Besides a scraper and a number of flint flakes, the pit contained an unpolished pointed-butted axe. The axe is two-sided with a pointed-oval cross-section, and it is 19 cm long and 6 cm wide. No certain skeletal colouring could be documented in the feature, but the rectangular shape means that we cannot rule out the possibility that the pit functioned as a grave and the post-holes are the remains of some kind of superstructure (Ericson Borggren, ms). Finds of unpolished axes in grave contexts are rare, however (Nielsen, P. O. 1977; Karsten 1994). Since the dating and function of other features on the site were never clarified, the grave hypothesis must be considered uncertain. Nor can we determine whether the adjacent features should be regarded as remains of a contemporary settlement.

## Votive sites

Within the investigation area, five places (Västra Hoby 18, Norrvidinge 22, Norra Nöbbelövs Mosse, Virke 3,

and Östra Karaby 11) have been interpreted as sites of Early Neolithic votive deposits in a context where no contemporary remains of settlements or graves have been found (fig. 11). The chosen sites no doubt lay in bogs or waterlogged ground when the deposits were made. The sacrificed objects are exclusively single pointed-butted axes, both unpolished and polished. Three of the axes are intact, two of them unpolished (Norrvidinge 22, Östra Karaby 11) and one polished (Virke 3). In two cases only the butt of the axe was deposited, one unpolished (Norra Nöbbelövs Mosse) and one polished (Västra Hoby 18). Four of the sites were later used for votive deposits on repeated occasions, in the Middle Neolithic as well, while Virke was used only during EN I. What they all have in common is that only one object, namely, the pointed-butted axe, was found at each place (Karsten 1994).

There are no Early Neolithic settlements – whether excavated or identified by surface survey – in the vicinity of these places. The find in the bog at Norra Nöbbelövs Mosse is at the shortest distance (approx. 700 m) from the nearest contemporary settlement.

## EN II–MNA II

**Settlement**  In the latter part of the Early Neolithic we notice a change in the settlement pattern in much of southern Scandinavia. Once again, our knowledge of Scanian settlement in this phase comes from the south-west and south-east parts of the province (e.g. Strömberg 1968, 1971, 1978, 1982a, 1982b, 1988a; Salomonsson 1971; Larsson & Larsson 1984, 1986; Larsson, L. 1985, 1989a, 1992a, 1992c, 1993, 1998; Larsson, M. 1984, 1985, 1987, 1988b, 1991; 1992; Svensson 1986; Björhem & Säfvestad 1989; Almquist & Svensson 1990; Billberg & Magnusson Staaf 1999). What characterizes these well-investigated regions is that settlement expanded vigorously during the period. In contrast, the settlement pattern looks partly different in different regions of Skåne. In the south-west parts of the province there is a shift in the settlements from the hummocky landscape of the interior to the

69

70

rich clay soils on the coasts. In other parts of the province, such as the Ystad area, we do not see the same change. Here the settlement areas show a continuity from the opening phase of the Early Neolithic into EN II–MNA II.

It was also at the end of the Early Neolithic that the sea reached its highest level, almost five metres above today's (Regnell, M., pers.com.), which meant that the bays reached further inland.

In the area around Saxån-Välabäcken and Lödde Å-Kävlingeån, eighty-eight settlements from this phase have been documented, thirty-three of them excavated on varying scales (fig. 22).

**Main settlements**   Within the investigation area there are some excavated places which, judging by the existing remains of settlement and the variation in find material, can be regarded as main settlements.

*Saxtorp 26 west (SU8)*   The dwelling site remains at Saxtorp 26 lay on a flat sandy height, about 10 m a.s.l., roughly 100 m north of the Saxån (fig. 22). East of the site the land starts to slope noticeably downwards what is now drained wetland but which in the Early Neolithic functioned as a votive site (see Saxtorp 26 east) (Lindahl Jensen & Nilsson 1999). The area was formerly documented in the register of ancient monuments as a Stone Age dwelling site, including a find of a fragmentary thin-butted axe.

The site was excavated in 1998 by the National Heritage Board Southern Excavations Department in connection with the construction of the West Coast Line. The almost 6,000 m² large excavation area contained a great number of features and houses. The density of features increased further up the slope, and all the house remains were concentrated within the northern and north-eastern part of the investigation area. In all probability the central parts of the dwelling site were on the plateau north of the excavated area. The remains of settlement consisted of ten long-houses, four sunken-floor huts, and at least one four-post

house. One of the long-houses, house 17, can be dated to EN II–MNA I on the basis of the design, ¹⁴C datings, and the appearance of the pottery, while the others are most probably from the Early Roman Iron Age and Migration Period (Artursson 1999).

The Neolithic house was roughly 20 m long and 6 m wide, a two-aisled structure oriented WNW–ESE (fig. 23). A total of three stout and deep post-holes were documented as traces of the roof-bearing structure. The distance between the roof-supports in the western part of the house was large, about 9 m, while in the eastern part it was about 4 m. The line of the north wall was almost entirely preserved and in certain sections doubled, while the southern wall line was more diffuse. The gables were less well preserved, but the parts that survive suggest that they were rounded. The inner area of the building was roughly 100 m². Finds of burnt clay and clay daub with clear impressions of wicker and other wooden structures were plentiful in the area of the house. It is thus reasonable to envisage that the walls were made of wattle and daub. Inside the house and outside the line of the south wall were a number of shallow pits or depressions with remains of a presumed demolition layer. The pits or depressions contained a large quantity of burnt clay and clay daub, as well as pottery of Funnel Beaker type. The clay daub in the pits could also be the vestiges of ovens. Archaeological remains of an oven, however, should consist of both remains of daub and signs of firing in the form of soot layers and fire-damaged underlying layers (Eriksson et al. 2000). The pits around the Neolithic house showed neither of these features, so the oven theory must be considered highly uncertain. The flint (1.2 kg) consists mainly of flakes and debitage. Only six tools were found: two flake scrapers, three retouched flint flakes, and a transverse arrowhead. The potsherds (1.3 kg) are of Funnel Beaker type, consisting mainly of pieces without decoration. The decorative techniques that do occur are lines, small stick impressions, cord, and whipped cord. Sherds from a richly decorated lugged beaker in Virum

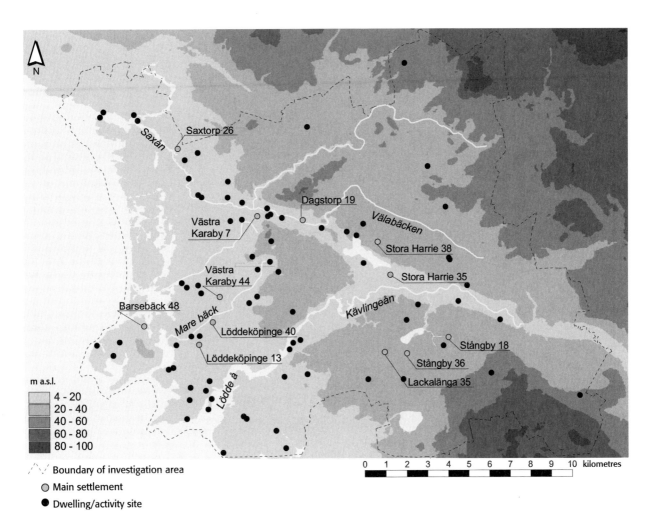

m a.s.l.

4 - 20
20 - 40
40 - 60
60 - 80
80 - 100

/‾\·/ Boundary of investigation area
○ Main settlement
● Dwelling/activity site

Fig. 22. Settlement sites in EN II-MNA II.

style were excavated from a pit (A14626) right beside the line of the south wall, and one fragment was found in the hole for a roof-bearing post (A15866) in one of the nearby Iron Age houses. The latter fragment is of thinner ware, and with finer whipped cord decoration; it could be a part of the pot that was found in the wetland (see Saxtorp 26 east). Pottery of Virum type is usually dated to EN II (Ebbesen & Mahler 1980; Koch 1998). The decorative elements on the other pottery agree with what was found in the adjacent wetland and can thus be dated with all probability to EN II. Of the bones (22 g), just over half are burnt and neither

the species nor the type of bone can be identified. The unburnt fragments consist of enamel fragments, most of which come from cattle (Artursson 1999).

The house can be dated on typological criteria and through the appearance of the pottery to the transition from the Early to the Middle Neolithic. This dating is confirmed by the $^{14}$C analyses. Charcoal from a wall post-hole has been dated to 4750±70 BP (3640–3380 cal. bc, Ua-9929), and charcoal from a roof-bearing post-hole to 4625±70 BP (3510–3130 cal. bc, Ua-9930) and 4685±70 BP (3620–3360 cal. bc, Ua-9931). The pit (A14626), which contained a relatively

72

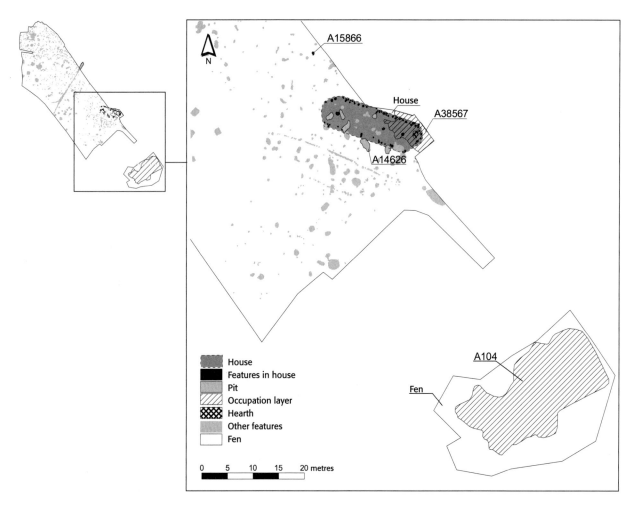

Fig. 23. Plan of Saxtorp 26 (SU8) in EN II-MNA II.

large amount of burnt clay daub and pottery of Virum type, has been [14]C-dated to 4710±70 BP (3630–3370 cal. bc, Ua-9927) (Artursson 1999; Artursson et al. 2003).

In the north-eastern part, the building was overlayered by an occupation layer (A38567), about 36 m² in area. The layer extends outside the line of the wall and continues outside the excavated area to the north and east. The flints (1 kg) are of Neolithic character but cannot be dated any more closely than this. The dwelling site could thus not be demarcated towards the east and north-east. South of the house, towards the wet-

land, there were no Neolithic remains (Artursson 1999).

***Västra Karaby 7*** About five kilometres south-east of Saxtorp 26, along the Saxån, was the next large settlement from this period, Västra Karaby 7 (fig. 22).

In connection with a planned house construction project in Dösjebro, the National Heritage Board Southern Excavations Department in autumn 1972 excavated a Bronze Age barrow. Under the barrow were found settlement layers from the Middle Neolithic. The dwelling site lay on a sandy height, 10 m a.s.l., and just over 300 m south of the confluence of the Välabäcken and Saxån. The sandy ridges in the area create great differences in level (Nagmér 1976).

The remains of the Middle Neolithic settlement documented by the excavation consisted of an occupation layer measuring about 150 m² and some small pits. The occupation layer could be demarcated to the south and east, but flint artefacts discovered by surface survey suggest that the settlement probably continued outside the excavated area to the north and west. The finds, both flint and pottery, are mainly concentrated in an area east of the barrow. Almost 35% of the occupation layer was excavated. Of the flint (5 kg), 16% consisted of tools or flakes with retouching. Flake scrapers dominated among the tools, which also included flake awls, knives, and transverse arrowheads. The majority of the pottery (12 kg) belongs to the Funnel Beaker culture. The most common decoration consists of vertical lines on the belly. Other decorative elements are whipped cord, cord, angles, and various forms of pits. Funnel beakers and bowls seem to be the most common vessel forms. Based on decoration and vessel shape, the pottery can be dated to EN II at the earliest, but the composition of the decoration indicates that the majority can be placed in MNA I. Fifteen grain impressions have been documented on pottery from the site. Hakon Hjelmqvist's analysis shows the following distribution of cereal types: five einkorn, four emmer, two einkorn or emmer, and four wheat. No organic material from the site is preserved. The occupation layer contained a funnel beaker which had been placed upside down, carefully enclosed by a clay packing. Only the rim and neck survived. The rim, which was decorated with double rows of pits, had a diameter of 0.4 m (Nagmér 1976; Löfwall 1977). The excavation did not uncover any surviving dwelling structures, but the varied finds suggest that the site may have functioned as a main settlement.

***Dagstorp 19 (SU21)*** Just over two kilometres to the east, immediately north of the Välabäcken, lay

Dagstorp 19 (fig. 22). The remains of settlement here make up a chronological sequence comprising EN I–MNA III. (Lagergren-Olsson & Linderoth 2000; Artursson 2003), and an account of the traces of settlement during the earliest phase of the Early Neolithic was given in the previous section.

In the western part of the excavated area, the largest occupation layer (approx. 3,700 m²), A150, was investigated (fig. 24a). The finds in the layer mainly came from EN I but a small element of MNA I is noticeable in the northernmost parts of the layer. In this part, especially under but also in the bottom of the layer, four houses could be discerned (houses 50, 51, 52, and 55). The house remains were trapezoidal and between 7 and 10 m long and with a maximum width of between 4.6 and 5.5 m. Three of the buildings ran roughly north–south and were very similar in shape. A characteristic feature of these three houses was the placing of the roof-bearing posts. One roof support was placed in the southern gable or just inside it, while two to three roof supports were found one or a few metres inside the north gable. In the northern part of the house there were pits (A53477, A53516, A84845, and A100162) which were probably contemporary with the houses. Finds from the pits in the trapezoidal houses have all yielded datings in MNA I. In addition, there is a ¹⁴C dating from a cereal grain taken from the wall-post of house 51. This gave a value of 4475±65 BP (3340–3030 cal. bc, Ua-25066), which corresponds to the start of the Middle Neolithic. In occupation layer A150 yet another building was documented. The structure, which was 8×7 m, consisted of irregularly placed post-holes and can be interpreted as the remains of a hut. This building (hut 56), based on finds in the adjacent occupation layer, should also be assigned to the early Middle Neolithic (Lagergren-Olsson & Linderoth 2000).

In the southern part of the site, closer to the Välabäcken, the excavation unearthed yet another occupation layer, A159 (fig. 24b). Access to the northern parts of the layer was restricted by modern-day

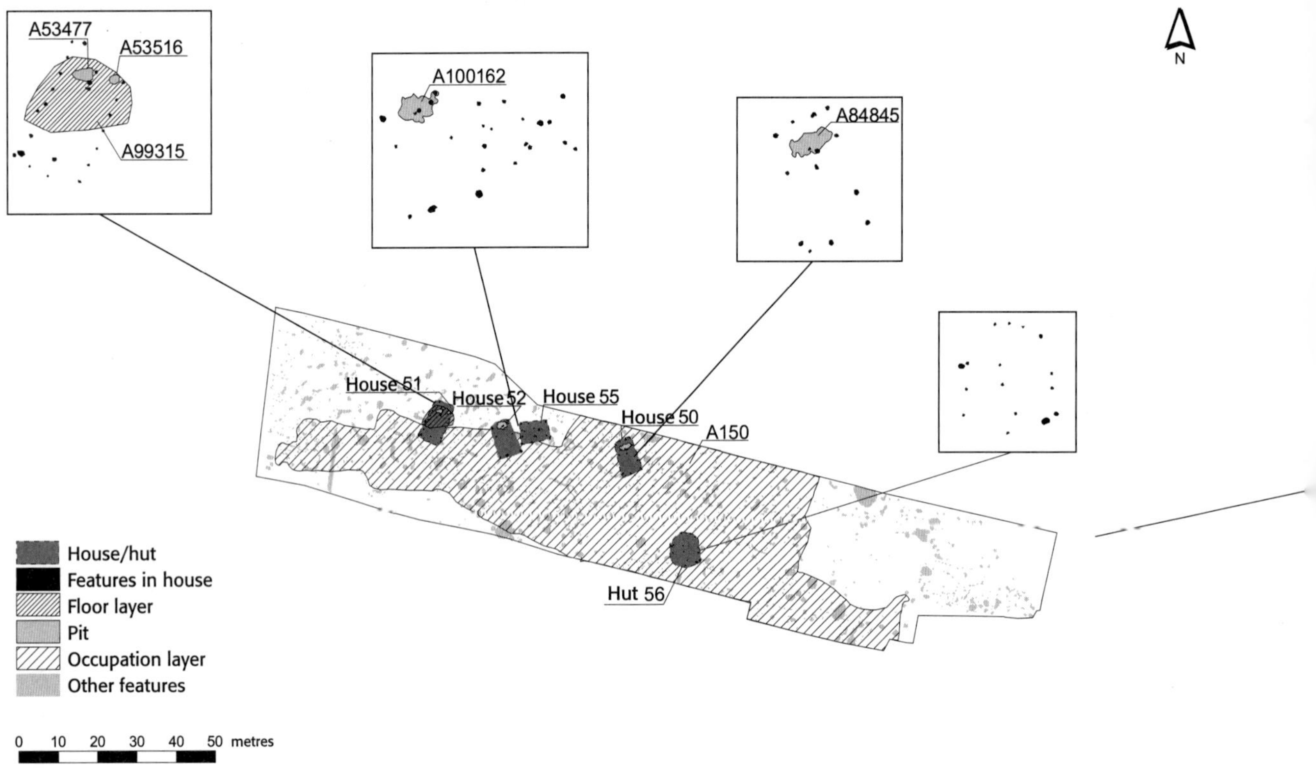

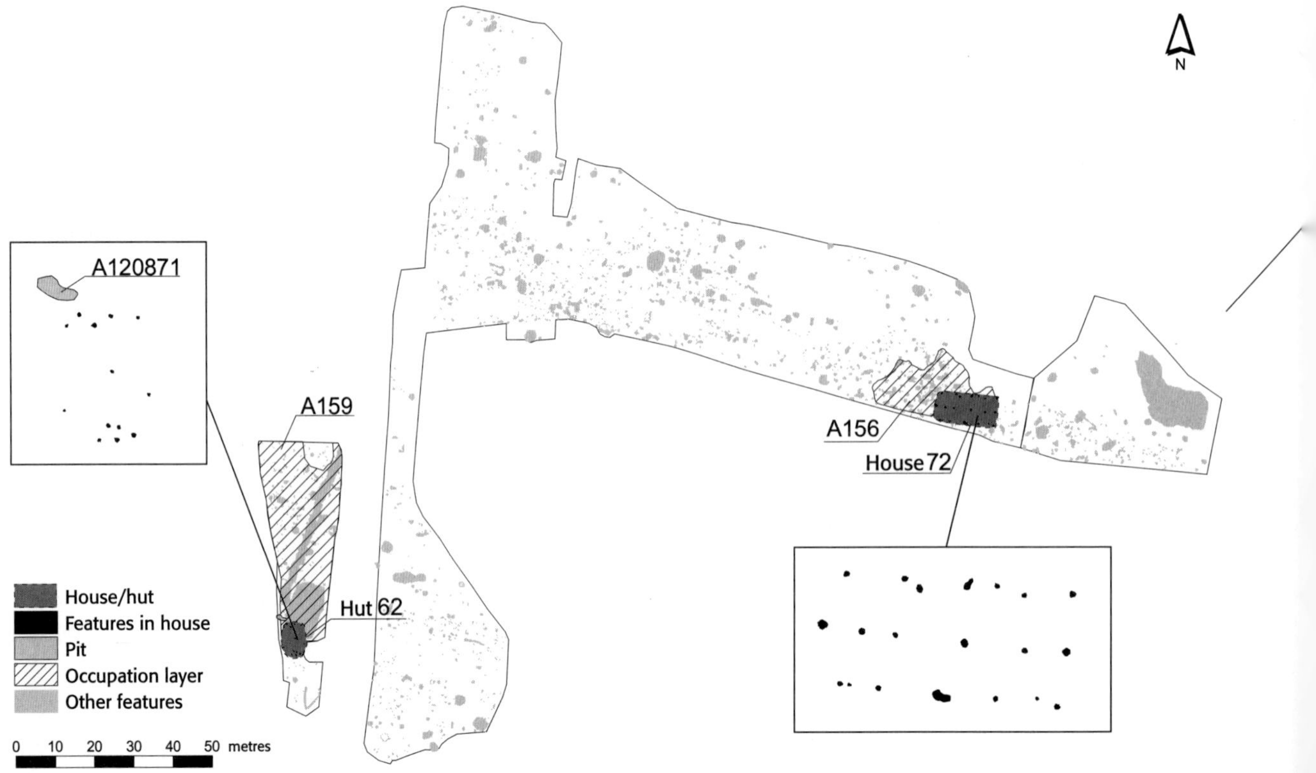

74

Fig. 24a and b. Plan of Dagstorp 19 (SU21) during EN II-MNA II.

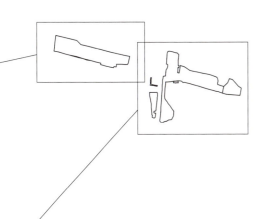

Fig. 25. Rock axe from Dagstorp 19 (SU21) (photo Cecilia Anderung).

Fig. 26. House 51 at Dagstorp 19 (SU21). Dagstorps Backar in the background (photo T. Johansson).

buildings, but the extent within the excavated area was estimated as just over 1,000 m². This was excavated in forty-four hand-dug 1×1 metre squares and then stripped in fifty 4×4 m squares. The flint material (7.8 kg) is numerically dominated by scrapers, but other tools include awls, knives, a transverse arrowhead, and fragments of polished flint axes. Parts of a polished rock axe were also retrieved. The pottery (3.4 kg) shows great variation in decorative techniques and composition. Line technique and cross-hatching dominate, but whipped cord, tooth stamps, and various types of pitted impressions occur. Based on the finds, the layer can be dated to the early MNA. Beside the southern part of the occupation layer was a concentration of post-holes which has been interpreted as the remains of a hut structure, hut 62. Just north of the hut an oblong pit (A120871) rich in finds was excavated. The filling was of varied character, with sooty, humic parts alternating with lighter-coloured, less humic parts. The pit measured 2.7×0.82 m, was bowl-shaped and 0.2 m deep. The finds mainly consist of pottery (2 kg). The flint (1.6 kg) included three scrapers, one transverse arrowhead, and two fragments of polished axes. Other finds are burnt bones (including two fragments of dog and one of sheep/goat) and two rock whetstones. The finds date the pit to MNA I. A charcoal sample from the feature gave an early Middle Neolithic dating, 4530±70 BP (3360–3100 cal. bc, Ua-25063) (Lagergren-Olsson & Linderoth 2000).

Roughly 300 m east of A150, parallel to the Välabäcken, an occupation layer measuring 300 m², A156, was excavated. The layer could be demarcated to the west, north, and south, but extended outside the development area down towards the Välabäcken in the south. Under and a little way outside the layer a two-aisled house was documented, house 72. It was oriented east–west, and it was about 15 metres long and 7 metres wide. After a surface survey, fifty-four metre-square trenches were dug. An area in the central part of the occupation layer, where the density of finds and

features was particularly high, was totally excavated. The layer was then stripped in eighteen 4×4 m squares. The flint tools (7.8 kg) were dominated by scrapers, but knives and an awl were also found. The pottery (6.6 kg) was concentrated in a limited part of the occupation layer. A great deal of the pottery is decorated, with the predominant ornamentation technique being lines, above all on the belly. Cross-hatching patterns and pits are also common. The finds date the layer to the early MNA (Lagergren-Olsson & Linderoth 2000).

The results of the excavation indicate a potential contemporaneity during the early MNA between several buildings (houses 50, 51, 52, 55, and possibly 72, along with huts 56 and 62) and occupation layers (A156 and A159 along with parts of A150), which suggests a contemporary habitation area corresponding to that of the big Danish Middle Neolithic settlement sites (cf. Madsen 1982, 1988; Skaarup 1985).

*Stora Harrie 38*   Four kilometres east of the Dagstorp settlement was yet another dwelling site from this period, Stora Harrie 38 (fig. 22). It was situated on a sandy south slope of a plateau, just over two kilometres north of the Kävlingeån and one and a half kilometres south of the Välabäcken. Immediately to the south of the plateau was a stream now channelled through a culvert. It flowed from a former lake northeast of the excavated area. Half a kilometre to the south was a large expanse of wetland. The sandy area of the settlement is surrounded by slightly heavier clayey soils (Persson 1988; Jeppsson 1996a).

On the site, which was excavated by the National Heritage Board in connection with the Sydgas project in 1984, there was a Neolithic occupation layer with an extent within the investigation area of almost 300 m², of which 225 m² was excavated. The layer contained dug features in the form of fifteen hearths, six pits, three post-holes, and one trench. Several of the features held Neolithic pottery. The occupation layer was limited to the west and east but continued outside the excavated area to the north and south (Persson 1988; Jeppsson 1996a).

The majority of the pottery (7 kg) can be dated to the early Middle Neolithic and possibly the late Early Neolithic. The decoration consists of cross-hatching, pitted impressions, whipped cord stamps, angle lines, vertical strokes, and triangles. The largest group of flint finds (43 kg) consists of flakes and debitage. The flint tools include scrapers, flake knives, transverse arrowheads, awls, cores, and polished axe fragments. Flake scrapers constitute the largest group of tools, with over 40%. The composition of the flint may be said to be typical of a Funnel Beaker site. The flint and pottery was concentrated above all in the area of the occupation layer where the features were also found. Neolithic pottery was found in a trench which had been disturbed by a trial dig and it was not possible to determine with certainty whether it was part of a Neolithic house structure. A feature adjacent to the trench was found to contain clay daub with impressions of wattle which could perhaps have come from the wall of a house (Persson 1988; Jeppsson 1996a). Remains of clay daub need not necessarily come from a wall; they may have been, for instance, part of an oven. Since there were no traces of ovens on the site, however, it seems reasonable to assume that the clay daub together with the trench represents a house from the early MN. The size and composition of the finds, the probable remains of a house, and the favourable ecological environment with the conditions for cultivation, animal husbandry, hunting and fishing indicate that the site should be regarded as a main settlement.

*Löddeköpinge 13*   Beside the stream called Mare Bäck it has been possible to identify some main settlements. Löddeköpinge 13, which was investigated in 1971 by the National Heritage Board Southern Excavations Department in connection with the construction of a road, was located in flat, sandy arable land a few hundred metres south of the Mare Bäck (fig. 22).

Within the excavated area an occupation layer 250 m² in extent and 0.2 m thick was documented, and 132 m² was excavated and machine-sieved. A test pit outside the area intended for development showed that the occupation layer covered a larger area than that documented inside the excavated area. The finds consisted of flint (10 kg) and pottery (9.8 kg). The latter was badly fragmented, consisting of both decorated and undecorated sherds. The decorative motifs were lines, pits, stick impressions, and whipped cord. The flint tools mainly consisted of flakes and debitage; the tools included scrapers, transverse arrowheads, awls, knives, and polished axe fragments. A pit measuring 3.2×1.5 m and 0.3 m deep, containing pottery, was excavated. The composition of the finds dates the occupation of the site to an early part of the Middle Neolithic (Wihlborg 1976).

The excavated area is small but the finds are numerous and varied, indicating that the site may have functioned as a main settlement.

*Löddeköpinge 40*   Just over a kilometre to the north-east, along the Mare Bäck, was yet another settlement which can be dated to the period EN II–MNA II (fig. 22). House construction led the National Heritage Board Southern Excavations Department to conduct excavations at Löddeköpinge 40 in 1990–1991. The settlement was beside the stream, which today is strictly drained and regulated, but which in prehistoric times flowed into the bay at today's Barsebäck Mosse. On the reconnaissance map of Skåne from 1812–1820, former wetlands and heights within the investigation area can be seen adjacent to the water system of the Mare Bäck. The remains of the settlement were on a sandy height about 9 m a.s.l. (Knarrström & Wallin 1999).

A total of 267 features were registered in the excavated area of 5,200 m², consisting of post-holes, hearths, and pits. A two-aisled house oriented NE–SE was documented, with four roof-bearing posts and a

78

system of wall-posts (fig. 27). In the north-eastern third of the house there was a semicircular short side consisting of about ten wall-posts. [14]C analyses of charcoal from two of the post-holes gave datings to 4185±65 BP (2880–2630 cal. bc, Ua-5472) and 4420±100 BP (3300–2920 cal. bc, Ua-5475). The composition of the flints (5.6 kg) suggests that the site was a main settlement in the Neolithic. The debitage reflects the manufacture of a great diversity of objects, and tools such as axes and scrapers paint a picture of the activities around the site. A great deal of the flint was collected during the work with the machine stripping. This clearly shows that the occupation layer was destroyed by ploughing and that the artefacts from the settlement ended up in the topsoil. Flakes and tools were concentrated in the central part of the site, where the finds included two large fragments of thin-butted axes. The majority of the pottery (0.7 kg) consists of coarse ware without decoration. Two ceramic fragments which were discovered in a hearth about 40 m south-west of the Neolithic house have datable decoration. On the bigger sherd the decoration is vertical bands consisting of repeated impressions with whipped cord and vertical cord-decorated lines. The smaller sherd has angular band decoration with cord-decorated lines forming fields with the tips of the angles overlapping each other (Knarrström & Wallin 1999). The sherds should probably be dated to the early Middle Neolithic (Ebbesen 1978). In the light of the [14]C datings and the finds from the plough layer above the house, it should be placed at the transition from the early Neolithic to the Middle Neolithic (Knarrström & Wallin 1999).

The first occupation of the site thus occurred at the Early/Middle Neolithic transition. The house and the composition of the finds suggest that the place can be

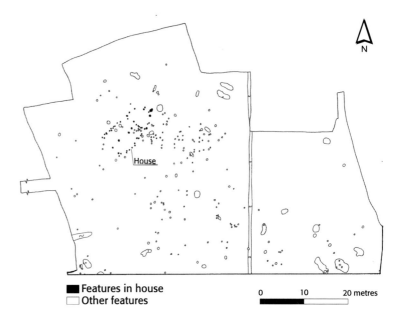

Fig. 27. Plan of Löddeköpinge 40 during EN II-MNA II.

Features in house
Other features

0    10    20 metres

described as a main settlement. This settlement, however, was not renewed by the construction of new houses or the reconstruction of the old house. A possible interpretation of this is that only one generation was active on the site. The sandy plateau does not appear to have been settled again until the Early Iron Age (Knarrström & Wallin 1999).

*Lackalänga 35*   Just over ten kilometres inland was the settlement of Lackalänga 35 (fig. 22). The site is on a flat rise, about 29 m a.s.l., consisting of light clay soils. North-east of the site is the bog Stångby Mosse, and the Kävlingeån flows a further 2.5 km to the north. In connection with the rerouting of road 108, the site was investigated in 1994 by the National Heritage Board Southern Excavations Department.

A total of 42 features were registered in the excavated area of roughly 1,000 m², most of them associated with EN II–MNA II. A number of post-holes were attributed to a probable house (fig. 28), not completely preserved. It was oriented east–west and was of the two-aisled type, with a trapezoidal form. It was diffi-

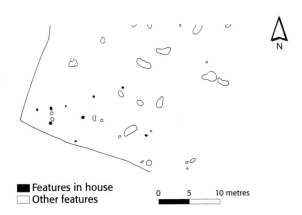

Features in house
Other features

0    5    10 metres

Fig. 28. Plan of Lackalänga 35 in EN II-MNA II.

cult to determine the length and width of the house since only a few post-holes from the wall were preserved. An occupation layer was documented inside the house. The finds included pottery, burnt clay, flint, and burnt bones. The pottery is coarse-tempered with several decorated fragments, in the form of stick impressions and vertical strokes. Both the fabric and the decoration indicate a dating to the transition between the Early and the Middle Neolithic. A $^{14}$C dating of a feature adjacent to the house gave a value of 4610±90 BP (3520–3100 cal. bc, Ua-7138), that is, EN II–MNA I (Olson et al. 1996). The site represents a limited area of a main settlement, with a probable house, a number of scattered post-holes, pits, and occupation layers.

*Stora Harrie 35*   The settlement was on a sandy plateau-like rise and a gentle southward slope some 400 m north of the Kävlingeån (fig. 22). The landscape is criss-crossed by several smaller watercourses. Just west of the site is the channel of a now drained stream, and there were once several wetlands in the area. In connection with the construction of housing, the Southern Excavations Department in 1988–1989 investigated remains of settlements from the Neolithic and the Late Bronze Age. The Neolithic remains consisted of a number of pits in the south-east part of the area. One of the pits contained the greater part of a

Funnel Beaker vessel with decoration in Virum style (Nagmér 1991). The flint tools included flake scrapers, awls, and knives. The occurrence of features in the area which could be dated to the Early and Middle Neolithic, together with flint material of Neolithic character, leads me to regard this place too as a main settlement. The occurrence of flint flakes in the topsoil suggests that a Neolithic occupation layer has been ploughed away.

**Votive sites**   During this period we see a distinct increase in the deposition of objects in wetlands compared with the previous phase (fig. 29). Of the 47 known wetland sites in the investigation area, only one has been excavated, namely, the fen at Saxtorp 26.

### Wetlands

*Saxtorp 26 east (SU9)*   The site is in the valley of the Saxån, at about 10 m a.s.l., on the slope of a sandy ridge (fig. 29). Towards the south-west the ground slopes down towards the Saxån, which flows about 130 m from the site. The site was investigated in autumn 1998 by the National Heritage Board Southern Excavations Department in connection with the construction of the West Coast Line (fig. 30). The former fen has now been drained, and at the time of the excavation the area was fully tilled. The fen drained towards the Saxån in the south-west. The layer sequence consisted of glacial clay, calcareous tufa, and several layers of peat with intervening layers of sand and gravel. Vegetation analyses show that in the Early Neolithic there was an established, relatively open, human-influenced landscape in the vicinity. The existence of the fen is manifested in the pollen through the presence of sedges, marsh horsetail, and water mint. The surrounding forest is dominated by lime and hazel, but occasional birch and alder also occurred near the fen. Adjacent settlements are indicated by the occurrence of plants typical of cultivated land, such as nettle, raspberry, sheep's sorrel, and knotgrass. Based on the pollen spectrum, the fen en-

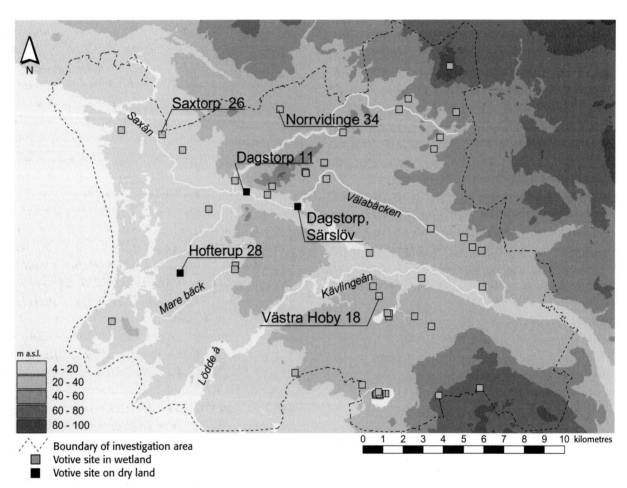

Fig. 29. Votive sites in EN II-MNA II.

vironment in the Neolithic is interpreted as relatively open, with the formation of fen peat and rivulets from a gushing spring giving small pools, at least during parts of the year. In certain circumstances calcareous tufa was also formed along the rivulets. The water from the spring was rich in iron, and a reddish-orange sludge containing iron built up in the rivulets (Lindahl Jensen & Nilsson 1999; Nilsson & Nilsson 2003).

Two find-bearing layers were excavated. A104 contained a rich and well-preserved body of finds from the Early Neolithic with objects of flint, pottery, worked sticks, bone objects, and bones of animals and humans. A103 overlayered A104, and in the northernmost part of the layer there was a concentration of finds from the Late Bronze Age consisting of a pot, wooden artefacts, and bones of both humans and animals. The Early Neolithic layer was located under layers of peat up to a thickness of some two metres, at levels between 6.5 and 9.3 m a.s.l. They covered virtually the whole extent of the fen, but there were small areas where the layer was missing, generally where the calcareous tufa had created small heights. The entire limits of the Neolithic layer, which comprised roughly 350 m², were documented within the investigation area (Lindahl Jensen & Nilsson 1999).

Fig. 30. The votive fen at Saxtorp 26 (SU9) during excavation (photo Ö. Mattsson).

The finds in the Early Neolithic layer consisted of knapped flint (35 kg), pottery (4 kg), animal bones (8 kg), human bones (0.8 kg), two bone artefacts, and three worked sticks. The majority of the finds were unearthed within a limited area in the southern part of the fen. With occasional exceptions, the finds of pottery and human bones were concentrated there.

The number of fragments of human bones is 39. Most of these have been identified as coming from the skull, chiefly the frontal bone and the parietal bone. Other common bones are parts of the long bones from both the upper and the lower extremities, including the humerus, radius, femur, and tibia. Other skeletal parts and regions of the body are more sparsely represented, such as the trunk, with two rib fragments, and

the foot, with one toe bone. Other bones from humans are half a mandible, two loose teeth, and a clavicle. The bones have been judged as coming from at least three individuals, but it is possible that they represent five individuals. Of individual I, only the skull is represented, which consists of 13 fragments which can be joined to make one large fragment. This comprises the greater part of the forehead with the superciliary arches and the two parietal bones. Two of the fragments have been [14]C-dated, one to 4520±80 BP (3350–3090 cal. bc, Ua-9811) and the other to 4760±75 BP (3690–3360 cal. bc, Ua-9810). The individual is judged to be an adult woman in her twenties or thirties. Individual II is identified solely on the basis of two fragments, a right and a left superciliary arch with a little of the frontal bone. One of the bones has been [14]C-dated to 4690±75 BP (3620–3360 cal. bc, Ua-9809). The shape of the superciliary arches suggests that the individual was a woman. The age is uncertain, estimated only on the basis of the thickness of the three different layers of the skull, giving the age range teenager/adult. Of individual III there are two fragments from the front part of the parietal bones towards the frontal bone. The bones can be joined together. One of the bones has been [14]C-dated to 4975±75 BP (3810–3660 cal. bc, Ua-9808). It has not been possible to ascertain with certainty whether other human bones belong to any of the above individuals or are parts of other people (Nilsson & Nilsson 2003).

The pottery consists mainly of sherds without decoration. The decoration that does occur consists above all of belly lines, but there are also examples of whipped cord, cord, and tooth stamp. Bone artefacts are represented by an ulna dagger, made from a bovine ulna, and a pin made from the bone of a pig. The ulna dagger has been [14]C-dated to 4810±75 BP (3690–3380 cal. bc, Ua-25501). The wooden artefacts consist of small fragments of pointed sticks of uncertain function. The majority of the flint tools and animal bones were found in combination with the above finds. The flint tools are dominated numerically by flake cores, retouched flints and blades, but scrapers, awls, microblades, knives, and polished axe fragments also occur. The animal bones are mostly from species such as cattle, pigs, sheep/goat, and red deer, but there are also bones from animals such as dog and roe deer. The bones are badly fragmented, although some whole bones do occur. A lumbar vertebra of sheep/goat has been [14]C-dated to 4470±60 BP (3340–3030 cal. bc, Ua-25499), a pelvic bone fragment of domesticated pig has been dated to 4550±60 BP (3360–3100 cal. bc, Ua-25500), and a tubular bone from a mammal to 4695±70 BP (3620–3370 cal. bc, Ua-9062) (Lindahl Jensen & Nilsson 1999; Nilsson & Nilsson 2003).

All in all, the finds give a uniform Early Neolithic impression, which is also confirmed by the [14]C analy-ses which date the Neolithic activities to EN I–EN II (Lindahl Jensen & Nilsson 1999). Based on comparisons with other votive fens, it is reasonable to interpret these finds as being deliberately deposited. A remarkable feature of the finds from Saxtorp is the absence of so-called traditional votive finds in the form of large tools. The most common votive object from the Early Neolithic in Skåne is the thin-butted flint axe (Karsten 1994), but at Saxtorp only small fragments of five axes were found. On the other hand, there were smaller flint tools and flakes/debitage, which have the character of more profane material. It should be pointed out, however, that "everyday waste" commonly occurs at other excavated wetlands such as Röekillorna and Hindby votive fen (Svensson 1993; Stjernquist 1997).

West of the wetland were remains of Neolithic settlement (fig. 23), including a house in the form of a two-aisled structure (see Saxtorp 26 west) (Artursson 1999).

**Offerings on dry land**   Adjacent to all the excavated megalithic tombs in the investigation area, remains have been identified which can probably be associated with special rituals to do with the monuments. At the sites of Hofterup 28, Dagstorp 11, and Särslöv (fig. 29) remains were documented which were not precisely beside contemporary graves but which should nevertheless be linked to the nearest megalithic tomb. It is uncertain whether there was a megalithic tomb at Dagstorp 11, but the proximity to Krångeltofta and the grave of Harald Hildetand (see below) shows that the site may have had a special meaning.

*Hofterup 28*   Close to the Hofterup dolmen (fig. 29) LUHM investigated a 5×2 m stone setting in 1959. The feature, which was about 20 m north of the grave, was oval and consisted of only one layer of stone of varying size. The area of some 6.5×4.5 m that was excavated around the feature was wholly covered by an occupation layer. The flint and the fragments of pottery decorated with tooth stamps and fish bones in the stone setting and occupation layer indicate that the two can be dated to the Middle Neolithic. According to the survey of ancient monuments, finds from the area include a thin-butted axe, two fragments of preforms for thick-butted axes, and flat-flaked sickles and daggers (Salomonsson 1960b). The function of the feature was difficult to determine, but one clue could be that similar features were excavated at Dagstorp 11 adjacent to the site of a presumed megalithic tomb (see below). Perhaps the stone packings are what is left of "altars" in connection with ceremonies performed at the burial monuments.

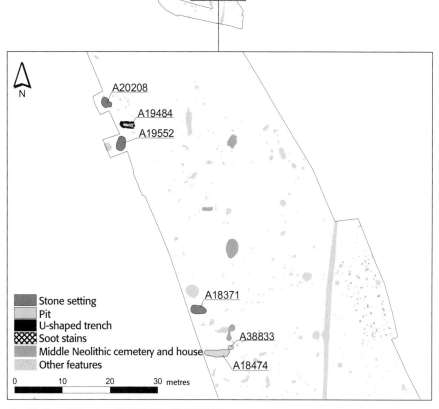

Fig. 31. Plan of Dagstorp 11 (SU17) in EN II–MNA II.

*Dagstorp 11 (SU17)* The Early and Middle Neolithic remains at Dagstorp 11, which were excavated in 1998 by the National Heritage Board Southern Excavations Department in connection with the construction of the West Coast Line, were beside the Välabäcken on a sandy south-facing slope and plateau at about 12 m a.s.l. (fig. 29). The area closest to the river was wetland in prehistoric times. North of the site, the terrain rises and the subsoil becomes clay. During the late MNA and early MNB there was a large settlement complex in the area, consisting of a palisade structure, axe-manufacturing places, houses, and a linear cemetery from the Battle Axe culture (see the sections on MNA III–V and MNB). Four urn graves and parts of an Iron Age settlement site were also documented. The features that can be dated to EN II–MNA II consist of

a concentration of pottery, a U-shaped trench, and three accumulations of stone (fig. 31) (Månsson & Pihl 1999).

In a pit, A18474, measuring 5.4×1.5 m and with a depth of roughly 0.2 m, a total of just over 14 kg of pottery was retrieved, much of it with decoration in the form of belly lines, pitted impressions, and different variants of stamp decoration. There is also pottery with decoration on both the inside and outside of the rim. The pottery comes from several different vessels. Judging by the decoration and fabric of the pottery, the finds can be assigned to the early MNA. Apart from pottery, the finds consisted of flint and occasional burnt bones. Most of the flint was flakes and debitage, but there was also a scraper and a few retouched flints. Just north-east of A18474 was yet another pit with pottery, A38833, from which one pot was excavated in a matrix. It is likely that this pit too should be regarded as part of the larger accumulation of pottery.

Otherwise, only occasional post-holes could be documented adjacent to the concentration of pottery, but without forming any distinguishable structure (Månsson & Pihl 1999).

In the western part of the area, 40 m north of the pottery concentration, was a U-shaped (A19484), partly stone-lined trench, with external dimensions of 3×1.4 m. The width of the closed western end was about 0.6 metres, while other parts were roughly 0.2–0.3 m wide. In the open eastern part there were two irregular sooty areas 0.5–0.6 m large. The depth of the trench varied between 0.2 and 0.3 m. Some of the stones along the edge of the trench were supported by smaller stones. At the bottom of the feature were small patches of soot in various places. These could possibly be the remains of a burnt wooden structure which could not be discerned in the otherwise homogeneous filling of the trench. A small quantity of pottery was found in the north-east part of the trench, beside a collection of stones. Otherwise, occasional potsherds and flint flakes were found scattered in the trench. The flint mainly consisted of flakes and debitage, but a blade and two flake cores were also found. The pottery consisted of small undecorated sherds. A charcoal sample from the eastern patch of soot in the feature has been [14]C-dated and given the value 4590±55 BP (3500–3120 cal. bc, Ua-9850), which corresponds to the period EN II–MNA I (Månsson & Pihl 1999).

North-west and south of the U-shaped trench were two accumulations of stone (A19552 and A20208). Both features consisted of single layers of stone located in diffuse colourings. The stones varied in size, but the majority were 0.2–0.3 m. Yet another collection of stones (A18371) of a similar character was found about 10 m north of the pottery concentration (Månsson & Pihl 1999). A chronological link between the pottery concentration, the trenches, and the stone collections cannot be ruled out. One possible interpretation is that these features are part of the activities performed beside a removed megalithic tomb. Outside megalithic tombs in both Skåne and Denmark, large

quantities of pottery/vessels are often deposited (Strömberg 1971; Hårdh 1982; Tilley 1996, 1999a). There are similarities in the composition of vessels and decoration between the Dagstorp feature and deposits at other megalithic tombs (Lagergren-Olsson 2003), and stone packings and dolmens seem to be the rule rather than the exception beside megalithic tombs in the investigation area (see below). An indication that there may have been a megalithic tomb in the area is the place-name Dösjebro. "Dysia" was the medieval name for the Välabäcken (Olsson 2000:26) and it may be connected to a megalithic tomb through the word for a dolmen (Swedish *dös*, Danish *dysse*).

***Dagstorp, Särslöv (SU22)*** The place is a glaciofluvial plateau of gravel and sand, about 100 m north of the Välabäcken, and at a height of roughly 15 m a.s.l. (fig. 29). The passage grave of Södervidinge 3 is about 800 m NNE of the investigation area. In connection with the construction of the West Coast Line within the area, the National Heritage Board Southern Excavations Department excavated remains, above all from the Iron Age and Early Middle Ages, but at least one Middle Neolithic structure was documented (Kriig 1999).

The Middle Neolithic feature was a U-shaped trench (A3585) with external dimensions of 2.7×2.5 m (fig. 32). It was partly overlayered by Iron Age remains and was partially damaged by a drain. Towards the NNE was an opening roughly 1.6 m wide. The filling consisted of homogeneous brown, slightly humic, gravelly sand and the depth varied from 0.04–0.22 m. The deeper parts probably consist of three post-holes. One post-hole is located at the opening to the east, and the other two are in the western part of the feature. Based on the shape of the feature and the occurrence of post-holes, it is reasonable to interpret it as some type of building. The finds from the feature were scarce. The flints were a few flakes/debitage, flakes from axe manufacturing, retouched flakes, flake cores, blades, and a flake scraper. A hammerstone of rock

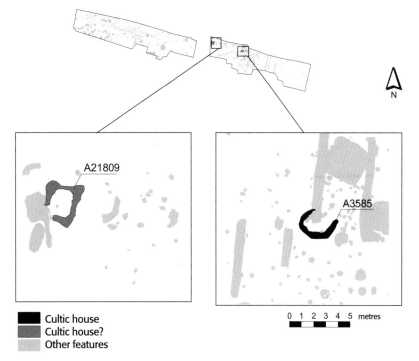

Fig. 32. Cultic house at Särslöv (SU22).

**Cultic house**
**Cultic house?**
**Other features**

85

was also found. In the north-west of the trench there were two decorated potsherds. The decoration consisted of large rhombi or angular bands filled with cross-hatching in line technique. This type of decoration is characteristic of the early Middle Neolithic (MNA I–II) and the sherds presumably come from a pedestalled bowl. These are normally associated with Middle Neolithic burial places and cultic sites. There were no other certain Neolithic structures in the area. A similar feature (A21809) was excavated about 40 m west of this, but it contained no finds and the dating is thus uncertain (Nilsson 2000). The features resemble the U-shaped trench at Dagstorp 11. The features at Särslöv, however, were slightly larger and more oval in shape than the one at Dagstorp.

In Denmark, northern Jutland has several parallels to the features in the so-called Neolithic cultic houses. The Danish examples, like those excavated at Särslöv, lack structures and finds usually associated with Neolithic dwelling sites. They have instead been interpreted as small sacred buildings, mortuary houses, or temples (Becker 1993; 1996).

**Graves**

**Excavated megalithic tombs**

*Barsebäck 12, Gillhög* Gillhög is at the highest point, about 25 m a.s.l., on a distinct hill rising above the otherwise flat coastal landscape (fig. 33). The hill is on the border of a foreland sticking out into the sound. The distance to today's coastline is just over a kilometre to the north and south and just under two kilometres to the west. To the south and east extends the plain of Lund and to the north the sandy plains around Saxtorp and Hofterup. The area at the passage grave differs from the rest of the coastal landscape in that the soils here are dominated by clay till. There is

one Stone Age dwelling site in the area registered by surface survey, with material indicating a dating to MNA III–MNA V.

The barrow measures about 36 m in diameter and reaches a height of slightly over 3 m. The chamber, which is 5.8×2.2 m with a height of 1.6 to 2 m, consists of a slightly rounded rectangular arrangement of twelve standing, uncut blocks (fig. 34). The chamber is oriented longitudinally SSW–NNE. The passage is 5.8 m long, 1 m wide, and roughly 1 m high, built of five pairs of orthostats topped by three capstones. It runs at a slightly oblique angle in the longitudinal direction of the chamber, which it enters at the southeast. In both the chamber and the passage the gaps between the orthostats are often filled with a carefully built-up packing of thin, horizontally laid flagstones. The spaces between the protruding parts of the orthostats are sealed on the outside with a mixture of clay and crushed flint. The floor of the chamber and the inner half of the passage consists of stamped clay. The outer part of the passage is covered by the cairn of earth and stone that surrounded the passage grave. The cairn ends towards the burial chamber in a large block which is placed in the middle of the passage, leaning against one of the side walls (Forssander 1932).

86

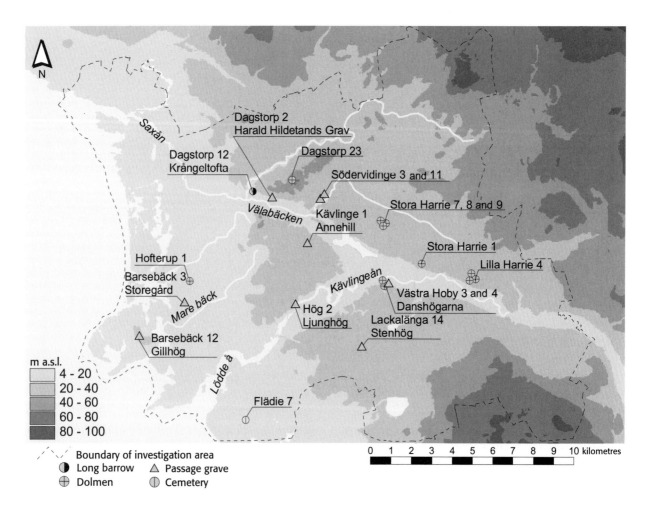

Fig. 33. Long barrow, dolmens, passage graves, and cemeteries.

The passage grave was excavated by LUHM in 1931–1932. The finds in the chamber are relatively sparse. Their fragmentary state and mutual relations suggest that they have been disturbed. Fragments of the same pot were found in different squares. Special circumstances indicate that the movement took place back in Neolithic times, since fragments of the same pot occurred both in the chamber and in the outer part of the passage, near the bottom of the huge cairn, which contained only finds from the Neolithic and was probably built in that period. There were few skeleton parts in the chamber and they were mostly

unidentifiable. On the other hand, plenty of human bones were identified in the inner part of the passage. One of the skull fragments shows traces of trepanning. Parts of six axes were found in the passage, two of them thin-bladed, both polished on four sides, and a hollow-polished edge fragment (Forssander 1932).

The cairn outside the passage was built up of stone and clay. The biggest stones were placed against the bottom and the size of the stones decreased towards the surface of the cairn. The finds are dominated by potsherds, roughly 40,000. Among the vessel types there are pedestalled bowls, funnel beakers, and hanging vessels. The flint contains just over thirty fragments of axes. Of those that could be identified, the thin-bladed and hollow-polished shapes predominate. In addition, a battle axe of type A is documented from Gillhög. The majority of the axe fragments were identified in the upper part of the cairn, above the greater part of the potsherds, which gives an indication of changed deposition traditions over time (Forssander 1932; Malmer 1962; Tilley 1999a).

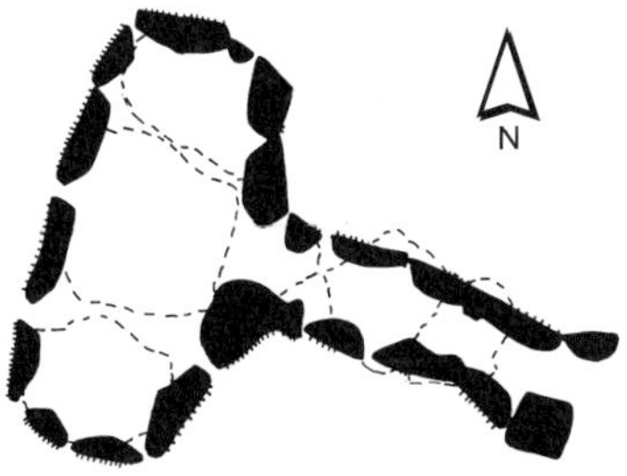

Fig. 34. Barsebäck 12, Gillhög. Dashed lines illustrate capstones (revised after Blomqvist 1989b). Scale 1:200.

*Barsebäck 3, Storegård* The passage grave at Storegård is located at a relatively high altitude, about 15 m a.s.l., on a flat, sandy height, roughly 3 km north of the Lödde Å and 2 km west of the Öresund (fig. 33). From the site today there is an extensive view and the sea can be glimpsed at two places. About half a kilometre south of megalithic tomb is the Mare Bäck with its surrounding wetlands. Just over a kilometre to the NNE is the Hofterup dolmen. There are no known Early or Middle Neolithic dwelling sites in the immediate vicinity of the grave. The closest is Barsebäck 36, half a kilometre to the east.

When the passage grave was excavated by LUHM under the leadership of Hansen at the end of the 1920s, it was observed that it was badly damaged. All that remained of the chamber was three undisturbed orthostats, two of which were shared by the passage and chamber, and the greater part of yet another orthostat, as well as small

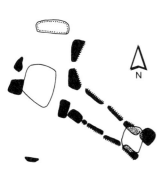

Fig. 35. Barsebäck 3, Storegård. Unfilled stones illustrate capstones while lines with parallel rows of dots indicate re-erected stones (revised after Blomqvist 1989b). Scale 1:200.

base parts of two stones. With the aid of packing stone in the ESE it was possible to estimate the shape and size of the chamber as about 6.5×2 m and roughly 1.6 m high. The chamber is rectangular, possibly with slightly rounded corners, and oriented SSW–NNE (fig. 35). Between the orthostats there was originally a packing of split flagstones, which survived at some places. The floor consisted of stamped clay which is preserved in most of the northern half of the chamber. The passage, which consists of five pairs of orthostats, is roughly 5 m long and 1 m wide with a height of about 1 m. Just as with Gillhög, the passage is not at right angles to the chamber, instead entering slightly obliquely to the south-east. Only the outermost capstone is preserved (Hansen 1930, 1931).

Although the grave was largely destroyed, seven virtually complete pots were found in it, parts of a further two pots, and small parts of ten more vessels. There were few flint tools in the chamber. We may mention a thin-bladed axe partially polished on four sides. In front of the entrance in the south-east there were no intact pots but a large number of sherds from an estimated 60 pots with rim ornamentation typical of MNA I–IV. Among the shapes are hanging vessels, pots with a tall cylindrical or conical neck, biconical vessels, and also clay ladles. A total of 227 amber beads were found in the chamber and 40 in the passage. The beads include different axe-shaped types. Outside the grave to the east, all that was found was parts of two beads and two axe fragments, one of which belonged to a thin-bladed axe (Hansen 1930, 1931).

No large skeletal parts were found in the burial chamber, just a few tiny pieces and about fifteen teeth. From this material it is not possible to say how many individuals were buried, just that there was more than one. Judging by the teeth, they could have been children or at least young individuals. A few pieces of

87

88

burnt bones were also documented in the chamber (Hansen 1930, 1931).

In 1986–87 the Department of Archaeology in Lund conducted seminar digs during four weeks in 1986 and two weeks in 1987 to investigate the barrow surrounding the megalithic tomb. At the time, probably all that was left of the barrow, about 25 m in diameter and almost 1.5 m high, was the lower part. The barrow around the megalithic tomb proved to consist exclusively of sand. In the southern side of the barrow, deposits of flint flake and pottery were observed, including a pot decorated with tooth stamps, in an accumulation of stone. In addition, parts of a probable kerb of a Bronze Age barrow west of the megalithic tomb were found (Hårdh 1993).

### Hög 2, Ljunghög

The passage grave in Hög is on a flat height 25 m a.s.l., west of a steep slope down towards the Lödde Å (fig. 33). The soils on the height consist of both clays and sand. The site affords a broad view of the surrounding landscape. Along the Lödde Å-Kävlingeån there are several Neolithic settlements. The nearest known one is less than 400 m to the north-west.

The megalithic tomb was excavated in 1919 by Hansen (1919a). The structure that was restored in 1967 is one of the best-preserved in Skåne (Petré & Salomonsson 1967). The rectangular chamber is 5×2 m in east–west direction and the passage is 5 m long. The chamber originally had three capstones (fig. 36). Around the chamber and the passage is a compact cairn covered by a thick layer of earth. One of the capstones is visible. Ljunghög is built up of round moraine blocks and the spaces between them are filled with horizontally laid flagstones. In the chamber some of the orthostats do not reach the desired height; the height of the wall was thus increased with blocks laid on top of and projecting out from the lower slabs. In the chamber were a large number of Late Neolithic

Fig. 36. Hög 2, Ljunghög (revised after Blomqvist 1989b). Scale 1:200.

objects which are typical grave goods, including flint daggers, and there was at least one Early Bronze Age burial. The grave was thus used during these periods as well, and older burials were probably cleared out. From the Middle Neolithic period there are only a few finds in the chamber. Most of these consisted of amber beads. In the passage there were two thin-bladed flint axes polished on four sides and a further polished fragment, along with three blade arrowheads of types A and B. The greatest quantity of Middle Neolithic was found outside the mouth of the passage. About 30 kg of potsherds was retrieved together with a fragment of a thick-butted flint axe. In connection with the restoration a semicircular cairn was excavated at the mouth of the passage. Under the cairn was a dark, sooty layer containing pottery, flint blades, amber beads, two flint axes, and a rock axe. The finds were concentrated in the entrance. The pottery from Hög consists of several hundred vessels, yet this is presumably only a small part of the original quantity. Vessel forms which could be identified include pedestalled bowls, funnel beakers, bowls, biconical pots, brim beakers, and hanging vessels. It seems as if the passage grave was used during much of the Middle Neolithic. The pottery represents phases MNA Ib–MNA IV (Hansen 1919a; Petré & Salomonsson 1967; Hårdh 1982).

### Kävlinge 1, Annehill

The megalithic tomb of Annehill is one of three double passage graves in Skåne. The other two, Östra Värlinge in Hammarlöv parish and Stora Kungsdösen in Östra Torp parish, are in south-west Skåne. Annehill has been excavated on two occasions, by Hansen in 1919 and as a seminar dig by the Department of Archaeology in Lund in 1986–87. The grave is located on a large plateau, 25 m a.s.l., roughly 1.3 km south of the Välabäcken and just over 2 km north of the Kävlingeån (fig. 33). The plateau is dominated by clay soils with small sandier parts. The area around the double passage grave is described as stony, clayey sand. The nearest Early and Middle Neolithic settlements are just over a kilometre to the north, beside the rivers.

Fig. 37. Kävlinge 1, Annehill (revised after Blomqvist 1989b). Scale 1:200.

The grave consists of two chambers. One is oval, measuring 3.5×2.5 m and oriented east–west, while the other is roughly the same size but more rectangular and oriented ESE–WNW (fig. 37). The 1919 excavation found that the structure was already seriously damaged. All the capstones were missing. The passage to the western chamber was missing, and only two stones were left of the passage to the eastern passage. The western chamber consists of seven orthostats with an opening facing the south-east, where the passage presumably lay. In both chambers there are remains of sealing in the form of pieces of sandstone between some of the orthostats. Eight slabs were documented in the eastern chamber and two belonging to the passage which led to the SSW. Between the chamber and the stone in the east side of the passage, according to Hansen, there was a door-post stone. Hansen's excavation in 1919 was confined to the chambers and the area of the damaged passages. He was able to observe that the soil was greatly disturbed, with recent material down in the bottom layer. In the eastern chamber there were occasional artefacts of flint, a slate pendant, and half an amber bead. In the bottom layer of the western chamber there were human bones, an undecorated sherd, a heart-shaped arrowhead, and a bone awl. Half an amber bead in the form of a double axe was discovered at the mouth of the eastern passage. The excavations in 1986–87 also comprised an area of 63 m² in front of the grave, with 53 m² as a continuous area and the rest as test pits. Under the topsoil eight features were documented, some of which could be from the re-erection of slabs

belonging to the passages. Part of the structure contained sealing stones; potsherds were found among some of them (Hårdh 1982; 1990a, 1990b).

A total of 9,000 potsherds were found in the area in front of the grave. Thirty-six per cent of the sherds are of Funnel Beaker type. It is clear from the rim sherds that about 260 pots were deposited in or near the grave. Among the vessel forms were pedestalled bowls, open bowls, and brim beakers. Chronologically the material comes from the greater part of the Middle Neolithic Funnel Beaker culture. It seems as if the material closest to the grave is older in character than what was discovered in the outer part of the excavated area. The flint is dominated by flakes and debitage. Among the tools are transverse arrowheads, flat-flaked arrowheads, three fragments of polished flint axes, and a reknapped thick-butted flint axe with a square butt. Two fragmentary rock axes were also found. Small fragments of unidentifiable burnt bones were collected. Among the bones were four fragments with scratched strokes. The decoration, partly in the form of zigzag lines and triangles, agrees well with the Funnel Beaker culture (Hårdh 1982; 1990a, 1990b).

*Lackalänga 14, Stenhög* The passage grave in Lackalänga is on the highest point, roughly 35 m a.s.l., of a sandy plateau (fig. 33). From the top of the hill there is an extensive view of the surroundings. A small bog and a watercourse are located just over 400 m south of the megalithic tomb. The nearest Neolithic settlement has been documented about 600 m to the north-east and dated to EN II–MNA II. Slightly more than 600 m to the south-west there is yet another settlement dated to the Early Neolithic.

Fig. 38. Lackalänga 14, Stenhög. Unfilled stones denote capstones and dotted stones indicate orthostats covered by capstones (revised after Blomqvist 1989b). Scale 1:200.

90

Stenhög was excavated and restored in 1923 by Hansen. Most of the chamber and passage was concealed before the excavation. The chamber is basically oval and extends 3.8×1.5 m north–south. It has three stones on one side and two on the other and one stone at each end. The chamber has three capstones. The passage in the east, which consists of twelve orthostats and four capstones, is 5.5 long and 0.8 m wide (fig. 38). The finds in the chamber included seven blade arrowheads of types A and B, flint daggers, flat-flaked arrowheads, a narrow chisel, blades, potsherds, and occasional human bones. The filling in the chamber, according to Hansen, gave the impression of having been disturbed. There were few finds in the passage, but they did include one fragmentary thick-butted, hollow-edged axe. A number of 1×1 m squares were excavated in the area immediately in front of the entrance to the passage. Within this area stone paving about 0.15 m thick was documented, containing almost 7,000 potsherds and two thin-bladed quadrilaterally polished flint axes (Hansen 1923). On the plan drawn during the 1923 excavation it may be noted that the passage grave is surrounded by a partly preserved stone floor with a diameter of approximately 25 metres. Parts of a kerb mark the limit of the stone floor to the north.

*Lilla Harrie 4*   In 1909 there was an excavation of three collapsed – and now removed – dolmens in Lilla Harrie (Karlin 1909). The site is on a flat, sandy ridge, 35 m a.s.l., just over 500 m north of the Kävlingeån (fig. 33). The nearest Early and Middle Neolithic settlement lies one kilometre to the west.

Dolmen I: A large block, about 4.2×2.6, functioned as the capstone resting on three or four large stones. An outer kerb of smaller stones surrounded the structure. Inside the presumed round dolmen were some human bones.

Dolmen II: About 6 m north-east of dolmen I was dolmen II. This had the same shape as the former. A stone block, about 2.7×1.7, was placed on top of four stones. Several cup marks were documented on the capstone.

Dolmen III: The third dolmen, which was situated just less than 4 m south-west of dolmen II, was probably the biggest. The capstone was about 5.2×3 m, supported by five upright slabs. This capstone likewise had cup marks.

The report states that there were a further two megalithic tombs in the area which had previously been removed. It is also reported that the dolmens in Lilla Harrie were the subject of legends (Karlin 1909).

*Dagstorp 12, Krångeltofta*   The ploughed-out long barrow was on the slope and crest of a ridge, 20 m a.s.l. The area is the western end of a fairly elevated range of hills known as Dagstorps Backar. To the west it gives way to the Saxån valley and in the south the valley of the Välabäcken extends with its many ancient monuments (fig. 33). To the east there are several Bronze Age barrows along the crest of the ridge.

The barrow was excavated by the National Heritage Board Southern Excavations Department in the winter of 1998–1999 in connection with the construction of the West Coast Line. The remaining stone structure consisted of three parallel lines of stones running north-east–south-west. The extent of the structure to the west could not be clarified, however, since it lay outside the excavated area. To the east, at right angles to the rows of stones, were two rectangular stone packings (contexts 4 and 9). The southern stone packing was slightly shifted to the east in relation to the northern one. These two stone packings were interpreted as façades for the long barrow. Furthest east was yet another rectangular stone packing oriented east–west (context 13). The three parallel rows of stones formed something that can be described as two rectangular stone frames. The middle line of stones was common to both the northern and the southern stone frame. The southern stone frame was not complete. Within the two stone frames were two large features interpreted as graves (contexts 6 and 11), characterized by outer and inner limits. The outer limits (contexts 5 and 10) consisted of stones laid in an oval pattern around the inner boundary of flat, split stones. It was striking that there were no stones inside the stone frames that were not part of the graves (fig. 39). Only fragments of burnt bones were encountered, but these were too fragmentary to allow identification. Just west of the northern stone frame was yet another grave structure which consisted of a stone packing overlayering a pit

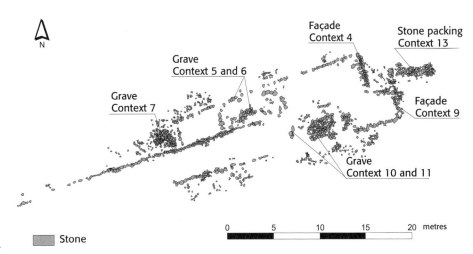

Fig. 39. Dagstorp 12, Krångeltofta. ▨ Stone

(context 7). Around the grave were scattered smaller stones. North and south of the outer rows of stones there were also scattered occurrences of stones. Adjacent to the western grave was a row of stones which linked the northern and middle rows. This can be interpreted as the vestiges of a room division or a west façade (Ericson Lagerås 1999).

The interpretation of the monument at Krångeltofta is mostly based on characteristic traits of the stone structure and the individual stone packings. The monument shares features with other long barrows: the trapezoidal shape, the location on a south-facing slope, and a mainly east–west orientation (Kaul 1988:64ff). The outer boundary consists of two stone frames, each with a façade in the eastern part, which is evidence that the structure was extended on at least two occasions. Within the stone frames were graves consisting of stone packings with flat and split stones. Floor-like stone packings which have been interpreted as graves in long barrows have previously been found in Sejerø (Liversage 1982) and Onsved Mark II (Kaul 1988) in Denmark, and in Britain (Liversage 1992:80). In many cases pottery is found in long barrows, for example, at the façade. It is often the sherds of just a few vessels. Very little pottery was discovered at the façades at Krångel-

tofta, which makes it difficult for us to give an exact dating of these characteristic parts of the long barrow (Ericson Lagerås 1999). Under the stone structure at Krångeltofta the excavation unearthed no dwelling site material in the form of house remains or occupation layers from the Neolithic. Fragments of a pointed- or thin-butted axe were retrieved immediately north of the feature (Ericson Lagerås 1999).

Very little charcoal was found in the façades, the graves, and the post-holes, which may be because fire was not a part of the rituals associated with the long barrow. The chances of finding relevant charcoal which can be used for [14]C dating these features were thus reduced. The filling in the north-eastern façade and the grave in the north-eastern part contained very little charcoal, which minimized the chances of finding charcoal from the time when the structure was in use. Moreover, the results of these samples, 8790±70 BP (7940–7700 cal. bc, Ua-9793) and 3375±60 BP (1740–1530 cal. bc, Ua-9795), did not correspond to the archaeological material. We probably cannot entertain great hopes of being able to date the stone structure with the aid of the [14]C method. To determine the date and phase of the long barrow at Krångeltofta, comparisons with other long barrows are likely to be more fruitful (Ericson Lagerås 1999).

Fig. 40. General view of the long barrow at Krångeltofta
(photo Å. Cademar).

*Södervidinge 3*  Two passage graves are located on the south slopes of Dagstorps Backar in Södervidinge parish, at a distance of about 250 m from each other (fig. 33). In 1919 Hansen excavated the more southerly one, Södervidinge 3. The grave is placed on a terrace on a sandy slope, 25 m a.s.l. The nearest Neolithic dwelling site is almost a kilometre to the south-west. The barrow is 10 m in diameter and up to 1 m high. The chamber is almost oval and measures 6×2–3 m from northeast to south-west. The floor of the chamber was covered with thin flagstones, some of which were still in position in the western part of the chamber when it was excavated. Of the capstones, only two large, broken

fragments survived. The passage is just over 5 m long and about 0.6 m wide (fig. 41). Between the first and second orthostat in the passage is a doorpost arrangement (Hansen 1919b).

In the chamber, which had been

Fig. 41. Södervidinge 3 (revised after Blomqvist 1989b). Scale 1:200.

plundered, the only finds were a dozen undecorated potsherds and a flint spearhead. In the passage, which was undisturbed, the excavation retrieved small quantities of pot fragments from both the Middle Neolithic and the Bronze Age and a blade arrowhead of type B. The largest amount of finds was discovered in a stone packing outside the passage. These included parts of pedestalled bowls and brim beakers, fragments of a thick-butted, hollow-polished flint axe, and yet another fragment of a thick-butted flint axe whose exact type cannot be determined (Hansen 1919b).

*Västra Hoby 3 and 4, Danshögarna*  The area in Västra Hoby consists of two long dolmens and a passage grave. The southern long dolmen and the passage grave were excavated by LUHM in the summer months of 1934–35. The excavated megalithic tombs are on a gentle sandy slope facing north, 200 south of the Kävlingeån. About 100 m north of these is the third grave, it too on a north-facing slope (fig. 33). Neolithic settlements lie both south and north of the river, although there is no settlement registered in the immediate vicinity of the megalithic tombs. Just over 500 m south of the site, parts of a Battle Axe cemetery have been excavated (Hansen 1917).

The southern long dolmen (RAÄ 3) measures 24×12 m in north–south direction and is 1–1.5 m high. The shape is virtually rectangular with rounded short sides. The barrow was erected on such sloping

⬆ Fig. 43. The passage grave and long dolmen at Västra Hoby, Danshögarna (photo M. Andersson).
▲ Fig. 44. Middle Neolithic pottery from the passage grave (RAÄ 3) in Västra Hoby (photo B. Almgren).

94

terrain that the base of the western side is 1.25 m lower than the opposite eastern side. The barrow is surrounded by a kerb of boulders. They are 0.2–0.5 m high and 0.5–1 m wide. The barrow surrounds a fairly centrally placed dolmen chamber, approximately 1.45×0.75–0.95 m (N–S), narrowing towards the south. At the time of the excavation what remained were the two end slabs and one side slab. Impressions in the sand showed that the chamber originally consisted of two stout side slabs and two slightly smaller slabs at the ends. A massive capstone probably covered the chamber. The bottom of the cist was lined with flagstones of alternating gneiss and chalk. The chamber is surrounded by an almost circular cairn, made of stones the size of a human head. The diameter of the cairn is 5.6 m. The chamber has been dug up all the way to the bottom in modern times, and there were no finds left in it. In the filling, however, there was a core axe and occasional potsherds of Neolithic character (Forssander 1937).

The barrow around the passage grave (RAÄ 3) is 11×15 m and 1.2 m high. The chamber of the passage grave is rectangular-oval and built of uncut slabs about 1.5 m high. Horizontally packed stone chips were documented between some of the slabs. The chamber measures 6.6×2 m and runs from north-east to south-west. The passage, which is 5.2 m long and 0.65 m wide, faces the south-east and consists of four pairs of orthostats (fig. 42). Between the first and second slabs is a doorpost arrangement. The capstones of both the chamber and the passage are missing. Around the barrow is a kerb consisting of about fifteen stones, 0.2–0.6 m high and 0.5–0.9 m wide. The

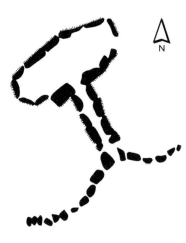

Fig. 42. Västra Hoby 3, Danshögarna (revised after Blomqvist 1989b). Scale 1:200.

chamber was excavated in the nineteenth century, and the excavation in 1934–35 therefore uncovered only occasional potsherds and flint flakes. Except in its innermost part, however, the passage was undisturbed. In it a lower Middle Neolithic later was documented, consisting of relatively few potsherds and a thin-butted axe. The axe was wedged between the two outermost slabs in the eastern side. The Middle Neolithic level was overlayered by a stratum of Late Neolithic material. Immediately outside the mouth of the passage was a flat cairn with a great admixture of gravel. In the direction of the passage it extended about 5 m, describing an almost semicircular arch with a diameter of 5 m. It seemed as if quite a few of the slabs in the kerb had been knocked down in connection with the building of the cairn, which would mean that the cairn is later than the passage grave itself. The cairn contained a large amount of pottery, about 50,000 sherds, which is the largest quantity from a megalithic tomb in south Scandinavia and probably in the whole of north-west Europe. Forssander claimed to be able to divide the find-bearing parts into two strata. In the layer closest to the entrance (stratum I) he found sherds belonging to pedestalled bowls, clay ladles, funnel beakers, and large bowl-shaped vessels. Stratum II was dominated by pottery decorated with tooth stamps. Among the vessel types are brim beakers and hanging vessels. The flint artefacts include nine flint and rock axes, one of them reknapped, and two fragmentary thick-butted flint axes, probably of type A, fragments of a probably hollow-polished thick-butted flint axe, an edge part of a thin-butted flint axe, fragments of a thin-bladed flint axe partially polished on four sides, two thin-butted axes, and a thick-butted rock axe, as well as two blade arrowheads (Forssander 1936, 1937; Tilley 1999a).

The long dolmen (RAÄ 4) closest to the Kävlingeån is 53×13 m in north–south direction and 2.4 m high.

The barrow is surrounded by 37 kerbstones (0.3–1.1 m high and 0.5–1.7 m wide), most of them standing. No burial chamber is visible, which means that it could in fact be a long barrow. The priest's report (1692) mentions that a warrior was slain on the spot. His body is supposed to be buried in one of the barrows (RAÄ 4?) and his head in the other (RAÄ 3?).

**Non-excavated megalithic tombs**  Some of the megalithic tombs in the area have never been excavated. In certain cases, therefore, it can be difficult to determine whether it is a long barrow/dolmen, round dolmen, or a passage grave.

*Dagstorp 2, the grave of Harald Hildetand*  The passage grave known as the grave of Harald Hildetand lies on a sandy south-facing slope of Dagstorps Backar, 20 m a.s.l. The Välabäcken flows approximately 300 m south of the megalithic tomb (fig. 33). There are no Neolithic settlements registered in the immediate vicinity of the grave. The grave has never been subjected to any archaeological investigation or restoration. The construction of the road to Södervidinge, south of the grave, has destroyed parts of the passage and any votive deposits there may have been there. The chamber measures roughly 6×2.5–3 m and is oriented from north-east to south-west with the passage to the south-east. The barrow is 9 m in diameter and 1 m high. On the upper side of one of the visible capstones of the passage there are about forty cup-marks.

*Dagstorp 23*  The presumed long dolmen is located at 50 m a.s.l. on a ledge of a clayey north-west slope with a position dominating the Saxån to the west (fig. 33). The structure is rectangular with noticeably rounded corners and is about 55×35 m and almost 3.5 m high. The long dolmen has a kerb, partly built like a cavity wall, almost 1.3 m tall, made of stone measuring 0.3–1 m. No Neolithic settlements exist in the immediate vicinity of the grave.

*Hofterup 1*  On a sandy terrace 10 m a.s.l. on a slope facing east down towards a depression, is the Hofterup dolmen. The site is just over a kilometre north-east of the passage grave at Storegård (fig. 33). The closest Early and Middle Neolithic dwelling site is about 350 m north of the megalithic tomb. The dolmen has a quadrilateral chamber measuring 1.3–1,9×1.2–1.5 m in a north–south direction. Five orthostats, 1.2–1.3 m tall and 0.7–1 m wide, bear up a capstone measuring 1.3×1.8 m (N–S). There are about twenty cup marks on the capstone.

*Stora Harrie 1*  The long dolmen is situated on a sandy plateau (30 m a.s.l.), right beside the slope down towards the Kävlingeån, which flows just over 500 m north of the grave (fig. 33). The closest Early and Middle Neolithic settlement is less than a kilometre to the north. The dolmen today consists of an orthostat measuring 1×1.3 m. Two metres south of this are two stone blocks, about 0.8–1.3×0.5 m in size. The dolmen is surrounded by an almost square stone setting, 11×11 m.

*Stora Harrie 7, 8, and 9*  On a flat, sandy height (30 m a.s.l.), roughly 800 m south of the Välabäcken, there are a dolmen and two long dolmens (fig. 33). Half a kilometre south-east of the site is a settlement dated to EN I, and a kilometre to the south-west, remains of settlement from EN II–MNA II have been excavated.

The dolmen (RAÄ 7) is 3×1×1.5 m and consists of three blocks, one of them smashed to pieces. The dolmen chamber is filled with stone and earth. There is no capstone. The long dolmen (RAÄ 8) measures 13×9 m from north-west to south-east. At the foot of the barrow there are eleven stone blocks 0.5–1.7 m high and 1–1.5 m wide, four on each long side, two at the south-east end, and one at the north-west end. No traces of the dolmen chamber are visible. The other long dolmen (RAÄ 9) is 52×7 m long from east to west. It is surrounded by kerbstones, 0.1–0.3 m high and 0.2–1.7 m wide. No dolmen chamber is visible. One of the blocks at the western end has a number of cup marks. The site of the long dolmen is popularly known as Galgbacken or "Gallows Hill". The area within the kerbstones is said to have been used as a place of execution (Hansen 1926).

*Södervidinge 11* The passage grave is on a sandy plateau, 25 m a.s.l. (fig. 33). The barrow measures 17 m in diameter and is almost 1.5 m high. The chamber is estimated to have measured 5×2 m, in north-east–south-west direction. The chamber has two capstones, the northern one of which bears about ten cup marks. The nearest Neolithic settlement is about a kilometre to the south, beside the Välabäcken.

**Data from archival studies** Archival studies, chiefly in the register of the Dialect and Place-Name Archive in Lund and early land survey maps, can supplement our picture of the stock of megalithic tombs. Research has been carried out, for example, by Hårdh (1982) in her study of the megalithic tombs in the area, and in connection with the second survey, to find special names indicating the existence of megalithic tombs. Particular attention was devoted to names containing elements such as *dös-, dysse-, stendös-, stendysse-, stenkiste-* and *kycklinge-*. The material is of course uncertain and can never be complete. It was no doubt common for megalithic tombs to give places their names, but it is difficult to know how names like *hög* or *höj* should be judged. They could be the remains of megalithic tombs or Bronze Age barrows.

A record of a passage grave or dolmen the exact location of which is not known, *Håstad 2*, is found in the Priest's Reports of 1692: "a mound called Puga-ugn ['fairy oven'] all covered with large stones..." located in the east field of Håstad.

The area where the passage grave in Hög is located, *Hög 2*, is called "stendöserne" (the stone dolmens) on a map from 1748. The register known as *Palteboken* from 1514 mentions *Stendösen* as the name of a part

of the east field in Hög parish. It is probable that these names can be associated with the passage grave in Hög and that the plural form "stendöserne" refers to several cultivation plots. It cannot be ruled out, however, that more than one megalithic tomb may have existed in the area (Hårdh 1982).

Sjöborg writes about a now destroyed *kummelgrotta*, literally "cairn-cave" and marks the place on a map, *Norra Nöbbelöv 1*, north-east of the bog of Nöbbelövs Mosse. On a map from 1774 the area is called "Kyck-lingeskiftet" (the chicken shift) and Sjöborg mentions the name "Kycklinghönan" (the mothering hen), an old term for a megalithic grave (Sjöborg 1824).

The land register mentions a dolmen in the north field of Norrvidinge. The place is right beside the Saxån, on a gentle sandy slope facing west, *Norrvidinge 76, Jungfrukällorna*. The priest's reports from 1729 mention that a man in the locality had five children, two sons and three daughters. One Christmas morning the three sisters were on their way to the early morning service when they were attacked and killed by their brothers who had failed to recognize them. The brothers buried their sisters on the bank of the river, where three springs rose: "the one bigger than the other. There is also a stone cairn, and these springs and the cairn can still be seen this day." When the place was surveyed in 1986, nothing was visible. The stone cairn (*stenvården*) that is mentioned could possibly be a dolmen.

At Stångby 3:1 there is a place, west of Stångby Mosse, which is called "Stendösseåkern" (stone-dolmen field) on the 1744 map, *Stångby 3*. It is mentioned by Bruzelius in his *Antikvarisk Beskrifning om Torna Härad i Skåne*. Even then the dolmen was totally destroyed (Bruzelius 1880).

Another area at Stångby is named "Stenkullen" (stone hill) on the 1744 map, which could indicate that there was once a megalithic tomb on the spot, *Stångby 5*. Remains of a mound can be seen today.

In Stävie there is a concentration of names suggesting that there were megalithic tombs in the area, *Stävie*

20. Today, however, there are no traces of any dolmens or passage graves. *Palteboken* from 1514 mentions "Stendösefältet" (the stone-dolmen field) in the west field. On maps from 1748, 1768, and 1776 the area is called "Stendösen" (Hårdh 1982). During the survey in 1985 there was nothing visible in the field. The area is a flat sandy height less than a kilometre south of the Kävlingeån.

On a map from 1775 there is a place marked "Stenkullen" (stone hill), *Vallkärra 37*. This is possibly the feature that Sjöborg records as "E of the village [Vallkärra] a line of standing stones [*domstensbana*] of the Danish quadrilateral form" (Sjöborg 1815). Sjöborg may be referring to a long dolmen. The site is on a flat sandy ridge.

On another sandy ridge (Karaby Backar), one kilometre south of the Välabäcken there is a barrow measuring 30×15 m (NNE–SSW) and almost 5 m high. A report from LUHM to Skånes Hembygdsförening (I 595/1959) mentions the remains of a kerb and that a couple of stones from it had rolled down the slope. The 1986 survey found nothing visible in the field. Dybeck mentions that there were eighteen large stones forming a triangle at the top of the mound (Dybeck 1840). The monument may possibly have been a long dolmen, *Västra Karaby 25*.

In the first survey in 1969 there is a record of a removed dolmen on Karaby Backar. By the time of the second survey in 1986 there was nothing visible in the field. On a map from 1755 a barrow is marked on the site, *Västra Karaby 113*.

On the same ridge, just over a kilometre south of the confluence of the Välabäcken and Dösjebro, is a barrow measuring 15×2–9 m (NW-SE), *Västra Karaby 34*. It is about a metre high and narrows towards the north-west. At the south-east edge there is a stone – possibly the kerbstone of a long dolmen.

Jennbert mentions in her dissertation that an area of 100 m² at *Löddeköpinge 8* contained some big stones. Their impressive size, together with the fact that the layers here were disturbed and that human bones were found, is strong evidence that there may have been a dolmen here (Jennbert 1984a:28).

As already mentioned, the name Dösjebro, the concentration of pottery, and the stone packings (see Dagstorp 11) suggests that there may have been a megalithic tomb at Dagstorp 11.

Since the data on the above megalithic tombs must be regarded as more or less uncertain, they will not be included in the discussion of the spatial distribution of graves in relation to other Neolithic remains. They are, however, a reminder that the number of megalithic tombs was probably greater in prehistoric times than those known today.

**Flat-earth graves**  Little is known about flat-earth graves from the latter part of the Early Neolithic and the start of the Middle Neolithic in the investigation area and in Skåne as a whole. Recently excavated sites in Flädie parish, however, have shown that this form of burial also existed during this period.

*Flädie RAÄ 7*  A more or less continuous complex of monuments was investigated by the National Heritage Board Southern Excavations Department in the autumn of 2000 in connection with planned road construction. The antiquities were on a sandy height beside the bay at Lomma (fig. 33). North and west of the site is the Lödde Å, the estuary of which in this period formed a deep bay. A Middle Neolithic flat-earth cemetery with seventeen securely attested graves (fig. 45) and a manufacturing place for flint tools located about 250 m north-east of the cemetery have been excavated. The sites, one of which, RAÄ 7, was previously known as a Stone Age dwelling site but also containing Iron Age remains, are in the parishes of Flädie and Borgeby in south-west Skåne (Pihl & Runcis 2001).

The cemetery yielded a rich amount of finds consisting of at least 180 amber beads and amulets, most of them shaped as double axes and clubs. Other forms occurred as well. At one of the graves a virtually intact decorated pot was found. In four of the graves it could

98

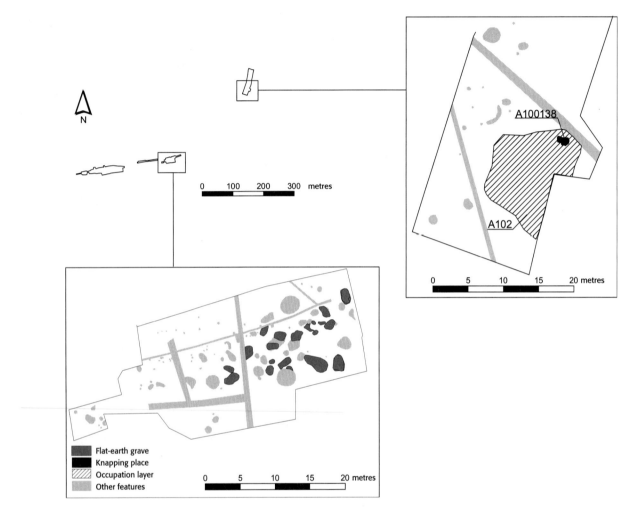

0    100    200    300   metres

0       5      10      15       20 metres

Flat-earth grave
Knapping place
Occupation layer
Other features

0        5       10       15        20 metres

Fig. 45. Plan of the cemetery at Flädie 7.

be demonstrated that whole pots had been deposited, while others contained only sherds. Some of the graves contained flint blades manufactured in an extremely refined technique. In one of the graves a little polished rock axe was deposited. Traces of the deceased were confined to reddish-brown stains in the ground and fragments of dental enamel. The buried individuals are judged by osteologists to be exclusively children or young individuals. The shapes of the amber objects and the pottery indicate that the cemetery was used at least during MNA I–III (Pihl & Runcis 2001; Runcis 2002).

The manufacturing place, where traces of Iron Age settlement were also observed in the immediate vicinity, stood out after stripping as an occupation area cov-

ering about 120 m² (A102) with numerous knapped flints on the surface. The dense concentration of flakes was demarcated in a total of twenty-three 0.5×0.5 m squares which were dug by hand. The distinct flint concentration (A100138) was slightly irregular in shape and measured roughly 1.8×1.1 m. The flakes lay on or near the surface of the layer, closely packed in a stratum a few centimetres thick. The total quantity of flint from the knapping place was just over 25 kg, with a great variation in weight between the squares, from less than 0.1 kg up to 7 kg per square. The flint is mainly of Senonian type, with flakes and debitage as the predominant category of finds. A large number of these are judged to come from the manufacture of quadrilateral flint axes. About ten flakes showed a

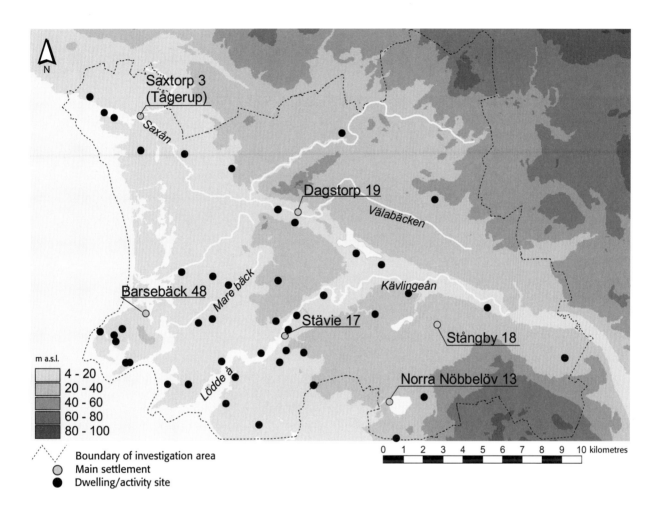

Fig. 46. Settlement sites in MNA III–V.

polished surface, and there were also occasional tools in the form of flake scrapers and a transverse arrowhead. Two of the polished flakes could be refitted to give a bigger edge fragment of an axe, whose narrow and broad side could both be distinguished. The angle between these, together with the arch, suggest that the flakes probably come from a thin-butted axe (Pihl & Runcis 2001).

## MNA III–V

**Settlement** Settlements, votive sites, and graves from this period in Skåne are not as well represented as in the previous phase. Just as in earlier parts of the Neo-

lithic, it is above all in the southern and south-west parts of the province that there is sufficient archaeological source material to allow us to carry on a discussion of the settlement pattern. In the Ystad area, there is settlement continuity within the old settled districts near the coast, but it seems as if the inner hummocky landscape was also claimed for settlement. Some of the earlier settlement areas were abandoned, however, which indicates that settlement was concentrated in certain areas. Archaeological excavations suggest that settlements continued to be small (Larsson, L. 1985, 1992a:94), but it should be pointed out that any assessment of the extent of settlements is

Fig. 47. Plan of Dagstorp 19 (SU21) in MNA III–V.

based on the excavation of rather small areas. Around Malmö the archaeological evidence shows that several smaller settlements were probably amalgamated in one bigger settlement, namely, Hindby Mosse (Svensson 1986:122).

Within the investigation area, fifty-one dwelling sites have been registered which can be dated to MNA III–V, and eighteen of these have been excavated.

**Main settlements** A number of the excavated sites have been interpreted as main settlements belonging to the period MNA III–V.

*Dagstorp 19 (SU21)* The period of the Neolithic settlement at Dagstorp 19 (fig. 46) that was most richly represented as regards the quantity of finds was MNA III.

In the eastern part of the area was the occupation layer with the greatest amount of finds, A153, which measured 500 m². The layer could be demarcated to the west, north, and east, but it extended beyond the excavated area to the south (fig. 47). After a surface survey, eighty-three 1×1m squares were dug by hand, concentrated in the central part of the layer, where the density of finds and features was high. The layer was then stripped in twenty-six 4×4 m squares. Among the flint (129 kg), the predominant categories of tools are flake scrapers and blade knives. Other types of tools include transverse arrowheads, awls, fragments of polished flint axes, and a large number of flake cores. About 8% of the total 26.4 kg of pottery is decorated. The decoration was rich and varied, with a wide range of execution and composition characterizing the material. Pits and stick impressions dominate, but tooth-stamp technique is also richly represented. Fragments of at least seven clay discs were retrieved. All in all, the finds indicate a dating of A153 to MNA III (Lagergren-Olsson & Linderoth 2000).

Two long-houses and a sunken-floor hut west and east of the layer (houses 71, 73, and 74) can probably be dated to MNA III. House 74 was oriented east–west on a slight slope down towards the Välabäcken. The building was roughly 15 m long and 7 m wide, with an internal area of just over 100 m². It was two-aisled and rectangular in shape. There were post-holes for at least six roof-bearing posts. All that remained of the northern long wall was four post-holes. The southern wall seems to have consisted of a double row of posts. In the features belonging to the house there were only a few finds of flint and pottery. The pottery, which is of Funnel Beaker character, consists of just two undecorated sherds. The flint is small quantities of flakes/debitage but there is also a flake core, a blade, and a microblade. The stratigraphical relation to layer A153 indicates that the house is probably contemporary with this. House 71 was built on a gentle slope down towards the Välabäcken. It was a two-aisled structure at least 13.5 m long and 5 m wide. The shape was rectangular and the orientation was WNW–ESE. The internal area is estimated as just under 70

Fig. 48. Layer 153 during excavation at Dagstorp 19 (SU21) (photo A. Lagergren-Olsson).

m². The row of roof-bearing posts consisted of five posts, three inside the house, and one in each gable. The northern wall line consisted of seven post-holes and the southern one of eight. In the line of the wall

102

Fig. 49. Section of pit A68613 at Dagstorp 19 (SU21)
(photo Y. Kristiansen).

some post-holes were missing in places, because recent pits and drains had destroyed parts of the structure. The finds in the features of the house were confined to occasional flint flakes and potsherds and small quantities of burnt bones and charcoal. In the south-western part of the house, beside the long wall, was a pit, A68765. It was irregularly rounded and had a diameter of roughly 1.5 m and a depth of 0.15 m. It had a fairly level bottom but sloped sides. The pit contained flint in the form of flakes/debitage and a retouched flake. The vast majority of the pottery is undecorated sherds. Three small pieces, however, have a tooth-stamped pattern and can be dated to MNA III. Adjacent to house 71 was an occupation layer (A158) with mixed pottery belonging to the Middle Neolithic. House 73 stood on a very gentle slope down towards the Välabäcken. The building had a slightly irregular round-oval shape. It may be described as a hut with a sunken-floor just over 4 m long and roughly 3.7 m wide and an area of nearly 15 m². The pit was about 0.3 m deep with a fairly level bottom and slightly sloping edges. In the middle of the house was a hole which could be a post-hole for a roof-bearing post. At the edge of the pit of the hut were three post-holes arranged in a triangle, which may possibly have been part of a wall. The flint in the pit consisted mainly of flakes/debitage and debris. The other flints were retouched pieces, blades, flake cores, knives, scrapers, awls, and two small polished axe fragments. The pottery was mostly undecorated, with only a small

number having any kind of decoration. In addition, there was a little piece of an undecorated clay disc. Among the decorated Neolithic pottery there were some fine-tempered sherds with small pits under the rim. A further few sherds have a double angle line both under the rim and on the shoulder. This vessel had a short neck and was therefore probably a bowl. In the pit of the hut there was also a quern rubber stone of rock and small quantities of burnt bones and red ochre. The bones were too fragmentary to allow identification of the species. All in all, the dated sherds together with the surrounding context probably allow the building to be dated to MNA II–III (Lagergren-Olsson & Linderoth 2000; Artursson et al. 2003).

A number of post-holes and pits were excavated in and under occupation layer A153, above all in the western parts. Right beside the occupation layer, two large pits, A68613 and A68431, were excavated. Large quantities of pottery (10 kg) and flint (15 kg) were retrieved from A68613. The pit measured 1.75×1.5 m on the surface; it was bowl-shaped and about 0.5 m deep. At the centre of the pit the filling in a likewise bowl-shaped section was very humic and sooty (fig. 49). The sooty part was demarcated to the north and the bottom by a concentration consisting of pottery and flint. The sherds in this concentration are of a thick, coarse-tempered fabric. The majority comes from a big vessel decorated with pits. Beside this stout pot was the greater part of a brim beaker. The placing of the pieces indicates that the brim beaker was originally placed in or perhaps right beside the bigger pot. Apart from the big pot and the brim beaker, fragments of a further fifteen or so decorated vessels were found. In addition, parts of nine clay discs were retrieved, three of them decorated with various types of stick impressions. One of the clay discs has a hole located at the edge. Among the flint tools there are scrapers, knives, above all blade knives, and awls (fig. 50). Further finds were a large fragment of a polished, reknapped, thick-butted axe, flake cores, and blades. The majority of the finds

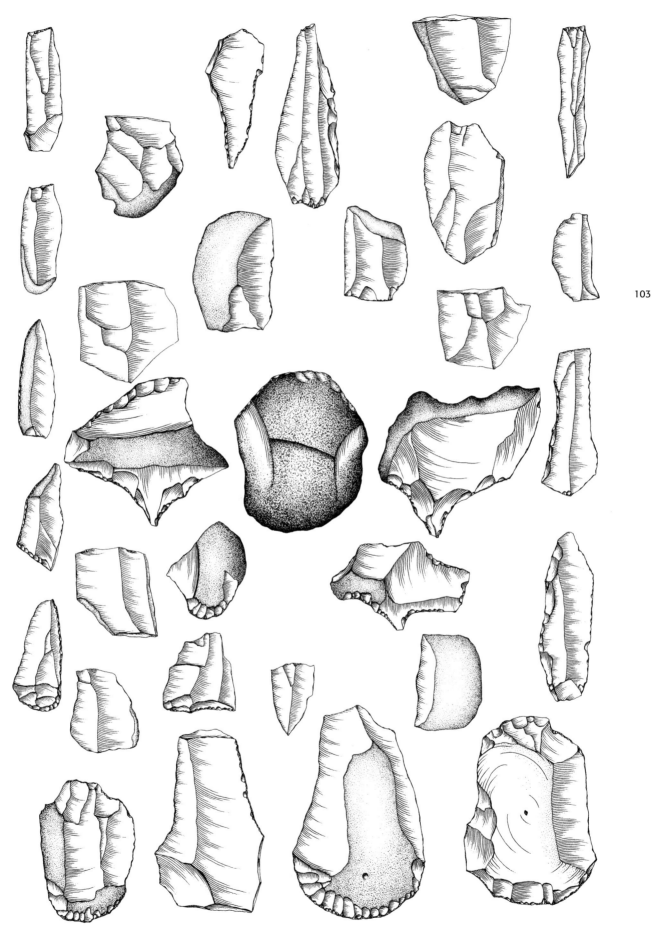

Fig. 50. Flints from pit A68613 at Dagstorp 19 (SU21). Drawings by Björn Nilsson.

come from the sooty part of the feature. The finds and the relation of the pit to the occupation layer indicate a dating to MNA III, contemporary with the deposition of the layer. Charcoal from a macrofossil sample gave a Middle Neolithic dating, 4360±70 BP (3090–2890 cal. bc, Ua-25062). Also found in the pit was 36 g of burnt bones, of which one fragment could be identified as coming from a domesticated pig. A68431 consisted of a funnel-shaped, stone-filled pit, which was also visible at the top of the layer. The pit measured 2.7×2.5 m at the surface, decreasing rapidly in size towards the bottom, which was 0.75 m deep. Three layers of stone were documented in the pit. The size of the stones mostly varied between 0.15 and 0.4 m. The middle layer of stone gave the impression that bigger stones had been placed along the edges of the pit and that the centre had been packed with smaller stones. The finds were mainly found in the top layer. They include a blade knife/blade sickle polished by use wear. Other flint material comprises scrapers, knives, and part of a polished axe. Fragments of at least ten different decorated pots were found together with about 1 kg of undecorated pottery. The relation of the pit to the occupation layer (A153) indicates that it was dug earlier or at the same time as the deposition of the layer (MNA III) (Lagergren-Olsson & Linderoth 2000).

It seems likely that Dagstorp 19 was a main settlement during the MNA III as well. The long tradition of the site, the extent of the finds, the size of the settlement, and the houses are clear indications of this.

*Barsebäck 48* The settlement was on a sandy height, about 5 m a.s.l., and according to the surface survey it comprised roughly 60,000 m². The distance from today's coastline is approximately 1.5 km. With the sea level at the time being about 4–5 m higher than today, the site was near the coast in the late MNA, when it was on a small peninsula by a lagoon right beside the narrow isthmus that connected the Barsebäck foreland with the mainland (fig. 46).

Parts of the site were excavated during seminar digs arranged by the Department of Archaeology in Lund in the autumn of 1987 and spring of 1988. No features were observed by the excavation, which was wholly concentrated on the massive occupation layer up to 0.5 m thick. Unfortunately, none of the documentation material in the form of plans and sections has been archived. Students at the department have, however, gone through parts of the material found in the 42 m² excavated in 1988. A total of almost 90 kg of flint was found, 8% of which consisted of tools, and there was about 3.5 kg of pottery. The tools are dominated above all by scrapers, which account for more than 50% of the total tools. No stratigraphical units could be distinguished in the occupation layer which was excavated in units of 0.1 m. On the other hand, a certain chronological difference could be discerned in the composition of finds between the upper and lower parts of the layer. At the bottom (unit V) the decorated pottery mostly shows tooth-stamp technique, bands, angle lines, and angle bands, small imprints at the rim, notches on the edge of the rim, holes, lines, rhombi, and chequerboard patterns. In units II–IV pits at the rim are most common. In these layers there were also Pitted Ware–influenced flint artefacts in the form of blade arrowheads and cylindrical blade cores. The uppermost unit (unit I) contained Late Neolithic flint tools such as spoon-shaped scrapers and flat-flaked arrowheads.

The layer sequence indicates more or less continuous settlement in the period MNA III–V. The extensive finds with a varied toolkit, the extent of the site, the favourable ecological environment, and the proximity to the passage grave of Gillhög mean that the site may be regarded as a main settlement during MNA III–V.

*Stävie 17* Just over seven kilometres east of Barsebäck 48 was the dwelling site of Stävie 17, immediately to the east of the Lödde Å (fig. 46). In 1972 the National Heritage Board Southern Excavations Department did an excavation of the site occasioned by plans for a gravel quarry. The settlement was located on a sandy height and the slope down to the Lödde Å. There was once an area of wetland north of the settlement.

The total area excavated was 150 m², distributed in four different trenches, which yielded similar find material and can be regarded as one and the same settlement. If it is, the remains cover an area of at least 10,000 m². The remains consisted of thick occupation layers and occasional pits and hearths. The flint amounts to 50 kg, of which 5% is tools. A large number of polished fragments were identified, of which four were thick-butted axes (3 A-axes and 1 B-axe). Eight cylindrical blade cores were found and about thirty fragments of blade arrowheads. The majority were deemed to be of types A and B. No certain blade arrowheads of group C or D were found. Other tools include flake and blade scrapers, awls, and knives. The pottery (17 kg) mostly consists of undecorated sherds. The decoration that does occur includes pit impressions, horizontal rows of vertical strokes, and comb stamps (Lindsten 1974; Nagmér 1990). The flints, with blade arrowheads and cylindrical blade cores, have a distinct Pitted Ware character. The pottery should probably be dated to the closing phase of MNA, that is, the Stävie group, showing clear similarities to the Danish Valby phase. The area of the settlement and the extent and varied character of the material give the impression that the site may have been a main settlement.

*Norra Nöbbelöv 13* The settlement was on a sandy place on the western edge of Nöbbelövs Mosse, about 23–25 m a.s.l. In the Neolithic this bog was probably an open lake (fig. 46). The site was excavated by the National Heritage Board Southern Excavations Department in 1994 in connection with work on road 108, and was found to have remains of settlement from both the Middle Neolithic and the Early Bronze Age. The extent of the Neolithic remains, which consisted of an occupation layer rich in finds with adja-

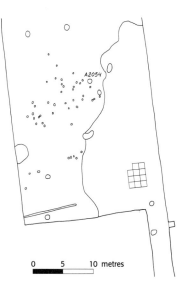

Fig. 51. Plan of Norra Nöbbelöv 13 in MNA III–V.

cent post-holes and pits, indicates that the site can probably be regarded as a main settlement. The location of the occupation layer, down towards the bog, and the fact that no features were observed under it, shows that it can be a refuse layer from the adjacent settlement. In total, only twelve 1×1 m squares in the layer were excavated. The flint (16 kg) consists mainly of flakes/debitage, but among the tools there are above all scrapers, knives, axe fragments, and cores. The scrapers are mostly flake scrapers and the knives are dominated by flake knives. The pottery in the layer is badly fragmented, making it difficult to draw any conclusions about vessel types. The decoration consists of tooth stamps and stick or nail impressions (Olson et al. 1996; Hellerström 1997). Analyses at the Ceramic Research Laboratory in Lund show that the pottery has a very homogeneous composition when it comes to the choice of raw clay and tempering, and differences in the size of temper have more to do with the function of the vessels. The same raw clay was used to make both pots and clay discs. This could suggest that the manufacture took place on the site (Brorsson 1996). The composition of the decoration and the total absence of cord, whipped cord, and vertical strokes

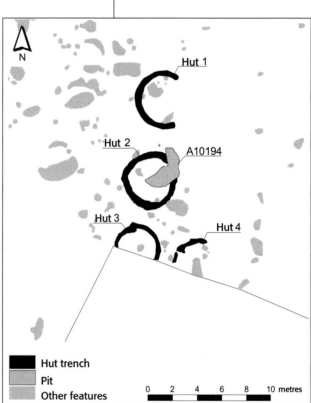

Fig. 52. Plan of Saxtorp 23 (SU10) in MNA III–V.

106

points to a dating in the late Funnel Beaker culture, no earlier than MNA III. Also found in the layer was a flint flake with scratchings on the cortex. The pattern consists of two concentric circles with cross lines and two angular bands. The pattern of the scratching agrees quite well with the decoration that we find on late Funnel Beaker culture pottery (Olson et al. 1996; Hellerström 1997). Among the bones in the layer which could be identified were cattle, sheep/goat, pig, and two fragments of human femurs (Nilsson 1996). Macrofossil analysis suggests that there was cultivation on the site. The occurrence of fat hen, black bindweed, common chickweed, and corn spurrey indicates spring-sown crops on nutrient-rich soils (Regnell 1996:93).

Immediately west of the occupation layer was a concentration of post-holes measuring roughly 12×5 m from east to west (fig. 51). The form and the filling suggest that the post-holes were contemporary. It is probable that they are the remains of some kind of building, the type of which could not be determined exactly in the field. A pit (A2054) just east of the post-holes contained a fragmented vessel. It was probably an open bowl with a weakly marked shoulder and decorated with at least three rows of oblique stick impressions in a zipper pattern. The vessel is likely to be no older than MNA III. It contained burnt animal bones and retouched flint flakes (Olson et al. 1996; Hellerström 1997).

**Dwelling/activity sites**

*Saxtorp 23 (SU10)* On the height between the Saxån to the south and the Kvärlövsån to the north (fig. 46) where Early Neolithic remains were documented, there were also traces of Middle Neolithic activity. In the southern part of the excavated area there were five trenches which were interpreted as having been dug for the walls of four hut structures (huts 1–4). The area with the huts has been heavily cultivated and damaged by recent activities. The trenches that could

be observed were probably only the last vestiges of the original structures. The huts were almost identical in design: circular with a diameter between 4 and 5 m. The width of the trenches varied between 0.5 and 0.6 m and the depth between 0.15 and 0.25 m. The cross-section was unevenly bowl-shaped and the irregularities can be interpreted as stick- or post-holes. Three of the huts had an opening towards the east. The two southernmost structures were cut by recent drains and could not be fully documented. The finds consisted of flint flakes/debitage, burnt clay, and small, unidentifiable potsherds. In the area closest to the huts several small trenches were noted. It is possible that these are the last traces of wall trenches destroyed by modern cultivation (fig. 52). The features contained no extant parts of animals or plants which could hint at the function of the huts (Andersson, M. 1999).

The four ¹⁴C analyses of charcoal particles from three of the wall trenches and the pit at hut 2 have yielded very different datings. Despite this, all four huts must be of roughly the same age since they are close to each other and give the impression of constituting a unit. The wall trench in hut 1 has been dated to 5315±90 BP (4240–4000 cal. bc, Ua-9846), that is, the end of the Late Mesolithic or possibly the start of the Early Neolithic. In hut 2 the wall trench has been dated to 9045±80 BP (8130–7970 cal. bc, Ua-9843), which corresponds to the Early Mesolithic. The pit (A10194) beside the same feature, however, was dated to 4000±85 BP (2850–2340 cal. bc, Ua-9845), that is, early MNB or possibly late MNA. The wall trench in hut 3 was dated 4485±85 BP (3340–3040 cal. bc, Ua-9844), which corresponds to the end of the Early Neolithic and the start of MNA. The preliminary investigation of 1997 excavated an occupation layer which subsequently ended up outside the area of the final excavation. Under the layer, excavation in squares documented two features, including part of a trench (A5538). The finds consisted of occasional flints. From this feature there is a ¹⁴C dating which gave the result 4160±90 BP (2880–2610 cal. bc, Ua-8985), corresponding to a dating to the transition MNA–MNB. The trench could possibly be part of a hut of the same type as those described above. Fragments of blade arrowheads were also retrieved within the area (Andersson, M. 1999).

Features of the same design as the huts on the site are known, for instance, from the village of Tuna on the island of Ven, where eight circular hut bottoms, about 3–5 m in diameter, were documented. These were dated to the Pitted Ware culture (Löfgren 1993). At Hagestad a dozen dwelling sites from the late EN and MN have been found, and hut-like structures have been excavated on some of these. On dwelling site 6 there were two probable hut bottoms, which had a diameter of three and five metres respectively. The pottery on the site was difficult to date since it retains traits of both Funnel Beaker ceramics and Pitted Ware.

A likely dating is the start of MNB. On site 7 there were six round hut bottoms, with a diameter varying between 2.9 and 3.3 m. These structures have only been schematically published, but in five cases they are supposed to have had remains of post-holes at the edges, while the sixth lacked post-holes. The huts were in a row, and since the excavated area was limited, it is not impossible that there were more huts on the site. These huts have been dated on the basis of the pottery to the transition between MNA and MNB (Strömberg 1988a).

The excavations at Saxtorp 23 show that the site has settlement remains from both the Early Neolithic and the Middle Neolithic. The circular huts probably belong to the latter phase. Finds of fragmentary blade arrowheads in the topsoil, parallels to the huts on Ven and at Hagestad, and at least two of the ¹⁴C analyses indicate a dating in the final phase of MNA and/or MNB. In addition, according to the register of ancient monuments, two thin-bladed axes and a B-axe have been found on the site. Whether all the huts are contemporary or should be associated with repeated visits to the site is difficult to judge. These remains probably represent brief, temporary activities on the site. The favourable environment, on a sandy tongue of land at the confluence of the Saxån and Kvärlövsån, may mean that the structures served as temporary dwellings or stores used by people when hunting, fishing, and collecting plants (Andersson, M. 1999).

*Lackalänga (Furulund)* The settlement was on the south side of the Kävlingeån, on a sandy plateau about 15 m a.s.l. (fig. 46). The landscape surrounding the site is gently undulating in character, broken only by the river and the ravine through which it flows. The closest megalithic tombs are "Danshögarna" at Västra Hoby, roughly two kilometres to the north-east. In connection with the rerouting of road 934, the National Heritage Board Southern Excavations Department excavated an area of 300 m² on the site.

Fig 53. Hut 2 at Saxtorp 23 (SU10) during excavation (photo Ö. Mattsson).

Fig. 54. Plan of Lackalänga (Furulund) in MNA III–V.

The area was covered by an occupation layer up to 0.5 m thick. Of the flint (27 kg), 2.3% consists of tools, if blades and retouched flints are included. Scrapers, above all flake scrapers, are the most frequent category of tool. Two blade arrowheads of type A2 and a transverse arrowhead were retrieved. Five large polished fragments could be identified, one of them from a B-axe, one from a repolished A/B-axe, and two from thick-butted, thin-bladed axes. In addition there was a fragment of a burnt flint chisel. Other tools included cores, knives, and an awl. The collected flint material from the occupation layer represents a traditional toolkit from the Middle Neolithic in southern Scandinavia, with Pitted Ware influences in the form of blade arrowheads. Generally speaking, the potsherds are small and fragmentary and cannot be more closely identified than as being of Neolithic character. A number of post-holes, in a round-oval formation measuring 15×9 m and running NW–SE, was documented under the occupation layer (fig. 54), but it was not possible to assign them to any distinct building. The occurrence of the post-holes and the form they made up nevertheless indicates that there may have been a building on the site. The majority of the flint

came from the occupation layer within this round-oval formation. Two $^{14}$C samples, one from the occupation layer and one from a post-hole, gave values of 4180±90 BP (2888–2611 cal. bc, Ua-7341) and 4060±70 BP (2823–2526 cal. bc, Ua-7642) respectively, which corresponds to late MNA or early MNB (Munkenberg 1996). Despite fairly varied flint material, I choose to regard the site as an activity site, like Saxtorp 23. The site seems to lack any long settlement tradition, the pottery was limited, and it is uncertain what the post-holes represent.

### A place for hoarding and axe manufacture

*Barsebäck 105, Stenbocksvallar* Along the north shore of the Barsebäck foreland, a very large amount of Mesolithic and Neolithic flint has been collected along a stretch of about 1.5 kilometres (fig. 46). It is likely that some of this material comes from several places which could not be distinguished by the surface survey. In the material collected here, Carl-Axel Althin, in his dissertation, documented 130 thick-butted axes (56 of them preforms), 22 thin-bladed axes (7 of them preforms), and 113 thick-butted chisels (95 of them preforms), together with a large number of flake axes, scrapers,

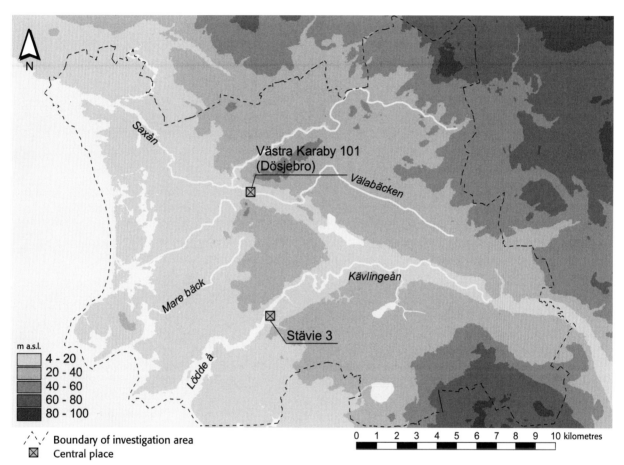

Fig. 55. Central places in MNA/MNB.

awls, knives, etc. (Althin 1954:19f). A new analysis of some of the axes found that, of the preforms whose types could be identified, there was a clear preponderance of thick-butted axes (Svensson, M., pers.com.). The huge quantity of axes and chisels gives the impression that there may have been a large hoard at some spot. One of the places probably functioned as a site for the production and distribution of axes and chisels.

A seminar dig in the area, performed by the Department of Archaeology in Lund in 1982, found that the material was mostly from the Late Mesolithic (Prahl & Streijffert 1994).

## Central places

At the end of MNA and the transition to MNB, places of central character were established within the investigation area (fig. 55). They no doubt had several functions, but the overall purpose must have been to assemble the people from a scattered settlement on special occasions.

*Stävie 3*   In a total of four stages between 1973 and 1978 and once during 1983, the National Heritage Board Southern Excavations Department excavated this site because of gravel quarrying and the laying of the Sydgas pipeline. The excavated area consisted of a sandy rise on the south bank of the Lödde Å (fig. 55).

The site can be described as a tongue of land between the Lödde Å to the north-west and a small ravine cut by a stream to the south-west. A total area of almost 70,000 m² was excavated with greater or lesser intensity. Within this area there were remains from most prehistoric periods, including a large cemetery from the Viking Age (Nagmér 1979; Larsson, L. 1982; Nagmér & Räf 1996).

In the eastern part of the area, a roughly 250 m long band of oblong pits was identified (fig. 56). These comprised a total of 14 pits whose length varied between 3 m and 40 m and the width between 1.3 and 4 m. The pits were between 0.4 and 1 m deep. The row of pits is at right angles to the tongue but ends in the middle of the sandy slope. One of the pits showed traces of burning in the bottom. Some of the pits were found to have an irregular bottom, which might suggest that they were dug in stages. The character of the filling indicates that the pits were filled in again after a short time when the edges collapsed. No traces of post-holes belonging to a palisade could be observed. The pottery in the oblong pits should probably be dated to the closing phase of MNA, that is, the Stävie group. The occurrence of finds in rather large quantities suggests that whole vessels were deposited. The pottery shows similarities in form and decoration to the pottery that characterizes MNA V, which is called Valby ware after the type site. Several of the smaller features within the pit system can also be dated to this period. Three presumed ovens were also excavated on the site; they were probably intended for firing pottery. The majority of the pots from the site which could be reconstructed have a slightly marked ledge between the neck and the belly and a straight, short neck. The clearly dominant orna-

Fig. 56. Plan of Stävie 3.

mental variable is finger impressions (Larsson, L. 1982). Impressions of cereal grains in the pottery show the use of mainly emmer and einkorn (Hjelmqvist 1982:108f). If the pottery can be placed at the end of the Funnel Beaker culture, then the flint shows a distinct character of Pitted Ware culture. Among other things, at Stävie there are numerous blade arrowheads of types A and B and cylindrical blade cores. There are also several fragments of thick-butted axes of both A- and B-type, a large quantity of scrapers, awls, polished fragments, and cores (Larsson, L. 1982). In one of the pits, which was part of the 250 m long system, flakes from axe manufacture were also identified. The amount of bones is limited, but pig is most common, with cattle, sheep/goat, and red deer also occurring (Persson 1982:114). There are [14]C datings of charcoal from an oven, a pit, and from a food crust on a sherd from a vessel with MNA V decoration from one of the pits in the system. These have yielded values of 4055±90 BP (2860–2460 cal. bc, St-6003),

110

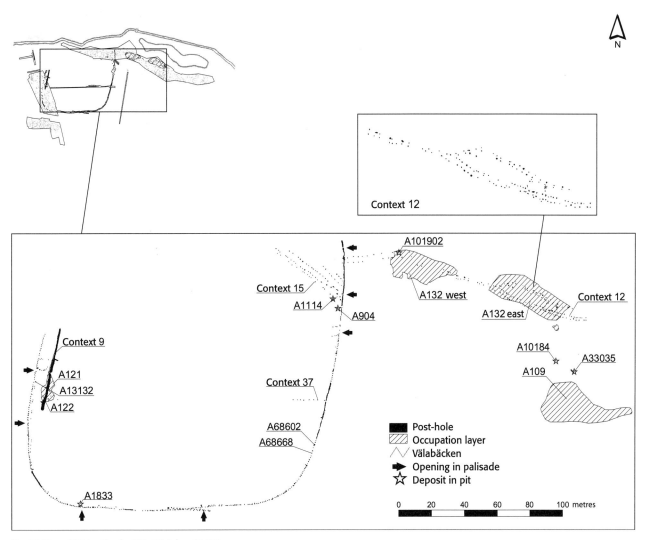

Fig. 57. Plan of Västra Karaby 101, Dösjebro (SU19).

3930±90 BP (2570–2280 cal. bc, St-6000), and 4360±85 BP (3260–2880 cal. bc, Ua-26016) (Nagmér 1979; Larsson, L. 1982; Nagmér & Räf 1996).

The site has been interpreted as an enclosure of Sarup type, but the finds and the [14]C analyses suggest a later dating than sites of this type found in Denmark (Nagmér 1979; Larsson, L. 1982; Nagmér & Räf 1996). Various scholars, however, have questioned whether this dating is relevant for the original phase of the structure, and doubts have been expressed as to whether the pits were excavated all the way to the bottom (Madsen 1988; Larsson, L., pers.com.). This question could only be answered by further excavations on the site.

*Västra Karaby 101, Dösjebro (SU19)*   The U-shaped palisaded enclosure at Dösjebro has been dated to an early phase of the Battle Axe period (MNB). I nevertheless choose to present the feature in this section since remains on the site show that it was of special

significance already during the late MNA. The palisaded enclosure was on a long, narrow, flat, sandy strip of land about 500 m long right beside the Välabäcken (fig. 55). This was one of the sites excavated by the National Heritage Board Southern Excavations Department in 1998 in connection with the construction of the West Coast Line. The roughly 100,000 m² strip was bordered to the north and east by the now straightened Välabäcken and to the south by a low, flat area which was once presumably wetland. The strip of land is centrally placed near the confluence of the Välabäcken and Saxån in the roughly two kilometre wide valley, which is lined by the hills of Västra Karaby to the south and Dagstorps Backar to the north.

The palisade was built of a single row of some 500 posts forming a U-shaped structure (fig. 57). The posts were free-standing, with a space of about a metre between them. Fragments of burnt clay in the filling of the post-holes suggest that the posts were probably joined by a wicker structure daubed with clay. Occasional sections, however, differ from this picture in that the posts were placed close together in trenches. The depth dug for the post-holes, up to 0.70 m, suggests that the palisade was at least of human height. The upper part of the stains left by the posts was sooty or mixed with charcoal, which shows that the posts burnt down rather than that they were singed before being set in the ground. In both the western and the eastern part of the palisade it was possible to follow the rows of postholes down to the wetland layers to the north. This could mean that the palisade was a structure of which the Välabäcken and the former wetland were the northern boundary. It cannot be ruled out, however, that the palisade took a turn right beside the wetland and formed a closed structure. All in all, the palisade and the river enclosed an area of roughly 30,000 m². Within the excavated area, inside the palisade, few structures could be associated with it. To the west was a circular, post-built structure which was joined in places to the palisade. Several rows of posts proceeded from the eastern part of the palisade down towards the Välabäcken (contexts 15 and 37). A number of openings in the palisade should be interpreted as entrances and/or exits. In post-holes belonging to the palisade structure there were deliberately deposited axes and flakes from axe manufacture. On several occasions the latter were found so densely packed that they must have been placed in the post-holes enclosed in a container. In two of the post-holes for the palisade there was pottery which, judging by the form and decoration, probably comes from the Battle Axe culture. Cord-decorated rim sherds presumably from two different vessels were found in A68602. The coarse cord decoration and the shape of the sherds indicates that they are likely to come from spherical pots of type C, according to Malmer's classification. A few metres south of this post-hole, in A68668, there was yet another sherd with cord decoration just under the rim. The slightly finer cord decoration suggests that this is a third vessel, presumably

of type A or B. All the sherds can be dated to the early Battle Axe culture (Malmer 1962). Parallel to the north-west part of the palisaded enclosure, a ditch was excavated (context 9). It was about 50 m long and 1 m wide. The feature had a U-shaped cross-section and the depth varied between 0.40 and 0.60 m. The ditch was surrounded by occupation layers to both the west (A122) and the east (A121). Four different strata could be distinguished in the ditch. Occasional flakes of axe manufacture occurred throughout the feature. The upper, very humic layer, with Late Bronze Age/ Early Iron Age pottery, should be regarded as an added layer connected with the later settlement on the site. The underlying layers, on the other hand, were older and seemed to be the same as the surrounding occupation layers (A121 and 122). Two deposits of flakes from axe manufacture were documented in layer 121 (Andersson et al. 1999).

In one of the pits (A1833), right beside an opening in the palisaded enclosure, there was an unpolished, thin-bladed, thick-butted flint axe. The pit had a diameter of 0.5 m and was 0.18 m deep. The axe was placed with the edge pointing upwards, right beside a 0.35×0.35 m stone. Three $^{14}$C datings have been obtained from post-holes in the palisade. The charcoal samples come from securely documented post-hole colourings. The dates they gave were 4130±55 BP (2870–2590 cal. bc, Ua-8790), 4165±70 BP (2880–2620 cal. bc, Ua-25094), and 4185±55 BP (2890–2670 cal. bc, Ua-8791), which correspond to the transition from MNA to MNB, thus firmly corroborating the archaeological dating. Two charcoal samples from the pit (A13132) beside the palisade with tooth-stamped Battle Axe pottery gave the dates 3980±70 BP (2580–2350 cal. bc, Ua-25098) and 3935±70 BP (2560–2310 cal. bc, Ua-25090) (Andersson et al. 1999; Svensson et al. 2001; Svensson 2002).

North of the palisade on the other side of the stream, nine graves were found in a linear cemetery from the Battle Axe culture (see Dagstorp 11, cemetery). A $^{14}$C dating of a wooden coffin from one of the

Fig. 58. The western part of the palisade marked with white paper plates. The hills in the background are Karaby Backar (photo M. Andersson).

Fig. 60. Axe in a post-hole at Västra Karaby 101, Dösjebro (SU19) (photo M. Andersson).

▼ Fig. 59. The eastern part of the palisade. Dagstorps Backar in the background (photo S. Carlsson).

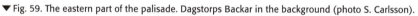

graves gave the value 4100±75 BP (2870–2490 cal. bc, Ua-9289), which suggests a close chronological connection between the cemetery and the palisade (Andersson et al. 1999; Svensson et al. 2001; Svensson 2002).

Just over a hundred metres east of the actual palisade, an occupation layer (A109) measuring slightly more than 700 m² was excavated; it was mostly characterized by the rich amount of flint flakes in relation to tools. Pottery was also scarce. A large proportion of the flakes showed features characteristic of the manufacture of quadrilateral axes and chisels. No intact knapping place was found, however. A total of just under 20 kg of flint and about 0.3 kg pottery was retrieved. In the total flint material the matt-grey Danian flint is slightly more common than flint of Senonian type. In contrast, the identified tools are almost exclusively made of Senonian flint. Among the tools may be mentioned transverse arrowheads, scrapers, occasional knives and awls, so-called gaming pieces, and retouched flakes. One of the transverse arrowheads was made from a flake from a polished axe. There were also a few flake cores. In terms of number, however, the tools make up less than 1% of the total flint. It is worth noting the relatively large number (71) of flint fragments with polished surfaces. Unlike the flint material as a whole and the axe manufacturing flakes in particular, this category of find is dominated by Senonian flint. Most of these mainly small axe fragments do not allow any identification of axe types. One of the axe fragments, however, consists of an edge piece with small sections of both the narrow and the broad side preserved. The polishing seems to be confined to the broad side, but it cannot be ruled out that the narrow side had also been polished. The flakes that could be securely associated with axe manufacture consist of a total of 774 pieces (approx. 2.5 kg), which corresponds to roughly 5% of the total number of flints. The majority of these are of Danian flint (just over 70%). The final stages in the axe-manufacturing process are overwhelmingly predominant (Svensson et al. 2001). North of the Välabäcken too, proper knapping places were documented (see Dagstorp 11). The palisaded enclosure, the cemetery, and the axe-manufacturing place should probably be regarded as a single complex of sites (Andersson et al. 1999; Svensson et al. 2001; Svensson 2002).

East of the palisade there was a complicated system of rows of post-holes (context 12), which could be followed in an east–west direction along the wetland. The rows of post-holes may possibly be viewed as a form of passage, the easternmost part of which expands to four rows of posts which form a pointed-oval "room". Within this area a large occupation layer was noted (A132 east) with a rich amount of flint and pottery of Karlsfält character belonging to the late Funnel Beaker culture (Lagergren-Olsson 2003). This layer and the post-hole system may therefore in all probability be regarded as being slightly older than the palisaded enclosure. The composition of the find material in the layers may be considered typical of dwelling sites from the Funnel Beaker culture. However, no houses or pits for waste or storage were found by the excavations. The traces of activity therefore probably do not represent permanent settlement on the site, which more likely saw short-term visits.

Both outside and inside the palisades there were several small pits which can be interpreted as votive deposits. One of the post-holes (A101902) west of "the room" contained a preform for a thick-butted axe of coarse Danian flint (fig. 60). The axe was placed with the butt facing upwards. A $^{14}$C dating from a charcoal fragment from this post-hole yielded the value 4510±70 BP (3350–3090 cal. bc, Ua-25091). Pits A904 and A10184 were similar in shape, size, and find composition. Both were round, about 0.5 m in diameter, and can be described mainly as rubbish deposits. Apart from the many scrapers there were retouched flints and flint flakes, which should be regarded as preforms for scrapers. Knives, flake cores, and an almost entirely disintegrated clay disc decorated with wavy lines were found in A10184. The latter can be dated to MNA V (Davidsen 1978). Right beside

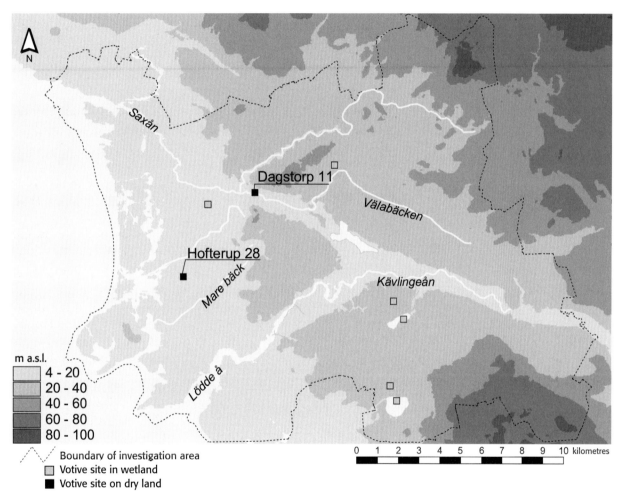

Fig. 61. Votive sites in MNA III–V.

A10184 was yet another bowl-shaped pit (A33035) with finds including a transverse arrowhead. A $^{14}$C analysis of a charcoal sample dates this feature to 4380±60 BP (3100–2910 cal. bc, Ua-25094). Pit A1114 differed in size from the pits described above. The feature was much larger, 0.8×1.0 m, but had a similar shallow bowl-shaped bottom (0.07 m). Occasional stones up to 0.15 m in size were unearthed. Despite its larger volume, the pit held fewer finds; they consist of a large butt part of a polished flint axe of Valby type, a scraper, a flake core, and small quantities of knapped flint.

**Votive sites** There are six documented votive sites in wetland contexts within the investigation area (fig. 61). All were found by people working with the soil and have thus not been archaeologically excavated. The pottery shows that the sites at both Hofterup 28 and Dagstorp 11 were also visited during this phase.

## MNB

**Settlement** We know the Battle Axe culture mainly from graves. There are not many excavated remains of settlement which can be dated to this period in Skåne. The finds are also of limited extent on these sites,

116

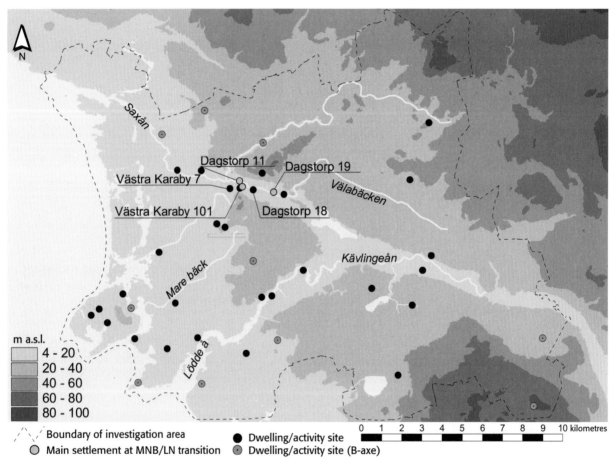

Fig. 62. Settlement sites in MNB.

which has often been interpreted as showing that the population were nomadic herders. Malmer, on the other hand, believes that agriculture was probably the main economic foundation for the Funnel Beaker and the Battle Axe cultures in Skåne, since their distribution essentially corresponds to the good soils for agriculture (Malmer 1975). Even though forty-two sites in the investigation area have been interpreted as settlement sites, the excavated remains are few and usually diffuse. Only five of the excavated sites can be assigned with reasonable certainty to the Battle Axe culture. It is not until the late MNB, at the transition to the Late Neolithic, that I have been able to identify places which can be interpreted as main settlements.

## Main settlements in the late MNB and early LN

*Västra Karaby 101, Dösjebro (SU19)*   In the spring of 2000 the Department of Archaeology at Lund University, in collaboration with the Southern Excavations Department, conducted a seminar excavation at the palisaded enclosure. The earlier excavation in 1998 had documented an opening with an adjacent passage in the southern part of the palisade. The structure was preliminarily interpreted as an entrance/exit (Andersson et al. 1999). For the seminar dig the trench was extended northwards and yet another row of post-holes was found parallel to the "passage", which meant that the earlier interpretation could be revised. The plan documentation and excavation of the post-

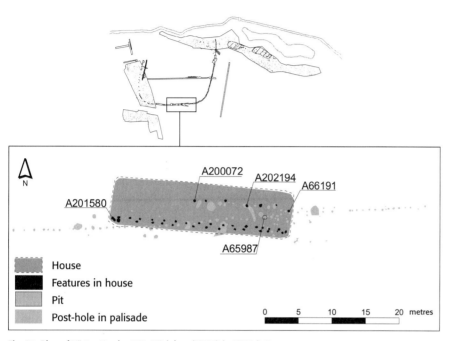

Fig. 63. Plan of Västra Karaby 101, Dösjebro (SU19) in MNB/LN.

117

holes showed that a long-house with a central row of posts overlayered the palisade (fig. 63). The northern row consists of the post-holes left by the roof-bearing posts, while the southern row is one of the wall lines. Only the south-east half of the house was exposed. The southern wall line, however, was uncovered in its entirety and found to consist of thirty-three post-holes. Several of the post-holes are doubled, which is probably a sign of repairs. The excavated eastern part of the row of roof-bearing posts consisted of nine central posts. Three of these (A200072, A202194, and A66191) were bigger and were dug deeper. These post-holes were evenly distributed along the roof-bearing construction, at distances of 6.3 m and 7.5 m. The stouter central posts were presumably an original structure that was subsequently reinforced. The fillings in the post-holes consisted of sooty humic sand. It was not possible to distinguish any colouring left by the posts; the filling was all homogeneously sooty. If the house burnt down, this suggests that the charred posts were pulled up and the holes filled with the surrounding occupation soil showing the effects of fire. Otherwise it should have been possible to distinguish the soot-filled post colouring from the holes. The house is oriented east–west, and from the excavated part it is calculated to have been about 26 m long and 6–7 m wide. The finds in the post-holes that could be associated with the house were limited, consisting

above all of occasional flint flakes and small, unidentifiable potsherds. In the post-holes in the south-west of the house (A201580), however, there were parts of a pot of Late Neolithic character together with indefinable burnt bones and flint flakes. In the eastern part of the house, two small, shallow, bowl-shaped pits were documented. One of them (A65987) contained a large quantity of charred seeds. One of the seeds (wheat) was sent for $^{14}$C analysis and gave the value 3785±60 BP (2290–2040 cal. bc, Ua-25614), which corresponds to the transition to the Late Neolithic. Charred seeds were also found in some of the post-holes belonging to the house (Svensson et al. 2001). The house is paralleled in its structural details by house no. 95 at Fosie IV, which has been dated to the Late Neolithic/ Early Bronze Age. The two houses are roughly the same size and have doubled post-holes in the walls, which indicates that they were repaired and reinforced (Björhem & Säfvestad 1989).

*Dagstorp 19 (SU21)*   Along with the extensive Funnel Beaker material at Dagstorp 19 (fig. 62) there were also some remains that can be dated to MNB. One of the houses at Dagstorp 19 may possibly be dated to the end of the Battle Axe culture.

The house (house 70) was situated on a gentle slope down towards the Välabäcken. The building ran from north-west to south-east and was a rectangular, two-

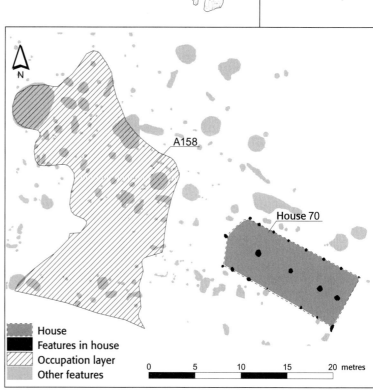

aisled structure, with slightly convex walls. The remains of the house had been disturbed by modern drainage and other recent digging, but the length could be estimated at about 15 m and the width at 6 m. The internal area was just under 90 m². The roof was supported by five stout posts, the westernmost of which was in the gable (fig. 64). The finds in the post-holes of the house consist of pottery and flint along with small quantities of burnt bones and burnt clay. The flint mainly consists of flakes/debitage, but there are also two flake cores, two blades, a knife, and a scraper. The pottery consists only of undecorated sherds, one of them with a type of fabric resembling Battle Axe ceramics.

There are two ¹⁴C analyses of hazelnut shells from the house. The sample from one of the wall post-holes gave the value 4784±75 BP (3650–3380 cal. bc, Ua-25061), corresponding to the transition between EN I and EN II. The other sample from one of the post-holes belonging to the roof-bearing structure was dated to 3950±75 BP (2570–2320 cal. bc, Ua-25060), that is, the end of MNB. The first dating must be considered early with regard to the regular design of the building and the large holes left by the roof-bearing posts. The latter dating may agree better with the appearance of the building, which is confirmed by the potsherd from one of the wall post-holes resembling Battle Axe ceramics. The nearby occupation layer, A158, also contained some potsherds which have been dated to the Battle Axe culture.

**Dagstorp 11 (SU17)** At Dagstorp 11, north of the palisaded enclosure and the Välabäcken (fig. 62), the excavation found not only the early Middle Neolithic structures but also remains from MNB in the form of occupation layers, houses, linear cemeteries and extensive axe-manufacturing places (Månsson & Pihl 1999).

The house was oriented NNW–SSE and was rectangular with a slightly trapezoidal form. The northwest part of the structure was overlayered by an occupation layer, 0.1 m thick, A105. The house was two-aisled, and at least two phases of building can be discerned. In addition, the roof-bearing posts appeared to have been replaced or reinforced once in each phase. The house was moved just over a metre when rebuilt. One phase, to the north, had three roof-bearing posts, all of them doubled. The other phase, to the south, consisted of four roof-bearing posts, two of which were doubled. The walls were straight and in a trapezoidal relation to each other, being wider at the north. The gables in both phases were straight in the southern part and slightly rounded in the northern part. The two phases of the building show a similar form apart from the fact that the northern phase was

Fig. 64. Plan of Dagstorp 19 (SU21) in MNB.

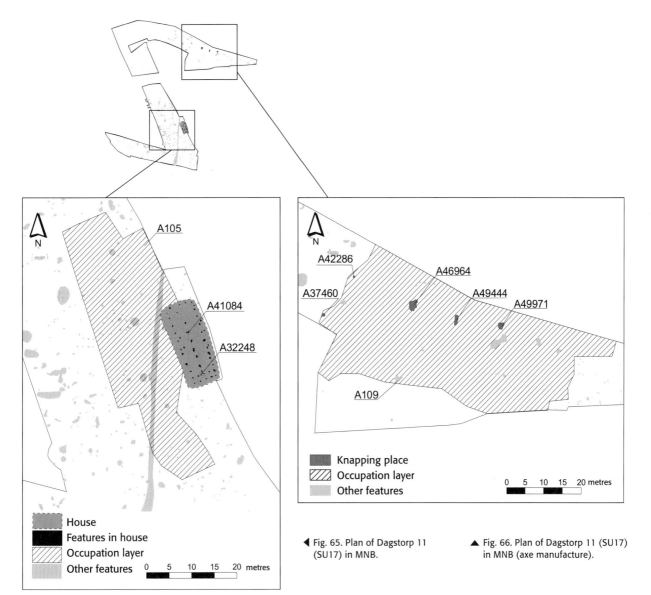

◀ Fig. 65. Plan of Dagstorp 11 (SU17) in MNB.

▲ Fig. 66. Plan of Dagstorp 11 (SU17) in MNB (axe manufacture).

missing a post-hole for a roof-bearing post (figs. 65 and 97). The flint in the post-holes mostly consists of flakes/debitage but there are also two flake scrapers, two flake cores, two polished axe fragments, and a flake from axe manufacture. One of the axe fragments probably comes from a hollow-edged axe. The pottery is mostly undecorated sherds, but two fragments have stroke ornamentation of Middle Neolithic character. Two [14]C analyses of charcoal from the holes of roof-bearing posts were performed. The sample from roof-bearing post A41084, in the northern phase, gave a date of 4280±55 BP (3020–2700 cal. bc, Ua-9848), while roof-bearing post A32248, in the southern phase, gave the result 3745±80 BP (2280–1980 cal. bc, Ua-25190). The first range is from the end of MNA to the start of MNB, while the second corresponds to the transition to the Late Neolithic. The latter dating seems most reasonable in view of the find of

the hollow-polished axe fragment in one of the roof-bearing post-holes and the design of the house which resembles the house structures found from the Late Neolithic.

The partly overlayering occupation layer, A105, contained chronologically mixed find material. Both Funnel Beaker culture and Battle Axe culture, and even later periods, are represented.

A noteworthy find in the occupation layer is two potsherds with geometrical decoration very like the Bell Beaker tradition and a tanged, flat-flaked arrowhead of the type common in Bell Beaker contexts (Vang Petersen 1993).

### Dwelling/activity sites

*Västra Karaby 7* In 1972 the National Heritage Board Southern Excavations Department investigated a barrow in Dösjebro from the Bronze Age in connec-

Fig. 67. The knapping place during excavation at Dagstorp 11 (SU17) (photo H. Pihl).

tion with planned housing construction. Under the barrow were settlement site layers from the Middle Neolithic (see chapter 4: EN II–MNA II). Västra Karaby 7 is just a few hundred metres south-west of the palisade complex in Dösjebro (fig. 62).

In the same place as the Funnel Beaker settlement, remains from the Battle Axe culture have also been documented. Pottery with a total weight of just over half a kilo, belonging to seven vessels, can be dated to this period. A vessel of which one-third has been reconstructed can be identified as spherical with all-over angular decoration (Löfwall 1977). The form and decoration place the vessel in the G, H, or J group of the Battle Axe culture (Malmer 1962). Battle Axe pottery was above all concentrated in the eastern part of the excavated area, where the largest quantity of knapped

flint was also found. No features could be shown to belong to this settlement phase (Löfwall 1977).

*Dagstorp 18*   The settlement at Dagstorp 18 was in the valley landscape, on a sandy hilltop and slope immediately south of the Välabäcken, just over half a kilometre east of Västra Karaby 101 (fig. 62). This Stone Age dwelling site was discovered at the start of the twentieth century, and was then completely obliterated in connection the extension of the arable land. A brief description together with the finds retrieved by ploughing was submitted to LUHM through the auspices of the landowner. According to the description, the occupation layer was oval in shape with the dimensions 20×6 m. The depth was 0.6 m. The flint included a large number of scrapers, awls, a fragment of a thick-butted axe, and a couple of fragments of hollow-polished axes. Among the pottery were pit-decorated sherds and a fragment of a clay disc decorated with a simple zigzag line (Althin 1954:109). Some of the pottery can thus be plausibly dated to the early Middle Neolithic, but the axe fragment shows that the site was also used in MNB.

### Axe-manufacturing place

*Dagstorp 11 (SU17)*   In the northern part of the excavated area at Dagstorp 11 there was a find-bearing layer (A109) mainly characterized by a rich occurrence of flint flakes and, in relation to the amount of flint, a relatively small proportion of tools and very little pottery. The flakes are wholly dominated by examples from axe manufacture. One intact (A46964) and two damaged knapping places (A49444 and A49971) were documented. These were at a distance of about 12 m from each other. Two further small concentrations of flint flakes were found at the western edge of the layer (A37460 and A42286) (fig. 66). The composition of the finds and the absence of dwelling site remains mean that the area is best described as a production place. The plentiful but relatively uniform flint material reflects extensive manufacture but also reknapping of flint axes. No evidence was found that axes were polished on the site, since no grindstones were discovered.

Knapping place A46964 was located in the northwest part of A109. The flint concentration was oval in shape, measuring about 3×2.3 m and 0.01–0.14 m thick. The place had flakes and debitage from axe manufacture, several polished fragments, and a butt part of a thick-butted, polished flint axe. The axe shows secondary working, but the narrow sides have traces of polishing and the cross-section of the butt is square. It can best be classified as a thick-butted axe of type B, dated to late MNA or MNB (Nielsen, P. O. 1979; Larsson, L. 1992a). In addition, a small number of flint tools were identified, including a hammerstone, transverse arrowheads, and scrapers. A few of

the flints are burnt. Several different types of flint are represented. Apart from variants of Senonian and Danian flint, there is also very coarse-grained, light-grey to dark-grey flint. A total of roughly 118 kg flint was retrieved from the knapping place, the majority of which is flakes from axe manufacture. A small quantity of pottery (0.4 kg) was discovered in the layer, including three sherds with horizontal cord decoration and a fragment of a clay disc. The other pottery mainly consists mainly of small, unidentifiable sherds. About twelve metres south-east of A46964, a badly damaged knapping place was exposed (A49444). Two ditches cut through the site. Between the ditches, the extensive excavation of the layer uncovered large amounts of flint within an area measuring 2.5×0.9 m. Here too, the flint mainly consisted of flakes from axe manufacture. Half of the preserved part of the knapping place was excavated and roughly 21 kg of flint was retrieved. The remains of yet another knapping place (A49971) were found about twelve metres east of A49444. The feature was damaged since the occupation layer had been bulldozed away, and its original extent is difficult to estimate. A total of 16 kg of flint and occasional potsherds were found within an area of 1.8×1.5 m. Here too, the finds are dominated by flakes from axe manufacture, but several transverse arrowheads and occasional potsherds were noted.

The axe-manufacturing site at Dagstorp 11 represents the largest assembled amount of finds in this category hitherto known in south Scandinavia, even though it is located outside the primary deposits of flint. The link to the axe-manufacturing sites documented at the palisaded enclosure, as well as the close chronological connection with the cemetery and the house, add a further dimension to the material. One of the few excavated manufacturing places for flint axes is Hastrup Vænget near Køge in Denmark (Vemming Hansen & Madsen 1983). Here a careful analysis of the finds and comparison with flakes from experimentally produced axes led to an estimate of the number of axes manufactured, of how long a time this corresponded to, and of how production was organized. Hastrup Vænget differs from the knapping place at Dagstorp 11, however, in that it is located within the primary area of flint, with a good supply of high-quality raw material.

## Graves

*Dagstorp 11 (SU17)* The linear cemetery at Dagstorp 11 (fig. 68) comprised ten graves from the Battle Axe culture. One of the graves (A227), however, can be placed in the Late Neolithic. The cemetery, which was oriented north–south, extended for about 70 m within the investigation area. The six southernmost graves lay in pairs in three groups. Grave A43708 was about 3.5 m west of the line of graves and was oriented east–west, while the other graves were oriented north–south (fig. 69). From roughly 500 m east of the linear cemetery there is information about a vanished Battle Axe grave, Dagstorp RAÄ 25, where a boat axe, a hollow-edged flint axe, and flint blades were found under a stone packing (Hansen 1920). Map studies have shown that the removed flat-earth grave was in all probability part of the now excavated cemetery. If so, RAÄ 25 would correspond to A25409, located nine metres west of the line of graves, which showed traces of recent digging. The graves differed greatly in terms of size, construction, orientation, depth, filling, grave goods, and number of burials. In cases where there was a stone packing, its depth varied, as did the size and number of the stones, and whether the packing was shaped like a frame or a funnel. Adjacent to two of the graves there were post-holes and a trench which were probably parts of the grave structure. There were also graves with different types of coffins, ranging from stains left by wood to slab cists, but there were also graves completely lacking a coffin. The number of grave goods per grave varied greatly. In four of the graves there were grave goods in the form of hollow-edged axes, battle axes, pots, amber beads, and blades. In five graves body colouring could be documented and

in two cases it was possible to ascertain that more than one person had been buried. The stains in the graves that are judged to have been left by bodies were all distinct, allowing identification of the head, trunk, and legs (Månsson & Pihl 1999).

**Inhumation grave:** (A25793), oval, roughly 2.8×1.8 m and 0.5 m deep. The grave was oriented north-east–south-west. No outlines of the deceased could be observed in the filling. In the southern part of the grave, within an area of 1.2×0.3 m and on either side of a stone, there were fragmented potsherds. Beside the stone, on a relatively even level, there were in addition ten amber beads which were in a very fragile state of preservation.

**Inhumation grave:** (A43708), oval, roughly 2.4×1.3 m and 0.35 m deep, oriented east–west. In the middle was a dark, rectangular stain left by a coffin, approximately 2.0×0.45 m. It contained flakes, burnt flint, pottery, and a thin-bladed, hollow-edged axe of flint corresponding most closely to Malmer's variant 3 (Malmer 1975:76). The pottery, including tooth-stamped sherds, was encountered in the eastern part. The axe was in the western part of the grave with the edge facing south. No skeleton colouring was noted. Four post-holes were found in either end of the grave, placed in a row. The filling indicates that the post-holes should be regarded as being contemporary with the grave, probably as part of some wooden structure which marked the grave above ground. Battle Axe graves with markings above ground are documented in Ullstorp, Skåne (Larsson, L. 1988a:81), and in Hagestad 44, Skåne (Strömberg 1989:82). Two charcoal samples from the bottom of grave A43708 gave the values 3850±75 BP (2460–2200 cal. bc, Ua-9854) and 4085±100 BP (2870–2490 cal. bc, Ua-25192). From one of the post-holes east of the grave (A43736), possibly belonging to a structure built over a grave, a charcoal sample was retrieved

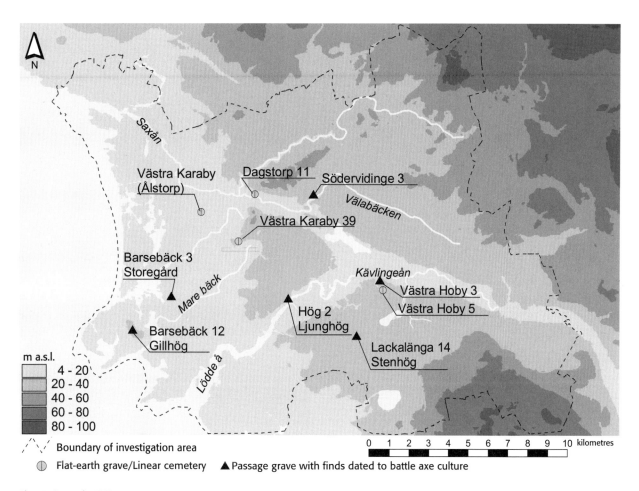

Fig. 68. Graves in MNB.

for $^{14}$C analysis, yielding the value 3975±70 BP (2580–2350 cal. bc, Ua-9855).

**Inhumation grave:** (A8184), oval, roughly 3×1.8 m and 1.15 m deep. The grave was oriented north–south. At the southern end of the grave were two post-holes which may have been part of a superstructure. The deceased had been laid in a frame-shaped stone feature. On a level with the lower part of the stone frame and 0.1–0.2 m above the burial level, there were coffin stains along the edges of the grave. At the burial level there were stains left by three individuals. The individual furthest to the south was placed in crouched posi-

tion, with the head to the south and the face to the east. Behind the head was a battle axe of rock corresponding best to Malmer's group C2 (Malmer 1975:95). In front of the head was a polished thin-bladed axe of variant 1 and an amber object. At the hip was a thick-bladed polished hollow-edged axe of variant 1, yet another amber find, two flint blades, and a small pot of type L. At the knee was yet another flint blade. Two vessels, one large and one small of type J, were found at the feet along with a flint blade. In the middle of the grave was an individual who had been buried in the same way, crouched. Behind the neck of the deceased was a thick-bladed, polished hol-

Fig. 70. Grave A8184 at Dagstorp 11 (SU17) (photo H. Pihl).

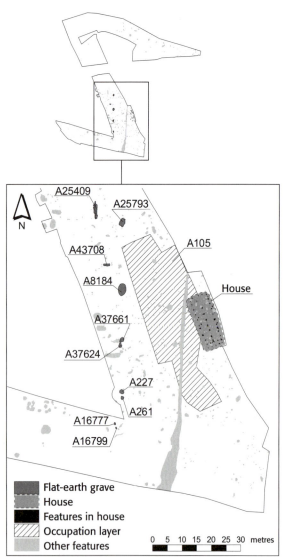

Fig. 69. Plan of Dagstorp 11 (SU17) in MNB (cemetery).

124

low-edged axe of variant 1. Slightly to the south of this was a battle axe, agreeing with Malmer's group D2. Just beside the battle axe lay a flint blade. The battle axe and the flint blade were placed in front of the head. At the knee was an amber object and at the foot a ceramic vessel. Furthest to the north, a colouring left by an individual was identified. The body was probably buried in crouched position in a north-west–south-east direction. West of the colouring was a pot and at the north-east edge a flint blade. Dental enamel and traces of the other anatomy of the skull show that the deceased was probably laid with the face to the east. Immediately west of the dissolved skull was a fragment of a milk tooth, a molar. This shows that the grave probably contained a child besides the three individuals attested by grave goods and colourings. The two $^{14}$C datings from the grave have given values of

Fig. 71. Grave A8184 at Dagstorp 11 (SU17) (photo H. Pihl).

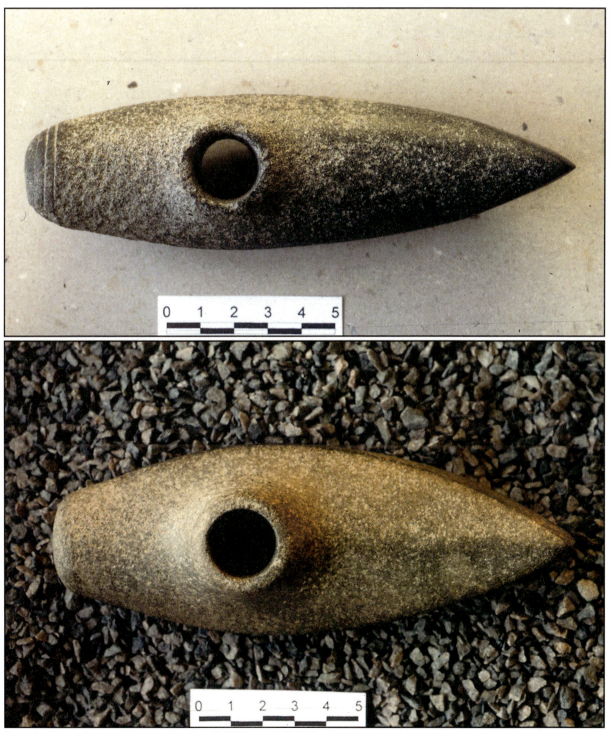

Fig. 72. Battle axes from grave A8184 at Dagstorp 11 (SU17) (photo H. Pihl).

4100±75 BP (2870–2490 cal. bc, Ua-9289) and 3905±75 BP (2480–2210 cal. bc, Ua-25194). The samples were taken from charcoal fragments found in the coffin stain. Despite the early $^{14}$C dating, the finds suggest that the grave can be assigned to the middle or later part of the Battle Axe culture (Malmer 1962; 1975).

**Inhumation grave:** (A37661), oval, roughly 1.4×1.3 m and 1.5 m deep, oriented NNE–SSW. A funnel-shaped stone structure was documented in the grave. Directly under the stones were colourings left by two individuals lying head to foot. The eastern individual stood out relatively clearly, with the head, trunk, and legs distinguishable. The individual was laid with the head to the north in slightly crouched position. Between the individuals was placed a large rectangular stone. Occasional undecorated potsherds and flint flakes were found in the filling of the grave.

**Inhumation grave:** (A37624), oval, roughly 2.15×1.1 m and 1.4 m deep, oriented NNE–SSW.

The frame-shaped stone packing consisted of stones at a total of eight levels. One individual was buried in crouched position in the south-west part of the grave, with the back to the west and the face looking south-east. In the north part of the grave, at the same level, there was yet another colouring. This was not so distinct, however, and it is unclear whether the stain represents a buried individual. No finds were found in the vicinity of the stains.

**Inhumation grave:** (A227), round, approx. 1.80 m in diameter and 0.5 m deep. A number of large stones were visible on the surface. The stone packing was about 0.5 m deep, and under it was a rectangular slab cist, oriented ENE–WSW, with a well-laid stone floor about 1.4×0.5 m. The floor consisted of 0.1–0.3 m flat slabs, most of them worked. The southern long side and the western short side were marked by orthostats on which capstones rested. Adjacent to the

south-east side of the slab cist was a "side chamber" measuring roughly 0.4×0.4 m formed of three large and a number of smaller stones. No skeleton colouring could be documented, whether in the slab cist or the side chamber. No grave goods were found, and the grave filling contained only a small amount of pottery and flint, including two polished fragments. The potsherds are probably from the same pot. The fabric is relatively thin, with fine tempering and with red granite as a dominant element. A small sherd is decorated with tooth stamps. The sherds can probably be ascribed to the Battle Axe culture. In Battle Axe graves, however, it is very unusual to find stone-paved floors, so the grave may possibly come from the Late Neolithic.

**Inhumation grave:** (A261), round, about 1 m in diameter and 0.9 m deep. After the ground was stripped, the grave stood out as a round, light colouring and with a number of large stones visible. All that was left of the stone packing were three large stones raised on edge along the western side. The colouring left by an individual in crouched position with the head to the south and the face to the east was documented. Some thirty pieces of undecorated pottery were retrieved, probably from the same vessel.

**Inhumation grave:** (A16777), oval, roughly 1.0×0.6 m and 0.5 m deep, oriented NNW–SSE. Four stones slightly larger than the size of a head marked the grave. Three of the stones were raised on edge to form an incomplete stone cist. The colouring left by an individual who had lain in crouched position with the head to the north and the face to the west was observed. Apart from the head, the trunk and legs could also be discerned. No finds occurred in the feature.

**Inhumation grave:** (A16799), oval, roughly 1.7×0.45 m and 0.45 m deep. Two stones stood on edge along the south-west side of the grave. Diffuse skeleton colourings were visible. No finds were discovered.

**Stone-filled pit/grave:** (A25409), about 5.5×0.85 m and 0.8 m deep, oriented north–south. The filling was recent, consisting of brown-speckled humic sand. Along the western side, however, there was another filling that was untouched, of an even grey colour and slightly humic. In the south-east corner some large stones were visible. The finds were knapped flint and pottery, relatively evenly distributed in the feature. The flint consisted of flakes and debitage. The pottery was exclusively undecorated sherds, but a large, thin-walled rim fragment was found in the northern part of the feature. Two ¹⁴C datings of charcoal taken from the filling of the western side yielded values of 4630±65 BP (3520–3340 cal. bc, Ua-9851) and 4570±85 BP (3500–3100 cal. bc, Ua-25195), corresponding to the period EN II–MNA I. The feature is probably the grave documented by Hansen (RAÄ 25) back in the 1920s. This would explain the recent filling, and the early ¹⁴C dates may be from material from the older settlement that ended up in this context (Månsson & Pihl 1999).

*Västra Hoby 5* In 1916 three flat-earth graves belonging to a linear cemetery from the Battle Axe culture and the Late Neolithic were excavated (Hansen 1917). A fourth grave which had been discovered 25 years earlier is probably part of the cemetery. The graves lay in a north–south direction on a flat plateau about 800 m south of the Kävlingeån (fig. 68). Some fifty metres to the west the land slopes down towards a now drained wetland. Further to the north and north-east of the find spot, the land likewise slopes down to the river. Only about 500 m north of the site is the monument called "Danshögarna", consisting of two long dolmens and a passage grave.

The southernmost grave measured 2×2.5 m and was 0.6–0.7 m deep. No skeleton parts were preserved, but the deceased had been laid in a frame-shaped stone structure. The grave goods were a hollow-polished flint axe and two pots of Malmer's type J:2. Roughly five metres NNW of this grave was yet another flat-earth grave, measuring about 3×2 m and almost a metre deep. A stain left by a wooden coffin was observed within the stone frame. Two pots of type H:3 and L:2 were documented as grave goods together with a hollow-polished flint axe. The third grave, which was about eight metres NNW of grave II, had a rather different stone structure consisting only of one layer of stones, laid in an irregular shape. A fragmentary flint dagger was found in this. Some fifty metres north-west of this there is information about yet another grave found in connection with clay extraction. The scant details state that there was a great deal of stone on the surface. The finds, which were not noticed until the extracted clay was to be used, consisted of a battle axe, a hollow-polished flint axe, and a thin-bladed flint axe (Hansen 1917; Malmer 1962).

*Västra Karaby 39* In connection with the National Heritage Board Southern Excavations Department's excavations for the Sydgas project in 1983, two flat-earth graves from the Battle Axe culture were discovered at Västra Karaby 39 (fig. 68). The site of the graves is a flat, sandy height about two kilometres south of the Saxån and Välabäcken (Jeppsson 1996b), where the nearest known cemetery from the Battle Axe culture is also located (Dagstorp 11).

The two Battle Axe graves were oriented east–west and lay about 10 m from each other on a little height. The grave to the south measured 3.1×1–1.6 m and was 0.56 m deep. No traces were left of the coffin or skeleton. At the bottom of the eastern part of the grave were grave goods consisting of a large pot of Malmer's type H:2 with base decoration of type 2:a. There was also a small vessel of Malmer's type G:2 with a slightly damaged bottom, but it was probably, like the preceding vessel, of type 2:a. The big pot contained two long flint blades, and outside the pot there were a further three blades and a blade scraper. Adjacent to the other grave goods were two blade arrowheads with a triangular section of type D. In the western part of the

127

grave were two hollow-edged polished thick-butted axes (Malmer 1962, 1975; Jeppsson 1996b).

The northern grave measured 3.35×1.22 m and was 0.9 m deep. It contained traces of a rectangular coffin. In the western part there were fragmentary parts of the skull surviving, which showed that the deceased, aged between 30 and 35, had been placed with the face to the north. Beside the skull there were 59 small cylindrical amber beads and 5–10 fragmentary ones. Seven large amber beads lay at the shoulder, and at the pelvis there were fragments of at least one big bead. At the head there was also a hollow-edged polished thick-butted axe and an undecorated pot of Malmer's type N. In the eastern part of the grave stood a large pot of type H:3, along with two long flint blades, a blade scraper, and a flake (Malmer 1962, 1975; Jeppsson 1996b).

*Västra Karaby (Ålstorp)*    About 400 m south of the Saxån and immediately north-east of the bog Ålstorps Mosse (fig. 68), a preliminary investigation conducted by the National Heritage Board Southern Excavations Department in October 1997 documented dwelling site remains and a flat-earth grave. A gentle sandy height runs through the area, about 14–16 m a.s.l. The bog was a lake in prehistoric times, so the site may be described as having a lakeside location. The flat-earth grave was an oval stone setting measuring 4.2×1.8 m, oriented NNW–SSE. The feature was never excavated during the preliminary investigation, but judging by the size and shape, and the size and orientation of the stones, the grave should probably be dated to the Battle Axe culture (Malmer 1975; Aspeborg 1997).

**Megalithic tombs**    Several megalithic tombs in south Scandinavia have been found to contain objects which show that they were also used during MNB (fig. 68). In the passage at Gillhög, the edge of a hollow-polished axe and two thin-bladed flint axes were found, and the cairn in front of the passage contained parts of a battle axe of type A and several thin-bladed and hollow-polished axe fragments (Forssander 1932; Malmer 1962:915). In Hög too, artefacts belonging to MNB were documented, including Battle Axe pottery of type H both inside and outside the passage grave (Hansen 1919a; Malmer 1962:917). At the mouth of the passage grave at Södervidinge, Battle Axe pottery of types GH and J:1 and a hollow-polished axe were retrieved (Hansen 1919b; Malmer 1962:922). The excavated passage grave at Västra Hoby held fragments of a thick-butted, probably hollow-polished flint axe, a thin-bladed flint axe with both the narrow and the broad side polished, and a thick-butted rock axe (Forssander 1937). The passage graves of Stenhög in Lackalänga and Storegård contained thin-bladed flint axes polished on four sides, which are usually dated to MNB. In Lackalänga there were moreover fragments of a hollow-edged thick-butted flint axe in the passage.

**Votive sites**    In the investigation area there are no excavated votive sites in wetland which can be dated to MNB. On the other hand, work with the soil at twenty-seven places (fig. 73) has turned up objects from this period which can be suspected to have been deposited in wetland where there are no parallel contemporary settlement remains or graves (Karsten 1994). ▌▌

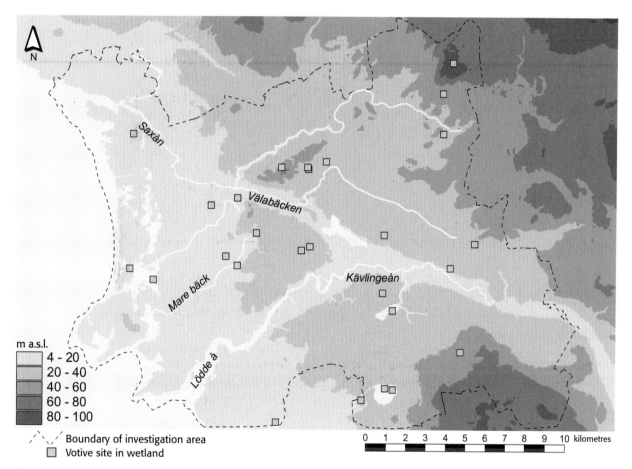

Fig. 73. Votive sites in MNB.

# Social organization

*The two valleys and the surrounding area were thus used intensively in the Neolithic. The adoption of agriculture did not mean that people lived a stationary life in one place throughout the year. Neither houses, cultivation, nor animal husbandry tied people to just one place. Hunting, fishing, and collection were probably significant in varying degrees throughout the Neolithic and required movement in the landscape. In addition, other special ritual or social activities were performed in places which were not always attached to the actual settlement. The remains in the landscape should be regarded as the traces of different activities of differing intensity, meaning, and duration. These different traces in different places in the landscape may be regarded as signs to be brought together and read by archaeologists in order to give meaning to prehistory.*

The northern Funnel Beaker complex has been regarded by many scholars as having its origin in the encounter between the Ertebølle-Ellerbek complex and various farming groups on the continent (Midgley 1992). A similar material culture was adopted over a large area in northern Europe, which should be viewed as an expression of a similar identity perception. This should not be understood, however, as being synonymous with "a people" or a homogeneous culture. Within this area there were several different societies with differing historical backgrounds and structural norms. I therefore consider it important that the interpretation of the social organization in the investigation area is based on the Neolithic remains in the region and that the manner in which the Neolithic way of life was adopted and developed here should be viewed on the basis of the distinctive regional conditions and the Late Mesolithic background.

## New ideas and old customs

The question of when and how the Neolithic began is a subject of constant debate which is closely connected with the discussion of what the Neolithic way of life meant and whether it led to changes in the material, economic, social, or spiritual sphere. I believe that in the Early Neolithic there was a change in all parts of society, but that this was a protracted process. The transition from the Late Mesolithic to the Early Neolithic was not a drastic event; it seems as if the really major changes to society did not take place until later in the Early Neolithic. What is clear is that the terms Mesolithic and Neolithic, referring to different cultures with distinct economies and social organization, should not be over-interpreted. The sharp boundary between the two periods is in part a product of precisely these terms. In addition, there have often been

two different schools of research, one studying the Mesolithic, the other studying the Neolithic, and each school proceeding from its own priorities and perspectives (Edmonds 1999). The archaeological record contains indications of both continuity and discontinuity, but it shows that there were gradual changes during the course of the Early Neolithic in all spheres of society.

A fully developed agricultural economy, to the extent that the major part of food was provided by cultivation and/or animal husbandry, is not attested in the initial phase of the Neolithic. In actual fact, wild food resources were probably of great importance during the Early Neolithic as well (cf. Madsen 1982; Larsson, M. 1984; Skaarup 1985). In the same way, there are indications that cultivation and animal husbandry on a small scale were introduced to south Scandinavia already in the Late Atlantic period (cf. Jennbert 1984a). As regards spatial organization, the archaeological evidence likewise shows that the transition from the Mesolithic to the Early Neolithic was characterized by both continuity and change. Several of the coastal sites of the Ertebølle culture in the investigation area, as in other parts of south Scandinavia, display traces of continuous use into the Early Neolithic. Eight of the total ten Early Neolithic coastal settlements are on Late Mesolithic sites. Some of the sites, moreover, have traditions of use going back thousands of years, in some cases back to the Late Palaeolithic (Andersson & Knarrström 1999). Sites were gradually occupied during the period in "new" environments inland as well. Unlike the coastal settlements, none of the Early Neolithic inland sites show continuity from the Mesolithic. At the same time, it is obvious that, in connection with the transition to the Neolithic, there were changes in parts of the material culture. It is above all in the form and decoration of the pottery that there are fundamental differences *vis-à-vis* Ertebølle pottery. The stock of flint in many ways shows continuity from the preceding period, although the polished flint axe does not occur until EN I (Stafford 1999).

## Settlement pattern

Traces of the earliest Neolithic in the investigation area are confined to settlements (27 of them) – in some cases probably combined with flat-earth graves – and occasional votive sites (5). The Neolithic is usually associated with the building of long barrows and megalithic monuments. However, there is no certain evidence that burial monuments were built in the investigation area in the very first phase of the Early Neolithic. Nor has it been documented that special places of assembly, corresponding to the Sarup sites, were arranged at the beginning of the Early Neolithic.

**Settlement** Several factors interacted in the choice of settlement locations in the Early Neolithic. Some of the underlying factors of significance were the availability of rich and varied economic resources, good communications, and the existence in the area of a tradition of well-known geographical landmarks which had acquired a symbolic meaning for the population.

It is obvious that tradition had a great influence when a settlement was established. In the areas where we find Mesolithic activities, in many cases we also find remains from the Early Neolithic. The coastal settlements were not abandoned at the transition to the Neolithic; most of the big Late Mesolithic sites were also used during the Early Neolithic. These were thus places with a long tradition of settlement. By repeatedly locating settlements in places where the ancestors had lived, their knowledge of and feeling for the place was carried on. A social landmark was created which constituted a permanent place in a partially mobile way of life. A long place-based tradition was crucial for the group's identity and for tracing and confirming its origin. I think that there was in this region an inherited knowledge of the coastal landscape which was shared by all the members of the community. This insight was not just a matter of the physical landscape but also of the landscape as a social construction. The activities of previous inhabitants were manifested in the landscape in that different places – natural formations or artificial constructions – were familiar and recalled past events. They thus constituted the norms or underlying structures that guided people in the annual use of all the parts of the landscape.

The inclination to locate their settlements by the sea, especially in bays and lagoons, was strong. Coastal sites – where land meets water, where the forest gives way to the open sea – appealed to the people. It is clear that two areas of coastal settlement can be discerned in the region. One of them, consisting of Tofta 17, Saxtorp 12, Saxtorp 3 (Tågerup), and Saxtorp 23, was centred around the former bay at the estuary of the Saxån. The other area, comprising Barsebäck 72, Barsebäck 54, Löddeköpinge 8, Löddeköpinge 17, and Löddeköpinge 33, was beside the rivers Lödde Å and Mare Bäck. The coastal strip between these two areas lacks traces of both Late Mesolithic and Early Neolithic activity. This can of course be due in part to the neglect of Early Neolithic coastal sites here in the survey of ancient monuments, but it is nevertheless a clear hint that coastal settlements were above all founded on the shores of bays or estuaries.

In an environment where the inland was filled with closed deciduous forests, we may assume that transports, seasonal movements, and social contacts were maintained by river and sea. The Öresund naturally was of major significance as a communication route in the area. A dwelling site should be viewed as a part of the landscape, not as separated from the surroundings. It therefore cannot be understood as an isolated phenomenon, but must be put in a landscape context. In this connection the value of places from the point of view of communications was important. All main settlements were situated along special communication channels in the landscape – beside river mouths or on tongues of land where two rivers merged, that is, at the encounter between land and water. From such places it was easy to move in several directions. The dwelling sites evidently represented points in the communication system.

Early Neolithic people took advantage of the topography to emphasize certain aspects of the dwelling site, through its spatial relation to other parts of the landscape. Places where communication channels met seem to have been of particular importance, in bays or at confluences of rivers. Another significant variable seems to have been the choice of prominent places in the landscape from which water routes could be observed. Settlements were always on small rises. Topographical features were used to reinforce and underline the prevailing structure of the community. The more permanent settlement areas can be regarded as nodes in the landscape.

With regard to the existing evidence of Early Neolithic dwelling sites it is very difficult to reconstruct a settlement pattern in which main settlements and activity sites are represented. There are no "pure" Early Neolithic settlements in the area. At occasional places the remains are nevertheless of such a scale that it is possible to discuss their character, and there are indications that some of the sites may have lasted longer than others.

Five of the excavated settlements in the area (Tofta 17, Saxtorp 12, Saxtorp 23, Dagstorp 19 and Löddeköpinge 8) which can be dated to EN I could be regarded as main settlements. From an economic point of view it is fully reasonable that a year-round settlement could have existed in these places. At least people could have stayed in the places for most of the year and only made short excursions for specific purposes. All the sites, with one exception, are on the open coast or in bays. The sole exception is Dagstorp 19, which is in the valley of the Välabäcken (fig. 11). The most diffuse traces are found at Tofta 17, where the admixture of remains of later settlement has seriously disturbed the Early Neolithic picture. The house and the probable flat-earth graves, together with the proximity to

Saxtorp 12 mean that the site may cautiously be regarded as a main settlement. At the other sites there were fairly large occupation layers with varied find material. Houses and huts were documented at Saxtorp 23, Tofta 17, Dagstorp 19, and possibly at Löddeköpinge 8, and there are good reasons for assuming that graves occurred at Tofta 17, Saxtorp 12, and Saxtorp 23.

It is evidently the case that certain groups in the initial phase of the Neolithic, of which Dagstorp 19 is an example, moved their more permanent settlement from the coast to inland watercourses. The inland settlements were mainly established beside rivers or wetlands. Contact with the familiar coastal regions was thus retained both physically and mentally via the water routes.

The main settlements constituted the fixed points, and the people took their identity from them. Apart from these sites there were other places intended for special purposes in certain periods of the year, temporarily visited by herders or hunters. It is of course difficult to recreate a settlement pattern in which temporary activity sites are linked to specific main settlements. Excavations of these places mostly reveal only one or two features, and this makes it hard to speculate about the function of a site. In the areas around the settlements by the Saxån bay there are no known minor sites which could represent short-term places with special functions. Around the inland settlement of Dagstorp 19, on the other hand, there are a number of sites identified by surface survey with a limited amount of Early Neolithic finds which may have been part of a settlement system of which Dagstorp 19 was the node. The evidence, however, is far too fragmentary to allow us to say anything about the function of these places. They are on the slopes of Karaby Backar, on sandy soils but close to clay soils. The advantage of these places is that the proximity to two different soil types gives variation in vegetation and game. In the sandy areas with late glacial and glacial glaciofluvial sediments, the vegetation consisted of a nutrient-rich wooded pastures with a relatively well developed undervegetation. This provided good living conditions for deer. An increased element of clay tills meant that the surface water found it difficult to penetrate the soil, so that there were at times damp patches where pools of water remained. In this environment the forest was probably dominated by ash, elm, and lime. The heavy clay soils with their deciduous forests offered optimal resources for extracting vegetable food. Trees could be ring-barked and thus made to produce shoots at a comfortable height for people and animals (Göransson 1988, 1996). A settlement in a "marginal area" like this, between different biotopes, made it possible to use several resources from one and the same place (cf. Larsson, M. 1984:204ff).

Lackalänga 36, Stävie 21, and Örtofta constitute a special category of place. Remains of huts at these sites show that a group of people probably used the sites for overnight stays in connection with special activities. There are no finds or other contemporary features to indicate that these were main settlements occupied for any length of time. All three are situated at a certain distance from the big river valleys, on clay soils beside sandy soils. These places can probably be said to represent temporary seasonal settlements intended for special purposes, perhaps animal husbandry.

The introduction of cultivation and animal husbandry, albeit on a small scale, entailed changes to the appearance of the landscape that subsequently had an impact on people and their relations. However, we can obtain no more than a fragmentary picture of the subsistence of the Early Neolithic populations in the area. Unfavourable preservation conditions for organic material restrict our chances of illuminating the economy. Through a combination of different kinds of source material one can nevertheless acquire some knowledge of the different economic pursuits. The location of settlements in the landscape, impressions of cereal grains in pottery, remains of animal bones, and pollen diagrams are all factors which can contribute information. The

scant organic material means that comparative evidence must be used.

The general picture in north-west Europe as a whole is that the proportion of elm pollen declines at the start of the Subboreal period. At the same time or slightly later, there is a tendency for other stands of deciduous forest, such as oak, ash, and lime, to decrease at the expense of grass pollen (Nilsson 1964; Berglund 1969; Digerfeldt 1982). In comparison with well-excavated areas, in a belt running from Ireland in the west via Scandinavia to the Baltic region, landscape development suggests an overall pattern for the emergence of the cultivated landscape, with the Neolithic being characterized by a wooded landscape with extensive, mobile agriculture and woodland grazing (Berglund 1999). The palaeobotanical investigations undertaken in the investigation area agree with this picture, since the spring at Saxtorp 26 and the wells at Saxtorp 23 have given a concordant impression of small cleared areas beside settlements during the Early Neolithic (Regnell, M., pers.com.).

Finds of cultivated plants from the Early and Middle Neolithic mostly consist of impressions in pottery. The Scanian material has been identified and discussed in detail by Hakon Hjelmqvist (1955, 1964, 1974, 1979). The overall picture is that varieties of barley and wheat predominate. In the Early Neolithic naked barley is more common than hulled barley. Three different species of wheat (emmer, einkorn, and wheat) are attested in the Early Neolithic finds. Impressions left by other species of plant occur, such as wild apple and hazel (Hjelmqvist 1955, 1964, 1974, 1979; Larsson, M. 1984; Jennbert 1984a; Tilley 1996). In the material from Löddesborg, the Early Neolithic sherds have nine certain impressions of identified cereals grains: five of wheat, two of naked barley, one of emmer, and one of einkorn. In addition there were impressions of apple pips, a little rounded impression which may be a bulbil of chive, an impression of lyme grass, an impression of a piece of a sedge leaf, and an impression of couch (Jennbert 1984a). There are of course problems involved in producing a picture of Early Neolithic cultivation on the basis of a few impressions of seeds in pottery. The evidence is far too small to allow us to ascertain the relative significance of the different species. It is also difficult to judge the scale of this early agriculture.

The relation between domesticated animals and game is poorly illuminated in the earliest phase of the Neolithic. There are few cases where the conditions on excavated dwelling sites are such that organic material is preserved. Among the attested domesticated animals in southern Sweden, cattle and pigs account for the largest share. Sheep or goats are rare in the material. It has been assumed that pigs were for a long time the most important source of protein (Bjørn 1988; Welinder 1998). This assumption, however, is not based on the faunal evidence but rather on the ecological conditions prevailing at the time, with a wooded landscape. These animals, which were really more like today's wild boar, blended very well in the forest environment, and the amount of work needed to maintain them was minimal. The available evidence in the investigation area, as in the rest of south Scandinavia, is scant. At Löddeköpinge 8 there are only a few finds of bones from cattle; wild species, such as various kinds of fish and bird, roe deer, red deer, and wild boar dominated (Jennbert 1984a). The Early Neolithic settlement of Saxtorp 23 was likewise dominated by remains of cattle in one of the wells. Although several of the sites were on the coast, there is little evidence of fish being of any great significance at the few Scanian sites where organic material is preserved. The bones from the late Early Neolithic site of Rävgrav in Östra Vemmenhög suggest that fishing was not an important economic activity (Larsson, L. 1992c).

The overall impression of the Early Neolithic economy is that it was highly varied. The siting of the settlements beside rivers and where different soil types meet nevertheless indicates that a varied and resource-rich environment was available. Hunting and collecting probably played a major role, while cultivation and animal husbandry perhaps, in several cases, accounted for only a small part of the total provision of food, mostly without any real economic significance. It is possible that some of the cultivation was for the production of alcoholic drinks for use on social occasions. Some of the Early Neolithic vessels may very well have been intended for use as drinking cups (Koch 1998; Fischer 2002:377).

Special dwelling sites as nodes used by people moving through the area were important for the way in which the landscape was ordered and perceived. We find that the places which seem to have been main settlements were located beside bays or, as in the case of Dagstorp 19, on rivers, while the smaller places, intended for some kind of specialized activity, mainly seem to have been located inland, usually along some watercourse.

This way of living was a tradition going back for generations; it gave the population a knowledge of the social and ecological structure of the landscape. This knowledge was constantly repeated and reinterpreted on the basis of the daily experience of the landscape.

The central significance of the main settlement is also expressed in the internal organization. Studies of the individual sites show, as we shall see, that there is a pattern in the way the Early Neolithic population organized itself in the micro-space (the place). Although we cannot explain in detail how they carried out their everyday activities, it is possible to detect several underlying motifs according to which the places were used. Different areas in which different activities were performed can be distinguished. The archaeological traces of at least three of the Early Neolithic coastal sites indicate that several societal functions were attached to one and the same place. The settlement was not just a site for social and economic activity; at these sites there was also a harmony between the everyday and the ritual activities. It therefore seems inadequate to make a strict distinction between profane and sacred when trying to understand people during the Neolithic.

*Houses and huts*  Remains of houses or huts were documented at Dagstorp 19, Saxtorp 23, Stävie 21, Lackalänga 36, and – with some doubt – at Tofta 17, Löddeköpinge 8, and Örtofta. In most cases the buildings are rather small and round or round-oval. The exceptions are houses 61 and 57/58 at Dagstorp 19, which are two-aisled buildings, and also possibly the incompletely preserved house at Tofta 17. All of the rectangular houses are oriented east–west with, in certain cases, a slight shift to WNW–ESE. The basic building material, as was customary in the Stone Age of southern Scandinavia, was wood. Remains of burnt clay at Saxtorp 23 suggest that the walls of some houses were of wattle and daub. Preservation is far too fragmentary to allow a detailed discussion of the internal structures of the houses. In the Saxtorp house, however, a hearth or oven structure could be linked to the internal design of the building.

At the Dagstorp settlement there were two longhouses and a hut which can be dated to EN I. It is not possible to determine with certainty whether it is a large household with accompanying houses for different functions or several contemporary households. Of course, there may also be a certain chronological difference between the buildings. The occurrence of several houses, however, might indicate dwellings for two or more individual family units.

The number of Early Neolithic houses is rather limited, but the few documented houses do confirm the picture of heterogeneous house structures in the opening phase of the Early Neolithic (figs. 20 and 74). The standardized house types that seem to occur in later periods have not yet been established.

136

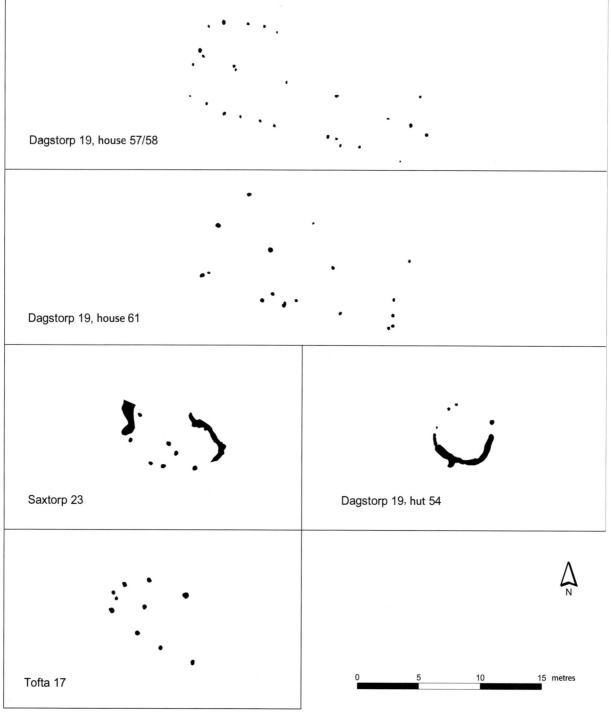

Dagstorp 19, house 57/58

Dagstorp 19, house 61

Saxtorp 23

Dagstorp 19, hut 54

Tofta 17

0    5    10    15  metres

N

Fig. 74. Houses and huts in EN I.

*Activity areas* Houses are only one element in a system of activities performed at a settlement. In studies of the organization of place it is essential to analyse how the house as one aspect of material culture relates to other activities. At some of the sites dated to EN I, special areas intended for specific activities can be distinguished outside the remains of the houses. The modest size of the houses suggests that the majority of the daily activities took place outside the houses. Moreover, the house interiors seem to have been kept fairly clean, since the finds are to a large extent outside the houses.

The clearest examples of the division of a dwelling site comes from the remains at Saxtorp 23, where it was possible to document, within an area of roughly 15,000 m², a dwelling, a manufacturing place, an area around a well, and flat-earth graves (fig. 12). The manufacturing place was just a few metres north-west of the house. The stratigraphical observations in the field show that the two phenomena may very well have been contemporary and that the production of tools was carried on right beside the house. Since the flint waste was registered in a dense accumulation, it is probable that people making tools gathered the waste on some kind of skins and then dumped it here. It therefore cannot be ruled out that the knapping place may have been inside a building which was cleaned when the work was finished. The activities at the well, on the other hand, were carried out a good distance from the house. For natural reasons, wells were dug where the groundwater was close to the surface. The heavy preponderance of scrapers among the tools beside the wells indicates that a specialized working process – the preparation of wood and skins – took place around them.

At some of the excavated sites there were surviving occupation layers of various sizes left by human activities. The quantity and variety of the finds at Löddeköpinge 8, Saxtorp 12, Saxtorp 23, and Dagstorp 19 strengthen the hypothesis about the character of these sites as main settlements. A common feature of the excavated settlements is that the flint, as expected, is dominated by flakes and debitage. Flake manufacture predominates, with some element of blades. Some flakes from axe manufacture were also retrieved, although they are only a small proportion of the total debitage/flakes. The tools are scrapers, knives, transverse arrowheads, and awls and axe fragments, together with a large quantity of "other" retouched flint. An analysis of the flint inventory shows that there was continuity in technology and tool types between the Late Mesolithic and the Early Neolithic. A slightly larger concentration of flint and pottery is noted beside, but not in, the Early Neolithic houses at Dagstorp (fig. 75). The settlement at Tofta has been too badly damaged by later activities to give us any clear idea of the Early Neolithic element.

At several of the Early Neolithic sites (Dagstorp 19, Saxtorp 23, Stävie 21, Örtofta) a number of small pits with sherds of Early Neolithic pottery, flint artefacts, burnt clay, and burnt bones have been documented. The function of the pits is of course difficult to judge. The composition of the material in the Early Neolithic pits, above all fragments of "everyday" objects, means that these have routinely been regarded as waste pits or storage pits. Some thought should nevertheless be devoted to the pits and their meaning. The majority of them are shallow and irregularly bowl-shaped, and the filling and section give the impression that the pits were filled in again immediately after the deposition. My view is that these features are in fact impractical as storage pits. A storage pit should have a distinct form in plan and section, with the sides straight or slightly sloping and the bottom flat (cf. Eriksson et al. 2000). It is reasonable to imagine that the almost beehive-shaped pit at Saxtorp 23, the sides of which were partly lined with clay, had a primary function as a storage pit. It has often been argued that pits with beehive-shaped sides were suitable for storing grain (Hill 1995:67). This, however, is one of the few pits that can be said to have been specially intended for storage. It also seems not to have been particularly appropriate

137

138

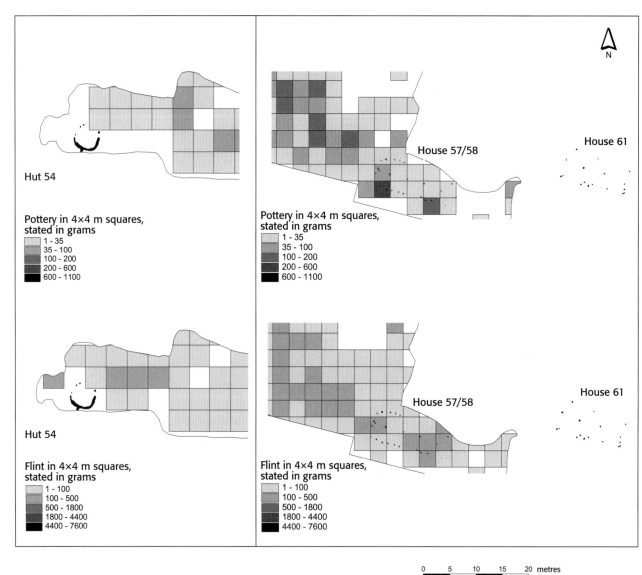

Fig. 75. Distribution of flint and pottery at the houses at Dagstorp 19 (SU 21) in EN I.

to perforate the ground surface at a dwelling site with shallow pits for waste products. Yet another argument against the idea that all pits functioned solely as storage containers or waste pits is that at both Saxtorp 23 and Dagstorp 19 there are potsherds from different pits with tempering and decoration which mean that they could come from the same vessels. Separating sherds from different pots and depositing them in dif-

ferent pits seems like a deliberate action, although of course it cannot be ruled out that a damaged pot could end up in two different waste pits.

Similar Early Neolithic pits are known from several places in southern Scandinavia. Nielsen has conducted a careful analysis of the finds from an Early Neolithic pit at Sigersted in Sjælland. Large quantities of pottery and knapped flint were retrieved here which could be chronologically linked to finds in the occupation layer of the site. He therefore interpreted the feature as a waste pit, since identifiable waste from diversified tool manufacture was found, together with remain of meals in the form of animal bones (Nielsen, P. O. 1985). It is tricky to determine what might be storage, waste, or accidentally dropped objects and what might be offerings on a dwelling site. Each find must be assessed separately. Ethnographic parallels show that the outlook on and treatment of dirt and waste vary between different cultures (Thomas 1991). It is obvious that the attitude to waste products prevailing in the Neolithic differed from that of our Western society. Deposits of flint flakes and debitage from Skåne are known from megalithic tombs and elsewhere in the south-east of the province (Strömberg 1971:320). The deposits can comprise everything from a few flakes to a couple of thousand. Besides flakes and debitage the deposits also contain blade fragments, transverse arrowheads, scrapers, and other small flint artefacts (Karsten 1994). These have been interpreted as reflecting cultic acts in connection with the construction of the grave (Strömberg 1971). Deliberate deposits of flakes/debitage from axe manufacture in the post-holes at the palisade in Dösjebro (Andersson et al. 1999; Svensson 2002) are yet another example of how so-called waste material is regarded as something more than just "dirt". It is possible that pits found on a dwelling site and containing habitation material or waste should not always be automatically considered as storage or waste pits. The composition of the material in the Stävie pit, including 95 scrapers and a stone packing on the bottom, gives a hint that the purpose may have been at least partly something else. Similar Neolithic deposits are known from elsewhere. Excavations in Fosie uncovered 32 scrapers together in the filling of a well (Björhem & Säfvestad 1989). By far the largest hoard was excavated as part of the Hagestad Project in eastern Skåne; it comprised 4,601 flakes and pieces of debitage, 770 flake scrapers, and 74 cores with a total weight of just over 76 kg (Strömberg 1982a:48ff).

*Graves* Remains of skeletons and clear grave goods are lacking in the graves in the area, which makes it difficult to establish with certainty that they really are graves. Some strong clues nevertheless suggest that they may in fact be Early Neolithic flat-earth graves. From Denmark several Early Neolithic flat-earth graves are known, and a comparative study of these can enlarge our understanding of the Scanian features as well. The majority of the graves were found in Jut-

land. The grave forms vary from simple, flat-earth graves without special structural details, to burials with various kinds of stone structures and/or adjacent post-holes. In Ebbesen's (1994) analysis of Early Neolithic graves he distinguishes eight types (A–H). Type A is defined as a simple oblong pit with no stone structure. The pit is usually a long oval or rectangular with rounded corners. The body was buried in a wooden coffin, wrapped in skins, or just laid in the earth. The orientation of the grave varies greatly, although east–west is most common. The length ranges from 1.6 to 3.0 m and the width from 0.45 to 1.5 m. The graves are between 0.45 and 0.6 m deep. At some of the features there were lone stones, and some have post-holes at the corners. The graves are dated to the entire Early Neolithic. This form of grave is most commonly found under flat earth. Some of the grave types are documented under long barrows. Ebbesen's study treats, above all, graves in which grave goods were found. However, he does not believe that this means that Early Neolithic flat-earth graves are particularly rich in grave goods. Graves without finds can only be dated to this time in cases where they can be securely associated with one of Ebbesen's eight types or if they are part of an Early Neolithic context (Ebbesen 1994). Unlike the situation in Denmark, there is as yet little sure evidence of Early Neolithic flat-earth graves in Skåne. At some places south and east of Malmö – Kristineberg, Oxievång, Petersborg, Skjutbanorna 1B, and Södra Sallerup – some probable flat-earth graves have been dated to EN I. The grave at Kristineberg was east of a ploughed-out, presumed long barrow (Larsson, M. 1980; Ekström 1999; Rudebeck & Ödman 2000; Sarnäs & Nord Paulsson 2001; Siech 2002).

The graves in the investigation area can be categorized as type A, that is, flat-earth graves without stone structures. Grave A642 at Saxtorp 23 does admittedly have stones along the north edge of the pit, which may be part of a simple frame structure. Post-holes found at the end of the same grave may also be part of the structure. The orientation of graves of type A varies greatly in the Danish material. This agrees with the excavated graves in our area, where both east–west and north–south occur. As regards length and width, all the graves in the investigation area fall within the dimensions measured in Denmark. The depth varies slightly, but this of course is connected to the degree of preservation. The shape of the features, fairly straight sides, a flat bottom, and traces of colouring left by a skeleton and/or coffin, corroborate the theory that these are graves. What is perhaps the least distinct grave at Tofta 17 is surrounded by post-holes forming a structure that resembles a house type of Mossby character. There are other examples of Early Neolithic burials in houses. At Bygholm Nørremark in eastern Jutland, under two long barrows placed one on top of the other, there was a burial inside a house. The house was a two-aisled structure with rounded gables and measuring roughly 12×5 m in east–west direction. An interpretation put forward by Preben Rønne is that a "ceremonial house" was built on the site. This was then demolished and the grave was placed within the demolished house and then the barrow was constructed on top of this. The structure has been dated to EN II (C) (Rønne 1979). At Tofta the grave and house are overlayered by a Bronze Age barrow (fig. 15). Although the barrow has preserved holes dug as postholes and graves, the actual construction of the barrow destroyed any other traces of Early Neolithic activities which might tell us what happened on the site. There are at least no clues that a long barrow preceded the Bronze Age barrow.

Ebbesen believes that the Early Neolithic flat-earth graves without stone structures are a continuation of Late Mesolithic mortuary traditions (Ebbesen 1994:80). At Skateholm it seems as if many more people were buried without grave goods in the later than in the earlier cemetery (Larsson, L. 1988b). There was possibly a decline in the tradition of burying the dead with grave goods at the end of the Late Mesolithic and the start of the Early Neolithic. This would explain the absence of finds in burials in the investigation area. Naturally, the grave goods may have been of material which has not been preserved. In the course of the Early Neolithic the grave forms become more complicated, with structures of wood and stone (Ebbesen 1994:80). A close spatial link between cemeteries and Late Mesolithic dwelling sites has been attested through different excavations in southern Scandinavia, for instance, at Bøgebakken on the Öresund coast of Sjælland, Skateholm on the south coast of Skåne, and Tågerup on the Saxån (Albrethsen & Brinch Petersen 1977; Larsson, L. 1995; Karsten & Knarrström

1999; Kjällquist 2001). A similar intimate relationship between graves and dwelling site seems to exist at some of the coastal Early Neolithic sites in the investigation area. At Saxtorp 23 the graves were placed within the highest part of the settlement area, while houses and activity areas were located further down towards the Kvärlövsbäcken. At Vallkärra it was not possible to determine the relation of any graves to contemporary settlements. The areas excavated there were too small and the finds too limited.

*The size of settlements* It cannot be taken for granted that Early Neolithic settlements were small in area. It seems in fact that both large and small sites existed in parallel. Both the excavations and the surface surveys in the investigation area show that some of the Early Neolithic dwelling sites were rather large. This may be a sign that space was needed for different activities and that there was successive expansion. It is difficult to calculate how large a group lived on each site at the same time. It may nevertheless be assumed, on the basis of the varying activities and the extent of the settlement, that, at least at Dagstorp 19 and Saxtorp 23, the groups could have been bigger than a single family. The different Early Neolithic activities at Saxtorp 23 comprise an area of at least 15,000 m² (fig. 12). The surface survey suggests that the site was much larger, more likely covering about 25,000 m². The excavated area at the Early Neolithic settlement of Dagstorp 19 comprises roughly 7,000 m² (fig. 18). The surface survey shows that the site probably continued down to the Välabäcken and was probably twice as large as the excavated area shows. Moreover, the finds collected from the site are so numerous as to indicate extensive activity. Of course it is impossible to determine with certainty the exact contemporaneity of the remains in the different places, but the spatial extent nevertheless gives the impression that the settlements were bigger than previous research has usually stated. The size of a settlement is of course closely connected to how we define a dwelling site. The big settlements during the Early Neolithic were not just used for dwelling, but also for burials and votive ceremonies, which meant that greater areas were claimed.

To sum up, it may be said of the organization of Early Neolithic settlements that there seems to have been a distinct and deliberate division into different activity areas on the site. The houses are relatively small and the distribution of the finds indicates that everyday chores were performed outside them. At both large and small settlements excavations have found small pits – often beside the houses – with contents which seem to represent the day-to-day activities of a dwelling site and which seem to manifest its significance. It seems as if there was an open area at the centre of the settlements at Saxtorp 23 and Dagstorp 19 (figs. 12 and 18), perhaps used for communal activities. At Saxtorp 23 this area is surrounded by a house and a well to the north and graves to the south. In Dagstorp the houses are in the eastern and western parts of the settlement.

**Votive sites** Alongside the deposits of votive character on dwelling sites there is also evidence that wetlands were used as votive sites. It appears as if this custom was practised to a rather limited extent in the opening phase of the Neolithic. Only at five places have objects been found in circumstances that can be described as votive finds, and in all cases the deposited object is an intact pointed-butted axe or a fragment of one. These finds are consequently found in contexts where there are no vestiges of burial or habitation.

The custom of depositing objects in wetlands is a recurrent feature throughout the Neolithic. It also seems as if the Early Neolithic votive custom has its roots in the Late Mesolithic, since there is great similarity between the Late Mesolithic and the Early Neolithic in the choice of the method and place for sacrifices. Karsten's studies of Neolithic votive finds shows that axes predominate in the votive bogs of Skåne (Karsten 1994). The fact that the axes are discovered as solitary finds may of course be due in part to the fact that the wetlands have not been excavated and that the find circumstances have therefore never been fully clarified.

## Society

As we have seen, the social and economic pattern follows largely the same lines as at the end of the Mesolithic. The archaeological evidence from the area indicates that the Mesolithic–Neolithic transition was not a dramatic event, but more like a continuous course of development.

Each society has its unique features. The specific culture-historical background means that the social organization and people's patterns of action vary from one society to another. By applying the archaeological evidence together with what we know about small-scale social structures from ethnographical investigations, there should nevertheless be good chances within the investigation area of reconstructing parts of the Early Neolithic social organization.

The settlement pattern shows nothing to contradict the prevailing view of Early Neolithic society as having been organized in kin communities where social relations were established and preserved through various bonds of kinship and friendship between individuals and groups (cf. Meillassoux 1972, 1981; Rey 1979; Terray 1975, 1979; Tilley 1984; Eriksen 1995). It is of course impossible to reconstruct in detail the structure of kinship relations. In the discussion below, however, it is sufficient to assume that people did not live in isolation and that their relations were steered by kinship. In societies of this type the individual household is the smallest and basic unit of production. Household or family units were tied together through one or more shared ancestors. Together they made up the kin group that was the fundamental social unit. Usually the local community consists of one or more kin groups governed by one of the elders. Collective work was socially organized or divided according to gender and age. The distribution of the products of labour was ensured via kinship ties and through a network of individuals extending beyond those who took part in the work process. It was mainly the younger members of the group who took care of production, while it was usually the older members who supervised and coordinated and who distributed resources to the economically unproductive members such as children and sick people.

There is evidence that people in the Late Mesolithic switched to an increasingly sedentary life. Coastal places like Saxtorp 3 (Tågerup), Skateholm, and Löddeköpinge 8 (Löddesborg) have been interpreted as more permanent settlement sites, possibly year-round dwellings (Jennbert 1984a; Larsson, L. 1988b; Karsten & Knarrström 1999). With the rich sources of nutrition available on the coast, people may have found it possible to settle permanently. It is uncertain whether these main settlements were inhabited all the year round or on recurrent visits, but it is clear that the sites functioned for hundreds and sometimes even thousands of years. Around the main settlements there were a number of places of a more temporary kind, used seasonally or for special purposes by small groups. The sedentary life that seems to have begun on the coast in the Late Mesolithic appears to have continued into the Early Neolithic. This gave the sites a symbolic emotional significance that was manifested in several places by burials beside the settlement.

It is perfectly reasonable to imagine that some of the bigger sites on the Saxån bay functioned at the same time (fig. 76). On the basis of the archaeological evidence, of course, it is impossible to achieve the absolute fine chronology required to establish that the sites were contemporary. If Tofta 17 and Saxtorp 12 are regarded as a unit, the distance to Saxtorp 23 is less than five kilometres. In between is Saxtorp 3 (Tågerup), the size and function of which are difficult to judge since the excavations never touched any Early Neolithic settlement horizons. A further six kilometres to the east, counting from Saxtorp 23, along the Saxån and the Välabäcken, is the inland site of Dagstorp 19. It ought to be perfectly possible that these places functioned simultaneously as self-sufficient units. Many ethnographically studied groups pursuing cultivation use a territory stretching 1–5 km (Chisholm 1968; Bakels 1978). One hypothesis is thus that it is possible

to identify at least three and perhaps four settlement groups in the valleys of the Saxån and Välabäcken.

In the area by the Lödde Å and Mare Bäck it is only Löddeköpinge 8 that has seen archaeological excavation, and here the extent of the occupation layer and the finds indicates that the sites functioned as main settlements. A further three sites in the area, identified by surface survey, with large amounts of flint and with traditions from the Late Mesolithic, could possibly be regarded as main settlements (fig. 77). Two of them are located close to the Mare Bäck, namely, Barsebäck 72 and Barsebäck 54. Almost five kilometres from there, at the mouth of the Lödde Å, there is not only Löddeköpinge 8 but also Löddeköpinge 17. Not having been excavated, these places are of course not proved to have been contemporary and their function cannot be determined with certainty. It may be observed, however, that Early Neolithic populations inhabited the Barsebäck foreland by the Mare Bäck and the bay formed by the

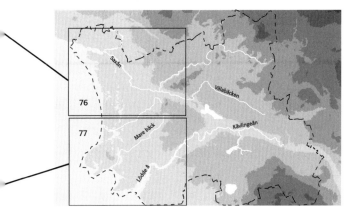

Fig. 76. Main settlements along the Saxån/Välabäcken in EN I.
Fig. 77. Main settlements on the Lödde Å and Mare Bäck in EN I.

estuary of the Lödde Å. There may have been one group of people in each area who moved between different settlement areas, Moreover, it is likely that these two settlement areas may have been in use simultaneously. If so, we can hypothetically imagine five or six settlement groups inhabiting the region around the Saxån–Välabäcken and Lödde Å-Kävlingeån in the opening phase of the Early Neolithic.

An analysis of the settlement organization in the investigation area gives the impression that more than one family may have lived together at some of the main settlements in the earliest phase of the Neolithic as well. The size of the individual house suggests that it was a dwelling for one family. A family may very well have consisted of three generations, with the grandparents also included in the household. Even though the excavated areas are not large enough to document the remains of all possible houses, the amount of finds and the spatial distribution of the sites, it seems that a number of family units could have existed simultaneously at the main settlements. The excavation at Dagstorp documented two long-houses and a hut from EN I, and finds of clay daub in several of the pits at Saxtorp 23 indicate that more than one house stood on the site. At least these two settlements were large enough to house several families, that is, a kin group.

In the wooded Early Neolithic landscape, small areas had been cleared for settlement, cultivation, and livestock. The location was optimal in that it commanded a view of large areas, not by creating closed territories but as a node linking several lines of movement in different directions. Although the landscape was largely covered by deciduous woods, the watercourses linked the region together. There are no traces yet of any permanent monuments in the landscape to manifest the specific territory or landscape spaces of a population. The row of post-holes and the ditches at Vallkärra, which may have been part of a long barrow, seem to have been constructed after the first phase when the grave/pit that could be dated to EN I was dug. There is likewise no secure dating for the excavated long barrow at Saxtorp 12 (Krångeltofta). Perhaps there were no clear territorial boundaries at all in this phase of the Neolithic. The wooded landscape was a socially open landscape in that the people moved freely in the area. It might have been possible for individuals to change group identity if they so wished. Kin groups may not have been closed, and the sense of "us and them" less pronounced. It is possible that ties of friendship were at times as significant as pure kindred relations for establishing networks of contact in the opening phase of the Early Neolithic.

With the idea of watercourses as a uniting link, it is reasonable to imagine that the main settlements along the Saxån–Välabäcken constituted a society in which one or more kin groups functioned together. In the same way, the dwelling sites on the Lödde Å and Mare Bäck may possibly be regarded as a cohesive society. Since the distance between the estuaries of the Saxån and Lödde Å is less than twenty kilometres by water, it is likely that there were contacts between these areas and that together they constituted a settlement district. Since the individual kin groups could not live independently, they were for several reasons dependent on the local community through the network of contacts. These social relations were necessary for the survival of the society. There was a need to maintain marriage contacts, trade, joint spiritual ceremonies, etc. Collective gatherings, when all the people in the area were assembled, probably occurred in connection with recurrent ceremonies which seem to have been connected to one of the main settlements. I thus believe that both the profane and the sacred acts were centred in the dwelling site and presumably open to the whole social community, even though the special collective ceremonies were probably conducted by a leading stratum. At this time the settlement was the most important point for the social network.

Through an increasingly sedentary way of life in the Late Mesolithic and the Early Neolithic, people became more tied to both time and place and thereby became dependent on what earlier generations had done in the area, such as forest clearance. A necessary condition for groups in these circumstances to be able to maintain a fair distribution of the most important resources was that more permanent relations were established and preserved between individuals through an expanded network of ties of kinship and marriage. The way in which this social order was maintained or changed depends on how power was legitimized. The archaeological traces of settlements, as regards how they were spatially organized, gives some, albeit vague, hints as to what the power structure may have looked like. Rituals concerning the life cycle, such as the mortuary ritual, could have the function of maintaining different interests of power and domination. Death and attitudes to death created a sphere of great symbolic and emotional power which could be exploited by the living. Mortuary practice was related to beliefs, which meant that burials could idealize, influence, and distort everyday social relations (Huntington & Metcalf 1979:122). It is probable that the power of the dominant groups in Early Neolithic society was legitimated and passed on through the burial ritual. Although important rituals were controlled by the social élite, it was not just these leading actors who were important, but also the onlookers, the passive participants. Through the burial, norms and values

were expressed in different ways and thereby also linked generation to generation. The cohesion between the members of society was reinforced. Since the ancestors had first made claim to the society's resources and land, there was also a close link in space between the settlement and the graves. The graves functioned as an expression of solidarity with the local group and of the geographical ties to the area (cf. Shanks & Tilley 1982). The close connection between dwelling site and burial place, I think, can therefore be seen as a territorial marker, with the concrete remains of the ancestors justifying the society's claim to the area. The ancestors established not just the solidarity and economy of the society, but also the rights of the society to the resources. This organization of space suggests that, just as with many historically known belief systems, there was no distinct difference between the living and the dead (Hertz 1960; Kopytoff 1971). The dead and the living were in a close relationship to each other. Life and death were categories of the same classification system. They were different categories, but life is a precondition for the definition of death and vice versa. Death and burial ceremonies were deeply involved in all spheres of society. The mortuary practice contributed to the reproduction of the social organization. Ideas about death and how to handle it were an important component in the aim of controlling time, space, and social relations.

Burial was also important because it was a symbolic transformation, a "rite of passage" (Gennep 1960), which changed a person's social position, in this case the move from the sphere of the living to the sphere of the dead. With its double meaning, the funeral ritual was an important element in the social process. Human bones are evidently special remains which do not only symbolize kinship; they also constitute it. They represent two fundamental principles of social relations, namely, individuality and collective. In the kin-based social organization, each person is at once a distinct individual and part of a larger collective. Burial is therefore important both for the individual in that it takes a person from one stage to another, and for the group in that the burial consolidates the relationship to the ancestors and the right to the place.

Alongside the recurrent but rarer "rites of passage", such as the funeral ritual, there are the more common rituals associated with annual, seasonal, and daily chores and actions. It is reasonable to imagine rituals on several social levels, from the collective, general ritual to the tasks of the individual or family group. We may assume that rituals entailed duties and actions on every level (Bradley 1990; Rudebeck 1998). Building houses, clearing areas of forest for cultivation and animal husbandry, or making a tool may also be regarded as transformative actions and may be occasions for special rituals. The ritual is often an action that exemplifies the ordinary and everyday. Ritual therefore cannot be placed in a separate pigeonhole from other activities, and neither the localization nor the content need express anything "special". Ritual is a social act that reproduces the structure and constitution of a society. It has often been argued that the distinction between ritual and everyday activities is a stereotyped, formalized, and repeated action (cf. Bell 1992; Rappaport 1999). It is nevertheless, as I have pointed out before, repetition and routine that characterize everyday chores and therefore the latter reproduce the prevailing structures.

Just like all human activity, such as arrangements in the habitation area, tool manufacture, or cooking, the handling of waste follows structured, deep-rooted cultural norms. Deliberate depositions of fragmented objects in pits is a form of symbolic behaviour which follows the prevailing cultural norms and structures. One problem in interpreting these "waste pits" is their household character, as regards both content and location. The difference between ritual and non-ritual can be very fine and difficult to discern in the archaeological record, but the important thing is to observe that the treatment of waste follows cultural norms and is a ritualized routine and therefore an act that reproduces the prevailing structural principles. It is therefore important to look at the pits in their context and not just focus on their form and content (cf. Hill 1995:96ff). By all appearances people in the Early and Middle Neolithic perceived dirt and hygiene differently from the way we do today. Unlike our Western attitude, their stance was not influenced by knowledge about hygiene and pathogenic organisms (cf. Douglas 1966). Potsherds, flint tools and debitage, and bones of cattle and pigs were in addition more than just dirt because these objects represented a Neolithic way of life (Thomas 1991). Dirt was formed by means of various ac-

tivities performed on the sites and was therefore considered a by-product of the creation of order. In such conditions, I therefore think it is possible that, for example, potsherds and bone waste could be left to lie at the settlement because they had acquired symbolic meaning. The often thick occupation layers at Funnel Beaker settlements may be the consequence of an ideology in which dirt was regarded as a natural part of the way of life belonging to the settlement, and so it was not cleared away. I consequently believe that the pits should perhaps not be regarded solely as waste pits (since much of the waste seems to have been left lying where it was) but as a procedure for further marking the symbolic meaning of the waste by burying a selection of it.

The material in the pits in the investigation area represented the most basic activities in people's social life, such as eating, cooking, drinking, and keeping fires burning. The actions performed during the ceremonies were reflected in the everyday activities pursued on the site. The deposited objects were fragments of action on the site and the pit was thus also a metaphor for the day-to-day chores. Everyday finds from several households may have been deposited on one and the same occasion. Social solidarity was enforced by a manifestation of everyday activity. The use of the same material, such as pottery, and the symbolism of destroying the vessels before depositing them, strengthened the bonds between the everyday activities and the actions that characterize ritual. A question that arises naturally is where the other parts of the objects were deposited. The majority, as we have seen, were probably left lying on the site, but perhaps some fragments were moved to other parts of the settlement. There are indications that sherds belonging to the same pot were deposited in different pits at both Saxtorp 23 and Dagstorp 19. Perhaps this should be regarded as an action intended to confirm the community between different households. It is also reasonable to imagine that fragments were exchanged between two different settlements with a view to reinforcing the solidarity between different groups, a state of affairs that is of course difficult to trace in the archaeological record.

On a higher level, the act of digging a pit and depositing fragmented objects in it is also a way to transform and strengthen the ties to the place. According to Claude Lévi-Strauss, sacrificial acts serve to create a relationship between the human and the divine (or the ancestral spirits). The relationship begins by breaking up the natural order of the world through the handling of objects in a special way. The establishment of a link between human and divine is proclaimed in several cases through the selection, justification, and destruction or deposition of an object, an animal, or a human. The transfer of a selected object from one stage to another is the goal of the ritual, which involves the act of picking out the object from its natural context (Lévi-Strauss 1987). In the same way as two persons establish a form of relationship by breaking and sharing a suitable object, the relation to a place is confirmed and strengthened by the deposition of parts of an object (cf. Chapman 2000). A locale acquired meaning and became a place when societal institutions transformed it by various rituals. I thus believe that depositions of objects in pits and the funeral ritual partly served the same purpose. In the Early Neolithic society in western Skåne it thus seems as if the dead were involved at some of the places which were also a forum for everyday activities – the production, use, discarding, and deposition of tools of stone and bone, of pottery and food remains.

Our Western conception of "individual" is a historical view which needs to be problematized. The human body should perhaps be viewed from one aspect as one of the material categories in the prevailing deposition structures during the Early Neolithic which belonged to the rituals for categorizing and understanding the world. The body as an incarnation of a lifelong process – from birth to death – can in this cultural context have been a twin source of an object's production (birth), consumption (life), destruction (death), and deposition (burial) (Kopytoff 1986; Bradley 1990; Tilley 1996). The strong bonds between people and objects in prehistoric times cannot be ignored. The production of artefacts was a process in which the craftsman's qualities were in certain cases transferred to the object. Material things were virtually animated, which is an outlook that can be recognized from several different ethnographical analyses (Carsten & Hugh-Jones 1995). Humans and objects should be seen as two distinct units but nevertheless related to each other. From this perspective, it is not surprising to regard the deposition ritual for the human body as a parallel to how artefacts were treated (cf. Wagner 1975; Chapman 2000). Artefacts may be viewed as events from the past which survive into the present. As authentic, primary, historical evidence, the objects can be revived, and in this way the past, the world of the ancestors, is brought into contact with the present and the prevailing structures are reproduced. Objects have the power to define the historical self-identity of the group, while simultaneously confirming for the living the strong bond between the group and the ancestors (Weiner 1985; Prown 1993). Depositing fragments of these artefacts gives a locale the value of being a special place and creates relations between the past and the present. This action can be of particular significance if one returns to a place which has been temporarily abandoned over a season. It is not necessary, however, for the object to have been deliberately destroyed. An artefact that has been broken in connection with use can subsequently acquire a symbolic role. For example, fire was important because of its transforming role and its symbolism in both sacred and profane contexts. Several of the flint objects in the excavated pits were burnt. I believe that the depositions of fragmented objects in the pits were deliberate, repeated actions which strengthened the relationship to the place by a manifestation of everyday activities.

The emphasis on the place, in my opinion, should be viewed as an expression of increased social control and the emergence of more or less permanent institutions. The maintenance of social relations between the living, the recently deceased, and the ancestors was ensured through several material forms – flint, pottery, and human bones.

Fragments of polished axes occur frequently on the dwelling sites in the investigation area, which shows, I believe, their importance as tools for clearing forest, for building houses. and so on. The well-shaped axes and the deposits of objects in wetlands also indicate that the axes had a meaning that went beyond the purely practical and symbolized some form of status.

146

Even though other material was also deposited which has not survived or been retrieved, the special role of the axe as an economic and social resource during the Neolithic is indisputable. In connection with the start of the Neolithic there is no evidence that axes were manufactured on the dwelling sites. Flakes from axe manufacture occur sparsely at settlements. It seems as if these objects were made by special craftsmen in special places. The manufacture of polished flint axes required much more time and energy than the making of Mesolithic core and flake axes. In certain cases the grinding and polishing of the axes was taken much further than what was required in practice. It is conceivable that axe manufacture, at least from raw nodule to plank, was carried out at places where the primary deposits of flint were found (Knarrström 2000b). Datings from the flint mines at Sallerup outside Malmö suggest that flint was extracted here as early as the very start of the Neolithic (Rudebeck 1994). The presence of axes in the investigation area and the absence of major traces of axe manufacture are thus evidence of contact and exchange of commodities taking place between different regions, since the flint must have been brought from the primary deposits. Quite lot of the flint probably came from the Malmö region, but there were also occurrences of flint on the raised beaches along the coast.

The flint as raw material and the axe with its symbolic meaning were probably important in the exchange of gifts. Ethnographical research has shown how various reciprocal relationships in societies maintained prevailing structures and gave the group a shared identity. This reciprocity is in turn based on different exchange systems on different levels which forged alliances within the society. The medium in the building of these alliances is "the gift", which has a built-in principle which means that a gift always requires a return gift. In his studies among peoples in Polynesia, Melanesia, North Asia, North America, and Africa, Marcel Mauss shows that exchange relations found expression in the form of gifts and return

gifts. Material objects, as we have seen, were animated. The circulation of goods created bonds and obligations which constituted the foundation of social relations. If someone stops returning the gift, the alliance is broken and hence the social communication. The exchange of gifts was perhaps not primarily an economic matter but was used in diplomacy and was a way to achieve prestige (Mauss 1925, 1950). Bronislaw Malinowski arrived at a similar picture when studying trading in shells in the Trobriand Islands (Malinowski 1922; Saunders 1991).

As ties to place increased in the Early Neolithic, as manifested in burials and sacrifices on dwelling sites, a more socially differentiated system was probably shaped. An incipient trend is therefore faintly detected, as people marked their group affiliation and position both within the group and in relation to nearby groups. A small surplus is produced to be used for feasts and rituals on the dwelling site and for the exchange of gifts. It is difficult to distinguish exchange commodities in the archaeological material, although similarities in the material culture reveal long-distance contacts. The occurrence of the axe in votive bogs shows its special position and its function beyond the purely practical. The pointed-butted axe may therefore also have acquired a position in the Early Neolithic as an important object in exchange relations. Kristina Jennbert's hypothesis about "the productive gift", assuming that grain and livestock came to southern Scandinavia through the exchange of gifts, also seems wholly plausible (Jennbert 1984a).

When axes were then placed in wetlands they ceased to circulate and took on a different meaning. They were given back to the earth from which they originally came. In this way the biography of the axe was completed. The role of the axe in the exchange of gifts was a matter of creating and maintaining relations between individuals and groups. The act of depositing the axe in a bog leads our thoughts rather to the sustenance of a relationship with a divinity. Depositions of single pointed-butted axes suggest that people in the Early Neolithic customarily used the votive sites on just one occasion, and that the act had a private rather than a collective character. The occurrence of both polished and unpolished examples and whole and fragmentary axes may indicate that the important thing was not the quality of the object but what the axe symbolized.

In chronological terms, EN I comprises almost a quarter of the Neolithic, whereas the votive deposits are only a small proportion of the total quantity of Neolithic votive finds. This picture prevails not only in the investigation area but in Skåne as a whole (Karsten 1994).

The available archaeological material consequently shows that collective activities, both profane and sacred, took place on the settlement site. The link between the group and the place, between the everyday activities and the social processes in society as a whole, is seen clearly on the dwelling sites. Smaller places or activity areas for some kind of specialized work – hunting, cultivation, animal husbandry, special sacrifice, etc. – performed by a smaller group of people, perhaps a family or a working group, were located at various places out in the surrounding landscape. Although the impact of the first so-called farmers on nature was rather marginal, cultivation and animal husbandry, albeit on a small scale, did of course affect the landscape. A changed view of the landscape subsequently had consequences for how people lived their lives. The human environment was increasingly shaped around permanent settlements, and within the socially constructed landscape the dwelling sites therefore also became the most prominent places. The settlement was the node where water met land, earth met air, body met soul, and time met place – a cosmology organized like a landscape. This is the angle from which we can see the landscape in the Early Neolithic. An ideology and a cosmology, a social network and an economy embodied by the creation of places with meaning in a landscape as an active cultural process. There was nothing of what we today would call a "ritual landscape" and a "profane landscape". Ritual activity was linked to everyday activities such as

hunting, fishing, gathering, and agriculture. The division into sacred and profane is thus irrelevant to a society where every aspect of life is interwoven.

## Further inland

The Early Neolithic period is characterized by a social organization already shaped in the Mesolithic. The individual's identity in time and place was linked to the settlement. Lasting structural principles prevailed in the Late Mesolithic and Early Neolithic, according to which the settlement was embedded in rich symbolic meaning reproduced through people's actions. The houses, the graves, and the pits may be seen as parts of this process, and ritual was a way to consolidate the central role of the settlements. The structure of society was based on kin groups where power probably lay with the elders of the group. Studies of traditional societies have shown that it was usually the elders who had the greatest power. Because of their age, they were considered to be in close contact with the ancestral spirits and the founders of the community, and it was the ancestors who once claimed the land. The ancestral spirits had a continued role to play by functioning as judges of how daily life should be lived, and here the old people in the community served as the intermediate link who could pass knowledge on to the young. It was to the elders that the power of the spirits was communicated, and the group's prosperity was dependent on the will of the spirits. In Early Neolithic society this view served to legitimate the prevailing social relations. The benevolence of the spirits was preserved through set, recurrent rituals controlled by the leading stratum of society (the elders) and the places in the landscape associated with them.

We have seen that the Late Mesolithic coastal sites continued to be used in the Early Neolithic. In the opening phase of the Early Neolithic, however, new settlements were also established, above all along the river systems further inland. Leaving a life by the sea must have been a rather big step. Along the coast, by lagoons and river mouths, people were active for most of the year, utilizing the diversity and variation of food resources both in the sea and on the land. There was a long tradition and knowledge of how to organize the landscape in the coastal region.

The transition from the Late Atlantic to the Subboreal has sometimes been characterized as a period of climate change, which supposedly had a negative effect on the marine resources and forced a change to agriculture and movement inland (Rowley-Conwy 1983, 1984, 1985; Zvelebil & Rowley-Conwy 1984). There are indications that the regressions and transgressions of the period caused a change in the marine environment and may have had an impact on the potential for oysters in particular to reproduce (Christensen 1982; Vang Petersen 1982; Liljegren 1982). There is nothing, however, to suggest that the climate changed to such a drastic extent as to have affected the ecological environment and access to the resources on which people lived. The economic conditions were surely no less favourable in the coastal region than inland. In addition, judging by the few preserved organic finds from Early Neolithic coastal settlements, it is not certain that the marine resources were used to any great extent. The Late Mesolithic economy was characterized by a full-scale broad-spectrum economy, and at Skateholm it was found that 87 different animal species were used as food (Larsson, L. 1984:14). Alongside these, there was probably a great variety of plants, fruit, and berries and a number of animal species whose traces have not survived because of decomposition processes. In such a flexible economy the decline in one resource ought not to have meant that people were fundamentally forced to change their way of life. It was the tradition and knowledge of the landscape rather than the resources of the sea that tied the population to the coast in the opening phase of the Neolithic, so the movements inland must have been provoked by other causes than purely economic ones.

The change in settlement pattern should probably be sought within the society. The reasons for change are always present within the group since there are constant oppositions in social relations which can lead to transformation. How serious the antagonisms become depends on the special relations prevailing between individuals, if one faction in the group exerts dominance over another.

Relations between the individual and the rest of society became increasingly tense as the Early Neolithic progressed. With greater sedentism, the population increased and hence also the social unit. The complexity of social relations increased, with more opposition between the individuals in the group as a consequence. A more stationary way of life gradually entailed not only a potential for new production conditions but also the rise of new social customs which utilized the depth of time and the social memory in a place. The social power that resulted from acquiring the past and using it with reference to the present and the future was attached to the settlement. Power was a matter of controlling other people and their resources, and it was based on social and esoteric control rather than economic control. Goods, labour, and land were evaluated within a symbolic system before they could be used as a basis for social dominance (cf. Hodder 1990). What happened at

the start of Neolithic was thus that a more settled life reshaped the landscape, albeit to a limited extent. Areas were cleared for cultivation and grazing. As a result, the view of the landscape was also changed. The need to assert one's sense of belonging to a place was intensified, and the power enjoyed by those (the elders) who exerted social control increased. A relation of dependence arose through the joint investment of labour in the soil. This entailed that the subsequent generation literally lived off the work of the previous generation. The same group that controlled the exchange of gifts probably also enjoyed access to the material symbols. Ties to place were displayed through rituals associated with ancestor worship, which affirmed the significance of the place and the social relations. The result is a structure in which the younger generation finds itself tied in one-sided dependence and obligations *vis-à-vis* the older generation. An inevitable consequence of the rise of a socially differentiated society is increased social awareness and suspicion of collective processes. As awareness of the new social compulsion grew, the social control also became more vulnerable. At the start of the Neolithic there were opportunities for the younger generation to avoid having the older generation exerting power or control over them. Migration and expansion to new, formerly unexploited areas meant that the bonds and obligations between the generations were weakened. The ancient system of norms, the underlying structures, changed. Perhaps this is what we see in the opening phase of the Early Neolithic. New sites and places came into use.

Although ties to place increased and led to increased internal social pressure between the different segments of the society, there still seem to have been no fixed territorial boundaries. The open ideology as regards territoriality may have facilitated the colonization process. Early Neolithic society had a great inherent freedom to colonize new landscapes. If people were not solely dependent on coastal sources of subsistence, but could also use other resources, there was no obstacle to populating new land.

## Establishment

In the latter part of the Early Neolithic and at the transition to the Middle Neolithic, changes in society are noticeable in several respects. Settlement expanded and seems to have gradually become established in more permanent districts. Apart from the settlements, other types of places with special meaning and function are a new element in the landscape. It was in the second half of the Early Neolithic that people began to build megalithic tombs. With their monumentality, these graves were to affect the picture of the landscape. Cultic and votive sites with deposits in wetlands increased significantly. There is also evidence for specialized workshop sites from this period in the investigation area. The landscape seems to have been divided up according to socially defined categories which meant that special social, economic, or spiritual activities took place at special times and specific places. Burials, votive deposits, cultivation, animal husbandry, hunting, and so on were all actions with their given place. Some of these activities were associated with the dwelling site while others were located in different parts of the landscape. In material culture too, there were changes, including the coming of a new form of axe – the thin-butted axe – and pottery with increasingly varied vessel shapes and combinations of decoration. It was probably also in this period that the first objects of metal began to circulate in the area.

### Settlement pattern

The remains from this period in the investigation area are extensive (fig. 78). In relation to the previous period, there is a noticeable growth in the number of places which can be defined as dwelling sites or activity sites. I have documented more than three times as many dwelling sites in EN II–MNA II than in EN I (88 versus 27), even though the length of the former period is only about 33% that of the latter (25% in calendar years) (see table I). Even more striking is the expansion of hoards and/or votive finds. In EN I five votive sites have been documented as against 50 from EN II–MNA II.

**Settlement**  The factors that were decisive for the choice of settlement location in the first phase of the Neolithic naturally applied in EN II as well, namely, tradition, communication, and ecology. The choice of settlement, however, is no longer tied to the coast and to the sites with a long tradition of occupation. The expansion of settlement inland which began in EN I increased significantly in EN II.

It is not the case that the coastal sites were abandoned at the end of the Early Neolithic. The number of settlement sites increased and all parts of the landscape, both coastal and inland environments, were claimed in a completely new way. At nine of the ten registered EN I sites on the coast, there is evidence that the place was also used in EN II–MNA II. They were known from before and continued to be used. It seems, however, that the late Early Neolithic and early Middle Neolithic element at several of these places is rather limited. They were used but had lost their crucial significance. The majority of the settlements established in the interior in EN I were visited continuously into the Middle Neolithic. Like the former period, locations chosen for settlement were above all on sandy soils close to a varied range of ecological and topographical features. The settlements mostly follow the rivers or wetlands, but areas outside these were also claimed.

As regards finds, features on dwelling sites, and the size of settlements, four main settlements can be identified along or close to the Saxån and Välabäcken (Saxtorp 26, Västra Karaby 7, Dagstorp 19, and Stora Harrie 38). The first three were located on sandy soil beside the Saxån or Välabäcken, while the rest were on a sandy south-facing slope, 1.5 km south of the Välabäcken, but beside a small lake (fig. 22). Houses were securely attested at Saxtorp and Dagstorp. At Stora Harrie a trench was documented and beside it clay daub with impressions of wattle was found. This is presumably the last remains of a house. The slightly earlier excavation of Västra Karaby did not systematically look for remains of buildings, so the function of this place must be considered uncertain. A large and varied amount of finds was registered at Västra Karaby, Dagstorp, and Stora Harrie. Five sites can be interpreted as main settlements in the area by the Lödde Å–Kävlingeån and Mare Bäck. (Barsebäck 48, Löddeköpinge 13, Löddeköpinge 40, Lackalänga 35, and Stora Harrie 35). The first three were beside the Mare Bäck and Stora Harrie is on the Kävlingeån (fig. 22). The site at Lackalänga differs by having been a few hundred metres from the nearest wetland. It is also the only place located on clay soils. Long-houses were

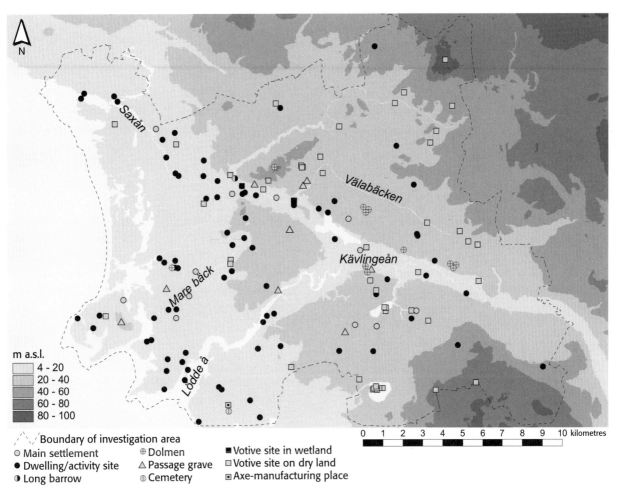

m a.s.l.
- 4 - 20
- 20 - 40
- 40 - 60
- 60 - 80
- 80 - 100

Boundary of investigation area
⊙ Main settlement        ⊕ Dolmen                ■ Votive site in wetland
● Dwelling/activity site  △ Passage grave        □ Votive site on dry land
◑ Long barrow            ⊕ Cemetery             ▣ Axe-manufacturing place

0  1  2  3  4  5  6  7  8  9  10 kilometres

Fig. 78. Settlement in EN II–MNA II.

documented at Löddeköpinge 40 and Lackalänga 35. All the settlements show a varied range of finds. The material from Stora Harrie 35 is limited, but several features were observed here in the form of pits and post-holes. Since only about 40% of the registered EN II–MNA II sites have been excavated, it is likely that not all the main settlements in the investigation area have been identified. Apart from the excavated settlements there are some sites identified by surface survey, with a varied collection of tools and waste indicating that they may have been main settlements. In the area by the Mare Bäck a site has been identified where the

collected flint, both tools and waste, is of such varied scope that it cannot be ruled out that the site functioned as a main settlement (Västra Karaby 44). The same applies to two places near Stångby Mosse (Stångby 18 and Stångby 36). In spatial terms the twelve main settlements are distributed to the west around the Mare Bäck, to the east around the Kävlingeån and Stångby Mosse, and to the north by the Välabäcken south of Dagstorp Backar.

The main settlements no longer seem to be solely on the coast; in many cases they were located on inland water systems. Small sandy heights or south-facing slopes were chosen as suitable settlement locations, with the exception of Lackalänga 35, which was on light clay soils. A clear breach of tradition in settlement is thus noticed in that the dwelling sites increase in number and their spatial placing is changed. It is noteworthy that only one of the main settlements (Dagstorp 19) shows continuity from EN I. The main settlements were thus still on slight elevations in the terrain but they do not have the same prominent role in the social landscape as before. In relation to the megalithic tombs they are mostly on a lower level, which also illustrates the somewhat different meaning of the settlements. I shall return to this later.

The majority of the places (76 in number), however, both the excavated ones and those discovered by surface survey, seem to be small and of a temporary character. The surveyed sites where only sparse amounts of flint have been observed may be assumed to be of a more temporary kind. These are along the watercourses and wetlands, spread all through the region, but with a concentration in the same areas as the main settlements.

Although settlement is no longer to the same extent on the coast, there was still access to water and different soil conditions with a variety of plant and animal life. The main settlements were thus located in favourable environments with rich variation, where the conditions were good for providing food. The picture of economic activity in Skåne and Denmark in EN II–MNA II is generally better illuminated than in the first part of the Early Neolithic. Pollen diagrams from different bogs in these areas show that woodland pollen decreases in the early and middle Early Neolithic and there is a corresponding increase in pollen from grass and other plants demanding light. In the closing phase of the period and at the start of the Middle Neolithic there is once again a rise in the proportion of woodland pollen in what is known as the regeneration phase (Berglund 1969, 1999). This need not necessarily reflect a decline in the intensity of the farming economy; it could just as well be the result of an emerging

coppice forest in the wake of forest clearance, a type of vegetation suitable for animal husbandry, giving both grazing and foliage for fodder (Göransson 1996). The pottery from this period has quite a number of grain impressions. The wheat varieties emmer and einkorn dominate, with a small element of ordinary wheat. Hjelmqvist's analysis of grain impressions from Västra Karaby 7 showed that it was precisely these three kinds of cereal that could be distinguished in the pottery (Löfwall 1977). Barley also occurs but to a lesser extent (Hjelmqvist 1982, 1985). In the osteological material from Danish Early and Middle Neolithic dwelling sites there are three species that dominate among domesticated animals, namely, cattle, pigs, and sheep/goat. Dog and horse have also been identified, but it is uncertain whether the horse in this period should be reckoned as domesticated. Starting in the Middle Neolithic, cattle seem to become the most important domesticated animal in economic terms (Madsen 1982:230; Nyegaard 1985). In Skåne the comparable osteological material from this period is rare. Bellevuegården outside Malmö yielded the largest amount of contemporary material from Skåne. The osteological analyses there, conducted by Evy and Ove Persson, agree with the findings from the Danish material (Larsson, M. 1984). Rävgrav in southern Skåne (Larsson, L. 1992c) and similar results have come from Hindby in Malmö (Nilsson & Nilsson 2003). Despite the Early Neolithic expansion phase, the impact on nature in this period was still marginal. The occurrence of game among the bones from dwelling sites indicates that hunting was still an important source of food. Roe deer and red deer are the most common species in the material. The role of fishing, on the other hand, is uncertain since very small quantities have been found on dwelling sites (Larsson, L. 1992c).

Despite the large number of settlements from the period EN II–MNA II in the investigation area, only a limited number have been so carefully excavated that a meaningful discussion of the internal organization of settlement sites is possible. Some important observations have nevertheless been made. The concentration of different societal functions in the settlement does not seem to be as great as at the start of the Early Neolithic. Functions were divided so that "new" places were created, such as the grave monuments and votive sites, for the performance of special ritual activities. This does not mean, however, that these activities totally disappeared from the dwelling sites.

Thanks to the most recent excavations along the West Coast Line in particular, our knowledge of Early and Middle Neolithic houses has increased. In the investigation area there are several more or less clear buildings from this period. An article on Early and Middle Neolithic houses in southern Scandinavia proposes a division into at least three different types occurring in EN II–MNA II (see Artursson et al. 2003).

The first group, known as the "Mossby house", consists of two-aisled houses with rounded gables and convex walls. They varied in length and in the number of roof-bearing posts, and sometimes had only a slightly rounded gable. As a rule there were no roof-bearing posts in the gables; the roof-bearing posts were instead placed along a more or less straight central line through the house. Three houses in the investigation area, house 17 at Saxtorp 26, house 57/58 at Dagstorp 19, and the house at Löddeköpinge 40, can be assigned to this group. This type of house seems to occur at least through the whole Early Neolithic. House 57/58 could be dated to EN I while the other two can be placed in the late Early Neolithic and possibly the early Middle Neolithic (Artursson et al. 2003).

The next group of houses consists of two-ailed houses with a trapezoidal shape – Dagstorp house type I. These are generally small houses, trapezoidal with the long walls straight. Depending on the size of the house, the number of post-holes left by roof-bearing posts varies somewhat, and they can also be placed in the gables. Five structures in the investigation area can be assigned to this type. Four of the houses, houses 50,

51, 52, 55 at Dagstorp 19, were uncovered by the excavations along the West Coast Line. The houses have been dated to the early Middle Neolithic. The house at Lackalänga 35 might also belong to this group (Artursson et al. 2003).

Two-aisled houses of rectangular form make up the third group – Dagstorp house type II. This category consists of long-houses with straight walls and gables. The majority of the houses had a length somewhere between 15 and 20 m. House 72 at Dagstorp is of this type and can be dated to MNA I (Artursson et al. 2003).

During the period, houses appear to have developed a certain regularity in their design (fig. 79). The basic materials for house construction were wood and clay, and the houses that seem to be dwelling houses have the form of small long-houses. At least four trapezoidal houses have been identified at Dagstorp 19, which can probably be dated to MNA I. In addition, there is a rectangular house here with a slightly less certain dating to the same period. The four trapezoidal houses show a striking homogeneity in their design. Built on a gentle slope running down towards the Välabäcken, the houses have an area of 32–50 m². Two of them are oriented NNW–SSE direction and one NNE–SSW. The fourth house runs east–west, placed almost at right angles to house 52. At least two of the houses are divided into two "rooms", a big one between the south gable and the roof-bearing posts in the northern part of the house, and a small room north of these posts. Three of the houses have pits placed in the northern part, in the small room. The houses were placed beside each other with no overlapping, which is an indication that they may be contemporary. Nor is there anything in the finds to suggest a difference in time between the buildings, that is to say, that the house was moved around on the same site. The division into two rooms could also be identified in the house at Löddeköpinge 40. It is noteworthy that the larger presumed dwelling section is in all cases in the southern part of the houses. The intention may have been to take advantage of the daylight and to keep the sunlight away from the other part of the house which may well have been used for storing food products. At the other sites where houses have been documented (Saxtorp 26, Löddeköpinge 40, and Lackalänga 35), only one sure building has been observed at each place. This may of course be because the excavation did not cover the entire settlement, but it nevertheless seems as if there were during the period both isolated farms with a single household and places where several households and farms existed at the same time. The size of the buildings from the different places which are interpreted as dwelling houses indicates that they were inhabited by a household or production unit, probably corresponding to a family.

Like the houses from EN I, the Dagstorp houses are relatively small and there is also little evidence of any kind of tool production inside the buildings. The mild climate that prevailed for much of the year during the Neolithic permitted outdoor activities. To take advantage of the daylight, a great deal of the cooking and the manufacture and maintenance of tools was done outdoors. It is also clear that the find concentrations are outside the houses (fig. 80a and b). This is particularly noticeable around houses 50 and 72 at Dagstorp. Immediately north-east of house 50, within an area of 2×3 m, large quantities above all of potsherds but also flint debitage were documented. There are no traces of any tool production in the immediate vicinity of the four trapezoidal houses.

The objects west of house 72, on the other hand, give the impression of being the remains of tool manufacture. This building was just over 300 m east of the other four dwelling houses in Dagstorp, and it is uncertain whether this house should be associated with the others or if it should be regarded as an isolated farm. Finds here included 26 flake cores and a hammerstone. The occurrence of 13 scrapers and 6 knives shows that other work was also carried on here. The pottery in the layer indicates that it belongs to a later part of MNA I (Lagergren-Olsson 2003). It is thus

possible that the house should be regarded as slightly later than the four trapezoidal buildings in the western part of the settlement.

Accumulations of post-holes were identified at Dagstorp 19 which do not seem to be proper dwelling houses; they are more likely to have been small huts or shelters which served other purposes than habitation (fig. 81). In and beside the irregular concentrations of post-holes (hut 56) only 20 m south-east of house 50 there is a noticeably increased find concentration, including a grindstone. Just over 200 m south-east of the four trapezoidal houses, down towards the Välabäcken, there was a feature that is also best regarded as a hut (hut 62) and beside it an occupation layer with concentrations of finds and features. Unlike the situation in the dwelling houses, there is a greater concentration of flint and pottery inside the huts. It is likely that workshops and activity areas were located a little distance away from the dwelling houses. The organization of the Dagstorp site seems to have involved placing the dwelling houses as far north as possible and the various general activities on the ground sloping down to the Välabäcken.

At the other site with more permanent settlement there are no traces of more than one contemporary farm unit as we find at Dagstorp. Where single houses have been documented (Lackalänga 35, Löddeköpinge 40, and Saxtorp 26) the excavated areas are of such a size (1,000, 3,500, and 4,400 m² respectively) that several buildings could have been identified if they had existed (figs. 23, 27, 28). The house at Saxtorp 26 is much bigger than other houses from this period. Perhaps more than one family lived here.

The phenomenon of pits on dwelling sites also occurs in EN II–MNA II. At the Saxtorp 26 site there were several pits inside the house and outside the southern wall. The pits were an irregular round or oval shape of a size varying from 0.76×0.57 m to 2.68×0.77 m. None of the pits was more than half a metre deep. They contained a large quantity of burnt clay and daub, pottery, knapped flint, and burnt bones. Among the vessel types there are fragments of a richly decorated lugged beaker. Beside the presumed wall trench at Stora Harrie 38 there were several pits with Neolithic pottery, knapped flint, clay daub, and occasionally bone fragments. At the Dagstorp settlement, pits could also be associated with three of the trapezoidal houses and right beside one of the so-called workshops. The finds agree with what was observed at Saxtorp and Stora Harrie. In form and content the pits are like those identified at settlements from EN I. On the other hand, it seems as

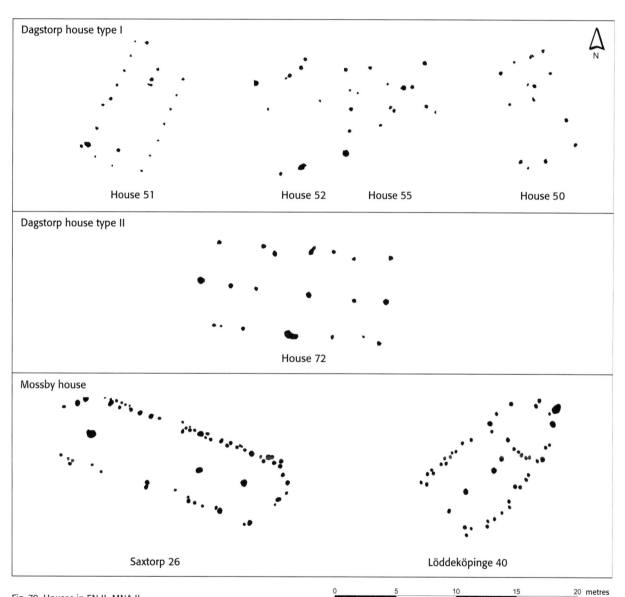

Dagstorp house type I

House 51 House 52 House 55 House 50

Dagstorp house type II

House 72

Mossby house

Saxtorp 26 Löddeköpinge 40

Fig. 79. Houses in EN II–MNA II.

0 5 10 15 20 metres

if at least some of these features in EN II–MNA II were more closely linked to the actual house than was the case in the preceding period. One deposition that stands out is the upturned funnel beaker at Västra Karaby 7. The custom of depositing funnel beakers upside down is known from other Scanian settlements, for instance at Burlöv outside Malmö

(Berggren 1999) and at Stora Herrestad north of Ystad (Andersson, T. 1997, 1999).

The number of dwelling sites at the end of the Early Neolithic increases in relation to the preceding period. However, it does not seem as if settlement generally grew in area. In most cases settlement consists of isolated farms, although the Dagstorp site shows

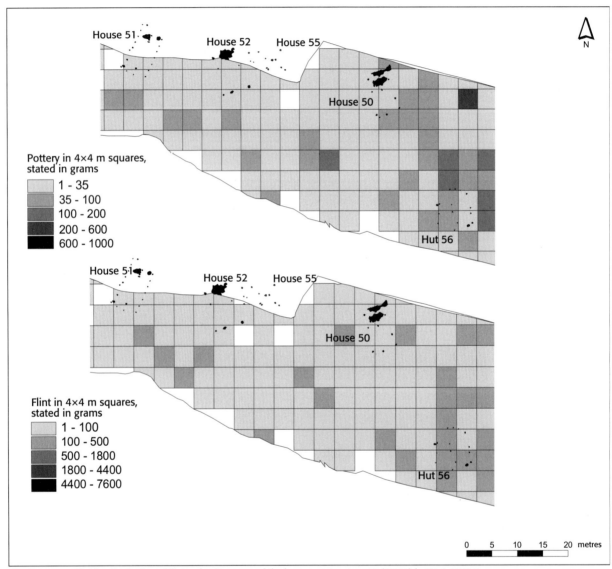

Pottery in 4×4 m squares, stated in grams

1 - 35
35 - 100
100 - 200
200 - 600
600 - 1000

Flint in 4×4 m squares, stated in grams

1 - 100
100 - 500
500 - 1800
1800 - 4400
4400 - 7600

0   5   10   15   20 metres

Fig. 80a and b. The distribution of flint and pottery around the houses at Dagstorp 19 (SU 21) in EN II–MNA II.

that this was not the only possible form. If we assume that the settlement at Dagstorp extended down to the Välabäcken, as the surface survey indicates, then it covered an area of 50,000–60,000 m². Judging by the excavated area together with the surface survey, the small main settlements had an estimated area of a few thousand square metres.

**Graves**   One long barrow, eleven round or long dolmens and nine passage graves are securely documented in the area. The second survey in 1985–1987 has shown by means of archive studies that the number was probably much larger. Twelve of the graves have been excavated in varying degree. One problem for the interpretation is that few megalithic tombs have been

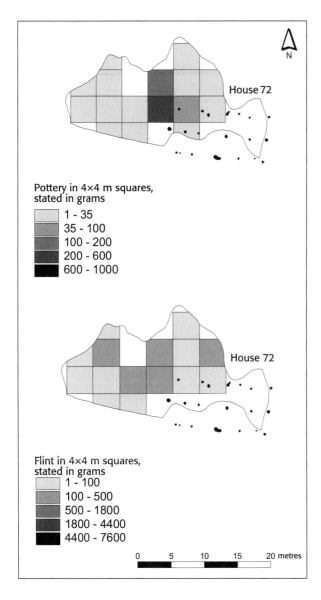

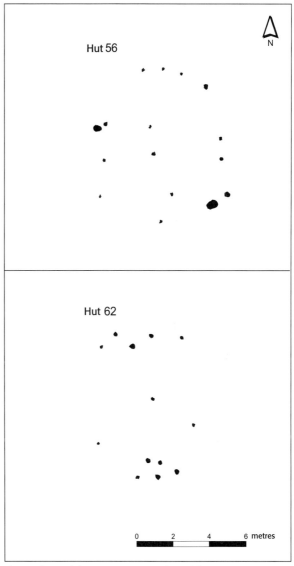

Fig. 81. The workshops at Dagstorp 19 (SU 21) in EN II–MNA II.

investigated by modern excavation methods, since a large share of them were excavated at the start of the twentieth century. Often these excavations focused on finds and paid no attention to features adjacent to the monuments. Apart from the megalithic tombs, a flat-earth cemetery consisting of 17 securely attested graves has been excavated in Borgeby parish.

The placing of the megalithic tombs in the landscape does not show a uniform picture. They were often placed at the highest point in the surroundings, but it is only Gillhög and Hög that can be said to have a monumental topographical location. Several of the graves were built on slopes or ledges on slopes. Nor is it possible to see any variations between how the different types of megalithic tombs were placed in the terrain. With the exception of the passage grave of Annehill, all the graves were beside or close to running water. Like the settlements, the megalithic tombs were above all located on sandy soils. Graves occur both singly and in groups. It is in the east and north-east of the area that the megalithic tombs are found in groups – three dolmens at Lilla Harrie, two long dolmens and a passage grave in Västra Hoby, two long dolmens and a dolmen at Stora Harrie, and two passage graves in Södervidinge.

The opinion still prevailing is that the long barrow is the earliest form of monumental grave, followed by the dolmen and later the passage grave (Nielsen, P. O. 1984; Blomqvist 1989a). However, there do not seem to be any distinct boundaries between the grave types; the different forms seem to overlap in time. In certain phases all three forms were probably constructed at the same time in different parts of southern Scandinavia. Early datings of human bones from passage graves in the Falköping district have shown that this type may have been erected here as early as the end of the Early Neolithic (Persson & Sjögren 1996). Dated material from grave chambers in Danish and Swedish dolmens and passage graves have also shown that they are partly contemporary, although the dolmen mostly seems to be the earliest (Blomqvist 1989a). Studies of the distribution of the different megalithic tombs in the investigation area show that those presumed to be oldest (long barrows, long dolmens, and dolmens), with Hofterup as an exception, lie in the east or north of the area.

In a study of the megalithic tombs in the area, Hårdh has analysed the pottery deposited at the monuments. By investigating the frequency of different combinations of decoration occurring at the different graves, a certain chronological difference can be demonstrated. At the four passage graves in the east and north of the area – Hög, Annehill, Södervidinge, and Västra Hoby – there is pottery with a high frequency of whipped cord, cross-hatching, arched impressions

and lines, which belong in an early part of the Middle Neolithic. This can be contrasted with Gillhög, Storegård, and Lackalänga to the west and south, where whipped cord is rare (Hårdh 1990b). It thus seems as if the first grave monuments, in the form of long barrows, long dolmens, and dolmens, were erected in the east and north of the area. It must thus have been in this area, judging by the ceramic deposits, that the first passage graves were built, and only after that was this type of grave established in the western and southern parts.

There are about twenty barrows in Skåne which may be long barrows, only a few of which have been excavated (Larsson, L. 1992b). In the investigation area only one long barrow (Dagstorp 12, Krångeltofta) has been excavated. In Denmark, by contrast, many more have been excavated, and it is in large measure from there that we derive our knowledge of the construction of long barrows (Madsen, T. 1993). The interpretation that the stone structure at Krångeltofta is the remains of an Early Neolithic long barrow is mainly based on the distinctive characteristics of this type of monument. Typical features are the trapezoidal shape, the east–west orientation, and the frequent location on the south slope of a hill. The east side has been perceived as a façade, sometimes in the form of a ditch with posts (Kaul 1988:64ff) and often with finds of pottery from one up to a dozen vessels. The actual burials, on the other hand, may be poor in grave goods (Madsen, T. 1993:98).

None of the dolmens in the area have been excavated in modern times, and it is only the Hofterup dolmen that seems to be undamaged today. Consequently, it is difficult to give a full account of their different structural details. The dolmen chambers were relatively small, about 1.5–3 m², consisting of three to five orthostats with a large capstone. In most cases the chamber was surrounded by a rectangle (long dolmen) or circle (round dolmen) of stones. These constituted the boundary of the mound of earth and stone packing that once probably covered most of the tomb up to the

lower part of the capstone. In several cases, however, the kerb has been removed and it is therefore impossible to determine whether it was originally a long or a round dolmen.

Since seven of the passage graves in the investigation area have been excavated, we have a better picture of them than of the long and round dolmens. The size of the chamber varies greatly from one monument to another, from Lackalänga at just over 6 m² to Gillhög at 18 m². In the cases where the shape is known, three of the graves have a rectangular chamber and three an oval chamber. The double passage grave of Annehill has one oval and one rectangular chamber. The chamber is usually oriented east–west, sometimes with a slight shift to either side of that axis. The exception is Lackalänga, whose chamber runs north–south. The passage, which is intact at six of the passage graves, is 5–5.8 m long. Generally speaking, the passage graves are carefully built and technically sophisticated. An interesting structural detail is that some of the wall slabs in the passage grave of Hög did not reach up to the desired height, which was therefore increased with extra slabs overshooting the lower slabs (Peter & Salomonsson 1967).

Several of the passage graves (Gillhög, Hög, Lacka-länga, Södervidinge, and Västra Hoby) have a more or less massive find-bearing cairn in front of the passage. It is not possible to determine whether Annehill and Harald Hildetand's Grave had a similar cairn, since recent cultivation and road construction have destroyed any traces. The excavations suggest that these cairns were accumulated in several phases and that deposits outside the graves were carried on in MNA Ib–MNA IV, with a concentration in the periods MNA Ib–MNA III (Hårdh 1990b).

It is rather rare for areas to have been excavated beside megalithic tombs. The digs that have been performed, however, show that activities took place not just in the immediate vicinity of the graves; a wider area in front of and around them was intended for various rituals. The different forms of stone packings found at Hofterup 28 and at the site of a possible megalithic tomb at Dagstorp 11 and possibly at Lackalänga and Annehill may be traces of sacrifices at the megalithic tombs. The U-shaped trench at Dagstorp may be the last traces of a cultic house. Perhaps the structures at Särslöv should also be interpreted as ritual buildings. The lack of contemporary features and ordinary Neolithic settlement site material suggests that the buildings did not serve as dwellings but had a specialized function. Moreover, the inner floor area of the buildings was only about 3 m², which must be considered small for a dwelling. The occurrence of sherds of a pedestalled bowl may corroborate the hypothesis that the buildings were intended for ritual purposes. The distance to the nearest megalithic tomb may seem large (800 m), but people in the Neolithic had a different way of viewing and shaping the landscape than we have today. Places that we would regard as isolated were viewed as being linked together. Parallels to these structures have been documented in some places in Denmark. In Jutland there are a number of features of varying size which have been interpreted as cultic houses. The remains consists of wall trenches with post-holes and are of rectangular/square form with the opening in one of the gables. They have all been dated early in the Middle Neolithic. Potsherds and flint axes have been found in most of them and they are, like the Dagstorp building, located close to megalithic tombs (Becker 1993; Andersen 2000). On the island of Strynø south of Fyn there was a building of the same shape and size as one of the buildings in Särslöv (A3585). Only one find was retrieved, a thin-butted flint axe placed on a flat stone in the centre of the house. In the vicinity there was a flat-earth grave, and the house has therefore been interpreted as a ritual building associated with the mortuary cult of the Funnel Beaker culture (Skaarup 1985:337ff). Like the Danish cultic houses, the feature at Dagstorp seems to have burnt down. Unlike the Danish counterparts, however, there are no finds of votive ceramics. One explanation for this, of course, is that later ploughing has removed any deposits.

**Votive sites** Deposits in the investigation area for which the find spot is exactly known, and where the finds cannot be linked to any dwelling site or burial place, seem to be mainly located in wetland areas such as bogs, fens, and lakes (cf. Karsten 1994). There are, however, records in which the find spot is described merely as a "hollow" and in these cases it is not clear whether it really is a drained wetland. These hollows may possibly represent former wetlands of limited size, which were sites for offerings of a private character performed by individuals.

Depositions of objects in wetlands, outside settlement contexts, increase significantly during this period. A clear distribution is noticeable in inland areas of wetland in the northern and eastern parts of the investigation area. In the Neolithic the area was full of bogs of varying size. The reconnaissance map of Skåne provides a picture of what the landscape might have looked like in the Neolithic (fig. 4). When the map was drawn (1812–20), 29% of the investigation area consisted of wetland, while the figure today is around 3% (Wolf 1956). Concentrations of deposits are observed in the bogs at Dagstorp, Västra Hoby, and Norra Nöbbelöv. None of the identified deposits are on the coast.

Of the forty-seven known votive sites in wetland environments in the investigation area, twenty-five consist of single finds, that is, finds of just one object. In all these single finds the deposited object is a thin-butted axe. Fifteen of the thin-butted axes were wholly or partly polished (of these two were thin-bladed, two of rock, and six fragmented). In addition, a miniature axe has been documented, made out of a thin-butted polished axe. Besides Saxtorp 26, twelve accumulated find spots have been documented, that is, places where finds of more than one object have been registered. In six of the cases the place was used on only one occa-

sion in EN II–MNA II but reused in later periods. The objects in the accumulated find spots that can be linked to EN II–MNA II consist of a total of 21 thin-butted axes (5 of them unpolished and 5 fragmented) and one thin-bladed, thin-butted quadrilaterally polished flint axe which can be interpreted as an imitation of a copper flat axe. At five places there are two or more objects interpreted as having been deposited simultaneously as hoards. Of the total eleven thin-butted axes in this category of find, two are unpolished and three of rock (Karsten 1994).

All of the deposited thin-butted flint axes whose type could be identified were of types I–IV. These types are usually assigned to EN II (Nielsen, P. O. 1977; Vang Petersen 1993). This dating is corroborated by the fact that all four axe types have been discovered in find combinations in Scanian hoards together with the pointed-butted axe of type 3 (Karsten 1994:137). Karsten's statement that axes found in hoards are longer than those probably deposited separately is confirmed in the investigation area (Karsten 1994:103–125).

A major problem is that only a few votive sites have been excavated. Most of the artefacts have been discovered in connection with peat cutting, drainage, or farm work (Karsten 1994). In these contexts it is of course above all the eye-catching objects – the axes – that are spotted. The fact that the thin-butted flint axes found in votive contexts are of types I–IV is an indication that sacrificial activity in wetlands culminated already in EN II and declined during the early Middle Neolithic. In the investigation area it is just the fen at Saxtorp that has been excavated. This investigation, together with the excavations of Hindby votive fen outside Malmö and Röekillorna in Löderup parish, shows that the deposits were highly varied in character and composition (Svensson 1993; Stjernquist 1997). It thus cannot be taken for granted that the objects unearthed from the different bogs in the investigation area are representative of what was once deposited. On the other hand, the wetland finds proba-

160

bly give a fairly good picture of their distribution in time and place.

It is difficult to describe the internal organization of the votive sites since so few have been excavated. There is much evidence, particularly from finds on dry land beside large stones or as house and pit offerings at dwelling sites, that votive acts in the form of deposits of a single object or a hoard exist as unique events (Karsten 1994). Without a total excavation, however, it is impossible to ascertain whether a votive site in wetland was used only once or on repeated occasions. Based on the excavations that have been done, there is good reason to suspect that several of the single finds from wetlands found during peat cutting or drainage should not be automatically interpreted as a single deposit, but rather as part of continuous, accumulating sacrificial activity in the same place. The Neolithic votive sites in southern Scandinavia which have been excavated to varying degrees, such as Hindby votive fen in Malmö, Röekillorna in Löderup parish, Salpetermosen in Sjælland, Veggerslev Mose I in Jutland, Lilla Aamosen in Sjælland, and Sludegårds Mose in Fyn, display partially shared features (Becker 1947; Albrechtsen 1954:4ff; Svensson 1993; Stjernquist 1997). We find deposits of varied character with occurrences of pottery, axes, animal bones, and sometimes human bones. The area covered by these accumulated find spots in wetland seems to lie between 300 and 1,000 m². Wooden structures such as platforms and piles, and occasionally even a footbridge leading out to the votive site, have been documented.

The area affected by wetland at Saxtorp 26 was about 1,200 m², of which the Neolithic layer comprised roughly 350 m². The wetland yielded a rich amount of Neolithic finds, mainly consisting of pottery, flint, and animal and human bones. The animal bones are chiefly remains from butchering and meals. The typologically datable pottery can be clearly assigned to EN II. Finds of two thin-butted axe fragments do not conflict with this dating. Despite the many aspects of source criticism to be considered, the distribution of the finds is interpreted as being largely undisturbed. The greater share of the objects were found in the southern part of the wetland. Maj-Lis Nilsson and Lena Nilsson argue in their article about the fen (2003) that the place should be interpreted as a votive site since specific categories of find occur only within a limited area. The assumption that the objects may be viewed as deliberately deposited offerings is corroborated by the that fact that the combination of human bones and pottery occurs frequently at Neolithic votive sites in wetlands (Becker 1947; Karsten

1994; Koch 1998). Flint and animal bones also figure in Neolithic votive contexts, and may have been part of the same context, but they could also have been deposited in an earlier or a later phase, as they have a wider distribution in wetland and may represent remains of votive acts of a different character, or they could be discarded material from a dwelling site. As regards the manner of deposition, it cannot be ascertained whether it was single or multiple objects that were deposited on one occasion. The archaeobotanical analyses have enabled a reconstruction of the environment, which corroborates the theory that the spring was used as a votive site. Both the striking topography and the occurrence of water have always been important in ritual contexts. The analyses present a picture of a complex and dramatic environment, where a spring with reddish water trickles through the ravine, over peat and areas of yellowish-white calcareous tufa, to form small pools in the deeper places (Nilsson & Nilsson 2003).

The absence of wooden structures at Saxtorp may be a sign that they were not needed. The spring was fairly accessible anyway, since the water mostly did not form any deep water mirrors. People could go out into the fen without any man-made structures; perhaps accumulations of stone prevented people from sinking into the fen. If the material had consisted of refuse from the settlement site, it would presumably have been dumped as close to the dwelling as possible, that is, in the northern part of the layer, but the majority of the finds were discovered within a limited area in the southern part. This was where all the objects of rock, wood, and bone were found, and virtually all the potsherds and human bones, and the greater share of the flint and animal bones. The house adjacent to the wetland can be interpreted on the basis of its design and the find material as a contemporary dwelling (fig. 23). [14]C datings from both the terrestrial environment and the wetland, and similarities in the finds, suggest that the remains are contemporaneous and that the area was used for at most 350 years in the latter part

162

of the Early Neolithic. The settlement was probably a single farm for one household, and the interpretation is that the people living on the site used the spring as a votive site (Nilsson & Nilsson 2003).

## Society

The start of the Neolithic saw the crystallization and formation of a number of ideas, social strategies, and networks whose roots can be sought in the Late Mesolithic. During this period the identity of the individual and the group was attached to the settlement. The prevailing structural principles reinforced the great symbolic significance of the settlement which was reproduced through people's action, and the houses, the graves, and the pits can be seen as parts of this process and the ritual of manifesting the vital role of the settlements. Later, in the course of the Early Neolithic, people's perception of places and landscape underwent a change. With increasingly permanent settlement, the complexity of social relations increased, leading to a tenser relationship between individuals and the rest of the community. These social relations were established in rituals associated with the ancestor cult, which also marked the significance of the place. Awareness of the growing social coercion meant that social control became more vulnerable. Some groups, mostly the younger people, therefore moved to settle in new areas. This meant that the landscape was used in a different way. Changes at places or monuments can be related to changes in the underlying structures of the population.

**Landscape spaces** The different categories of places (fig. 82) should be regarded as parts of a whole which were closely interlinked in the Neolithic person's world-view. In the social landscape it is reasonable to imagine that people's identity was closely connected to the house and the dwelling site. Beyond this there were places visited at special times for special purposes (Cooney & Grogan 1999). A spatial analysis of the distribution of large and small settlements, grave mon-

uments, and votive sites allows some observations to be made. It is striking how well the distribution of main settlements and megalithic tombs coincides. All main settlements, with the exception of Saxtorp 26, are at a distance of between 500 and 1,500 metres from the monuments. In contrast, there is no contemporary settlement, whether large or small, that is located right beside the grave monuments. According to the register of antiquities there were Stone Age dwelling sites adjacent to Gillhög, Stora Harrie 8, and Södervidinge 3. The surface finds at Gillhög, however, can be dated to MNA III–V and those at Stora Harrie to EN I, while the material at Södervidinge cannot be dated any more exactly than to the Stone Age. The finds at these megalithic tombs should perhaps be primarily associated with activities connected with various mortuary rituals. This hypothesis is corroborated by the excavations hitherto conducted beside megalithic tombs. The distribution of votive sites in the landscape is not as clearly connected to the settlements or the graves. Even though the areas with the greatest concentration of dwelling sites and graves also contain most votive sites, these occur both in the immediate vicinity of settlements and, in certain cases, several kilometres from the nearest known contemporary dwelling site or burial place. If one studies the spatial distribution of all known places, that is, even the smaller and presumably temporary activity sites, it is difficult to discern specific settlement concentrations. It is natural if the temporary sites have a wide distribution, since they may in many cases be overnight camps used when moving in the landscape. If the analysis is confined to the probable main settlements, megalithic tombs, and votive sites, on the other hand, different settlement concentrations associated with different spatial contexts can be distinguished. These "landscape spaces" can be identified by studying the chronological and chorological distribution of settlement together with the character of the landscape. It may be reasonable to assume that it is within a landscape space that a society consisting of one or more kin groups maintained its annual activities.

Judging by the evidence of dwelling sites, graves, and votive sites, the first inland area in the valley landscape to be permanently settled during the Early Neolithic seems to have been the Välabäcken valley (fig. 83). It is no exaggeration to claim that this valley landscape constituted a geographically well-demarcated area. At Särslöv the Välabäcken, flowing from the north, takes a westward turn and meanders just over three kilometres through the valley until it then joins the Saxån. There is a distinct elevation here on either

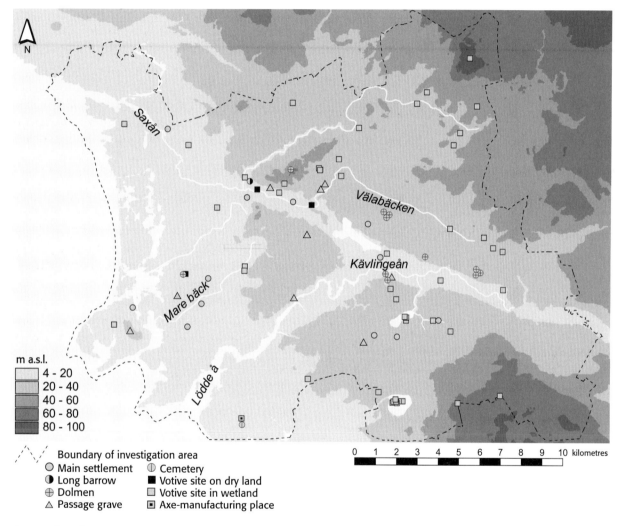

m a.s.l.

4 - 20
20 - 40
40 - 60
60 - 80
80 - 100

Boundary of investigation area
○ Main settlement    ① Cemetery
◐ Long barrow    ■ Votive site on dry land
⊕ Dolmen    ☐ Votive site in wetland
△ Passage grave    ▣ Axe-manufacturing place

0  1  2  3  4  5  6  7  8  9  10 kilometres

Fig. 82. Main settlements, graves, axe-manufacturing places, and votive sites in EN II–MNA II.

side of the Välabäcken. North of the river are the hills called Dagstorp Backar and to the south are Karaby Backar. The former wetland area in the valley at Dös-jebro is beside the Välabäcken where it turns to the west. The topographical conditions may be said to have pressed settlement into the confined space of the river valley. This means a heightened sense of being in an enclosed space between the two groups of hills and the wetland. Several dwelling sites, megalithic tombs, and votive sites are concentrated here, on sandy spots

along the river. The character of the valley, together with the composition of the settlement, thus suggests a socially constructed landscape space with a physical and mental extent and boundaries. A large settlement was established at Dagstorp already in EN I, when several households seem to have existed at the same time. This place was probably used, at least in periods, throughout the Early Neolithic and subsequently. During the early Middle Neolithic we see once again a concentration of settlement in this place. Together

164

with Västra Karaby 7, these two settlements may be regarded as main settlements. They are just over two kilometres apart. Västra Karaby 7 seems to have been established in EN II but continued into the early Middle Neolithic. The Dagstorp site was probably the larger of the two, with several cooperating farm units. It may actually be the case that this place is the only main settlement in the valley, and that it is here that the household units were assembled. At Västra Karaby there are no traces of house remains, but there were extensive finds, and the lack of buildings may be due to the excavation techniques. It is therefore difficult to assess the place. It is reasonable to assume that the four trapezoidal houses at Dagstorp represent four separate and perhaps contemporary production or household units. A factor suggesting that they are contemporary is that the houses do not overlayer each other but lie side by side (fig. 24a). Their virtually identical shape also hints that they were built at the same time. The similarity in design of the houses could also symbolize the equal position of the households; in other words, none of the household units ranked higher than any of the others. The settlement is centrally located within the "enclosed space" formed here by the Välabäcken valley. Several places where only a small amount of finds are documented lie higher up on Karaby Backar and along the river, both east and west of the Dagstorp settlement. Their function and meaning cannot be determined on the basis of the meagre finds and the lack of osteological material. They were most likely places which were visited on a temporary basis in connection with cultivation, animal husbandry, or food gathering. That the valley confirmed its importance at an early stage is noticed in the occurrence of a long barrow and a long dolmen. The custom of burying the dead on the dwelling site seems to have ceased at the end of the Early Neolithic. At least, there are no traces of proper burials on the sites. This ritual now seems to have largely been moved to special places in the landscape – to the big grave monuments. In the Välabäcken valley it is clear that the central settle-

ment was located on the river down in the valley while the grave monuments were placed on the plateau of southern slopes of the Dagstorp hills. This location of the graves, chiefly on the south side of the hills, probably made it possible for the inhabitants of Dagstorp to see the monuments every day, at least if the areas around the graves were cleared. The megalithic monuments are three passage graves (Dagstorp 2 and Södervidinge 3 and 11), one long dolmen (Dagstorp 23), and one long barrow (Dagstorp 12). In spatial and chronological terms the long barrow and possibly the long dolmen could be associated with Västra Karaby 7 while the passage graves belonged to the Dagstorp site. The placing of the long dolmen on a north-west slope down towards the Saxån indicates that this monument was perhaps built to face settlements along the Saxån which have not yet been discovered. Several votive deposits have been registered beside the bogs at Dagstorp Backar. In all cases these are separated from the settlements.

West of the Välabäcken valley, along the Saxån, there are separate sites virtually all the way out to the coast. A small concentration can be noted around the main settlement at Saxtorp 23. The terrain here is rather flat but is interrupted by the Kvärlövsbäcken where it flows into the Saxån. The area is distinctive in that there are no megalithic tombs and no archival data about any removed graves. Votive sites are documented, however, and one is located right beside the Saxtorp site.

During the Early Neolithic the expansion of settlement continued eastwards, along the rivers. Around the Kävlingeån as far as its tributary the Bråån, and to the south along the tributary from Stångby Mosse, there is a concentration of settlements, votive sites, and megalithic tombs (fig. 84). The terrain is gently undulating but is cut through the centre by the valleys of the Kävlingeån and Stångby Å. Along the northern part of the Stångby Å the steep valley is a striking feature of the landscape. In prehistoric times there was a continuous area of fen along the river, from today's

Västra Hoby to Lackalänga, around which settlement was concentrated. The area of this settlement concentration is bigger and not as clearly demarcated by the physical geography as the Välabäcken valley, although the settlement density decreases to the north-east by the Välabäcken and to the south-east at Stångby, where the land rises. In the north-west the wetland in the Dösjebro valley forms a natural boundary. By adopting a central position in the area today, at Stångby Mosse, one gets a good general view of the character of the district. The "outer limits" may be said to correspond to the location of the churches which can be seen from here on their heights, Kävlinge to the north-west, Stora Harrie to the north, Lilla Harrie to the north-east, Stångby to the south-east, and Lackalänga to the south-west. It seems as if the hilly area around the Kävlingeån and Stångby Mosse constituted a landscape space with a mental boundary coinciding with what could be visually surveyed. Unlike the "enclosed space" in the Välabäcken valley, the area is a more open landscape space. Nor do the different household units in the area seem to be concentrated in a single settlement like the one at Dagstorp. Settlement here seems to have consisted of several "small spaces", that is, single farms with surrounding activity sites and close to one or more megalithic tombs. Three of the excavated settlements, which can be assumed on good grounds to have been of permanent character (Stora Harrie 38, Stora Harrie 35, and Lackalänga 35), seem to have been established in EN II but the material also indicates, at least at Stora Harrie 38 and Lackalänga 35, that the settlement continued during MNA I. Two passage graves (Lackalänga and Västra Hoby) and seven round or long dolmens (Västra Hoby, Lilla Harrie, and Stora Harrie) are located in this part of the region. All three settlements are at a distance of about a kilometre from the nearest megalithic tomb. The megalithic tombs are at slightly higher locations that the settlements, and in all cases it must have been possible to see the graves from the settlement. It would thus be perfectly reasonable to link Stora Harrie 38 to

the group of graves at Stora Harrie 7, 8 and 9; Stora Harrie 35 to the megalithic tombs in Västra Hoby; and Lackalänga 35 to the passage grave in the same parish. Several votive sites are registered in this area. As in the Välabäcken valley, these are grouped around, but nevertheless separate from, the settlements.

The south-west settlement group is on the Barsebäck foreland and along the Mare Bäck (fig. 85). The area is topographically demarcated to the south-east by the bay formed by the estuary of the Lödde Å, to the west by the Öresund, and to the north-west by wetland areas at Hofterup. To the north-east the settlement extends to the bog of Karaby Mosse. The terrain is flat, interrupted only by the distinct ridge on which the Gillhög passage grave is located. Apart from Gillhög, the megalithic tombs of Storegård and Hofterup are also located in the area. Within this area it is possible to distinguish smaller spaces. In the Neolithic the foreland at Barsebäck was a peninsula connected to the mainland by a narrow isthmus. Within this area there are several coastal dwelling sites and a main settlement (Barsebäck 48) just under a kilometre north-east of Gillhög. Two main settlements close to Storegård (Löddeköpinge 13 and Löddeköpinge 40) can be dated to the early Middle Neolithic by means of the pottery and [14]C analyses. Near the Hofterup dolmen, less than a kilometre to the east, there is likewise a presumed main settlement (Västra Karaby 44). The place has not been excavated, but the survey of ancient monuments registered a copious amount of flint. One or two main settlements seem to be associated with a megalithic tomb each. The organization of the excavated sites indicates that settlement here consisted of isolated farms (fig. 27). As in the other areas, the settlements are placed at such a distance and level that it was evidently possible to see the monuments from the habitation area. Unlike the northern and eastern parts of the investigation area, where several votive sites have been registered, only one votive site in a wetland environment is known in this south-west part of the investigation area.

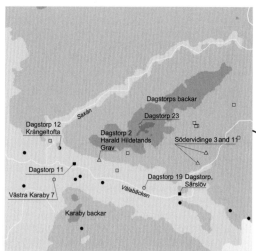

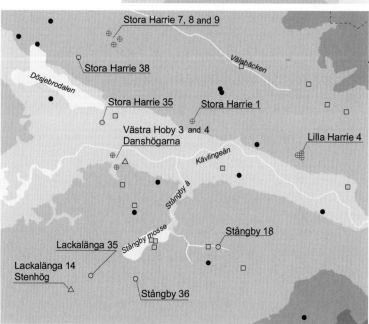

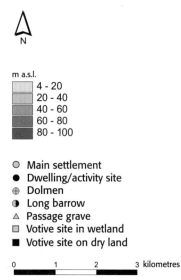

m a.s.l.

4 - 20
20 - 40
40 - 60
60 - 80
80 - 100

○  Main settlement
●  Dwelling/activity site
⊕  Dolmen
◑  Long barrow
△  Passage grave
▢  Votive site in wetland
■  Votive site on dry land

0        1        2        3 kilometres

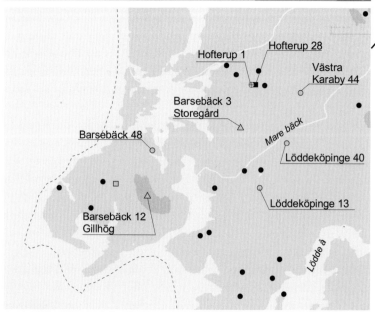

Fig. 83. Settlement in the Välabäcken valley in EN II–MNA II.
Fig. 84. Settlement on the Kävlingeån and at Stångby Mosse in EN II–MNA II.
Fig. 85. Settlement by the Lödde Å and Mare Bäck in EN II–MNA II.

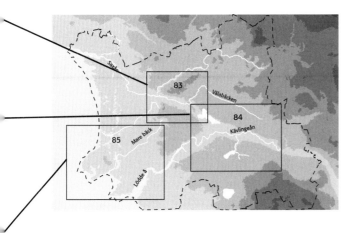

Datings of the dwelling sites, votive deposits of thin-butted flint axes of types I–IV, megalithic tombs, and ceramic deposits beside these, suggest that it was in the northern and eastern parts of the investigation area that the bigger settlement districts were first established at the end of the Early Neolithic. This tendency is noticeable already in EN I when the first big inland settlement was founded at Dagstorp. Unlike the open landscape that existed in the initial phase of the Early Neolithic, however, in the later part of the period there was more permanent localization in special landscape spaces. The triad constituted by the dwelling sites, megalithic tombs, and votive sites reflects a society that established more permanent settlement in special districts. The spatial distribution of settlements, graves, and votive sites suggests that there may have been three or four different districts or landscape spaces in the valley in the early part of the Middle Neolithic. However, differences between different areas are noticeable in the structure of the dwelling sites. The central settlement site at Dagstorp in the Välabäcken valley consisting of several household units has no counterpart in the other areas where the isolated farm seems to have been the prevailing form of settlement. These latter landscape spaces also seem to have been divisible into small spaces consisting of one or a few households around one of the megalithic tombs or groups of graves.

**Social organization**   The size of the houses in the investigation area indicates, as we have seen, that they served as a home for a household or extended family. The house should be seen as a cultural construction, with house forms illustrating tradition and social organization (Parker-Pearson & Richards 1994:7). Ethnographical studies have shown that a society and its values are reflected in the house and the dwelling site, with the house as an idea comprising food, security, social belonging, heat, and rest, as well as the family, family production, kin continuity, and kinship ties (Tilley 1999b). In stratified societies houses often function as a marker to distinguish élite groups from the rest of the population. Larger, more richly decorated houses manifest prosperity, power, and status (Waterson 1995). In the existing house evidence from the period EN II–MNA II in the investigation area, however, it is not possible to detect social differences between households. Both the houses at the Dagstorp settlement and the various isolated farms display structural similarities and seem in large measure to have been divided in a similar way. I would interpret the slightly smaller buildings at Dagstorp not as dwelling houses but as workshops or stores. In these buildings there is a greater quantity of pottery and flint debitage than in the surrounding areas, which would suggest some form of tool production.

The division of the trapezoidal buildings into two sections presupposes a deliberate internal spatial organization of the house. There was probably a functional and symbolic difference between the larger central dwelling section and the smaller peripheral part. In the northern part of the house, in the smaller room, pits have been documented. This part was probably used as a store, but the composition of deposits also indicates that there may be a more symbolic element. The fact that an activity has an economic function need not mean that it could not simultaneously have a ritual or symbolic character. Even if the small room in the houses functioned as a store, this does not rule out the possibility that we can detect traces of actions tell-ing us about the underlying ideas the people had about the house and the place. The finds in the pits, flint debitage/tools, potsherds, burnt clay, and occasional bones, resemble the composition in the pits at settlements from EN I.

The discussion above of dwelling site pits in the opening phase of the Early Neolithic is therefore relevant for this period as well. Deposits in pits are more frequent in the Early Neolithic and the early Middle Neolithic (Karsten 1994:162). I believe that the placing of waste in small pits on the dwelling site, just like all human activity, was governed by structured, deep-rooted cultural norms (cf. Chapman 2000). In this phase of the Neolithic too, it is clear that waste was in large measure allowed to lie on the dwelling site. As a by-product of the establishment of order, it became a symbol of the Neolithic way of life and had its given place on the site. Some of the "dirt" was buried in pits but it is still just a small portion of the settlement's total waste. This reinforces the hypothesis that only a representative selection of the waste was deposited in pits. Deposits of fragmented objects in the pits were deliberate, repetitive actions, that is, rituals which manifested the everyday activities and reinforced the relationship to the place. The ritual is an action that exemplified the ordinary and everyday. This means that ritual cannot be lightly placed in a pigeonhole separate from other activities, and neither the location nor the content need express anything "special". It is important to observe that even the treatment of waste follows cultural norms and is therefore an action that reproduces the prevailing structural principles. Several of the pits on the settlements, in or beside the houses, consist of material that can be designated as waste, but which also represents a cross-section of everyday activities. What the things had in common was that they were part of a daily process intended to transform natural products from the landscape into food, clothes, and building materials, and the objects are products of precisely this process of transformation. The objects produced and used in different social activities are

identified with special ideas through ritual. These are objects employed in agriculture, tool manufacture, cooking, etc. They were not made specifically to be part of rituals but to be used in a series of mundane tasks. The majority of the objects in the pits are fragmented and used, and may be regarded as "dead". By "burying" the objects, people strengthened the link between everyday and ritual activities and thereby also confirmed their own relation to the place (cf. Hill 1995:96ff; Chapman 2000).

There is a tendency for find-rich pits in EN II–MNA II to be more clearly linked to the dwelling houses than they were in the initial phase of the Early Neolithic. That houses function as political and ritual units as well as household units has been noted by several ethnographical studies (Carsten & Hugh-Jones 1995). The ancestors are often present, literally in the form of skeletal parts or through supernaturally charged heirlooms kept in the house (Waterson 1995). In the same way as EN I pits manifested the everyday activities at the settlement and reinforced the community between the households, the pits in this case may also have functioned as a marker of the individual household's work. The similar design of the houses suggests a more formalized site community in which it may have been important to assert the individual household, despite the seeming equality.

The equal relationship between households expressed by the houses did not mean the absence of relations of dominance between different groups within the society. There are other indications in the archaeological record of an unequal power structure. At the end of the Early Neolithic and the start of the Middle Neolithic, just as in EN I, society was probably organized on the basis of kinship. The power structures that can be traced back at least to the Late Mesolithic were not broken up when new lands were occupied; they were instead concealed or toned down, possibly in a phase when the new settlements were still not fully established in the interior. My study has shown that each landscape space was built up of several households or families which were probably related to each other through kinship ties. In some cases one or perhaps more kin groups were assembled at a settlement, as at Dagstorp, where several families probably lived on the same site. In other circumstances only one family lived on each site and the kin group was scattered in several settlements. The construction of grave monuments and the activities around these testify, as we shall see, to the existence of relations of dominance. An élite, probably consisting of the elders of the community, acquired control of spiritual and ritual knowledge.

168

An attempt was made above to link the bigger settlements to specific megalithic tombs. It is only a model, but it shows at least that the grave monuments had a spatial relationship to cultivation and to the dwelling sites as different parts of an organized landscape, which was probably established with reference both to economic strategies and to social and spiritual traditions. It is likely that the monuments had different functions such as burial places, ritual sites, and symbols of power and memory. It is therefore not feasible to regard the grave monuments as uniform phenomena. The concept of mortuary practice may be said to include both the external and the internal design of the grave, the burial method, the grave goods, and traces of funeral rituals (Gräslund 1991:84). The grave should be seen as a structure of ideas in which the different structural details, both external and internal, can be understood as parts of a whole reflecting the spiritual and social conceptions of Neolithic people. The significance of the megalithic tombs probably varied in time and place. Each region has its specific historical conditions in which the graves acquire their role. There may have been common traditions and rituals over wide areas, but these may have been performed and expressed differently in different regions. What is interesting in the following discussion is the significance of the grave monuments when they were erected late in the Early Neolithic and at the start of the Middle Neolithic in the valley landscape of western Skåne.

The construction of the monuments suggests a new view of the landscape. It is an activity which involved remodelling the landscape – moving boulders, clearing forest, and levelling surfaces. Unlike the Early Neolithic flat-earth graves, the megalithic tombs were visible in the landscape in a new way. The permanence of the monuments is a reminder that Neolithic people were not just engaged in the past but also in the future. The aim of defining places with monuments may have been primarily to create a sense of permanence between the society and the landscape – a way of socializing the landscape. If we want to understand the relationship between the megalithic tombs and the landscape it is important also to consider the contemporary settlement. In the course of the Early Neolithic partly new settlement districts were established in the interior, probably as a consequence of internal tensions in the society but perhaps also due to population growth. In connection with the colonization of the interior, the time was also right to adopt the western European tradition of building megalithic tombs. The really interesting thing from the point of view of the landscape is the visibility of the monuments. They probably functioned vis-à-vis two different categories of population and with two different messages. They were a symbol directed against the outer world and also an internal identity symbol for the society within which the monuments were erected. In the gently undulating landscape of western Skåne there were no natural cliff formations. In this terrain the monuments had a manifest physical impact. Building creates a visual effect in the landscape, to and from which attention was directed. The architecture of the graves and the topography of the place interact. The placing of the monuments in the landscape determines from where and from what distance they could be observed and what could be seen from them. Control of the new land could be confirmed by the monuments, which then functioned as a social and ideological signal to passers-by. The megalithic tombs, with the exception of Annehill, were located on the rivers that probably served as communication routes in the Neolithic: the Välabäcken, Lödde Å–Kävlingeån, and Mare Bäck. Although they are rarely right beside the rivers, they could in most cases be seen from them because of their location on the slopes running down to the water or on high plateaus. The construction of the megalithic tombs can probably be associated with one aspect of what is popularly called the domestication of nature (cf. Hodder 1990; Thomas 1991; Bradley 1993; Tilley 1994). At the start of the Early Neolithic, the central settlements were linked to ancient lands established back in Mesolithic times. The relation to the landscape and to other population groups was traditionally regulated through rituals at the dwelling sites. In connection with the migration to the interior, I believe it became necessary to create new "spaces". Before this the landscape along the valleys had only seen sporadic visits and therefore had not been modelled according to ancient traditions in the way the coastal areas were. It was thus essential to domesticate the landscape through the creation of new places in important topographical locations. These places can very well have previously been reference points in the terrain, but with the construction of a monument, the landscape was reshaped and the people forged a lasting relationship to it. Creating and shaping a meaningful order in the surrounding space through new places is an attempt to make the world comprehensible and meaningful. This seems to be why some of the activities formerly associated with the dwelling site in the Late Mesolithic and Early Neolithic, such as burials and other ritual acts, were transferred to various points in the landscape in the course of the Early Neolithic. The microplaces within the settlements were moved out and became places in the landscape but with partly the same function in a larger space. The landscape spaces were like a macro settlement comprising dwelling, votive activities, and burial.

The man-made "space" was a scene of social reproduction. Control over the creation of space therefore led to power over the practice of social reproduction, that is, to the maintenance of power relations between individuals and groups. In the parts of the valley landscape which were relatively densely populated at the end of the Early Neolithic and the start of the Middle Neolithic, the megaliths were presumably not primarily to be regarded as territorial markers; they more likely regulated the social relationship within and between the different local groups. They served to define the social identity of the group and functioned as a stabilizing factor symbolizing the permanence of the social identity.

The lack of extremely monumental positions suggests that it was not the intention that the graves should be seen from far afield. They faced inwards towards the groups that built the monuments. This indicates that the monuments were perhaps chiefly intended to keep the group together instead of demonstrating power towards an outside observer. An important aspect is that the megaliths were located in more prominent places in the landscape than the settlements. From the dwelling sites in the valleys, the people were able to look up at the megalithic tombs on the slopes. Daily life proceeded at the settlements with the megalithic tombs in the background, representing the past, the ancestors, and a sense of permanence. Death is of course an individual occurrence but it is simultaneously a social occasion. Since death means that an individual is separated from the society and the collective of which he was once a part, the social order must be restored or reproduced in a changed form through funeral rituals (Huntingdon & Metcalf 1979). I have shown that, in the first part of the Early Neolithic these actions were performed beside the dwelling site itself, to which the group's identity was linked. When new lands were later colonized, it was necessary for the group to mark the existence of a larger space through the megalithic tombs and the rituals associated with them.

People's physical surroundings influenced settlement and the way in which spaces were created. Settlement patterns also show different features in different landscapes. It is only at Dagstorp, in the Välabäcken valley, that there is evidence of the existence of more than one contemporary farm unit on the same site. The "enclosed space" formed by the valley seems to have had a unifying effect in that the farms were concentrated in one place. Three to four households or extended families may have lived together on the site. There are three passage graves on the slopes of Dagstorp Backar. One possibility is that the construction of the monuments was done communally within the kin group but that each megalithic tomb originally corresponded to one household. Outside the Väla-bäcken valley, where the landscape does not form a closed space in the same way, only single farms are attested. Their position in the landscape is also such that the nearest megalithic tomb, located on a higher slope or plateau, is visible from the settlement.

Most of the excavated megalithic tombs in Skåne and Denmark have been the scene of recurrent activities of various kinds in both prehistoric and historic times. This makes it difficult to restore the original burial. Finds of bones in grave chambers, however, often show that women, men, and children are all represented (Strömberg 1971; Kaul 1992; Tilley 1996). This corroborates the idea that the graves were originally intended for the whole household and perhaps not just for the leading stratum of society, even though the actual funeral ritual was performed by some of the leaders of the kin group.

It is necessary once again to stress that the megalithic tombs are a complex and heterogeneous phenomenon. The probably gradual change of the megalithic tombs from the long barrow via long and round dolmens to the passage grave may illustrate a partly changed meaning of the monuments. In EN I, when burials were performed at dwelling sites, the rituals in connection with this were open in that the whole community took part throughout the course of events, both the passive spectators and the leaders officiating at the ritual. When at least parts of the funeral ritual were moved out to places in the landscape, to the long barrows and long/round dolmens, this was presumably still open to everyone in the community, who could participate because the remains of the ancestors were enclosed in these monuments. Their presence could then only be recreated in the memory through the visual effect of the monuments. With the construction of the passage graves a new dimension was added to the ritual through the passage leading into the chamber. The passage emphasized the difference between the outer and the inner world, between the rituals performed outside the grave and those performed in the chamber itself. This was marked by the long, narrow passage, often with a threshold (cf. Cooney 2000). It was probably only a few of the select members of the community who now had access to the inner sanctuary. Contact between the living and the ancestral spirits now no longer took place in the presence of the whole community but in concealed form, inside the grave chamber. I believe this may have been an expression of growing social control. Preservation conditions in the excavated passage graves have not been good enough to allow us to give sure answers about

the treatment of the dead. It is probable, however, that at least some of the megalithic tombs were used as primary graves. Evidence for this comes from the black, sticky soil that has been documented around the bones in several passage graves, which could be the remains of the soft parts of the body (Gräslund 1989; Kaul 1992). The treatment of the dead person's bones evidently did not cease with this, and it is rare to find the parts of a skeleton in their correct anatomical position in the chambers. This can partly be explained in terms of later burials having disturbed earlier ones. However, the bones are often in such a location that it seems likely that they were arranged according to specific rules. Excavations have also shown that it is not always complete skeletons that are found in the graves. Various parts of the skeletons were probably removed some time after the burial to be used in sacrificial rituals in other places. Perhaps the complete skeleton was not always buried. In certain cases the deceased may have been placed elsewhere first until the soft parts had decayed and the megalithic tombs were thus used as ossuaries for the deposition of the skeletal parts (cf. Tilley 1996:221ff). There are several ethnographic parallels to such a procedure (Malinowski 1922, 1929; Weiner 1976; Munn 1986). It seems clear, however, that special rites were performed around the ancestors' bones.

Deliberate deposition of whole or fragmented objects – sacrifices – occurred, as we have seen, both at settlements and burial places and in wetlands outside these two contexts. Above all we see a noticeable increase in the frequency of deposition in the wetlands during this part of the Neolithic. The later part of the Early Neolithic is thus characterized by the growing frequency of votive activities outside settlement contexts compared with the early part of the period. Although some of the votive sites were still used on only one occasion, it seems as if we now also see a tendency towards the establishment of permanent votive sites. The tradition from the start of the Early Neolithic of single deposits on one occasion can be interpreted as offerings of a purely private character performed by individuals or small groups. The permanent votive sites, on the other hand, to which people returned several times, may have been used for more collective sacrificial activities. It is still the flint axe that is the most commonly deposited object, although the excavations at Saxtorp show that the composition of votive finds is much more complex than this. In certain cases it seems as if people preferred to visit wetlands located far from the settlement, where they deposited their offerings in private, while in other cases it is obvious that the bog beside the dwelling site was used for sacrificial activity. I would regard the objects deposited in wetlands beside the dwelling place as "dwelling site offerings", to be treated as a separately category from the deposits in places removed from the dwelling site.

We can thus distinguish two different contexts of wetland offering: deposits in wetlands right beside the settlement and offerings away from the settlement of both private and collective character. Although the representativeness of votive offerings must be treated with great caution, since only a few votive sites have been excavated, there is nevertheless a tendency for whole axes to dominate in the votive finds not linked to settlements, whereas votive deposits on or near dwelling sites consist of more varied and fragmented material which seems to be a reflection of the everyday tasks. If this difference is real it is an indication that different value or significance was ascribed to the different offerings associated with different contexts.

The excavations showed that the votive fen in Saxtorp can be associated on good grounds with the adjacent settlement (Nilsson & Nilsson 2003). No whole axes or pots were found here, but a large quantity of flint flakes and tools such as scrapers, awls, and knives, potsherds, and bones of animals and humans. At first sight, the composition of the finds resembles ordinary dwelling site material. The proportion of human bones and the fact that the objects seem to have been deliberately placed in a limited part of the fen nevertheless suggests a deposit with a particular purpose – a ritual act. The objects deposited in the wetland is comparable in certain respects with the finds documented in Early Neolithic votive pits at settlements in that they seem to represent everyday life, being a cross-section of some of the basic activities in people's social life, such as eating, cooking, drinking, and lighting fires. I believe that the "dwelling site offerings" deposited in the adjacent wetland probably had partly the same purpose as the Early Neolithic votive pits. The social community was strengthened by a manifestation of everyday tasks. The votive deposits

should also be seen as a way to transform and reinforce the bonds with the place. A locale acquired meaning and became a place by means of various rituals which transformed it. Just as two persons establish a form of alliance by breaking and sharing a suitable object, the relationship to a place is confirmed and strengthened by the deposition of parts of an object (cf. Chapman 2000). The occurrence of human bones in the votive fen at Saxtorp is a confirmation that the burial ritual was not just performed at the megalithic tombs. It has long been a well-known fact that scattered human bones occur at places of differing character, such as dwelling site features or occupation layers, wetlands, and places of assembly (Svensson 1993; Kaul 1992; Koch 1998). By all appearances, it was considered important to place parts of the dead in other places than the grave. One explanation for this may proceed from the discussion above about the localization of the graves adjacent to dwelling sites in EN I. The idea that objects were animated and, just like the human body, could be followed from birth to death – production (birth), consumption (life), destruction (death), and deposition (burial) – no doubt prevailed in the later part of the Early Neolithic and the Middle Neolithic as well. People and objects may be perceived as two distinct units, yet still closely related to each other. It is therefore not especially strange to consider the ritual for depositing the human body as a parallel to the way in which artefacts were treated (cf. Wagner 1975; Chapman 2000). The fact that different parts of the ancestors were used in rituals in connection with the different places of the group signalled that the different categories – the settlements, the votive bogs, the graves – constituted separate parts of a societal whole. The relocation of the ancestors' bones confirmed the significance and role of the places in the network of activities in which the group was involved. This is possibly why we see that parts of the skeleton seem to have been removed from the megalithic tombs some time after the burial. Only two more votive deposits in wetland (Västra Hoby 18 and Norrvidinge 34) are adjacent to probable contemporary settlements (fig. 78). However, these sites have not been excavated, so it is not possible to paint a clear picture of their link with the settlements.

The vast majority of wetlands with votive finds, however, are rarely located adjacent to the nearest known contemporary settlement. The distance varies from a couple of hundred metres to several kilometres. Evidently the location of the settlements in these cases was crucial not for where the deposits were made; it is instead the place itself, its scenery and special environment that offered the optimal votive setting. There is a great similarity between different peoples in different parts of the world as regards sacred places. They are constantly associated with what we in the West regard as special natural formations such as cliffs, wetlands, or watercourses (Carmichael et al. 1998). There are several examples of groups who view wetlands as holy places. The Sto:lo Indians in south-west Canada have several different types of sanctified places, chiefly lakes or wetlands, which are believed to be inhabited by supernatural forces. They are often rather large areas with an uneven distribution in the landscape (Mohs 1998). The situation in Canada, or among other small-scale societies, of course cannot be directly transferred to the Neolithic in western Skåne. However, it gives an indication of how different places in the landscape may have been perceived. The fact that it is the place itself that was important and not the relation to the dwelling site also explains the varying distance to the settlements. Slightly more than half of the votive deposits are single finds. Despite the aspects of source criticism mentioned above, there is a hint here that offerings of a private character were still of great significance. Also, it is often rather small wetlands that were used for offerings, which might not have been suitable for large crowds of people. Individuals or small groups, such as a household or a work group, may have gone to a sacred place before some special event in order to appease higher powers.

In cases when it can be documented that two or more whole axes were deposited at the same time, one can envisage that the offering was performed by a larger group, perhaps a kin group. It seems improbable that a single individual would have been able to spare and deposit several axes for private purposes. One hypothesis is that some of the accumulated votive sites may have functioned during a period in the second half of the Early Neolithic as meeting places in connection with collective rites. It is probable too that the first votive finds of copper objects are from the Early Neolithic. From Västra Karaby there is a find of a cop-

per dagger dated to late in the Early Neolithic, but unfortunately the exact find spot is not stated (Oldeberg 1974; Magnusson Staaf 1996). Lutz Klassen, in his work on early copper in Scandinavia (2000), says that it may have been extracted in central Sweden as early as the Early Neolithic. The technological know-how, however, must have come from continental Europe, which is evidence of the long-distance contacts established during this period.

It is interesting that deposits in wetlands seem to cease or at least decrease at the transition to the Middle Neolithic. All of the flint axes found in the wetlands whose type can be determined are thin-butted axes of types I–IV, which according to Nielsen can be dated to EN II (Nielsen, P. O. 1977). The concentration of votive deposits in the northern and eastern part of the valley landscape, where the earliest settlements and megalithic tombs are probably found, reinforces this hypothesis. The decline in the use of bogs as votive sites coincides in time with the increasing frequency of ceramic deposits outside megalithic tombs. A clear redistribution and rearrangement of the sacrificial ritual is thus noticeable at the transition to the Middle Neolithic. Deposits chiefly of axes in wetlands were replaced by deposits above all of pottery but later also axes outside megalithic tombs.

The polished axe that was used in several different contexts was probably of great practical and symbolic significance during the Neolithic. The axe was important for clearing areas for settlement and cultivation, and it was used for working wood for building houses and making fences, canoes, wooden bowls, etc. The axe was probably also an important object in exchange relations between different groups. The raw material at least for the axes had to be obtained from areas with a better supply of flint. Just as in the initial phase of the Early Neolithic, however, axe production cannot be linked to any of the excavated settlements. Instead, knapping seems to have been done in special places, sometimes presumably right beside the sources of the raw material, such as the flint mines in Ängdala outside Malmö. However, there is no sure evidence of any production of thin-butted axes at Ängdala. Moreover, the size of nodules found from the mines in Malmö shows that they probably would not have been big enough to function as raw material for thin-butted axes (Rudebeck 1994, 1998; Jansson 1999). Perhaps nodules were brought from the other side of the Öresund, in Denmark.

On the axe-manufacturing site at Flädie, production seems to have been geared to thin-butted flint axes (Pihl & Runcis 2001). The flakes from this place show that the axe was given its final shape here, while the rough knapping into a quadrilateral plank presumably was done at the source of the raw material. The fact that special places were chosen for axe manufacture testifies to the significance of the axe for many different activities in people's lives. The production of an axe could even be compared to important stages in a person's life (see the discussion above), such as birth, puberty, or marriage. In many cultures these events, when an individual is transferred from one state of physical development to another, are accompanied by a rite of passage (Gennep 1960). It was therefore necessary that axe manufacture, perhaps like some rites of passage, was performed away from the settlement in order to avoid "impurity" (cf. Strassburg 2000:412). People probably chose places which already had a special meaning, and axe production could further emphasize the significance of a site. The axe-manufacturing site in Flädie, which is located close to a children's cemetery, reinforces this hypothesis. An interesting factor is of course the almost 200 amber beads deposited as grave goods, many of them in the shape of axes. The symbolic meaning of the axe is also illustrated by the long and carefully shaped examples which are often found deposited in votive bogs. Often the long axes are better made than the shorter ones (Olausson 1983, 1997:271). The axe may thus be said to link production, consumption, exchange of gifts, and ritual. They tied different spheres of human activity together and were a medium for alliances and exchange relations between different groups (cf.

Tilley 1996:101ff). In the same way, pottery was important for several different activities such as cooking, storage, and in ritual contexts. The varying shapes and decoration of the vessels, however, emphasized the differences between different groups in a way that the axe did not. In her study of the pottery from megalithic tombs in western Skåne, Hårdh thinks that the relatively free choice of patterns on the pottery, despite a certain basic norm, suggests that ceramic production was not centralized but local (Hårdh 1986, 1990b). The variation between the different graves in the way decorative patterns are combined on the pottery could be a reflection and manifestation of group affiliation.

I think that there are various signs that social control increased at the transition to the Middle Neolithic. As the settlement areas were established in the interior, there was a greater need for institutionalized rituals to consolidate the prevailing order. The leading stratum of society therefore marked its position by fully adopting the leadership of these rituals. The passage graves are an indication of this. Only a few leading individuals had access to the chamber through the passage. The fact that offerings and rituals were performed at specific places, at the monuments, is further evidence of the need for control. It is perhaps at this point in time that the megalithic tombs also acquired a major role as meeting places. The pottery, which seems to mark group affiliation more clearly than the axes, became more important in votive deposits. There are several, admittedly diffuse, traces of activities around the monuments. Although the obscure character of the remains makes it difficult to understand what happened on the sites, it is a clear indication of their function as meeting places for various ritual activities. The U-shaped trench at Dagstorp can probably be interpreted as having had the same meaning as the Danish cultic houses. The pottery in these is of the same type (e.g. pedestalled bowls and clay ladles) as the ceramic deposits at the entrance to the passage graves. It is reasonable to interpret them as small ritual temples (Andersen 2000). The stone packings around several of the megalithic tombs in the excavation area (Hofterup, Annehill, and Dagstorp) can probably also be associated with votive rituals.

On the basis of the design of the chamber in the passage graves, they have sometimes been divided into different phases. The oval shape is believed to be older than the rectangular (Strömberg 1971; Hårdh 1990a). In cases where it has been possible to reconstruct the chamber, it has been found that Gillhög, Storegård, and Hög have a rectangular chamber while Västra Hoby, Södervidinge, and Lackalänga have oval chambers. The theory may agree with the state of affairs in the area since the passage graves in the north-east are assumed to have been erected earlier than those in the south-west. The centrally placed double passage grave at Annehill is distinctive in several ways. It has one rectangular chamber while the other one, which is partly destroyed, seems to have been rounded. Annehill is also the only megalithic tomb that was placed over a kilometre from the nearest river. There are no contemporary settlements in the immediate vicinity as there are around the other megalithic tombs. Perhaps different societies from the different landscape spaces met here and manifested their social affinity, expressed in the passage grave. In Skåne the tradition of building Sarup enclosures does not seem to have been established in this period. The place most frequently discussed is Stävie on the Kävlingeån in western Skåne (Larsson, L. 1982). Stävie includes a north–south ditch system which, like the Danish sites, demarcated a topographically distinct tongue of land beside the river. However, the system of ditches has been dated to MNA V. The different monuments in the separate landscape spaces may have functioned alternately as meeting places for the local groups. The big deposits of pottery at Västra Hoby and Gillhög indicate that these may have functioned periodically as local places of assembly. At large gatherings, when groups from perhaps the entire region met, Annehill may have functioned as a kind of central place. The factors speaking in favour of this are the location of the site and the design of the monument. The amount of finds is much smaller than at Västra Hoby and Gillhög. This of course may be due to preservation conditions or technical factors to do with the excavation. In addition, it is reasonable to assume that the local meeting places like Gillhög and Västra Hoby were visited much more often than any regional central place.

## Bringing under shared leadership

In the opening phase of the Early Neolithic, the settlement was a central place in the world, a node linking people both geographically in relation to the surrounding world and chronologically in a continuous relationship to the ancestors, to contemporaries, and to coming generations. Votive deposits and burials on the sites demonstrated the opposition between what was within the site and what was outside it. The second half of the Early Neolithic was a period of vigorous settlement expansion. The increasingly permanent way of life, together with a probable popula-

tion growth, increased the internal pressure in the society, and groups moved inland. In the archaeological record it is possible to follow how settlements were established from west to east along the Saxån and Välabäcken, and south from there to the Kävlingeån and Stångby Mosse, finally also colonizing the area around the Mare Bäck and Barsebäck. When permanent new settlement districts were established, it required the creation of landscape spaces; in other words, the group had to mark its social identity in the area by setting up new places, possibly at previously known topographical landmarks. It is in this context that the western European tradition of building megalithic tombs was adopted in the valley landscape and the tradition of depositing offerings in wetlands increased dramatically. In connection with the creation of the new landscape spaces, the view of the landscape was also changed. In certain respects the dwelling site may now be said to have comprised the entire landscape space in that various functions were now moved out into the surroundings. For the first time, major interventions were made outside the settlement itself and the cultivation plots. The construction of the monuments meant that large areas were cleared and that the landscape acquired a different profile. Not just the building but presumably also the clearance of the vegetation meant that special bonds to the place were forged and much of the landscape was socialized through these measures. It is clear that the different places in the landscape were parts of a complete unit – the unit that was formerly concentrated on the dwelling site. Settlements, megalithic tombs, votive and cultic sites had different meanings, but at the same time we see that the same phenomena partly recur at the different places. The primary burial of the dead presumably took place at the megalithic tombs. The occurrence of human bones both on dwelling sites and at votive sites shows that either only parts of the skeleton were buried in the megaliths, or else certain parts were taken from the passage graves to be used in rituals at other places. The burial or deposition of fragments of an ancestor at different places in the landscape space is a symbolic action and a clear signal that there was a need to mark that places belonged together, that they were parts of a whole. In the investigation area, no human bones have been identified in settlement site contexts from this phase. Studies of other areas, where human bones occur frequently in settlement contexts, suggest that this is due to the unfavourable preservation conditions for bones. The burnt bones retrieved from several of the pits are too fragmentary to allow the species to be identified.

Another indication that the places belong together is the similarity of the material composition between dwelling site pits and the deposits in several of the wetlands. Excavations of megalithic tombs in south-east Skåne have shown that hoards of flint flakes and small flint tools also occur in the grave chambers. These have been interpreted as cultic acts in connection with the construction of the grave (Strömberg 1971:320). The passage graves in the investigation area were disturbed when excavated, and no certain deposits of waste were noticed by the excavators. On the other hand, in most cases, flint flakes and potsherds were documented which could have come from votive pits of the same type as those at the settlements.

The social organization was still that of a kin society. The growing social coercion that arose in EN I in connection with the increased permanence of settlement was relieved when people moved out to colonize new districts. At the transition to the Middle Neolithic it seems as if the "new" landscape spaces had been stabilized. It was therefore necessary once again that the ritual should be institutionalized in the sense that the leading stratum in each kin group took a firmer control of the ritual. This is noticeable above all in the establishment of specific places for different rituals at the megalithic tombs. The private rituals at the scattered wetlands seem to have ceased, and instead this activity was concentrated at central meeting places at the megalithic tombs. The megalithic tomb with a passage leading into

the burial chamber illustrates how presumably only a few leading people had access to this "sacred space". The fact that pottery, which marks group affiliation more clearly than axes by virtue of the different forms of decoration, is increasingly asserted in the ritual shows that it may have been important to emphasize the identity of the group. The increased influence of the ancestors, expressed in the megalithic tombs and the treatment of the bones of the dead, probably also meant that biological kin categorizations became the prevailing form in group formations.

## Consolidation and dissolution

In the same way as a distinct change was noticeable in the organization of society at the end of the Early Neolithic, the transition to what we call MNA III may also be said to be a time of change. This makes itself felt above all in the settlement organization, with a reduction in the number of settlements and deposits in wetlands compared with the previous period. These transformations can be traced back to the start of the Middle Neolithic, when the custom of depositing objects in bogs declined in favour of votive rituals at the megalithic tombs. Although new grave monuments were no longer erected in this period, they were still used as burial chambers and "sacred places". In the material culture the thick-butted axe replaced the thin-butted one. MNA III also entailed a clear change in the ceramic tradition. Lines on the belly of the pot disappeared, while pitted and tooth-stamped decoration became very common. Vessel forms are more varied than in earlier periods; besides funnel beakers there are now open bowls of various kinds and brim beakers.

In the closing phase of the period it seems as if three different material cultures partly existed in parallel in southern Scandinavia, which complicates the picture of the archaeological remains. Alongside the Funnel Beaker culture there are now also the Pitted Ware culture and the Battle Axe culture. The Pitted Ware culture, as it is represented, for example, in north-eastern Skåne, with forms characteristic of the culture such as pointed-bottomed, pitted vessels, does not seem to occur in the investigation area. In contrast, a flint inventory influenced by the Pitted Ware culture is found in Funnel Beaker contexts and known as the Stävie group. The Battle Axe culture, as in many other places, is chiefly represented in the grave finds and seems to come after the Funnel Beaker culture, possibly with a certain overlap. The encounter between the two material cultures is best seen at the palisaded enclosure in Dösjebro.

## Settlement pattern

The period MNA III–V has a much shorter duration than EN II–MNA II (see table I), and the number of documented settlements is also much smaller (51 versus 88). We thus see a numerical reduction in settlements during the period, which could of course be explained in part by the shorter duration of the period. The fall in the number of dwelling sites should not be solely ascribed to the length of the period or a reduction in the population; it is more likely due to a concentration, with the main settlements growing in size. Votive deposits in wetlands also decline noticeably in this phase, from forty-seven known in EN II–MNA II to six in MNA III–V (fig. 86). As we have seen, this votive activity had probably already started to decline at the start of the Middle Neolithic. It is necessary to point out, however, that seven votive sites, apart from the six mentioned above, yielded the thick-butted B-axe which can be associated with either the Stävie group or the Battle Axe culture. Some of these deposits may thus possibly have been made in the late MNA.

**Settlement**  About half of the settlements are on sites that were also used in EN II–MNA II, but settlement is no longer scattered over the whole landscape; it seems as if the population was concentrated to a greater extent than before in special areas along rivers and near the coast. As in the preceding periods, people mainly chose to locate their dwelling sites on sandy soils, although some of the smaller places are on clay soils. Above all at the end of the period it seems as if the tendency to settle on the coast increases. The majority of sites with elements of the Pitted Ware flint inventory are coastal.

Most of the sites from the period have not been excavated, which makes it more difficult for us to obtain a picture of their function. Of the excavated sites, five can nevertheless be regarded on good grounds as main settlements on account of their extent and the quantity of finds (Saxtorp 3 (Tågerup), Dagstorp 19, Barsebäck 48, Stävie 17, and Norra Nöbbelöv 13) (fig. 46). It was only at Dagstorp 19 and Norra Nöbbelöv 13 (figs.

47 and 51) that houses could be documented, but these places were also the only ones where large areas were stripped around the actual settlement. The excavations at Saxtorp 3 (Tågerup) touched only the Mesolithic remains, but the surface survey showed that the Early and Middle Neolithic settlements were higher up on the plateau. Several fragments of thick-butted axes of type A show that the site was occupied in the late MNA (Althin 1954:104). At Barsebäck 48 and Stävie 17 the excavations were concentrated on the finds in the occupation layers. Some of the surface-surveyed places also contain a large quantity of knapped flint, which would indicate longer permanent settlement. In most cases, however, it is difficult to determine which period to assign most of the artefacts to. It was found that some of the sites on the Barsebäck foreland had a large number of whole and fragmentary thick-butted flint axes together with a large amount of other flint. One of these places may also have functioned as a main settlement. Stångby 18 beside Stångby Mosse, with continuity from the Early Neolithic and a large volume of flint detected by surface survey, including several fragmented thick-butted flint axes, should, in my opinion, be regarded as a main settlement.

The main settlements are all centrally located in areas with a high density of dwelling sites on sandy heights along the coast and rivers. The distribution of the settlements partly resembles the situation at the start of EN I. Unlike the wide distribution of dwelling sites in all parts of the landscape, as in EN II–MNA II, there has once again been a contraction to places on the coast or around watercourses. The main settlements are surrounded by smaller sites, in most cases not excavated, but identified by surface survey. These places do not seem to have necessarily been placed beside the rivers in the valleys; in several cases they are at higher points on sand or clay soils. The localization of the main settlements in the landscape seems in large measure also to have been influenced by where earlier generations lived. At Barsebäck 48, Saxtorp 3 (Tågerup), and Dagstorp 19 there is evidence of occu-

177

178

pation in the Early Neolithic as well, and in the case of Tågerup also in much of the Mesolithic. It is highly likely that the people knew of the earlier use of these places. At least, earlier activities should have been obvious in the waste material left behind. It is not inconceivable that the occurrence of this material gave the place a special charge which was significant for the choice of dwelling site. Consideration for the activities of the ancestors is hinted at Dagstorp 19, where it seems that people in MNA III deliberately placed their habitation activities alongside the preceding settlement. Perhaps there was uninterrupted continuity, with successive moves along the river, or perhaps there was a desire to return to places with an ancient tradition, but without making any interventions in or "disturbing" the work of past generations. At also seems as if each main settlement had a special relationship to some form of ritual place. The most common feature is the close relationship of the main settlements to a megalithic tomb, but at Norra Nöbbelöv 13 and Stångby 18 the old votive sites still seem to have functioned as meeting places. It is only at Saxtorp 3 that there is no documentation of any contemporary ritual site. This may be due to technical factors to do with the excavation, but perhaps the site in this period was in fact only a temporary camp used for activities such as hunting or animal husbandry.

The general picture in south-west Skåne and Denmark is that cattle increasingly dominated among the livestock in the course of the Middle Neolithic. Hunting is less visible in the evidence and it is therefore possible that animal husbandry acquired a significant role in the economy (Kristiansen 1988:49; Welinder 1998:98ff). Cultivation still occurs on a small scale, and analyses of grain impressions, for instance at Stävie and Karlsfält, suggest that emmer and einkorn predominated (Hjelmqvist 1982:13; 1985:63). The material from Piledal in southern Skåne, however, shows a different picture. Of the 963 grains which have been identified, naked barley is more common than hulled barley and varieties of wheat (Welinder 1998:99). Ad-

mixture of later elements on this site means that we must show some caution about the dating of this material. However, among the thousands of charred grains from the Alvastra pile dwelling, naked barley also predominates (Welinder 1998:99). The finds thus show that barley may have been more common than the impressions in pottery usually suggest.

Some of the places surrounding the permanent settlements may be the result of an economy partly based on transhumance, that is, a stationary settlement combined with the seasonal use of grazing land away from the base site. This could be an explanation for the decline in plants favoured by cultivated land which is noticeable in pollen diagrams from this period (Digerfeldt 1975). The sometimes stiff clay on which some of the smaller sites were established was hard to till but would have been fine for animal husbandry. In the Ystad area Lars Larsson has observed a concentration of settlement at the transition to the Middle Neolithic which he believes could be connected with a greater significance for animal husbandry (cf. Larsson, L. 1989, 1992a, 1998), and it is possible that the same form of production prevailed in western Skåne.

In the course of the Middle Neolithic we notice a shift of settlement towards the coast. Right at the start of the Middle Neolithic there are hints that people in the marginal areas of the Funnel Beaker culture made greater use of the marine resources along the coast, first in central Sweden and Gotland, but later also on the west coast and further south (Malmer 1969; Welinder 1971, 1976, 1978; Löfstrand 1974; Kaelas 1976; Nielsen, S. 1979; Åkerlund 1996; Edenmo et al. 1997). In the investigation area we can likewise observe a pull of settlement towards the coast at the end of the period, when the sites show the clear influence of the Pitted Ware culture on the flint material. Unfortunately, there is no organic material at the coastal sites in the investigation area, which makes it difficult to estimate the extent to which marine resources were used here. It is possible that the deterioration in climate at the end of MNA led to an increase in the stock

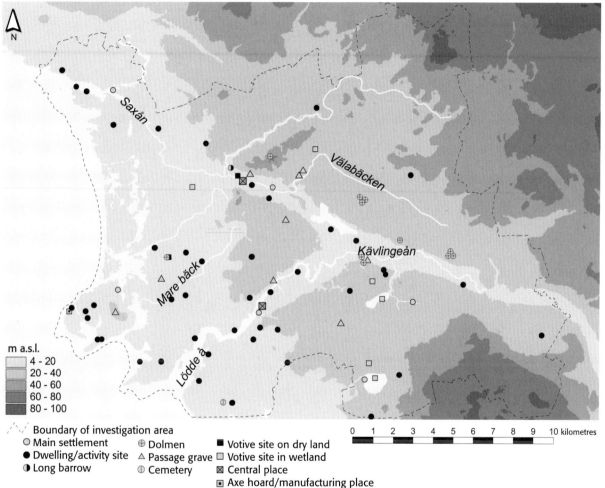

m a.s.l.

4 - 20
20 - 40
40 - 60
60 - 80
80 - 100

∿ Boundary of investigation area
○ Main settlement          ⊕ Dolmen              ■ Votive site on dry land
● Dwelling/activity site   △ Passage grave       □ Votive site in wetland
◑ Long barrow              ◐ Cemetery            ⊠ Central place
                                                 ⊡ Axe hoard/manufacturing place

0  1  2  3  4  5  6  7  8  9  10 kilometres

Fig. 86. Settlement in MNA III–V.

of seal in southern Scandinavia as well. The material from western Skåne in general shows that a mixed economy prevailed at the end of MNA, when cultivation and animal husbandry were combined with coastal fishing and inland hunting (Hjelmqvist 1982:108f; Persson 1982:114; Welinder 1998:100f; Burenhult 1999:321f).

The main settlements were evidently used more intensively during the period than earlier in the Neolithic. The finds in the occupation layer at Dagstorp 19, in relation to the size of the site, are much more numerous than in the occupation layers from other periods.

The period does not have a longer duration than other periods in MNA. The large quantity of finds in the occupation layer indicates instead that activity on the site was more intensive than in other periods. One explanation is that in MNA III more people lived on a permanent dwelling site than before. At Barsebäck 48 and Norra Nöbbelöv 13 too, the extensive finds are an indication that settlements were bigger than before. This picture can be connected to the distribution of settlements, with a greater concentration which could be the result of more people moving together to fewer but bigger dwelling sites.

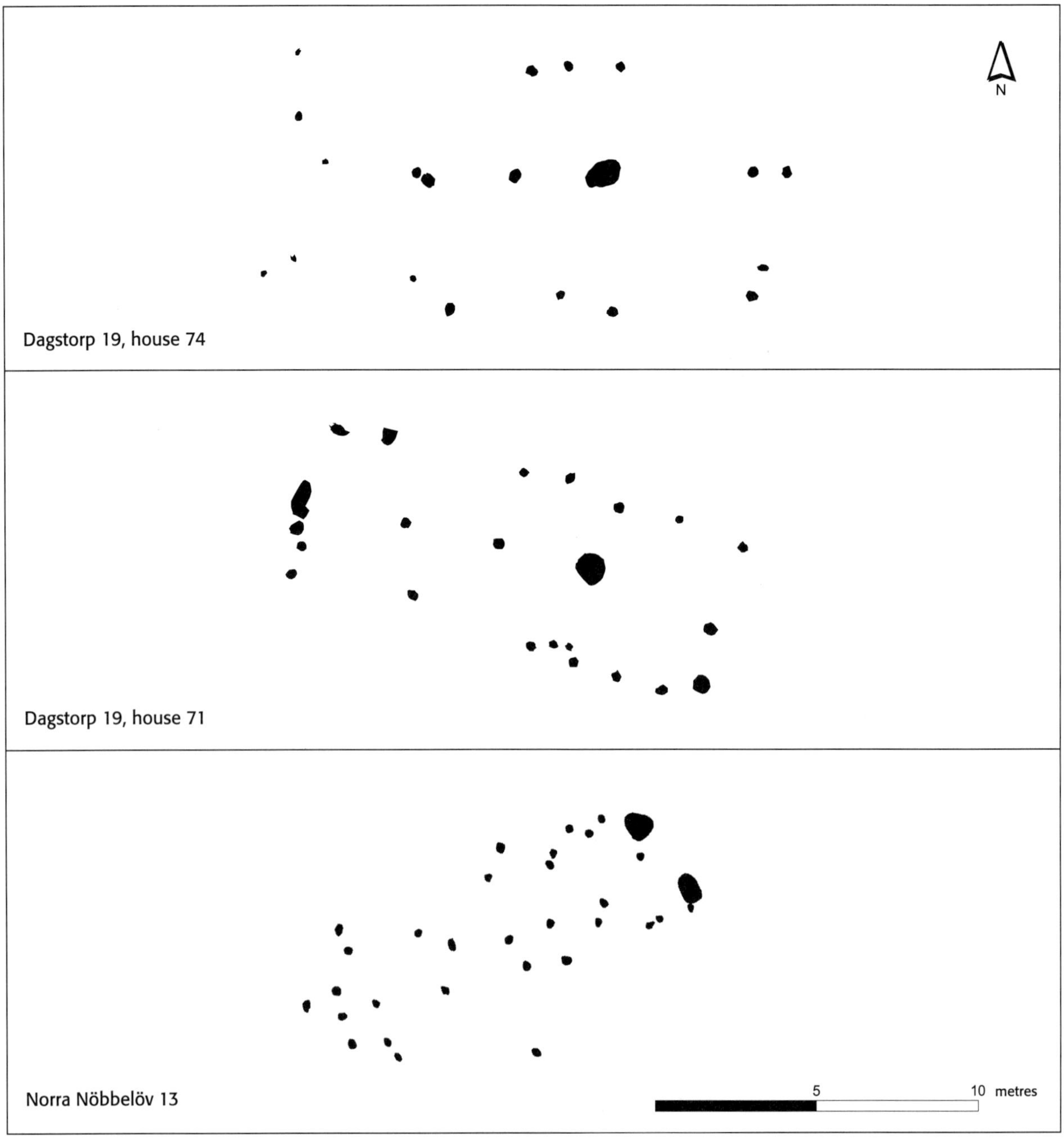

Dagstorp 19, house 74

Dagstorp 19, house 71

Norra Nöbbelöv 13

5    10 metres

Fig. 87. Houses in MNA III–V.

The documented buildings in the investigation area show that the dwelling house was probably a rectangular long-house (fig. 87). Dagstorp house type II, which can be dated to MNA III, is a clearly rectangular structure, while the building in Norra Nöbbelöv is more difficult to interpret, although it also displays a rectangular ground plan. The number of houses is small, but the tendency is for dwelling houses to be bigger in MNA III than in the previous period. The dwelling area in the rectangular houses is 90–100 m², while trapezoidal house types from MNA I at Dagstorp 19 (Dagstorp house type I) were no more than 50 m². The Mossby house at Saxtorp 26, which has been dated to EN II, is an exception, however, with a

dwelling area of roughly 100 m². Perhaps the bigger houses are an indication that two or more families shared a dwelling.

There are no structural details in the form of hearths, pits, or post-holes to reveal how the house was internally organized. The type of room division documented in the house remains from EN II–MNA I at Löddeköpinge 40 and Dagstorp 19 has not been identified. It is difficult to determine whether this shows that the houses were not divided into different rooms or that they were built to a design that has not left any traces.

There are no known long-houses, or dwelling houses, in the investigation area which can be dated with certainty to the closing part of the period, MNA IV–V.

It must be considered uncertain what the round-oval post-hole structure at Lackalänga (Furulund) represents. On the other hand, the hut remains at Saxtorp 23 can probably be assigned to late MNA. The structures were poorly preserved and no finds, whether organic or inorganic, survived to give any clues about their function. A comparisons with the hut remains in Hagestad, however, may be fruitful. The huts here, like those at Saxtorp, were circular and placed close to each other. The finds, with elements of both Pitted Ware and Funnel Beaker cultures in the form of objects such as blade arrowheads, cylindrical blade cores, clay discs with arch decoration, and tulip-shaped beakers, date the huts to the late MNA. Among the bones, both wild and domesticated species were identified. Strömberg believes that the huts functioned as seasonal dwellings in connection with hunting and fishing on the coast (Strömberg 1988a). Although no finds could be directly linked to the hut remains at Saxtorp, a number of fragments of blade arrowheads were retrieved from plough furrows. It is reasonable to regard the structures at Saxtorp, like those in Hagestad, as remains of brief seasonal activities.

It is of course problematic that none of the excavations in the investigation area has uncovered house structures from the final phase of the Funnel Beaker culture or indeed any remains showing the organization of settlements in the period. The finds, both from surface surveys and excavated occupation layers, have shown that the period is nevertheless richly represented in the area. It is only at a few places in Bornholm and Skåne that we have houses which can be dated to late MNA at all. The dwelling sites at Limensgård and Grødbygård have yielded extensive material with a large number of house remains, in the form of two-aisled rectangular structures with wall trenches, from the end of MNA and the start of MNB (Nielsen & Nielsen 1985; Nielsen, P. O. 1999:155). An uncertain house, dated to MNA V, was documented by a small excavation of the late Funnel Beaker site of Karlsfält (Larsson, L. 1992a:94ff). Only parts of what might be

a house were within the excavated area, which makes interpretation tricky.

If we study the distribution of finds at long-houses, we see the same pattern as observed at the dwelling site of Dagstorp 19 for EN II–MNA II (fig. 88). There is a tendency for the houses to have been kept clear of waste, but the occupants were not as careful about cleaning the area around the house. The occupation layer in the eastern part of house 71 at Dagstorp 19, however, is hard to interpret since it was badly disturbed by Iron Age settlement. The distribution of finds in the occupation layers indicates that most of the everyday activities were pursued in the area between the two houses at Dagstorp 19. It also seems natural that tool manufacture, cooking, and so on, were done in a shared open area between the dwelling houses if they functioned simultaneously. The densest accumulation of finds was observed just east of house 74. This probably indicates either that several household activities were performed right beside the house or else that waste was only dumped outside the home. The composition of flint finds in this area is mixed, dominated by flakes/debitage with scrapers and knives as the most common categories of tool. They thus do not give a clear picture of what happened there. At both Dagstorp 19 and Norra Nöbbelöv 13 there were pits containing so-called waste material. Two pits at Dagstorp distinguish themselves particularly through their size, design, and quantity of finds. In one of the pits a brim beaker was placed in or right beside a bigger vessel, and in the other pit there were three layers of stones, with the bigger stones placed along the sides. This shows a deliberate deposition which rules out the possibility that the pits were waste containers – or at least that they were only regarded as "refuse chutes". That these pits had a significance going beyond that of ordinary refuse containers is confirmed by the fact that people on Funnel Beaker sites generally do not appear to have bothered to keep the habitation area clear of waste. At the same time, it is obvious that a

182

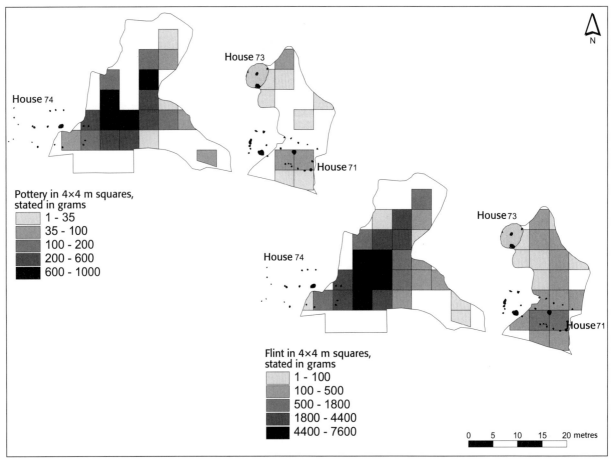

Fig. 88. Distribution of flint and pottery around the houses at Dagstorp 19 (SU 21) in MNA III–V.

large share of the objects in the pits are "everyday objects", and the material in the pits agrees with the composition of finds on the rest of the site. Knarrström's analyses of the flint from one of the pits (A68613) also shows that several of the tools were used in everyday work (Knarrström 2000b).

Although a much smaller area was excavated at Norra Nöbbelöv 13, it is still possible to discern certain similarities between Dagstorp 19 and Norra Nöbbelöv 13 as regards the internal organization of the settlement. We find activity areas and refuse layers outside the well-cleaned rectangular dwelling houses. Beside the houses and activity areas, both sites had pits

containing flint, pottery, and bones. All of the excavated main settlements showed a similar tool composition, with the disc scraper being by far the most common artefact, followed by the knife.

It is difficult to assess the area of the sites since none of them has been completely excavated. The excavated area with material from MNA III at Dagstorp 19 comprises roughly 5,000 m². The surface survey indicates, however, that the settlement extended down to the river and that the site was in reality much larger. The surface-surveyed habitation area at Barsebäck 48 is about 60,000 m², while Norra Nöbbelöv 13 and Stävie 17 both have an area of some

20,000 m². The area at Tågerup 3 is hard to judge since the evidence of the surface survey does not allow us to draw any clear boundary with the Mesolithic remains. It thus seems as if the main settlements in MNA III–V were bigger than in the earlier phases of the Neolithic in terms of both the area and the amount of finds.

**Votive sites**  The tradition of depositing axes in wetlands declined in significance during MNA. There are only six documented votive sites with finds of material that can be certainly dated to MNA. The deposits are still located in bogs in the interior, and it is only the one at Norra Nöbbelövs Mosse that is adjacent to a known contemporary settlement (Norra Nöbbelöv 13). The few votive deposits registered in wetlands in the investigation area from the period MNA III–V seem to be spread in accordance with the distribution of deposits in the preceding period, for they occur in the northern and eastern parts of the area. In the south-west, on the other hand, around Barsebäck with its density of dwelling sites, there are no known votive bogs. This indicates that in the areas where the tradition of depositing objects in wetlands was strongest in EN II–MNA II, the custom survived in MNA III–V as well, albeit in reduced form. Four of the six votive deposits are also located in wetlands which were used during the preceding period. None of the votive sites has been excavated, but it seems as if it is still the axe that is the most important artefact to deposit.

In this account I have not included deposits consisting solely of B-axes since this type is usually assigned to MNB. The excavations in the area, however, have shown that the B-axe has been found both in places where the flint is influenced by the Pitted Ware culture and at Battle Axe culture sites. There may possibly be a new rise in the number of votive deposits at the end of MNA. It should be stressed, however, that B-axes were deposited in places which largely agree with the distribution of Battle Axe settlement in the province.

## Society

At the transition to MNA III there were changes which are reflected both in the material culture and in the spatial distribution of settlements and votive sites. This is the second palpable change in the Early and Middle Neolithic Funnel Beaker culture around the Saxån–Välabäcken and Lödde Å-Kävlingeån. The first was noted in connection with the expansion of settlement at the end of the Early Neolithic, when people moved to new areas. I argue that the internal social pressure created in the initial phase of the Early Neolithic with the establishment of more permanent settlements now decreased. Rearrangements in the spatial pattern in the landscape and in the material culture can be ascribed to changed conditions in the social organization, which was in turn influenced by the new circumstances. As the new settlement districts were established and confirmed, there was again a growing need to maintain social control. The first visible sign of this phenomenon in the archaeological record is noticed in the changes in votive ritual. The more private sacrifices in wetlands were increasingly replaced by collective events at the megalithic tombs. Pottery, with its decoration more clearly expressing group affiliation, became more common in the ritual than the axe. Later, during MNA III, there was also a gradual change in the settlement pattern. Dwelling sites became fewer in number and more concentrated around some big main settlements. Towards the end of the period there was a reduction in the number of inland settlements, while settlement intensity on the coast and on the shores of bays remained or even increased in certain areas. Several of these sites have finds with clear Pitted Ware influences, known as the Stävie group. In cases where sites with material associated with the Funnel Beaker culture (TRB) and sites with finds from the Stävie group occur within the same area, I mark this on the maps showing the different landscape spaces in MNA III–V.

**Landscape spaces**  The valley of the Välabäcken was still important in MNA III (fig. 89). The Dagstorp site

183

remained as a main settlement and seems to have had the largest population during this period (fig. 47). Only two other dwelling sites in the valley can certainly be placed in MNA III–V: one of them was by the Välabäcken a kilometre west of Dagstorp 19 and the other lay half a kilometre south of the main settlement. The material from these, however, is too limited to allow us to speculate about their function. Pottery deposits at the passage grave of Södervidinge 3 show that this was the scene of rituals into MNA III. It is uncertain whether Harald Hildetand's Grave still had a function during the period, since it has not been excavated, but it is likely that this grave, just like the other passage graves in the investigation area, served as a venue for rituals in much of MNA. The social relation between the main settlement of Dagstorp and the passage graves on the slopes of the hills is thus noticeable during this phase as well. A votive find in wetland has been documented close to the valley. It is a single find of a thick-butted axe, located at least two kilometres from the nearest known contemporary settlement.

At the end of MNA the finds suggest that the valley was no longer used in the same way. Dagstorp 19 was abandoned as a main settlement, and no comparable dwelling site is known from this area. However, a site of a different kind arose less than two kilometres to the west, Västra Karaby 101 in Dösjebro. The pottery found beside the eastern post system (fig. 57, context 12) displays similarities to the late MNA material from Karlsfält. It is doubtful, however, whether this place really functioned as a traditional dwelling site. Although the finds in the layer were of dwelling site character, careful documentation failed to uncover any other features, in the form of remains of houses, hearths, or pits, indicating the presence of settlement. The material probably represents the everyday activities carried out in connection with other happenings of a more collective kind. The post system, which makes up a pointed-oval room measuring 50×8 m, could perhaps be interpreted as a "predecessor" of the palisaded enclosure that was later built on the site during the

early Battle Axe culture. It is unclear, however, whether the "room" is a separate structure or part of a larger palisade system. Ploughing and damming have destroyed any continuation of the rows of posts. Several deposits on the site have been dated to the late MNA, reinforcing the impression of the significance of the place already in the late Funnel Beaker culture and before the construction of the palisaded enclosure.

In the area around the former wetland area at Stångby Mosse, rather few settlements from this period are documented (fig. 90). With the exception of Stångby 18, the surface-surveyed sites are fairly small. The large ceramic deposits at the passage grave in Västra Hoby and two votive finds of thick-butted axes, type A, in the area nevertheless suggest that the surroundings were also used in the late MNA. Stångby 18 may possibly have been a main settlement. The site is on the gentle north- and south-facing slopes of a stream that has now been drained, about a kilometre east of Stångby Mosse. In the Neolithic the bog was probably an open lake. The surface survey at Stångby 18 has yielded a large number of flint flakes and blades and several fragments of thick-butted axes. It is one of the few inland settlements with finds of both cylindrical blade cores and blade arrowheads. Moreover, the site had a tradition of occupation since the Early Neolithic. Without excavations, however, the significance of the place remains uncertain. The votive site at Stångby Mosse, with a tradition going back to EN I, may still have been an important meeting place in the late MNA. Its location in the dramatic valley would probably have made it an imposing scene for sacrificial ceremonies. It is reasonable to assume that the rituals at Danshögarna in Västra Hoby likewise assembled the local population, and perhaps it was not until the end of the period that deposits in the wetland were resumed. Both Stångby 18 and Lackalänga (Furulund) show that the area was inhabited in the late MNA and early MNB.

A few kilometres south of the settlement at Stångby Mosse, we see in the late MNA a re-establishment of settlement in the areas around Nöbbelövs Mosse (fig. 91), a bog which was probably an open lake in the Neolithic (Olson et al. 1996). I have identified two settlements dated to EN in the area but no known examples from EN II–MNA II. However, several votive deposits from the late Early Neolithic have been documented in Nöbbelövs Mosse (Karsten 1994). The area around the lake was thus used more or less continuously throughout the Early and Middle Neolithic but its significance varied. Judging by the existing archaeological evidence, the settlements in the area ceased to exist at the end of the Early Neolithic, when the lake was only visited for special sacrificial ceremonies. In MNA III the area was once again settled. A main settlement (Norra Nöbbelöv 13) has been identified together with some smaller sites. The terrain is rather flat with no noticeable topographical variation. In this landscape it is likely that the lake, with the gentle but distinct slopes down to it, was a central point. The many votive deposits above all in EN II, but also occasional finds from MNA III, indicate this. Since no megalithic tombs are known in the immediate vicinity, sites beside the lake may possibly have functioned as places of assembly for special collective rituals. These must have been visible to everyone standing on the slopes around the lake. Nöbbelöv 13 was on a flat rise from which it was possible to survey the lake.

The area that seems to be most densely settled during this period is the valley of the Lödde Å, between Hög and Stävie. In a stretch of about three kilometres along the river, a dozen settlements of varying size have been documented (fig. 92). The terrain is slightly undulating but is interrupted by the valley of the river and its adjacent wetlands. The landscape resembles the Välabäcken valley to some extent. Although the hills at Hög and Stävie are not nearly as prominent as Karaby Backar and Dagstorp Backar, the character of the topography, together with the distribution of settlement, give the impression of a landscape space. The centre of gravity of settlement here seems to be at the end of MNA, when the central place Stävie 3 and the

main settlement of Stävie 17 were established. Stävie 17 lay on a sandy rise that stands out from the immediate surroundings, with water to the north and west. From here it was possible to command a view of the valley landscape. In the northern part of the landscape space is the passage grave at Hög. The large quantity of pottery found in front of the passage shows that the place was the scene of shared rituals until at least MNA IV. After this, collective gatherings were probably moved to the central place in Stävie.

As in the preceding period, we notice denser settlement around the megalithic tombs of Gillhög, Storegård, and Hofterup 1 on the Mare Bäck (fig. 93). On the peninsula formed by the Barsebäck foreland in the Neolithic, there were seven settlements in MNA III–V. At all these sites, surface survey has discovered large amounts of flint. Apart from Barsebäck 48, however, only a few can be dated to MNA III–V, and much of the material probably belongs to earlier Mesolithic settlements. At five of the settlements, blade arrowheads and cylindrical blade cores have been identified, which may suggest that the area was used continuously in the last phase of MNA as well. Excavations and surface surveys of the main settlement of Barsebäck 48 have yielded a large body of material from the late MNA. In this period the site was beside a lagoon in the shelter of the ridge running to the south and west. The peninsula was dominated by the ridge on which Gillhög lies. There is a clear relationship between the main settlement, which was established in EN II–MNA II, and the passage grave. As previously pointed out, the megalithic tomb "faces" the dwelling site, from where it was possible to look up towards the grave. The pottery at Gillhög is copious, showing its significance as a place of assembly in much of MNA. Along the coast, at Stenbocksvallar, a large number of thick-butted flint axes and flint chisels, several of them preforms, have been collected. The finds are a clear indication that the area was important for the production and distribution of axes and chisels. Outside the Barsebäck foreland, at the mouth of the Lödde Å and Mare Bäck, several late MNA sites have also been registered.

The bay at the mouth of the Saxån and the Tågerup promontory at the confluence of the Saxån and Bråån were likewise used in the late MNA (fig. 94). Just as on the Barsebäck foreland, several sites have a flint inventory influenced by the Pitted Ware culture. The big site in the area, the main settlement, may have been Saxtorp 3 (Tågerup). The excavations here touched only the Mesolithic parts of the settlement, but there is a considerable collection of surface finds from here which can be dated to the late MNA (Althin 1954). The bay probably reached all the way to the Tågerup promontory throughout the Middle Neolithic and functioned as a link between the different sites. There are no known megalithic tombs or votive sites in this area, so it cannot be ruled out that the bay was only visited on a temporary basis, for hunting and fishing expeditions. An excavation of the Middle Neolithic remains at Tågerup would be required to answer these questions.

In each area or landscape space there seems to have been one main settlement around which settlement was concentrated. In the vicinity there is also a site which functioned as a place of assembly for collective ceremonies, perhaps with the participation of people from other landscape spaces as well. These central places could have been megalithic tombs, wetlands, or special structures like those at Stävie and Dösjebro. The main settlements cover a larger area and yield more finds than in previous periods. On the other hand, there are fewer places for special activities. It was probably not just habitation but also various activities that were concentrated at the main settlements. The location of these, often where different ecological niches met, shows that hunting, fishing, and gathering could be managed from here. Macrofossil analyses from Norra Nöbbelöv suggest that cultivation may have been carried on adjacent to the settlement. Some of the sites surrounding the

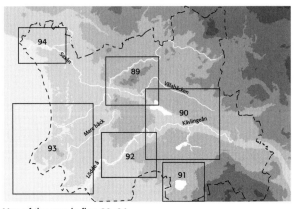

Map of the area in figs. 89–94.

main settlements may be the result of an economy partly based on transhumance, that is, a stationary settlement combined with seasonal use of grazing land located at some distance from the main settlement.

In the closing phase of the period we note the start of a dissolution of the inland settlement districts or landscape spaces established at the end of the Early Neolithic. The settlements were increasingly located by the sea in bays, as at Stävie, Barsebäck, and Tågerup (fig. 95).

**Social organization** Only Dagstorp 19 has preserved remains indicating that more than one dwelling house may have existed simultaneously (fig. 47). This is probably due to the excavation methods and the size of the excavated areas. The extent of the archaeological material at all the main settlements of the period can be interpreted as showing that several families moved together to an even greater extent than in the preceding periods. Judging by the existing house remains, there is also a tendency for houses to be built slightly larger during the period and with a regular rectangular form. The changes in house architecture may be a sign of modifications in the social organization. The size of the existing house remains may show that households consisted of more than one nuclear family. The hypothesis must be consid-

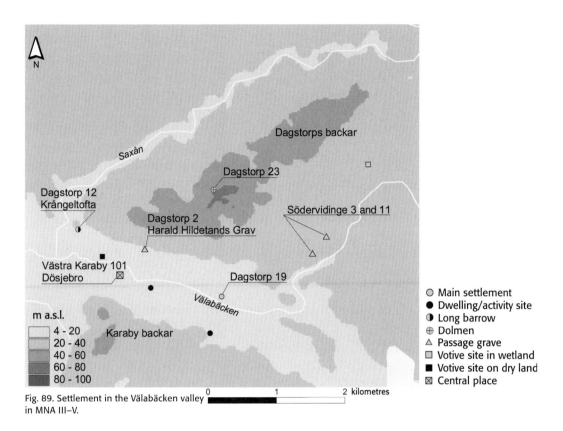

Fig. 89. Settlement in the Välabäcken valley
in MNA III–V.

○ Main settlement
● Dwelling/activity site
◑ Long barrow
⊕ Dolmen
△ Passage grave
□ Votive site in wetland
■ Votive site on dry land
⊠ Central place

187

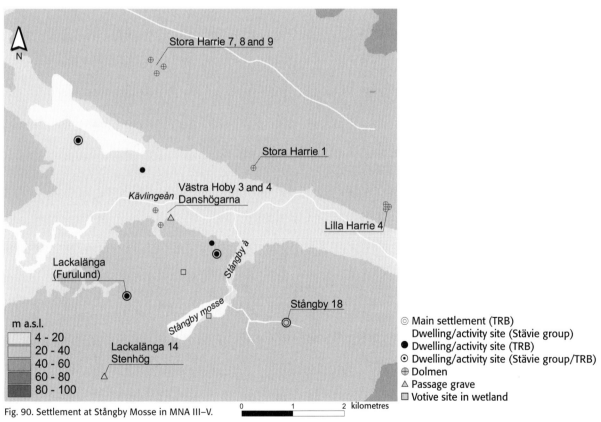

Fig. 90. Settlement at Stångby Mosse in MNA III–V.

◎ Main settlement (TRB)
  Dwelling/activity site (Stävie group)
● Dwelling/activity site (TRB)
⊙ Dwelling/activity site (Stävie group/TRB)
⊕ Dolmen
△ Passage grave
□ Votive site in wetland

ered uncertain, but the fact remains that the rectangular houses (Dagstorp house type II) from MNA III are up to twice as big as MNA I houses (Dagstorp house type I). Since I have interpreted both types as

dwelling houses, the difference in size must have an organizational explanation. It should be emphasized that houses of greater size (Saxtorp 26 and house 72 at Dagstorp 19) were also documented during the

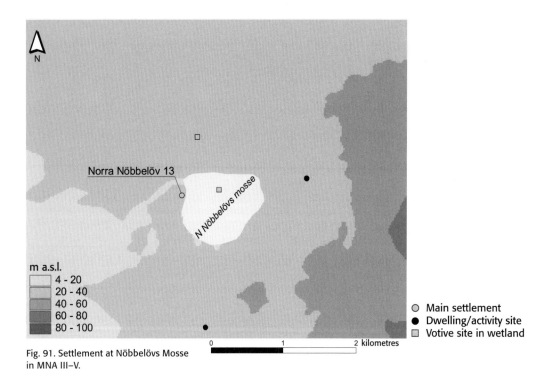

Fig. 91. Settlement at Nöbbelövs Mosse
in MNA III–V.

188

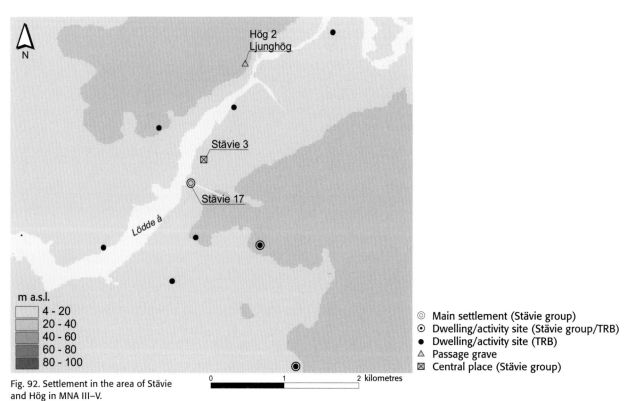

Fig. 92. Settlement in the area of Stävie
and Hög in MNA III–V.

preceding phase, but these seem to have functioned as isolated farms. It is only at Dagstorp 19 in MNA III that there are remains indicating that multi-family houses could have existed on the site at the same time. There may of course be other functional reasons why the houses are bigger than before, for example, that various manufacturing processes were moved indoors. However, there are no traces of this,

since occupation layers with finds are mainly outside the houses, which suggests rather that these activities were performed outdoors. Even if the social group grew, as several families moved together, there is still nothing in the architecture of the houses or the organization of settlement to indicate any social differences between households. The society was probably still organized in the form of kin groups. Individual

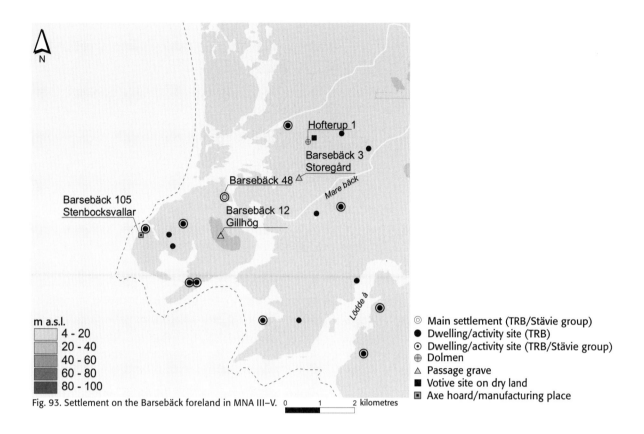

Fig. 93. Settlement on the Barsebäck foreland in MNA III–V.

⊚ Main settlement (TRB/Stävie group)
● Dwelling/activity site (TRB)
⊙ Dwelling/activity site (TRB/Stävie group)
⊕ Dolmen
△ Passage grave
■ Votive site on dry land
▣ Axe hoard/manufacturing place

189

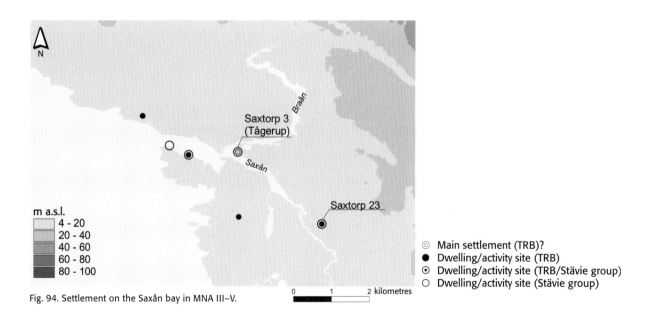

Fig. 94. Settlement on the Saxån bay in MNA III–V.

⊚ Main settlement (TRB)?
● Dwelling/activity site (TRB)
⊙ Dwelling/activity site (TRB/Stävie group)
○ Dwelling/activity site (Stävie group)

families were the base, linked to each other through one or more ancestor, and together forming a kin group under the leadership of one or more of the elders (cf. Meillassoux 1972, 1981; Rey 1979; Terray 1975, 1979; Tilley 1984; Eriksen 1995). It seems as if the significance and power of this group of leading older men and/or women increased in connection with the consolidation.

Private sacrifices in wetlands almost totally ceased at the very start of the Middle Neolithic; instead the votive ritual was in most cases diverted to collective ceremonies at the megalithic tombs. In EN II, areas in the interior were colonized and new settlement districts were established. As part of the consolidation phase of these areas, sacrificial activity in wetlands increased and monumental graves were erected in order

190

to define places and socialize the landscape. When the settlement areas were gradually stabilized, it became necessary to maintain and confirm the newly founded economic and social relations. If the relations involving social dominance were to be preserved, it was necessary for various strategies to be implemented regularly in order to mask and distort the true conditions and legitimize the unequal relations. The institutionalized public ritual had already been important in EN I–MNA II for legitimizing the social order. As yet another stage in the consolidation of the power structure, the old traditional votive sites were abandoned early in the Middle Neolithic and the votive rituals were instead focused wholly on the megalithic tombs. The increased ritual focus on the megalithic tombs can be interpreted as the monopolization of the sacred by an élite, who thereby completely took over the role of link between the community and the divine world. A more explicitly hierarchic organization crystallized. It was also in MNA II–III that the activities involving ceramic deposits at megalithic tombs culminated and pottery acquired the most complicated vessel forms and decorative patterns of the whole Neolithic (e.g. Tilley 1984). It can be said that the structural changes in society that began in MNA I–II were completed at the same time as the manufacture of the thin-butted flint axe ceased in favour of the thick-butted axe. As the custom of private offerings decreased in importance, the role of the axe as an attribute in the collective religious ceremonies declined. Also, the thin-butted axes are often better made than the thick-butted ones, showing a greater degree of craft skill (Petersson & Nilsson 1999). The emphasis on pottery in the ritual signalled group affiliation more clearly (see above) and demonstrated the stronger collective character of the society.

The finds from the megalithic tombs show that burial and the cult of the dead acquired increasing importance in the social and religious pattern. It was during the preceding phase that the monuments were erected, but their significance for the members of the society did not decline in this period. In fact, it seems as if the rituals at the graves became increasingly complex. Exactly what the actual burial process looked like has not been wholly clarified, since reburials and later activities have in many cases destroyed the traces of the earliest burials. It seems clear, however, that several of the major ceremonies took place after the construction of the passage graves (Kaul 1988:78). The deposition of human skeletons at the monuments involved a series of activities. All in all, the results of excavations of Danish and Scanian passage graves show that they were probably used to a large extent for primary burials. Evidence for this comes from observations in several graves of a dark, fatty layer of earth which suggests that a considerable number of bodies rotted in the chamber. There are also quite a few small bones in the graves, and it is not likely that these bones would be found to such an extent in secondary burials (Kaul 1992). In addition, personal ornaments such as amber beads, which were part of the dress or necklaces, often occur in the chamber (Strömberg 1971; Ebbesen 1975; Gräslund 1989: 72f). After the decomposition process removed the soft parts from the skeletons, they underwent different kinds of treatment. Burnt bones have been documented in the chamber, the passage, and outside the opening of several megalithic tombs. There are few finds, and it is not likely that they represent cremation at the graves, but a special treatment of selected parts of the remains (Tilley 1996:223). The destruction of the skeleton through fire and the deposition of selected bones in and around the grave was only a part of the burial ritual. Another seems to have been to sort and move the bones. When the chamber was used for a long time, the bones were moved to the side to make room for new ones. Often this clearance seems to have followed a certain order, and on several occasions we find specific categories of bones, such as skulls, thigh bones, and shoulder blades stacked. Evidently, certain categories of bones were taken away to other places (dwelling sites and votive bogs) to be used in rituals there. Another characteristic feature of passage graves is that the chamber was divided into sections by means of long, narrow stones. Unfortunately, it has been difficult to determine how many individuals the bone fragments in each section represent (cf. Strömberg 1968, 1971; Tilley 1996). Even though it is not possible to reconstruct the treatment of the skeletons exactly, it is obvious that the manipulation of the ancestors' bones was a significant element in the ritual at the grave monuments. Anthropologists have often pointed out how the human body has contributed a multitude of symbols in rituals intended to create order and reproduce the world (e.g. Mauss 1973; Huntingdon & Metcalf 1979). The body is intimately associated with personal identity and therefore functions as a natural link to the world outside. Death is an individual occurrence but also a social happening. A death means that an individual is separated from the collective world of which he or she was once part, but the funeral ritual also restores the social bonds broken by death and creates the conditions for the social order to survive by emphasizing the prevailing social positions. The death of an individual thereby becomes an instrument for reinforcing the social values of the community. In modern nation states continuity between generations is ensured through existing institutions such as the state administration, courts, armies, police, and so on. In societies lacking this state apparatus, traditional values are maintained partly through rituals invoking the ancestors and the past. The rituals to do with the dead are thus at least as much about the living. By making the individual's death into a social event, death and the funeral ritual are simultaneously associated with the renewal of life. In many low-technology societies, it is the dead ancestors who renew the world of the living and forge social bonds. Several scholars believe that there is a correlation between the type of social or-

ganization and how the body is perceived in the burial ritual (Douglas 1973; Needham 1973; Ellen 1977). The treatment of the bones in the passage graves reveals the symbolic value of the human body in MNA II–III, when some of the bones were sorted and cremated, or in some cases moved, after the body had decomposed. A dead body undergoes changes, and the transformation of the body, regardless of whether it takes place through natural mouldering, skeletalization, or cremation, is a source of symbols. The separation of the flesh from the bones may be the crucial event that carries a person to his or her final rest and/or permits the soul to leave the material world. As symbols, the bones can represent the ancestors, continuity, order, fertility, or community. Control of the ancestors' bones has been important in different ways in many societies. In China the bones were put in prominent places to give symbolic control of the environment, while in New Guinea the bones were stored in "head-houses" and considered to give access to the ancestors' souls. Just as with the relics of Christian saints, the physical bone remains can be moved and circulated to maintain contact with the ancestors (Thomas 1999b:136). I therefore believe that the ceremonies to do with the bones of the dead in the Middle Neolithic should probably be regarded as a reflection of the growing significance of the ancestors' cult. The social élite, consisting of a group of elders, ensures its power position in the collective by means of complex rituals in which they invoke the ancestors and legitimize their own position.

In addition, the ceremonies served to camouflage social inequalities. Both cremation and the stacking of bones destroyed individual identity. The process of breaking up the skeleton meant that the individual body was transformed into a social body represented by the accumulation of bones in the chamber. The social differences that they expressed in life, in the form of age, gender, or status, were thus repressed. Collective rather than individual identity was accentuated in death (Tilley 1999a). The fact that some of the ancestors' bones circulated in the society, both at settlements and at the megalithic tombs, indicates that they were indeed an integral part of the social community.

It occurred already in parts of the Neolithic that a number of households or families lived on the same site. On the other hand, there now seems to have been a more deliberate concentration in special places. This phenomenon is also documented in the Malmö area, where several small settlements seem to be combined on a large site, namely, the Hindby site (Svensson 1986). The big main settlements should not be compared with the economic units of later periods, the traditional villages with communally farmed fields and meadows and organized fallow systems (cf. Olsson & Thomasson 2001). Although the livestock grazed the same lands, the individual households could still have functioned in large measure as independent production units. In an economy in which hunting and fishing were probably still of significance, and cultivation was confined to small "garden plots", it is difficult to see any economic advantages of large group settlements. If the group was not brought together to generate economic gain, the question is why individual households chose to move together to an area where the social hierarchy was expressed more clearly. The settlement pattern should probably be understood as the product of a social system and an ideology in which collectivism assumed more permanent forms. The assembly of several households in a main settlement can, I think, be seen as yet another expression of collective thinking and increasing social integration. The agglomerated settlement should be interpreted in terms of the successful strategy of an élite to establish social control, which was legitimized in the collective ritual. The whole point of dominance is to master other people and their assets, and it was based on social and esoteric control rather than economic control (cf. Hodder 1990). As an element in the exercise of control, the élite makes the different households in the district move together to one main settlement. When several households were combined on one site, the conditions were better for the élite of elders to legitimize and exercise their social and economic control through various rituals. In addition, it is likely that competition between different local groups in the region had increased. Through the consolidation, each group's area was more clearly defined, and people chose to move closer to each other to strengthen the group identity.

As settlement was consolidated and the number of inhabitants of the main settlements increased, with growing complexity in social relations as a consequence, strict rituals were required on the dwelling site as well. Pit offerings on the site are represented at Dagstorp 19 and Norra Nöbbelöv 13. The quantity of deposited objects and the size of the pits at Dagstorp 19 are a reflection of conditions on the dwelling sites. Just as in the preceding phases, the material is a representative cross-section of the tools and artefacts of a settlement. The special combination of vessel forms in the pits on the site suggests a deliberate selection for deposition. The set of vessels represents a portion of "everyday ceramics" but deposited in combination with special pots such as the brim beaker. The purpose of the pit offerings was probably the same as in the Early Neolithic and the start of the Middle Neolithic. The deposited objects were fragments of activities on the site, so the pits were a metaphor for the daily tasks. Through a manifestation of everyday work, the sense of social community was reinforced and differences were concealed. Digging a pit and depositing fragmented objects in it is also a way to transform and strengthen the bonds to the site. Votive actions help to create a relationship between the human and the divine (or the ancestral spirits). Communication between human and divine is proclaimed in several cases through the selection, justification, and destruction or deposition of an object, an animal, or a human being (Lévi-Strauss 1987). In the pits at Dagstorp 19 the ritual was further reinforced through deposits of a brim beaker in A68613 and the stone structure in A68431. This should probably be interpreted as meaning that digging pits and filling them with objects was no long-er just the result of the use of the place but an event in itself. This might be a sign that the ceremony on the dwelling site increased in significance.

**The dissolution of the landscape spaces** In the ar-chaeological record at the end of MNA we notice changes from the preceding phase which indicate a breach with earlier traditions. The occupation of the big main settlements in the interior ceased, and habita-tions in general were more confined to the coast. In the material culture we see changes in the flint inventory, which in several places takes on distinct Pitted Ware influences, and in the pottery, which shows partly dif-ferent vessel forms and decorative patterns. Votive rit-uals at the megalithic tombs decrease considerably, and instead large central places are established, as at Stävie and Dösjebro. The societal process that began in the Late Mesolithic, with increased permanence of settlement, the adoption of agriculture, and ancestor worship can be said to culminate in MNA III. When more permanent main settlements were established in EN I, people were more bound to time and place. Sow-ing and harvesting were planned, and people became dependent on what former generations had done, for example, by clearing forest. An area had been created and was then inherited by the succeeding generation. The care of the ancestors' spirits therefore became an important part of people's lives. The ancestors were not just the source of a society's solidarity; they also asserted the right of the society to the resources. The relationship to the place was marked through various rituals at the main settlements, such as burial ceremo-nies and pit offerings. People were buried in flat-earth graves with an individual in each grave. The elders, who were considered to be closest to the deceased kin, led the rituals and thereby established a kind of power in the society. Population growth, together with heightened internal tension because of the increasing social control, meant that some groups moved to colo-nize new areas. These new landscapes were socialized

and defined by the triad formed by the dwelling sites, the votive sites, and the megalithic tombs. They were places with different meanings but closely interwoven as parts of the same system, in which each part could not function without the other two. The functions that were formerly confined to main settlements were relo-cated at places out in the landscape space, which can thus be regarded as a macro settlement site. The first monumental graves in the form of long barrows and dolmens were intended for single individuals in the upper stratum of society. After the burial the graves were closed and the dead were physically inaccessible to the survivors. Shared rituals in memory of the an-cestors were nevertheless carried on at the monu-ments. The consolidation of settlement gradually had the effect that the prevailing power relations were le-gitimized. For this purpose, the ritual performed at the graves was made more complex. The ceremonies were enacted by an élite who made increasing claims on the control of ritual knowledge and relations with the sa-cred, and hence also on social and economic control. The passage grave gave access to the ancestors' bones, but only for the select few. To conceal the increasing inequality, an ideology was advocated which empha-sized the collective and sought to strengthen the sense of solidarity. The Funnel Beaker society had developed a system whereby large resources were channelled into rituals which conformed the prevailing order. In MNA III this policy seems to have been taken to its extreme, and the situation finally became untenable, as a larger production surplus was required for these ceremonies. The finds at megalithic tombs show that large quanti-ties of pottery were made for the purpose of being used in the rituals there. The number of potsherds at Västra Hoby and Gillhög is among the largest in the whole of north-west Europe (Tilley 1999a). It is not impossible that grain and livestock were used as sacri-fices. The osteological material is limited, but burnt animal bones occur together with burnt human bones at several graves in Skåne, e.g. Gillhög, Trollasten, Tågarp, and Jarladösen (Tilley 1996).

The expansive and centralized tendency of the organization had exacerbated inherent tensions between generations and kindreds – within and between groups. A state was reached where the quantity of the material and human resources required to maintain and conceal social inequalities went beyond the pain threshold. This social environment favoured the growth of alternative power relations. The archaeological evidence suggests that society at the end of MNA was not as cohesive as it had formerly been. In Skåne and Denmark there is often talk of several variants of late Funnel Beaker culture and/or Pitted Ware culture (cf. Edenmo et al. 1997). Several ceramic styles with partly different geographical distribution have been found in Denmark. The MNA IVb style defined by Ebbesen is above all concentrated in southern Sjælland (Ebbesen 1975:136), while the MNA V/Valby pottery has its main distribution in the eastern and northern parts of Jutland and in north-west Sjælland (Davidsen 1978:11). In Bornholm a number of places have been documented with pottery which resembles the Danish MNA V but which also shows shared features with Funnel Beaker ceramics in Skåne (Nielsen & Nielsen 1985). Partly contemporary with these groups there are thus sites, such as Kainsbakke and Kirial Bro in north-eastern Jutland, with finds showing influences from the Pitted Ware culture (Rasmussen 1984). In Skåne Pitted Ware material is represented at sites like Nymölla and Siretorp in north-eastern Skåne and Blekinge, Jonstorp in north-west Skåne, and Pitted Ware–influenced flint at Stävie in south-west Skåne (Bagge & Kjellmark 1939; Malmer 1969; Wyszomirska 1988; Larsson, L. 1992a, 1998). The late Funnel Beaker culture is represented by places like Karlsfält and Långåker (Larsson, L 1992a). Variations in ceramic styles between these sites may, in my belief, indicate the emergence of more independent groups which marked their group identity. Evidently the late MNA saw a break with the organization through which social relations were maintained by a group of elders legitimizing their social and economic control through sacred knowledge and ritual activities.

Places with material which can be placed both in the Stävie group (Stävie 3 and Stävie 17) and in the Karlsfält group (Barsebäck 48 and Västra Karaby 101) have been documented in the investigation area. In addition, there are several sites where surface finds of flint of Pitted Ware character indicate that these sites should be assigned to the Stävie group. The pottery at Västra Karaby 101 in Dösjebro and Barsebäck 48, as mentioned previously, shows great similarities to the pottery from Karlsfält in southern Skåne. Two crusts of food and a cereal grain from Karlsfält have been [14]C-dated and yielded the results 4100±125 BP (2880–2490 cal. bc, Ua-81), 4370±220 BP (3400–2650 cal. bc, Ua-82), and 4190±60 BP (2890–2670 cal. bc, AA-1842) (Larsson, L. 1992a:102). From Stävie we have [14]C datings from an oven, a pit, and food encrusted on a potsherd. These have given the dates 4055±90 BP (2860–2460 cal. bc, St-6003), 3930±90 BP (2570–2280 cal. bc, St-6000), and 4360±85 BP (3260–2880 cal. bc, Ua-26016) (Nagmér 1979; Larsson, L. 1982; Nagmér & Räf 1996). It is also reasonable to imagine that the huts at Saxtorp 23 and the possible building at Lackalänga should be placed in the Stävie group. The two [14]C analyses that can be presumed to date the huts at Saxtorp have given values of 4000±85 BP (2850–2340 cal. bc, Ua-9845) and 4160±90 BP (2880–2610 cal. bc, Ua-8985), that is, MNB and the end of MNA (Andersson & Pihl 1997; Andersson, M. 1999). The feature and the surrounding occupation layer at Lackalänga have given the dates 4180±90 BP (2888–2611 cal. bc, Ua-7341) and 4060±70 BP (2823–2526 cal. bc, Ua-7642), which also correspond to late MNA or early MNB (Munkenberg 1996).

With the exception of the dating of the food crust (Ua-26016), the [14]C results from Stävie thus hint that the Stävie group is slightly later than the Karlsfält group. However, it cannot be ruled out that we are really dealing with two different groups which may partly have existed simultaneously, but that the Stävie group continued to exist – parallel to the early Battle Axe culture – after the Karlsfält group had disappeared. The datings may thus mean that the characteristic ceramic style of the Stävie group can have existed at the same time as parts of both the tooth-stamp period and later also the early Battle Axe culture. According to the $^{14}$C datings of MNA V/Valby sites in Denmark, this phase too existed over a relatively long period. Danish material has placed the MNA V/Valby pottery in the time-span 4300–4100 BP (Malmros & Tauber 1977:81; Davidsen 1978:170; Tauber 1986:table I). This indicates that the manufacture of MNA V/Valby pottery in Denmark began at an early stage, partly contemporary with "earlier" styles belonging to the Funnel Beaker culture (cf. Lagergren-Olsson 2003).

The growing social tensions may possibly have brought out the incompatible interests of different factions, leading to an inevitable conflict in which groups or families who found the situation more and more strained broke out of the Funnel beaker society. It is in this connection that the depopulation of the interior should be understood. Disfavoured groups left the district and the landscape spaces were dissolved. In the closing phase of the Funnel Beaker culture we consequently see a period in which collective manifestations were less important. Rituals at the megalithic tombs decline, and where they do occur they seem to be on a limited scale. At the end of MNA (IV–V) and also in MNB it seems to be chiefly flint axes that were deposited at megalithic tombs. This is shown by the occurrence of thick-butted, thin-bladed, and hollow-polished flint axes at several of the passage graves. The deposits are nevertheless more limited than the pottery, indicating that they might be of a more private character. Deposits of objects in wetlands are still rare in this period. The occurrence of B-axes in votive bogs, however, is an indication that deposits in wetlands did increase in the late MNA and that the private ritual became more significant. The emphasis on the collective as the prevailing societal ideology probably col-

lapsed, and the individual households broke out of the community. The majority evidently made their way to the coastal areas. The move may have been further impelled by the deterioration in climate at the same time, with the transgression that is assumed to have favoured marine food resources (Christensen 1993). It is now also clear that elements of the Pitted Ware culture made their entry into areas which had formerly been exclusively characterized by classical Funnel Beaker culture. Perhaps there were structural similarities between the Funnel Beaker and Pitted Ware cultures and possibly a common origin, which enabled an assimilation between the two traditions (cf. Larsson, L. 1998:443). Several scholars have claimed that the rise of the Pitted Ware culture should be explained as an internal development within the Funnel Beaker culture. They were supposedly groups which largely based their subsistence on marine resources and gradually developed a material culture and a social system of their own (e.g. Nielsen, S. 1979; Burenhult 1991, 1999). Arguments in favour of this are that the Pitted Ware pottery seems to be a continuation of Funnel Beaker pottery and that Pitted Ware dwelling sites are usually in areas previously inhabited by the people of the Funnel Beaker culture. The hypothesis seems probable since the groups in the Funnel Beaker society (the Stävie group) that later moved to the coast seem to have incorporated parts of the material culture that characterized the coastal Pitted Ware culture.

Unlike the increasingly hierarchical organization of the Funnel Beaker society, it seems as if the Pitted Ware culture maintained a more egalitarian form of society. At least, there is nothing in the Pitted Ware mortuary practice – as it is known from central Sweden, Öland, and Gotland – to indicate a more stratified society. As a rule, burials were in simple flat-earth graves, where we sometimes find red ochre and simple stone structures. The grave goods chiefly have the character of personal belongings such as simple tools and ornaments. The graves often cut across each other and they are oriented in most directions, seemingly regardless of gender or age, and they lack markers above ground (Knutsson 1995). I believe that the egalitarian social system of the Pitted Ware culture was perhaps a temptation for the groups that broke away from the increasingly centralized social system of the Funnel Beaker culture. If the two traditions derived from a common origin, with partly similar social and ideological structures, there could also have been an assimilation within certain regions. Basic underlying structures and values, which can be traced back to Late Mesolithic and Early Neolithic times, survived in both cultures. The close association between graves and dwelling sites in the Pitted Ware culture (Malmer 1962, 1975; Wyszomirska 1984; Knutsson 1995) shows us that the ancestors were significant for the surviving kin. Although a hierarchical order like that in the Funnel Beaker culture never arose in the Pitted Ware culture, the veneration of the ancestors here too was probably a way to assert rights to land and to legitimize the prevailing order. The organization of the settlement also displays similarities between the cultures. At dwelling sites like Jonstorp (Malmer 1969), Nymölla (Wyszomirska 1988), Kainsbakke, and Kirial Bro (Rasmussen & Boas 1982), large occupation layers on the site indicate a liberal attitude to dirt. Neither Ertebølle, Funnel Beaker, nor Pitted Ware dwelling sites were cleaned – a striking difference from the subsequent Battle Axe culture and Late Neolithic culture. The waste was a by-product of their way of life, and in the creation of order dirt was therefore regarded as a natural part of the settlement.

The fact that the collective votive ceremonies declined at megalithic tombs indicates the start of a time when power relations were no longer built up on the basis of the same hierarchical structure. The decoration on pottery became more spare, which may mean that the need to express group affiliation had declined (cf. Tilley 1984). At the same time, as we have seen, there were variations in ceramic styles between different regions, which could suggest the development of independent groups. A transformation from homogeneous to heterogeneous style would thus indicate a transition from a collective to a personal or individual identity. Although it is not self-evident that different ceramic styles indicate the formation of more independent groups, the hypothesis is also strengthened by the settlement pattern, with a tendency to division and more settlements being located on the coast, which paints a picture of more independent household units. There are few remains of houses from this period to reveal how permanent settlement really was. Perhaps people moved between several different places and therefore did not leave distinct traces behind them. Saxtorp 23, with its small circular huts, can be envisaged as having been one such place, used for short periods. There are, however, two larger sites, probably main settlements (Barsebäck 48 and Stävie 17) documented in the investigation area from the closing phase of the period. Since collective places of assembly do not seem to have functioned as before, some of the settlements are likely to have served as meeting places. Barsebäck 48 had presumably had a crucial role as a main settlement back in MNA III. A large proportion of the pottery from the site has great similarities to the Karlsfält pottery, thereby showing that the site was also occupied in the latter part of MNA. In addition, there is flint showing influences of Pitted Ware culture which further reinforces the role of the site at the end of MNA. At Stävie 17 the finds seem to be fully comparable to those from the adjacent Stävie site (Stävie 3) and can be securely placed in the late MNA. Unfortunately, the excavations at the two places focused only on the occupation layers, which means that any traces of buildings have not been documented. To some degree the organization of society in the late MNA resembles what prevailed at the start of the Early Neolithic. It was a partially coastal population with autonomous household units, and authority lay with some elders in the kin group, whose identity was linked to the settlement. After the dissolution of the landscape spaces formed late in the Early Neolithic and early in the Middle Neolithic, the landscape once again became socially open for a period, without fixed settlement districts or distinct landscape spaces. There was no longer an obvious triad of dwelling site, votive place, and burial place in the closing phase of MNA (fig. 95a and b).

This new order of social segregation gradually contributed to the rise of the big central places intended to bring about integration once again. They came to represent the symbolic integration between autonomous household units. The people who at the end of MNA lived scattered in the landscape could not live in isolation from each other. The reproduction of each group was of course dependent on the establishment of wider contacts. The construction of the central places at Dösjebro and Stävie in the late MNA served to institutionalize the links between the groups. It is likely that regular assemblies were held at fixed times at these places and that they were the scene of a number of different activities and events which formalized alliances between different kindreds. It is also evident that the ideology behind the assembly places was different from the ceremonies at the megalithic tombs. The rituals associated with the monumental graves aimed to legitimize the supremacy of the élite through the sacrifice of a production surplus to the ancestors. The megalithic tombs were in themselves also symbols of permanence. The stone monuments were a mediator between past, present, and future. The palisaded enclosures, on the other hand, were an expression of something that was impermanent. Their function was to serve as a venue for present events. The excavations in Dösjebro, south of the Välabäcken, also showed that the palisaded enclosure there probably only functioned for a brief period (Andersson & Svensson 1999). It was in the later part of MNA that the site at Dösjebro seemingly acquired a special significance. The activities in "the pointed-oval space" are difficult to interpret, but they were obviously not of ordinary dwelling site character. Perhaps the site had already functioned in the closing phase of the Funnel Beaker culture as a place of assembly for those who had not

yet left the united community. The Stävie site, and the finds there, show that this place was used as a node by the people of the Stävie group. In connection with the transition to MNB the actual palisaded enclosure was built in Dösjebro and, as we shall see, probably by population groups who had adopted new continental ideas. Mac Svensson has pointed out that the axe-manufacturing places at the palisade in Dösjebro, together with the deposits of axes and flakes from axe manufacture at Dösjebro and other contemporary palisaded enclosures such as Hyllie outside Malmö, Sigersted I in central Sjælland, and Helgeshøj outside Copenhagen (Svensson 2002), show that the places had an important role in the manufacture, distribution, and consumption of axes. It was probably at Stenbocksvallar that the first stages of axe production from blank to quadrilateral plank took place. At any rate, the large quantity of preforms of axes and chisels from there is a hint of that. The supply of flint at Stenbocksvallar may have been sufficient for this production. Anders Högberg has discussed in an article (2002) the occurrence of a large number of axe preforms at three special places along Järavallen in Skåne: Sibbarp and Östra Torp in south-west Skåne and Stenbocksvallar on the Barsebäck foreland. He believes that the first steps in axe production were taken at these places and that the preforms were then transported to other places for continued working. At different periods, however, a large part of the production was deposited on the sites at Järavallen. Högberg shows that this is not a matter of discarded items; the deposited preforms would have been perfectly suitable for continued working. The act of leaving some of the production at these places should instead be viewed as an act to manifest the significance of the places. This hypothesis harmonizes with my idea put forward above, that it was customary in Funnel Beaker society for parts of the production to be left or buried as a way to strengthen bonds with the site. It is also conceivable that there many have been some flint import along the coast from the Malmö area. From there the distribu-

197

198

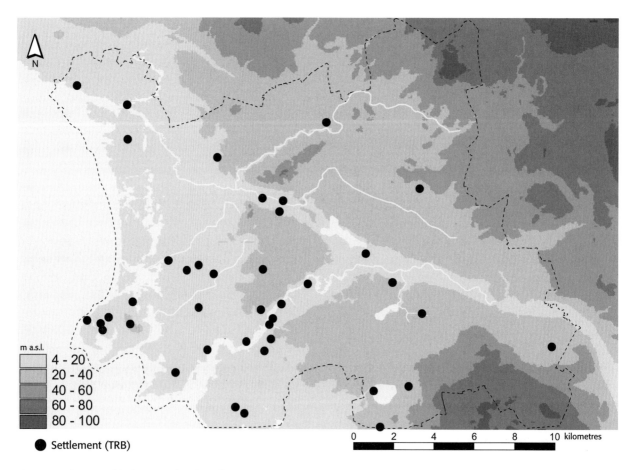

m a.s.l.
4 - 20
20 - 40
40 - 60
60 - 80
80 - 100

● Settlement (TRB)

0    2    4    6    8    10 kilometres

Fig. 95a. Settlements of the late Funnel Beaker culture.

tion could have continued to the palisaded enclosure at Dösjebro, which was a node in the handling of axes.

Although the axe may have lost its role at the collective ceremonies at the megalithic tombs at the start of MNA, its practical significance and symbolism for personal status was probably still important. Axes continued to occur, to a more limited extent, at rituals which were probably of a more private character at the monuments and votive bogs. The exchange of goods in low-technology societies is a matter of maintaining diplomatic relations and therefore cannot be regarded solely in economic terms (e.g. Mauss 1950; Sahlin 1972). This activity should rather be understood as the creation, preservation, and manipulation

of social relations. The management of axe distribution probably had a central role in the mediation of marriages, in the maintenance of kinship ties, and as a symbol of status. What we see manifested at the palisaded enclosure at the transition to MNB can be changed power relations in the community. In the old power structure, leadership was based on sacral control, through direct links with the ancestors' spirits, which thereby also exerted power over the social and economic aspects of the society. When this authority, which emphasized social integration, was broken, control was transferred to individuals and families. Instead of emphasizing the collective, the stress was now on individual prestige, personal networks, long-

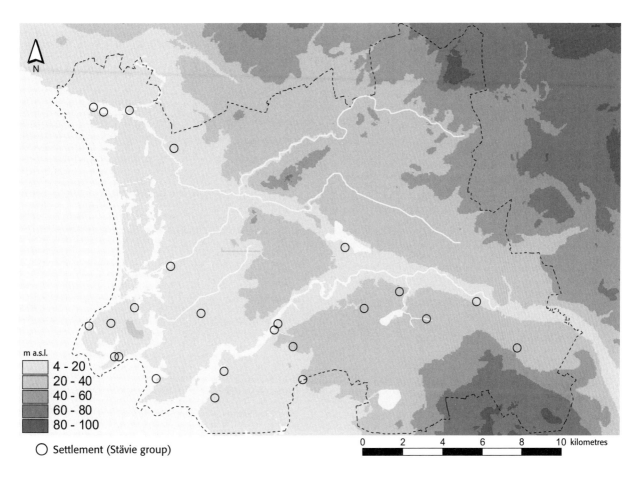

m a.s.l.

4 - 20
20 - 40
40 - 60
60 - 80
80 - 100

◯ Settlement (Stävie group)

0   2   4   6   8   10 kilometres

Fig. 95b. Settlements of the Stävie group.

distance exchange, and specialized craft. As we have seen, this found expression in the break-up of settlement. A hint that there was also a change in mortuary practice comes from Flädie 7, where flat-earth graves from MNA have been documented. Perhaps it was much more independent families and individuals that now met at the central places than in earlier phases of the Middle Neolithic. I shall develop this line of thought in the next chapter.

## Two ways

The landscape spaces created at the end of the Early Neolithic were maintained through the triad of dwelling sites, burial places, and votive sites. Things which

had largely been done at the dwelling site in the initial phase of the Early Neolithic were moved out into the landscape, where they defined and socialized "space". The landscape spaces were established in the formerly open countryside. Power was gradually concentrated in a few selected elders. With the aim of controlling and maintaining the prevailing social relations, the ritual was collectivized and focused on the megalithic tombs and settlements. Collectivism gradually led to settlement being concentrated around a main settlement.

The increased social coercion, however, caused families and groups to break out of the united community. The landscape spaces were dissolved, and once again we see a tendency to a more open landscape. The old traditional way was abandoned and the population sought alternative ways. Influences from the more egalitarian Pitted Ware culture enticed some groups to make their way to the coastal zones, making up what we know as the Stävie group. Other population groups, in connection with the transition to MNB, as I have already hinted as regards the palisaded enclosure in Dösjebro, would adopt continental ideas with completely different power structures. It was no longer a stratum of elders that dominated through sacral control and reference to the ancestral spirits; positions in the community were offered to individuals and groups possessing special social and economic skills. Large central places were established which functioned as centres for commerce in axes and other goods, but also as places where the population of the district met to form and maintain social bonds.

## New ideas and different customs

In connection with the transition to MNB and the rise of the Battle Axe culture in southern Scandinavia, changes in the settlement pattern, site organization, grave forms, and material culture can be detected. The known Battle Axe settlements are small and poor in finds, there are few house remains, burials are now mostly in flat-earth graves, and new types of artefacts such as hollow-edged flint axes, boat-shaped battle axes, and spherical pots are noticeable in the material culture. Scholars claimed for a long time that the changes were brought by immigrating peoples (e.g. Müller 1898; Almgren 1914, 1919; Rydbeck 1930; Forssander 1933; Glob 1944), whereas the more recent view has usually been that instead of actual immigration there was a cultural change, as new customs were adopted by the old Funnel Beaker culture (e.g. Malmer 1962; 1975). In the next section I will show that the late Funnel Beaker culture in the investigation area was a society that was receptive to new ideas which were able to take root in the existing society.

## Settlement pattern

In the investigation area, 32 settlements have been documented as belonging to the Battle Axe culture during MNB. In addition there are a further ten sites where the only datable artefact is the B-axe. Fragments of B-axes occur both on sites with Pitted Ware flint and on sites with Battle Axe material. It is obvious that the axe type was used in both the Stävie group and the Battle Axe culture, which may also have existed partly parallel. This of course entails problems in determining the culture of sites where the only datable object is the B-axe. For this reason, the places in the investigation area with fragments of B-axes as the only identifiable artefact must be rather vaguely described as belonging to the late MNA (the Stävie group) or MNB. Remains from MNB are dominated by surface-surveyed sites, since only a few have been excavated. There is a noticeable decrease in the number of settlements in relation to the preceding phase, although the period is much longer than MNA III–V (see table I). It should be pointed out, however, that several of the coastal sites where flint with Pitted Ware influence has been identified (the Stävie group) may very well have functioned as settlements into MNB.

Battle Axe graves have been excavated at four sites, and at least six of the passage graves in the area have evidence of use in MNB as well. Deposits in wetlands once again increase significantly, with 27 known deposits from this period (fig. 96). In five of the cases the only deposited object is a B-axe, which means that the sacrifice may have been made already in the late MNA.

**Settlement**   The distribution of settlement in MNB shows no clear departure from that in the late Funnel Beaker culture. Dwelling sites are found in the same areas as in the Funnel Beaker culture (fig. 96). It seems, however, as if the distribution in the investigation area was slightly more limited; at any rate, there are no remains from the north-west parts of the area, along the Saxån bay. In this area, however, the Pitted Ware influences on settlement site material are clearly visible. The majority of the Battle Axe settlements (65%) are on sites previously occupied in EN or MNA. Just over 30% were built in places where settlement has been documented in the preceding period, MNA III–V, so that direct continuity is theoretically possible.

With only the scanty material found by surface survey it is difficult to establish a fine chronology for the settlements from MNB. It is therefore hard to determine with certainty which parts of the region the Battle Axe culture was first established in. The indications that we have, however, show that the earliest Battle Axe culture is found right from the start in the traditional core areas of the Funnel Beaker culture. The [14]C datings and pottery finds show that the palisaded enclosure in Dösjebro was probably built in an early phase of the Battle Axe culture. A battle axe that typologically is likely to belong in the early Battle Axe culture has been identified at the passage grave in Gillhög. All in all, this indicates that the bearers of the Battle Axe culture populated the same districts as the Funnel Beaker people right from the start. Anna Lagergren-Olsson's studies of the Middle Neolithic pottery from Dösjebro have also demonstrated that *"There is no TRB [Funnel Beaker] pottery in the material from the Saxån/Välabäcken valley to indicate the presence of yet another style between the later tooth-stamp period and SYK [Battle Axe culture]. This and the early SYK datings mean that it is possible that SYK immediately succeeded the period of tooth stamps in the local area"* (Lagergren-Olsson 2003:207).

The settlement pattern thus shows that the bearers of the Battle Axe culture used the same parts of the landscape as the earlier population in the Funnel Beaker culture, and, as before, the dwelling sites were located on sandy soils beside lakes and rivers. However, it is not possible to identify any dwelling sites like the big main settlements that arose in MNA III – at least not in the first part of MNB. The site at Västra Karaby 7 contained pottery from seven pots and a varied range of flint which indicates that this place could have been a main settlement. The material is too small, however, to allow any certain assessment. The pottery dates the site to the middle or latter part of the Battle Axe culture. In the other dwelling site material from the period it is difficult to detect any main settlements. The Battle Axe culture mostly occurs on a very limited scale at excavated Neolithic sites, usually in the form of occasional potsherds or a fragment or two of a tool. It is obviously the case that the Battle Axe culture has left fewer visible traces in the landscape than the preceding Funnel Beaker culture. This tendency was also seen at the end of MNA, when some of the bigger settlements were abandoned. It is not until the closing phase of the period and the transition to the Late Neolithic that remains of stable houses are found in the investigation area (fig. 97) and that some of the sites may have functioned as main settlements. Whether the houses at Dagstorp 11, Dagstorp 19, and Västra Karaby 101 should be placed in MNB or the Late Neolithic is uncertain. Based on the [14]C datings it is reasonable to assign at least the house at Dagstorp 19 to a late phase in MNB and, if so, this indicates that the typical Late Neolithic rectangular long-house has its roots in MNB. At the same time, the houses suggest that population had once again become more sedentary.

The limited amount of finds means that it is unusually hard to grasp the economy of the period. The few grain impressions from Skåne show that people mainly grew barley, and the domesticated animals they kept were cattle, sheep, and pigs. A rise in sheep breeding can be documented (Welinder 1998:100f). Various pollen diagrams show that the later part of the Middle Neolithic is a period of clear decline in trees and bushes in favour of an increasingly open grazing landscape (Digerfeldt 1975; Berglund 1991:111, 1999). This expansion phase for plants indicating meadow and pasture is probably due to intensified animal husbandry (Kristiansen 1988; Larsson, L. 1989, 1998; Welinder 1998). As previously suggested, this process was presumably started early in the Middle Neolithic, when the so-called regeneration phase in the development of

202

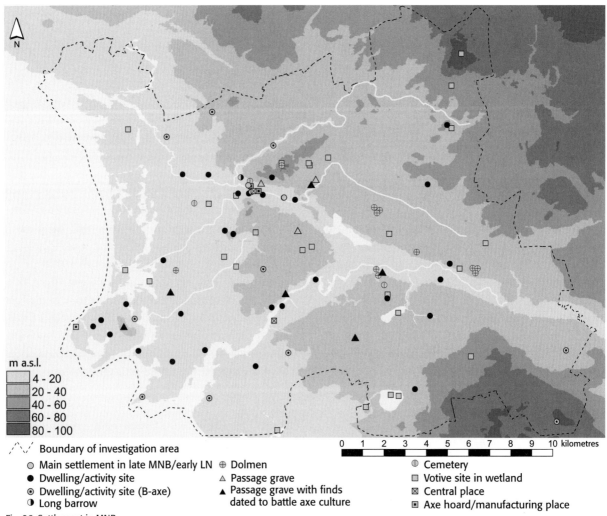

m a.s.l.

| | 4 - 20 |
| | 20 - 40 |
| | 40 - 60 |
| | 60 - 80 |
| | 80 - 100 |

/⌐\ㄴ/  Boundary of investigation area

○ Main settlement in late MNB/early LN ⊕ Dolmen

● Dwelling/activity site △ Passage grave

◉ Dwelling/activity site (B-axe) ▲ Passage grave with finds
                                    dated to battle axe culture

◑ Long barrow

⊕ Cemetery

☐ Votive site in wetland

⊠ Central place

▣ Axe hoard/manufacturing place

0 1 2 3 4 5 6 7 8 9 10 kilometres

Fig. 96. Settlement in MNB.

the Neolithic landscape need not necessarily have meant a total regrowth of the forests; it may illustrate a phase of coppice forests used intensively for grazing and leaf foliage (Göransson 1996). The continued expansion of animal husbandry and the need for open grazing land in MNB gradually also reveals itself in the pollen diagrams. The osteological material from the graves shows that people hunted, among other animals, red deer and roe deer. The material is small and it is difficult to determine how large the element of hunting, fishing, and gathering was in relation to agriculture and animal husbandry.

It is probably in the light of the increasing livestock keeping that many of the smaller settlements should be perceived. It is reasonable to assume that animal husbandry in the initial phase of the Battle Axe culture was pursued in a way that corresponds to true nomadism (cf. Larsson, L. 1989:73). Brief stays at different places at different parts of the year can be a partial explanation for the often diffuse remains of settlement.

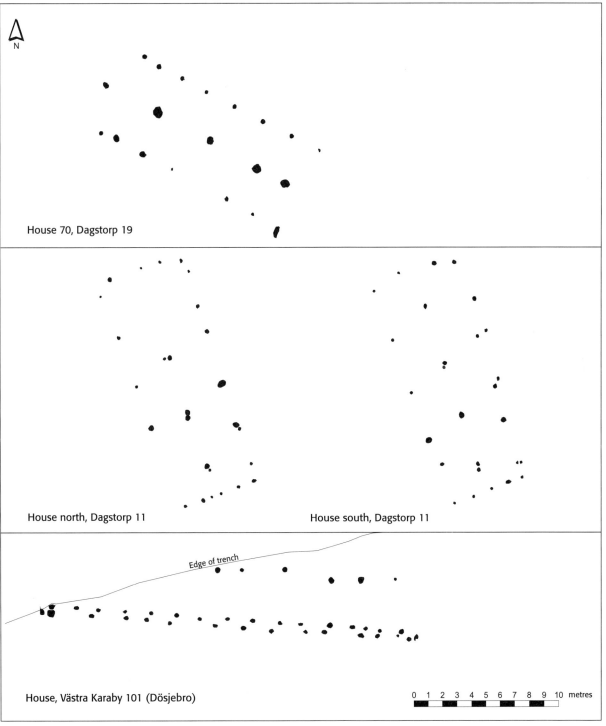

House 70, Dagstorp 19

House north, Dagstorp 11

House south, Dagstorp 11

Edge of trench

House, Västra Karaby 101 (Dösjebro)

0 1 2 3 4 5 6 7 8 9 10 metres

Fig. 97. Houses in the late MNB or early LN.

Since the Battle Axe culture settlements have left such vague archaeological traces in the landscape, it is tricky to speculate about the organization of the dwelling site. Nevertheless, it is perhaps precisely the lack of dwelling site remains that can lead to speculations as to how the settlements were organized – at least if the culture is put in relation to the Funnel Beaker culture. That the bearers of the Battle Axe culture to a high degree lived as herding nomads is probably not the whole explanation for the lack of settlement site remains. Even though a group of people had a mobile way of life, traces of their different activity sites should be visible in the form of tool manufacture, huts, hearths, etc. We have seen this among Mesolithic hunter-gatherer populations. Malmer has argued that, since the population was settled on the best arable soils, which are still farmed, only the deepest pits, such as the graves, are preserved. After a number of centuries, the organic material decomposed and the pottery crumbled (Malmer 1975:53). I believe that this too is only part of the truth. At several of the Funnel Beaker culture settlements in the region, which were also located on the best agricultural land, large occupation layers and house remains have been documented. It is more likely that the attitude to waste was different in the Battle Axe culture than in the Funnel Beaker and Pitted Ware cultures (cf. Svensson 2002:47). The dwelling area was cleaned in a completely different way from the customs in the preceding phases. At Västra Karaby 101 no occupation layer could be documented adjacent to the house. An occupation layer was excavated which partly overlayered the house at Dagstorp 11. However, it contained a relatively small amount of pottery and flint in relation to excavated layers from the Funnel Beaker culture in the investigation area. The pottery with decorative elements in the form of pits, impressions, lines and stamped decoration, and finds of flat-flaked arrowheads and a fragmentary sickle show, moreover, that some of the finds were deposited both during the Funnel Beaker culture and in later periods. The situation is the same on other

sites where finds from the Battle Axe culture have been discovered. Usually the material is dominated by finds which can be assigned to the Funnel Beaker culture, as, for example, at Dagstorp 18, Dagstorp 19, and Västra Karaby 7. The dwelling areas were probably cleaned and the majority of the objects taken away. Unlike the funnel beaker, the spherical Battle Axe pots were designed so that they could be set down in each other and were thus easy to transport (Lindahl 2000:170).

It may also be observed that pit offerings of the kind we know from the Early and Middle Neolithic Funnel Beaker culture are rare in the Battle Axe culture. A characteristic of the Funnel Beaker culture settlements is the pits whose function may vary, but the actual occurrence of them illustrates the permanence of settlement and the marking of a place. In the eastern part of the house at Västra Karaby 101, two shallow pits were documented, one of which contained charred seeds. The dating, however, is at the transition from MNB to LN, and these are pits which can probably be connected to the actual house. At the other Battle Axe settlements in the investigation area there are no pits in the dwelling area which can be securely dated to the period. An excavation at Västra Karaby 21 (about 200 m west of the cemetery Västra Karaby 39) documented a pit containing pottery of Battle Axe type (Olsson 1971). The documentation, however, provides no information about whether the objects are primary deposits or ended up there in connection with later activities: the site also has remains from the Late Bronze Age and Vendel Period.

Surface survey finds of fragmentary hollow-edged flint axes, quadrilaterally polished thick-butted, thin-bladed axes and thick-butted rock axes show that Battle Axe sites occur frequently in the investigation area, while excavations simultaneously reveal that ground structures on these sites are diffuse. The reasons for this are presumably that the population in the Battle Axe period largely lived as nomads and stayed for brief periods in each place, but also because the attitude to the dwelling site and its activities was different. The significance of the site did not have to be marked through pit offerings, and the waste left by dwelling site activities was not left as it had been in the Funnel Beaker tradition.

**Votive sites**   In MNB and possibly already in the late MNA there is a revival in the custom of depositing objects of stone – above all axes – in wetlands (fig. 73). The distribution of votive activities in the landscape agrees in large measure with what was seen in earlier phases, since it is in the northern and eastern parts of the region that the deposits occur with the greatest frequency. In several cases continuity of deposits in the same wetland is attested. At almost 40% of the wetlands used in MNB there are deposits documented from earlier Neolithic phases, and EN II is always represented among these. Just as Karsten pointed out in his study of Neolithic votive finds, there are similarities between MNB and EN II in the frequency of deposits and the choice of site (Karsten 1994:181). The great difference from the immediately preceding phase is of course that votive activity in wetlands almost ceased in much of MNA since the votive ritual was instead steered chiefly towards the megalithic tombs. It is nevertheless not the case that the old votive sites were totally abandoned. Occasional axe deposits are also documented from MNA III–V, and in four cases of six these are located in wetlands that were also used in both EN II and MNB. It is in particular the wetlands at Norra Nöbbelöv and Stångby that were used as votive sites in MNA III–V, where there probably were no grave monuments.

There are no excavated wetlands in the area with deposits that can be dated to MNB. This means that it is difficult to understand what the deposition tradition really was like, since it is only whole stone objects that are noticed by people working the land. It is difficult to determine whether fragmented objects were deposited to the same extent as in certain periods of the Funnel Beaker culture.

There is great variation as regards the types of artefacts deposited in wetlands in MNB. The most common are different types of axes. Nineteen thick-butted, hollow-edged flint axes occur in votive contexts, fourteen of them as accumulated single finds, three as single finds, and two in hoards. Ten of the axes were unpolished and nine were polished. Of the nineteen hollow-edged axes, six were fragmentary. Seven quadrilaterally polished thick-butted, thin-bladed axes have been documented as deposited in wetland, five of them as accumulated single finds, one as a sin-

gle find, and one in a hoard. All the thin-bladed axes were polished and only one was fragmentary. Twelve B-axes have been found deposited in wetlands, six of them as accumulated single finds, three as single finds, and three in hoards. Only one of the B-axes was fragmentary and seven of the twelve axes were polished. Three rock axes have been found as accumulated single finds in wetlands. In addition, there is a medium-bladed flint axe, a grindstone shaped like a thighbone, a blade arrowhead of type D, the butt section of a battle axe documented as accumulated single finds. The majority of the votive finds are single finds, just as Karsten has shown for the whole of Skåne (Karsten 1994). This does not mean, however, that they were the sole object to be deposited; this is just the registered find circumstances. Since none of the votive sites have been excavated, it cannot be determined with certainty whether one or more object was once deposited. There do not appear to have been any set rules for which objects could be combined in hoards or in what context an axe had to be polished or unpolished.

**Graves**   In the investigation area there are sixteen documented flat-earth graves from the Battle Axe culture, distributed in four places, one of which, the grave at Västra Karaby (Ålstorp), must be considered uncertain (fig. 68). It is likely that only a few of the presumed Battle Axe graves in the region have been discovered. Unlike the megalithic tombs, they did not leave any trace above ground. Even when topsoil has been stripped, the graves can be difficult to detect if they have no stone structure. After the burial, the graves were mostly filled again with the original dug-up earth, which makes them difficult to distinguish from the surrounding subsoil. With this insight, it is not likely that our picture of the distribution of Battle Axe graves in the landscape is fully representative. It can nevertheless be observed that the graves are located in two of the areas where settlement was densest during the period, namely, at the confluence of the Välabäcken and Saxån and around Stångby Mosse.

205

206

This picture can be supplemented with the inclusion of activities at passage graves in MNB. Artefacts which can be associated with MNB have been found at Gillhög, Storegård, Hög, Lackalänga, Södervidinge, and Västra Hoby. The finds at the first three passage graves show that burial activities took place even in the densely settled areas around the Mare Bäck and Lödde Å.

As in the rest of southern Scandinavia, the placing of the graves in the landscape is not entirely uniform. At Västra Hoby 5, Västra Karaby (Ålstorp), and Västra Karaby 39 they are on a flat sandy rise, while the Dagstorp cemetery is on a sandy, south-facing slope. They are all located close to rivers or wetlands.

The datable graves can be placed in the middle or later part of the Battle Axe culture on account of their design, the pottery, and the battle axe types. Some of the graves with a stone structure or grave goods could hypothetically be older, but in the absence of datable material this cannot be determined. The earliest grave find, in the Gillhög passage grave, comes from a battle axe.

The cemeteries at Dagstorp 11 and Västra Hoby 5 corroborate the view that Battle Axe culture graves were usually placed in lines (Malmer 1962:239, 1975:47). This means that the excavations which uncovered only one or two flat-earth graves probably did not discover the whole cemetery. For that reason, the graves at Västra Karaby 39 and the possible Battle Axe grave at Västra Karaby (Ålstorp) may very well be part of a larger linear cemetery. It is also possible that the cemeteries in Västra Hoby and Dagstorp comprise more graves than those excavated. The topographical conditions at Dagstorp nevertheless indicate that the cemetery was demarcated to the south by the Välabäcken and to the north by the rise in the terrain with the soil changing to clay.

Excavations of the linear cemeteries in Lilla Beddinge, Svarte, and elsewhere show that they were often used for a long period of time (Malmer 1975:46). It is also common that the longitudinal axis of the graves is in the same direction as the line of graves of which it is part. The position of the oldest was thus known to the people making later burials. There are also several indications that Battle Axe graves had a visible marking above ground. At least one of the inhumation graves at Dagstorp had post-holes which could be associated with the grave structure, indicating some form of superstructure. A grave at Ullstorp in southern Skåne was surrounded by four post-holes whose profile showed that the posts seemed to have been angled towards the centre of the grave (Larsson, L. 1988a:87f). At grave 53 in Lilla Beddinge there were stains which may have been part of a wooden structure (Malmer 1975:157). Adjacent to a grave at Löderup 15 and one at Hagestad 44 in south-east Skåne, post-hole stains have also been observed which have been considered to belong to the grave structure (Strömberg 1989:83). Nor can it be ruled out that small barrows or cairns originally covered the graves, just as in Denmark (Hansen & Rostholm 1993).

Several scholars have put forward hypotheses that the cemeteries were placed along contemporary communication routes (e.g. Müller 1904; Malmer 1962; Jørgensen 1977; Svensson 2002). The localization of the cemetery in Dösjebro in the direction of the Välabäcken indicates that there was a ford here during the Middle Neolithic. Unfortunately, there were no remains of Neolithic roads, but today's bridge is in the vicinity just as the medieval one was. Reconstructions of the Viking Age and medieval road network have moreover shown that one of the main roads in Skåne during this period probably ran immediately south of the palisaded enclosure and the cemetery while another ran west of the cemetery in Västra Hoby (Blomquist 1951; Stenholm 1986; Svensson 2002).

**Central places** It seems likely, as Svensson has pointed out in his article about palisaded enclosures in northern Europe, that the palisaded enclosure in Dösjebro (Västra Karaby 101), the axe-manufacturing sites north and south of the Välabäcken, and the cemetery (Dagstorp 11) should be regarded as belonging to one and the same activity complex (Svensson 2002). The axe-manufacturing sites were documented adjacent to both the palisaded enclosure and the Battle Axe cemetery. At least the palisade and one of the knapping places seem to be contemporary. The close spatial association between the palisaded enclosure and the axe-manufacturing place is further accentuated by the deposits of flakes from axe manufacture which have been documented in pits and post-holes belonging to the palisade.

The dating of the manufacturing sites south of the Välabäcken rests on finds and on the find context. The occurrence of flakes from the manufacture and re-knapping of quadrilateral flint axes and chisels give an unambiguous dating to the Neolithic. The other find material in the form of transverse arrowheads, scrapers and so-called gaming pieces supports this dating. Exactly which type of axe or chisel was made is more difficult to determine, however. Since Danian flint predominates among the axe-manufacture flakes, this gives some support for a Middle Neolithic dating, since the properties of this type of flint seem to have been preferred for the manufacture, above all, of certain types of thick-butted axes (Vang Petersen 1993:111). At the knapping place north of Välabäcken 11, moreover, a small axe fragment has been identified as belonging to a thick-butted flint axe of Nielsen's group B (Månsson & Pihl 1999). The existing basis for the dating thus shows a contemporaneity between the palisade and axe manufacture.

Although some of the ¹⁴C datings from the cemetery indicate an overlap in time with the palisade, the pottery and the form of the graves suggest that at least parts of the cemetery are slightly later than the palisade and axe-manufacturing activities. The burials should nevertheless be regarded as a part of the central events that took place on the site in the Battle Axe culture. The significance of the site as a meeting place in connection with the activities that went on at the palisaded enclosure probably lay in the awareness of the people who used the area as a burial place.

The location of the Dösjebro complex is central in relation to how the MNB settlements are distributed along the Saxån and Välabäcken. As a meeting place it was easy to reach. The placing of the palisaded enclosure in the valley is natural in a longer temporal perspective as well. The site was important at least since the early Middle Neolithic, as attested by such things as the pottery deposits and the U-shaped trench beside the cemetery. Pit offerings and post-built structures east of the palisade can be dated to the late MNA. It was natural for the bearers of the Battle Axe culture to take over a site of traditional significance.

In a similar way, the site in Stävie is centrally located along the Lödde Å. It is not impossible these two central places may have functioned partly simultaneously at the transition from MNA to MNB. The palisaded enclosure in Dösjebro was a meeting place for the Battle Axe culture people, while the Stävie site was the place where the people of the Stävie group assembled. The majority of Stävie group sites are located in the south-west parts of the area and the valley of the Lödde Å. It is reasonable to assume that the two sites had an overall function as places of assembly, but the variation in the form of the two sites also suggests that they had partly different functions and/or that they mark two different groups with different cultural features.

Unlike the palisaded enclosure, which was built with posts, the feature in Stävie demarcated a tongue of land by means of a ditch or pits. This structure can best be compared with the Sarup sites. If the dating in Stävie is correct, it means that this feature is about 500 years later than the Danish counterparts. This is not so strange, however, in view of the fact that the site at Sarup was also used in the late MNA. There is evidence of settlement on the site in MNA V and traces of ditch systems, at least in MNA III–IV (Andersen 1997). This type of feature appears to have been known in the late Funnel Beaker culture as well, and when there was a need to assemble the people of an area, outside the context of megalithic tombs, one such structure was erected in Stävie. Flakes from axe manufacture were documented in one of the pits, but above all it seems as if people deposited whole pots or large parts of them in the pits. It is interesting that a fairly large number of pits with flint and pottery dated to the late MNA were also found on the Stävie tongue (Larsson, L. 1982). At the palisade in Dösjebro there were only a few contemporary features inside the enclosure, and these were right beside the row of posts.

The palisade, which was built of a single row of posts, shows no traces of repair or rebuilding. Moreover, soot stains in the top layer of the post-holes show that the whole feature burnt down. The lack of reset posts in the palisade and the fact that the complex was destroyed by fire and not rebuilt suggests that the enclosure was used for only a short period. The excavation covered a rather small part of the interior of the enclosure. In this part there were no remains that could be associated with the palisade. This agrees with other excavated palisaded enclosures from the Battle Axe culture, such as Hyllie (Svensson 1991, 2002). It seems as if the activities – at least those which have left traces – were carried out at the actual row of posts and the entrance areas. The finds from the post-holes and the trenches in the palisade consist of flint and small quantities of pottery and burnt clay. Apart from a small number of tools, the flint is totally dominated by small flakes and debris. Among the flakes, many can be diagnosed as residual products from the manufacture of quadrilateral axes/chisels. It is noteworthy that the proportion of burnt flint (approx. 30%) is much higher in features belonging to the palisade than in surrounding structures and in Neolithic finds in general. This high proportion of burnt flint in combination with the find circumstances and the stratigraphy must surely show that the majority of the finds were in the post-holes/trench when the palisade burnt down. Moreover, the fact that the finds almost exclusively occur in the upper part of the filling of post-holes/ trenches and in clear concentrations shows that the objects are deliberate primary deposits and not older

material which ended up in the post-holes secondarily. The placing of the objects also shows that they were deposited in the foundation pits and ditches of the palisade when the holes were refilled and the posts stabilized (Svensson 2001 et al.). In certain cases flakes from axe manufacture were found close together, vertically standing in conical piles. The find circumstances gave the impression that the flakes had been placed in a container of organic material which has not survived, beside the posts in connection with the construction of the palisade. In certain cases, however, flakes were also found in the colouring left by the posts, but only in the very top part of the filling. These finds may have primarily derived from the now ploughed-out top filling of the post-holes and through mechanical processes secondarily ended up in the post-hole colouring. However, the find circumstances may also indicate that objects were placed on the ground surface immediately beside the palisade and then secondarily ended up in the depression formed in the ground surface as the post rotted away (Andersson et al. 1999).

The significant proportion of debris in the deposits may indicate that flint knapping took place right beside the post-holes where the finds were placed. Several of the flakes in one and the same post-hole were also struck from the same nodule, but flakes from several different planks/nodules are represented in the larger concentrations of finds, which shows that the finds do not come from just one knapping session but are parts of several events, and perhaps the flakes were gathered together to be deposited together. Traces of the manufacture of axes undoubtedly occupy a prominent place among these events, and the deposits of axe-manufacture flakes emphasize the close chronological, spatial, and functional relationship between the enclosure and the axe manufacture. This is further emphasized by the unpolished, thick-butted axe that was placed in a shallow pit right beside one of the openings in the palisade (Svensson 2002).

The axe-manufacturing areas at the palisade and at Dagstorp 11 show both similarities and differences. The composition of the flint is similar in the two areas, although the find material from Dagstorp 11 is much larger. Above all it is characterized by a low proportion of tools in relation to the total amount of flint (approx. 1%). This can be compared, for example, with the excavated Middle Neolithic dwelling site of Dagstorp 19 where the proportion of tools varies between 4 and 8%. Also noteworthy is the almost total absence of flakes from axe manufacture on the sites. The distribution of the size of axe-manufacture flakes in the two areas is similar, with a clear predominance for the later phase of the manufacturing process. Big flakes from the start of the manufacturing process are totally lacking, which suggests that this part of the production took place elsewhere. A clear difference between the manufacturing areas is seen in the choice of raw material, with a dominance of Danian flint in the manufacturing area at the palisade and Senonian flint at Dagstorp 11 (Svensson 2001 et al.).

## Society

Towards the end of MNA it is clear that an ideology with an emphasis on collectivism weakened in favour of a more individualistic society. This is noticeable both in the material culture and in the organization of dwelling sites, burial places, and votive sites. In the mid MNA power had been increasingly centralized with an élite who legitimized their supremacy through sacral knowledge in which they were considered to stand close to the ancestral spirits. This was accentuated in the rituals performed for the ancestors, which simultaneously concealed the inequalities by emphasizing the collective and the cohesion of the society. The rituals at the megaliths became increasingly refined, the ceramic decoration was further elaborated, and the settlements grew. People's actions in everyday life and their rituals reproduced and reinforced the underlying structures in the society which asserted the right of the collective above that of the individual. This order can be said to culminate in MNA III. The dominance in society, however, gradually heightened the internal tensions between different groups. The social and economic resources required to maintain the swelling rituals went beyond the limits of what the population was able to produce. Small groups left the community and adopted a way of life which had been maintained by the coastal Pitted Ware populations in north-west Skåne, forming the Stävie group. The structures of the society fell apart and receptiveness to outside influences grew. The continental currents that usually go under the name Corded Ware culture grad-

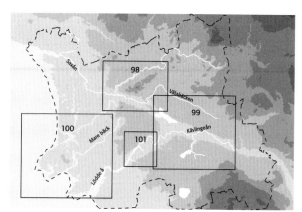

Map of the area in figs. 98–101.

ually reached southern Scandinavia and were assimilated in the form of the Battle Axe culture.

**Landscape spaces** It is likely that the bearers of the Battle Axe culture were not bound to the "space", in the same way as the population of the Funnel Beaker culture, at least in the sense that they led a more mobile way of life. The visible traces in the landscape both above and below ground level are more diffuse than in earlier (and later) periods. It is nevertheless clear that people occupied the same parts of the landscape as in the Funnel Beaker culture, since the settlements, the graves, and the votive sites are partly distributed in the same areas. The Välabäcken valley, the bays at the estuaries of the Mare Bäck and Lödde Å, the valley at Hög, and the gently undulating landscape at Stångby Mosse were evidently most densely settled.

The continued settlement concentration around the Välabäcken valley is striking in MNB (fig. 98). In the valley there are settlements, graves, votive sites, and a central place in the form of the palisaded enclosure. The dwelling sites lie like a necklace along the Välabäcken and Saxån. It is also within this area that the most distinct remains of structures can be distinguished on the sites. This can of course be explained, at least in part, by the fact that it is here that Battle Axe settlements have seen most excavations. Houses were documented at Västra Karaby 101, Dagstorp 11, and

210

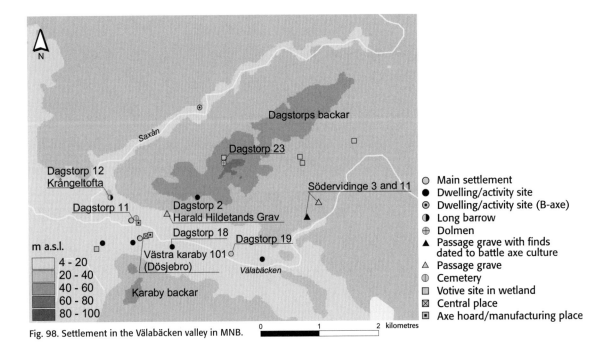

Fig. 98. Settlement in the Välabäcken valley in MNB.

Legend (Fig. 98):
- ○ Main settlement
- ● Dwelling/activity site
- ⊙ Dwelling/activity site (B-axe)
- ◑ Long barrow
- ⊕ Dolmen
- ▲ Passage grave with finds dated to battle axe culture
- △ Passage grave
- ⦶ Cemetery
- ☐ Votive site in wetland
- ⊠ Central place
- ▣ Axe hoard/manufacturing place

m a.s.l.
- 4 - 20
- 20 - 40
- 40 - 60
- 60 - 80
- 80 - 100

0    1    2 kilometres

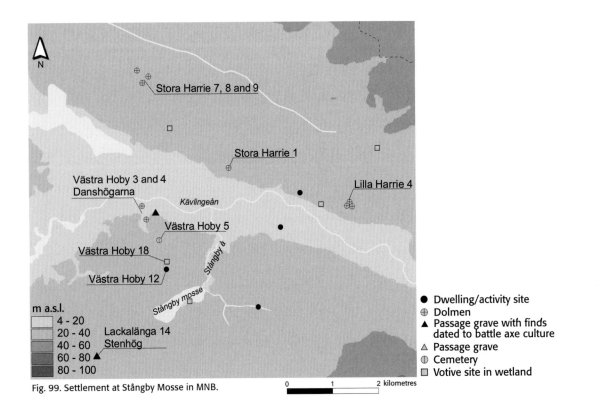

Fig. 99. Settlement at Stångby Mosse in MNB.

Legend (Fig. 99):
- ● Dwelling/activity site
- ⊕ Dolmen
- ▲ Passage grave with finds dated to battle axe culture
- △ Passage grave
- ⦶ Cemetery
- ☐ Votive site in wetland

m a.s.l.
- 4 - 20
- 20 - 40
- 40 - 60
- 60 - 80
- 80 - 100

0    1    2 kilometres

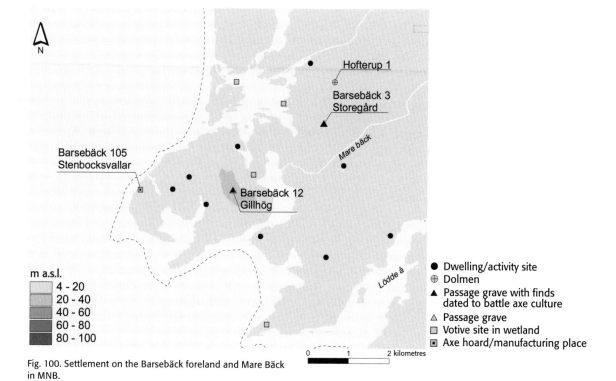

Fig. 100. Settlement on the Barsebäck foreland and Mare Bäck
in MNB.

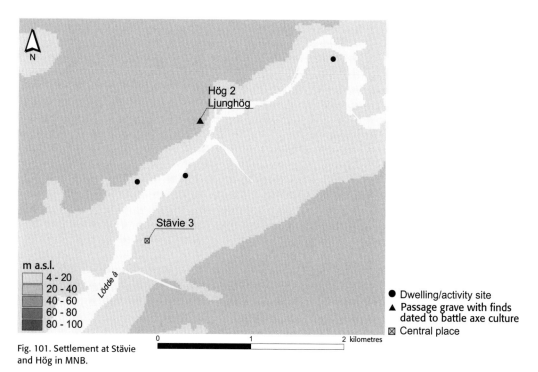

Fig. 101. Settlement at Stävie
and Hög in MNB.

Dagstorp 19 (figs. 63, 64, and 65). These structures are late, however, probably from the transition to the Late Neolithic. The only structure that can with certainty be placed in the early Battle Axe culture is the palisaded enclosure at Västra Karaby 101 in Dösjebro. The structure is probably proof of continuity in the area, emphasizing that this place was for a long time not considered suitable for settlement. The early Middle Neolithic remains, in the form of the pottery deposit, the stone packings, and the U-shaped trench north of the Välabäcken, indicate that the land on either side of the river here had a special meaning beyond the ordinary dwelling site functions. In a mobile settlement system the site was probably an important meeting place at the MNA/MNB transition. In the middle and later parts of MNB the site north of the stream acquired the function of a cemetery, and it seems to have been at the transition to the Late Neolithic that ordinary settlements were first established on either side of the river. Ceramic finds at the mouth of the passage grave in Södervidinge suggest that this was still the scene of rituals in MNB. Objects deposited in wetlands, separated from the dwelling sites, show that they functioned as votive sites.

The increasing density of settlement in the Välabäcken valley indicates that the landscape space that arose there at the very start of the Early Neolithic nevertheless continued into the Battle Axe culture. Although the settlement pattern in MNB was more mobile, the demarcated, enclosed spaces in the valley had a special attraction for people.

The area around Stångby Mosse and Västra Hoby is yet another district populated at an early stage by bearers of the Funnel Beaker culture, but also displaying plentiful remains from the Battle Axe culture (fig. 99). The settlements are on either side of the bog and in the wetlands along the Kävlingeån. The dwelling sites in the area are known from flakes found by surface survey, including fragmentary hollow-polished axes or chisels. Even whole hollow-polished flint axes have been found at Västra Hoby 12. This can, of

course, also be an indication of ploughed-up graves or votive deposits. Just over 500 m north of Västra Hoby 12 is the linear cemetery of Västra Hoby 5. It cannot be entirely ruled out that these two sites do in fact make up a unit, that is, a continuous elongated linear cemetery. Between these two places, about 100 m north of Västra Hoby 12, is the votive site of Västra Hoby 18. Both fragmentary and whole hollow-edged and thin-bladed axes were found here in dried-out wetland. The find spot is interpreted as a votive site (Karsten 1994:249). The landscape context could mean that some of this find instead belonged to ploughed-up graves which may have been part of a linear cemetery. Reconstructions of the Viking Age road network indicate that the road between Lund and Kävlinge ran in a north-west to south-east direction west of the three sites (Blomqvist 1951). Since the linear cemetery is also oriented in this direction, it may be hypothesized that the graves were laid along a contemporary road. A long time elapsed between MNB and the Viking Age, but the Late Iron Age road network may in any case be a hint of the location of even older communication routes.

It is difficult to find any link between dwelling sites and burial places. Based on the available archaeological material, it does not seem as if graves were dug right beside the settlements. If anything they were placed beside and along communication routes (as at Dagstorp 11 and Västra Hoby 5). Finds of axes in the passage graves at Västra Hoby and Lackalänga show that these were a part of the community in this period too. The votive deposits in wetlands, just like those in the Välabäcken valley, seem to be located away from contemporary settlements and perhaps also away from the roads.

The former bays at the estuaries of the Mare Bäck and Lödde Å were still important for settlement in MNB (fig. 100). Several places which were occupied in the late MNA were also visited during this period. It is above all on the Barsebäck foreland that we see continuity in settlement. The find of a battle axe of type A in the passage grave in Gillhög is a sign that the Battle Axe culture gained an early foothold here. The few excavations which have touched on Battle Axe settlement in this area have not identified any remains of houses. Nor have the excavations here been of a sufficiently large area to identify the buildings. There are no known flat-earth graves which can be dated to this period. The difficulty of discovering this type of feature may explain the lack of graves. The tendency towards a decline in wetland offerings in this part of the investigation area seems to apply to MNB as well. In his work on Neolithic votive finds, Karsten mentions three places where blade arrowheads have been found in bogs, one of type A and two of type C (1994). It is uncertain which culture these belong to, and they could also have been shot away by people hunting. Votive deposits in which the object is an axe, on the other hand, are completely missing in the area.

Continuity can also be discerned in the settlement at Stävie and Hög (fig. 101). A number of settlements were located in the valley of the Lödde Å. The central place at Stävie probably ceased to function some time in the course of MNB. Finds of Battle Axe pottery at the passage grave in Hög nevertheless show that the area was still of significance for the population.

**Social organization**   The lack of remains of structures at the settlements, as we have seen, means uncertainty about how the sites were organized and makes it difficult to interpret the social organization. As a whole, it is only in exceptional cases that excavations of Battle Axe sites in southern Scandinavia have given such results that it has been possible to discuss dwelling site organization (Adamsen & Ebbesen 1986; Larsson, L. 1989a). I nevertheless believe that the few traces that exist, together with the remains of graves, votive sites, and central places, give some clues to an understanding of MNB society. At the transition between MNA and MNB and in the early MNB there are only occasional remains of settlement in the investigation area. The circular huts at Saxtorp 23 and the round-oval

concentration of post-holes at Lackalänga can probably be ascribed to the Stävie group. Houses thus seem to be wholly lacking in the archaeological material from the early Battle Axe period in the investigation area. The palisaded enclosure and the find in Gillhög are nevertheless clear evidence that bearers of the Battle Axe culture were represented in the region. The occurrence of these remains also presupposes that some of the surface-surveyed settlements, where artefacts usually dated to MNB have been identified, could probably derive from an early part of the Battle Axe culture. The existing traces of Battle Axe culture settlements are scarce, however. I have interpreted this as a combination of a relatively brief use of each site together with an attitude to waste different from that prevailing in the Funnel Beaker culture, that is, a different deposition tradition. The element of animal husbandry in the Battle Axe culture seems to have been large and may have been pursued in a way that is comparable with nomadism (cf. Larsson, L. 1989b:73). Thus, nothing in the existing settlement site material suggests the existence of large sites where households lived simultaneously. Presumably people moved in rather small groups the size of one or two nuclear families.

I believe that there are indications that the old form of organization of kin groups was dissolved at the transition to MNB. In Funnel Beaker society the single family was the base that was united with others via shared ancestors. One or more kin groups formed a local community under the leadership of an élite consisting of some elders from special families. These power structures had been reproduced and reinforced ever since the opening phase of the Early Neolithic through shared rituals in which the collective was emphasized and inequalities were concealed. The scene and the design of the rituals varied, but the aim was to legitimize the power vested in a few by asserting the bonds to the ancestors. In this way the leaders affirmed their power over time and place. I discussed the reasons for changes in Funnel Beaker society in the that the structural principles for power relations had changed.

The scattered and small settlements contributed to the avoidance of relations of dominance between different groups. There were opportunities for the individual, the household, or the little local group to improve their social position as far as the prevailing social system permitted. The more mobile way of life was expressed in the way that places were no longer so clearly marked. Battle Axe sites seem to lack the pits of various kinds that characterized many Funnel Beaker sites. Whether these pits were primarily used for waste, storage, or votive activities, they mark a sense of belonging to the place. In certain cases we may suspect that the deposited objects were a cross-section of the everyday activities as a manifestation of these tasks. The deposits were a ritualized routine which reproduced the prevailing structural principles that tied the individual and the group to the place. Waste at Funnel Beaker sites was regarded as a product of the maintenance of the prevailing order on a site. There was no need to clean the area. For the people of the Battle Axe culture, on the other hand, who only set up short-term camps, identity was not linked to the site. Belonging to a place did not need to be expressed in the form of special rituals whereby objects were buried in the ground, and people probably carried the majority of their everyday artefacts with them. Perhaps their mobile way of life meant that the landscape did not need to be permanently reshaped and socialized in the way expressed by the Funnel Beaker culture with its grave monuments of stone. If there are no distinct traces in the landscape, this may of course be because people deliberately chose not to reshape their surroundings. Natural formations in the terrain could function as nodes in the landscape, and some of the old monuments could still be used for private rituals. While it is true that the palisaded enclosures meant a major reshaping of the landscape, as I have pointed out before, they were not of a permanent nature but were raised for special events in the present.

The changed mortuary practice, with the flat-earth grave as the form now prevailing, can also be seen as an expression of changed power structures. Although some of the megalithic tombs were also used in MNB, it was not at all on the same scale as in earlier parts of the Middle Neolithic (MNA I–III) and of a more private character. The large ceremonies assembling many people at the monuments had ceased. Instead the linear cemeteries should perhaps also be seen in the light of a more mobile pattern of life and individual thinking. As I have previously pointed out, there is some

preceding chapter. Several groups within the Funnel Beaker culture gradually adopted a way of life practised by the coastal populations who had formerly lived further to the north (the Stävie group). Others, presumably the majority, assimilated somewhat later ideas prevailing on the continent (the Battle Axe culture). Two groups with different cultural features thereby came to coexist during a period of MNB. By this I mean population groups who regard themselves as belonging to a delimited category of people and who share fundamental cultural values.

During this period of internal division, the Funnel Beaker society was in a state where new influences from outside had greater opportunity to make themselves felt. The unifying forces, in the form of a stratum of leading elders, were weakened, as was the collective ideology. The communal ceremonies at the megalithic tombs ceased and the settlement was split up into smaller units. I therefore believe that the new elements noticeable in society at the transition to MNB were not the result of large-scale immigration; the seedbed of change probably existed within the Funnel Beaker society. Similarities in mortuary practice and in material culture over much of northern and central Europe show that there were wide-ranging contacts. The increased links with the people of the continent are also noticeable in a growing number of metal objects of various kinds in the middle and later part of the Battle Axe culture (Janzon 1986:126f). In addition, battle axes made of volcanic rocks have been found in the Hagestad area and elsewhere, which can probably be traced to central Europe (Strömberg 1975:267; Hulthén, B. pers.com.). It is thus reasonable to assume that influences and innovations were spread within an existing and well-developed network of contacts without large movements of people.

The society that emerged – alongside the coastal populations that I have chosen to call the Stävie group (cf. Larsson, L. 1989b) – was built up just as before, with the family as the smallest unit of production. The archaeological evidence nevertheless contains hints evidence that the linear cemeteries were placed along contemporary roads. For a people in movement it was natural that the graves should lie where communications ran. The older grave monuments were also probably located on communication routes, but these did not express a movement forwards in the terrain in the same way as the linear cemeteries must have done. The Battle Axe graves may also be said to emphasize the individual or the family. Unlike the collective burial space which the passage graves probably constituted, the Battle Axe graves were intended for one or just a few individuals. When the collective ideology broke down, burial customs changed. The leading stratum no longer consisted of elders who legitimized their power through a close relationship to the ancestors.

The new power relations seem to have been based on secular and economic experience rather than on sacred knowledge. At the MNA/MNB transition a new form of central places was established, with a design and finds showing other activities and values than those prevailing at the megalithic tombs in an earlier phase of the Middle Neolithic. A general aim of the sites at Stävie and Dösjebro was of course to maintain regional and perhaps supraregional social contacts. In a kind of society where there were no large settlements consisting of several household units and where the megalithic tombs no longer functioned as formal ceremonial sites, the new meeting places satisfied the need to achieve social integration. A closer study of the sites indicates special functions. The complex at Dösjebro reveals an environment where the production and distribution of axes played a major role. Both east and north of the palisaded enclosure, on other side of the Välabäcken, axe-manufacturing places have been documented which have been assumed on reasonable grounds to be contemporary with the palisade. Deposits of flakes from axe manufacture at the palisade posts and of whole and fragmentary axes beside the enclosure also illustrate the important role of the axe on the site. At the Stävie site there are ovens which may possibly have been intended for firing pottery

(Larsson, L. 1982:88). Over a hundred fragmented axes have been retrieved from here, and a new look through the finds showed that axe-manufacture flakes occur in the occupation layer and in one of the pits. The craft seems to have been important at these central places. The production, distribution, and deposition of axes and axe waste gives insight into the new ideology in MNB. They also demonstrate the existence of a comprehensive network.

The manufacturing process was not just a matter of shaping axe blanks; it also produced a quantity of waste. At the knapping places at the palisaded enclosure in Dösjebro can we observe the last two steps in the process of manufacturing flint axes. The large amount of polished fragments suggests that production also included the reknapping of axes. The total absence of big flakes from the initial manufacturing sequence indicates that this took place elsewhere. I believe that the flakes should not be regarded as waste but as a product of cultural value like the axes. The deposits of some of the axe-manufacture flakes corroborate this, and may be seen as a procedure whereby the flint was returned to the earth (Cooney 2000). As a whole, the production and distribution of axes should be regarded as a significant activity surrounded by various rules. The choice of manufacturing sites illustrates that this activity was not linked to the settlement but to significant places in the landscape. The knapping places around Dösjebro are located in an area that had been characterized since the end of the Early Neolithic by ceremonial activities. It is likely to have been a part of the mythology long before axe production was started. The location of production beside the palisaded enclosure suggests that it was an integral part of large social gatherings. The fact that large flint nodules for axe manufacture are lacking in the area of the Välabäcken valley means that they must have been brought from the areas where the raw material could be found, namely, on the raised beaches along the coast. It may have been on the shore at Barsebäck, at Stenbocksvallar, that the flint nodules were reworked into quadrilateral axe planks before they were transported further to places like Dösjebro. Some nodules were perhaps brought from the flint mines in the Malmö area or even from flint-rich areas in Denmark.

The axe-manufacturing places were thus centrally located in the landscape, the knapping places show that production was probably on a large scale, the treatment of flakes from axe manufacture suggests strict rituals in connection with the manufacturing process, and production took place outside the primary flint areas – all of which is evidence of a well-developed distribution network. There are powerful reasons to assume that those who controlled this activity enjoyed a powerful position in society. Renewed interest in depositing axes in wetlands in the late MNA and MNB highlights the significance of the axe as a prestige object. Deposits of axes at the megalithic tombs reinforce this picture. This also shows an ideological change, with the emphasis shifted from the collective to the single family or the individual. As I discussed above, pottery and complicated decorative styles may indicate an emphasis on belonging to a group, while an axe is better regarded as a personal attribute. The axe was an object to be carried on the person, and was probably of great significance in the exchange of gifts and the forging of alliances (Tilley 1996:101; Cooney 2000). The custom of private sacrifices thus seems to have undergone a renaissance in MNB. An interesting difference from previous periods is the occurrence and deposition of several different axe types (hollow-edged, thin-bladed, medium-bladed, and B-axes). In EN I it was the pointed-butted axe that was sacrificed, while the thin-butted axe and the thick-butted A-axe were the most commonly deposited types in wetlands in EN II–MNA II and in MNA III–V. In addition, deposits of battle axes and faceted grindstones have been documented in the investigation area in MNB. The battle axe, the hollow-edged thick-butted axe, and the thin-bladed flint axe also occur frequently in the flat-earth graves of the Battle Axe culture. Regardless of functional differences between the axe types, their occur-

rence means that the number of prestige objects increased. An increase in individual status objects may be connected to the changed power relations. It was now important for individuals to mark their position or status, partly through these artefacts.

Unlike the situation during the Funnel Beaker culture – possibly with the exception of its initial phase – it thus does not seem as if status positions in the Battle Axe culture were kin-based and given from birth. This is noticeable, among other things, in the way the population is no longer as tied to place. In the Funnel Beaker culture people had made communal investments in newly colonized land, with the result that subsequent generations lived on the work of the previous generation. The elders in society, who were closest to the ancestral spirits, acquired a position of power and controlled the means of production and the productive resources. This had given rise to a one-sided dependence and obligations for the young vis-à-vis the old. The megalithic tombs and the collective ceremonies held at them were an expression of this. Instead, in the Battle Axe culture, an individual or family probably acquired prestige and status in the eyes of other members of the community through different types of social strategies. The scattered and mobile settlement broke the hereditary dominance, and the mortuary ritual asserted the individual or the family rather than the collective. Acquired status was based on the special knowledge of certain individuals (cf. Nordquist 2001:29f). The prominent position of the flintsmith is noticeable through the localization of knapping places in the landscape and the link to the palisaded enclosure, as well as through the ritual treatment that seems to have been associated with the axe manufacture. Those who controlled this activity presumably had a significant power position and represented the unity of the local community. In reciprocal relations between communities, they represented the economic interests of the group, and the most important task of this leading stratum was probably to establish and maintain alliances which satisfied the group's need for necessary

216

resources. The ceremonies at the central places in Dös-jebro and Stävie were important because different groups met here to forge alliances. The meetings between the groups were an opportunity to strengthen the respect and prestige of one's own group. Competition was also expressed in efforts to better one's position in relation to the spirit world. Deposits of axes-manufacture flakes at the palisade posts should probably be viewed in this light – as a deliberate act to create and reinforce bonds with the gods. Fragments of axes or pots identified adjacent to the enclosure may be the result of deliberate destruction of some of the surplus production with the aim of asserting one's own importance and that of the group and favouring the relationship to higher powers.

The renewed tradition of depositing offerings in wetlands can probably be associated with the new individual ideology. Since individuals and families had the opportunity to acquire social status independent of kin affiliation, the private relationship to the gods was once again important. In his work on Scanian Neolithic votive finds, Karsten shows that it was to a large extent the older votive sites that came into use again after an interruption of a few hundred years. He says that "*The oral tradition that enabled the content of the rituals to be passed on thus did not only have information about which wetland people used to make offerings in, but the exact location of the votive site in it*" (Karsten 1994:180). This is of course an argument that the Battle Axe culture, in combination with continental influences, evolved within the framework of the Funnel Beaker tradition. The material that we associate with the Battle Axe culture signalled a breach with an older social system (cf. Damm 1993:200). The new groups that emerged locally wanted to show their social and symbolic distance from the old traditions and people in power. It was important for the new leaders to free themselves from the preceding Funnel Beaker society, which can explain the material differences between the two cultures. One way for the new power group to show its

rivalry and distance openly was to use material culture to stress their differences.

The material culture that grew up was not a local phenomenon; it had its foundation in a shared cultural complex which in central and eastern Europe goes under the name of the Corded Ware culture, whereas in western Europe it is known as the Bell Beaker or Beaker culture. In Denmark, Holland, and western Germany, the mortuary practice has given the name Single Grave culture, while the Swedish, Norwegian, and Finnish counterparts were originally called the Boat Axe culture, but in recent years the term Battle Axe culture has become the most common designation for the culture in this area (Malmer 1962, 1975; Larsson, L. 1989b). The wide distribution should not be seen as reflecting large-scale migrations; instead, when the local social structures broke down and a new identity was built up, it was natural to adopt already existing symbols. The European network was well developed and innovations spread rapidly. People thus showed their solidarity with other continental groups while simultaneously being in opposition to the old system.

I thus believe that the population group that broke away from the Funnel Beaker culture and followed the continental currents had its origin in the Funnel Beaker culture. The foundation had been laid for new ideas to grow as a consequence of the changes in society and shifts in power that had begun at the end of MNA. This explains why the earliest Battle Axe settlement seems to have gained a foothold in the old core areas of the Funnel Beaker culture (fig. 102). The fact that the palisaded enclosure in Dösjebro, which can be dated to the early Battle Axe culture, was built on the same site as the late Funnel Beaker culture's place of assembly also demonstrates similarities and continuity in the organization of society. The structures are a form of central place which functioned during the period when the settlements split up. To a certain extent the megalithic tombs were still used for votive and/or funeral ceremonies during the Battle Axe culture. This can be seen as a way for the new people in power to

217

218

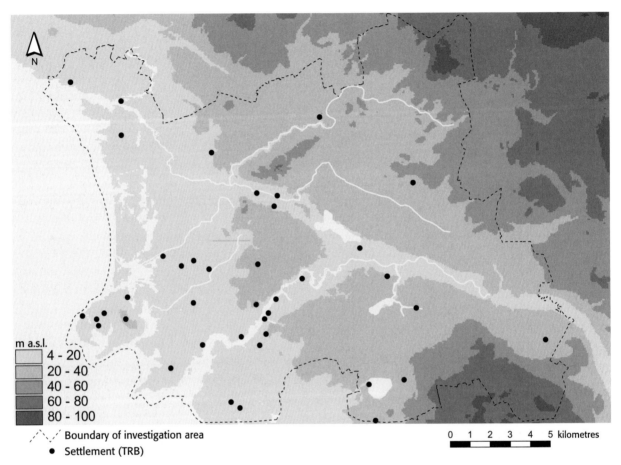

m a.s.l.

4 - 20
20 - 40
40 - 60
60 - 80
80 - 100

0  1  2  3  4  5 kilometres

⌒\_⌒ Boundary of investigation area
● Settlement (TRB)

Fig. 102a–c. Settlement sites in the late MNA and MNB.

take over the sacred places of the Funnel Beaker culture and thereby confirm the change of power. But it also shows that there seems to have been a hereditary solidarity and kinship with the old sacred places and that perhaps more private votive rituals were performed at the monuments.

On the basis of the finds, the Stävie structure should be linked to the Stävie group. The site at Stävie shows structural similarities to Sarup sites (causewayed enclosures) and the customs of the Funnel Beaker culture. The ditches and the pits with objects on the tongue of land follow the deposition traditions of the Funnel Beaker culture. The Stävie group seems to have arisen through an assimilation of Pitted Ware and Funnel Beaker populations. The two cultures probably had a shared origin in the early Funnel Beaker culture, so it is not surprising that their assembly places had a structure corresponding to that of the earlier Sarup sites. The Battle Axe culture was likewise a local development from the Funnel Beaker culture. The difference is that the Stävie group consists of populations who had broken out of the Funnel Beaker society already in the late MNA and adopted and assimilated a Pitted Ware way of life, while those who turned to the traditions of the Battle Axe culture at the start of MNB totally broke away from the older kin-based social organization and identified with currents on the continent.

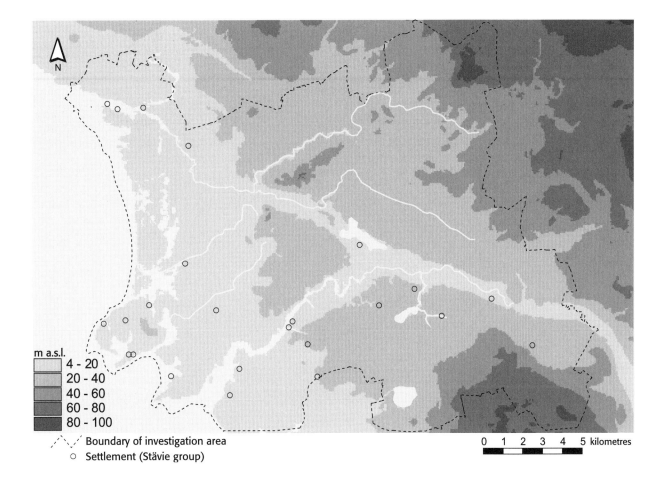

m a.s.l.

- 4 - 20
- 20 - 40
- 40 - 60
- 60 - 80
- 80 - 100

/˙\.˙/ Boundary of investigation area

○ Settlement (Stävie group)

0   1   2   3   4   5 kilometres

Parts of the Stävie group probably continued to exist at least in the early MNB. Datings from Stävie 3, Saxtorp 23, and Lackalänga suggest this. The settlement pattern can also be interpreted in this way. Whereas the Battle Axe populations mainly moved within the core areas of the Funnel Beaker culture in the interior in the south and north-east, the Stävie group lived in the coastal areas in the west and also along the Lödde Å. The two populations evidently inhabited partly different areas, although they overlap, above all in the south-west. Ideologically these two groups were probably quite far removed. The Stävie group, which partially adopted the lifestyle of coastal Pitted Ware people, practised a mixed economy in which coastal hunting and fishing was probably important. Although they had broken with the hierarchical power relations of the Funnel Beaker culture which were legitimized through lavish ceremonies at the megaliths, several of the older principles of power structure originating in the Ertebølle culture still survived. In the Pitted Ware culture there is often a close association between graves and dwelling site (Malmer 1962, 1975; Wyszomirska 1984; Knutsson 1995). The ancestors were probably significant for the descendants, and as in the Funnel Beaker culture, the veneration of their spirits was a way to assert one's rights to land and legitimize the prevailing order. The organization of dwelling sites, as we have seen, also

220

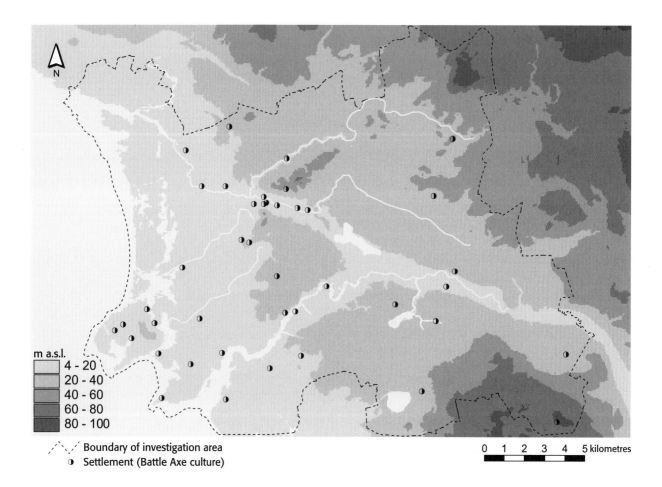

m a.s.l.

4 - 20
20 - 40
40 - 60
60 - 80
80 - 100

/˄\˅/ Boundary of investigation area
◑ Settlement (Battle Axe culture)

0　1　2　3　4　5 kilometres

shows similarities between the culture groups. In the Battle Axe culture, on the other hand, the old power structures had been completely changed, and status was instead acquired through various skills. The material culture clearly shows that the world of symbols had continental influences while the artefacts of the Stävie group incorporated elements from the older Funnel Beaker and Pitted Ware cultures.

The finds, together with differences in the structure of the two central places, indicate, as I have pointed out, that their aim, alongside the unifying function, was partly different. It is likely that the production and distribution of axes did not have as significant a position at the Stävie site as at the palisade in Dösje-

bro. The commercial activities that took place at the palisaded enclosure were perhaps not as prominent at Stävie. Instead, the focus may have been on older traditional forms of ceremony. The deposition of pottery in particular in pits on the tongue of land and in systems of ditches follows the deposition tradition of the Funnel Beaker culture. The aim was no longer to legitimize ancient power structures but still to achieve integration in a divided settlement through traditional ceremonies.

There is nothing in the evidence at the Stävie site or the palisaded enclosure to suggest extensive contact between the two groups. There is no Battle Axe pottery at Stävie and there is no pottery characteristic of the Stävie group at the enclosure. Perhaps the ideological antagonisms were too great to allow profound contacts to be maintained. The Stävie pottery also displays great differences from the pottery of the Funnel Beaker culture and the Battle Axe culture in the Välabäcken valley as regards vessel forms, decoration, and technique (Lagergren Olsson 2003; Stilborg 2003). It seems as if different population groups developed different ceramic traditions. Of course two groups cannot live so close to each other without some kind of mutual influence. Different cultural groups are not built up from the absence of interaction; this is in fact the basis on which a society is built (Barth 1969b). Distinct material differences may exist between groups even if there is an exchange of goods and services. Material culture is used as an active element in social interaction. Different groups with distinctive cultural features can use material culture to emphasize their differences, while a group wishing to use a different group's resources can try to tone down the material expressions of such differences (Hodder 1982:119ff). To some extent the two populations probably used different parts of the landscape and different ecological niches. Both presumably practised a mixed economy, but the Stävie group exploited marine resources to a greater extent while the Battle Axe people carried on animal husbandry. Although it was important to emphasize one's ethnic affiliation through material culture, there may have been an exchange of goods in any case. Anthropology has many examples of coexisting groups using different ecological niches but still trading with each other (see e.g. Barth 1969a, 1969b; Tilley 1982a).

It is clear that the process that gradually led to what we know as the Late Neolithic was started during the Battle Axe culture. New crops in the form of barley were grown on a significant scale. There was probably also an increase in the importance of sheep as wool was used more for spinning and weaving (Hedeager & Kristiansen 1988:83f; Larsson, L. 1989:74). The new design of houses probably took shape in the

late MNB. At the same time the Stävie group probably lost people to the Battle Axe culture. In the long run the rather small groups of people living along the coast could not resist the continental influences that gained an increasingly strong foothold through growing long-distance contacts at the end of MNB.

In the closing phase of the Battle Axe culture the population seems once again to shift to a more permanent settlement pattern. It is precisely in the late MNB or early Late Neolithic that there is evidence of large houses in the investigation area. The three buildings at Dagstorp 11, Dagstorp 19, and Västra Karaby 101 show clear similarities to Late Neolithic houses, but the $^{14}$C analyses and the finds, at least at Dagstorp 19, show that this should be dated to the late MNB. It is during the Late Neolithic that a uniform and almost standardized building tradition emerged in much of southern and central Scandinavia (Björhem & Säfvestad 1989). This Late Neolithic building tradition can evidently be traced back to the late Battle Axe culture. The manner of building changed in that considerable labour was devoted to making houses more durable. This change is probably connected not just to the increased permanence of settlement but can also be associated with a change in the view of the buildings as such.

It seems as if continental influences increased at the end of the south Scandinavian Battle Axe culture. Three houses excavated at Myrhøj in northern Jutland have shown the link between the late Single Grave culture and the continental Bell Beaker culture. Pottery of Single Grave type occurs on the site together with pottery showing clear similarities to that of the Bell Beaker culture. Apart from this there are other artefacts, such as a wrist guard of stone and flat-flaked arrowheads, which display a clear connection between the Bell Beaker culture and the late Single Grave culture (Jensen 1973). In Jutland there are a number of other houses and graves containing Bell Beaker material (Skov 1982; Simonsen 1983; Apel 2000:47). From Sjælland and Skåne too, there are occasional finds sug-

221

gesting that the Bell Beaker culture may have had an influence on development in these areas. The occupation layer at the house at Dagstorp 11 contained a flat-flaked arrowhead with a short tang which is considered characteristic of the Bell Beaker culture (Vang Petersen 1993:92). In addition, two potsherds with Bell Beaker–inspired decoration were identified in the layer. About a kilometre south-west of Dagstorp 11, Bell Beaker pottery was excavated from a post-hole near a Late Neolithic farm consisting of a long-house and a small outhouse (Västra Karaby 35) (Pettersson 2000:53f). There were evidently contacts between the Bell Beaker culture and the Battle Axe culture which may have been of crucial significance for the emergence of the Late Neolithic culture in southern Scandinavia.

It is interesting that the houses we know from the late MNB/early Late Neolithic in the investigation area were built on sites with a long continuity and a special significance. The house at Dagstorp 11 was built virtually parallel to the linear cemetery. The cemetery must surely have been known when the house was built, at least if the graves had some marking above ground. South of the Välabäcken a long-house was built, cutting across the southern side of the palisaded enclosure, and the house at Dagstorp 19 was placed on a site where settlements had existed more or less uninterrupted since EN I. The Bell Beaker influences in the Välabäcken valley and other parts of southern Scandinavia illustrate how the long-distance social network continued to grow. In the Välabäcken valley, which was a centre for the production, consumption, and distribution of axes, particularly successful groups may have been established, in tougher competition. These groups founded settlements in places with a tradition, which shows their awareness of the past. The original significance of the place gave the new settlements a special status, thereby legitimizing the prevailing political organization. The permanence of the existing structures and a more stable way of life were constructed through the new houses and later in the new form of grave, the stone cist. This came at a time when people were once again starting to be more or less settled compared with the more mobile way of life in the Battle Axe culture. The stone cist, alongside the houses and like the megalithic tombs, thus symbolized a link to the land, investments made in it, and access to its resources. Once again, people thus began to make collective graves in the form of megalithic structures, although the stone cist differs in design and size from its Middle Neolithic counterparts.

At the end of MNA the Funnel Beaker society had within it the seeds of the changes which meant that new continental ideas could gain a foothold in southern Scandinavia in the form of the Battle Axe culture. The social organization that emerged in the Early and Middle Neolithic had developed a system with increasing central control, the structures of which were legitimized and concealed through collective rituals at the megalithic tombs. The resources required to maintain these ceremonies were a strain on the people, some of whom broke out of the organization. They adopted the more egalitarian way of life of coastal groups in south Scandinavia. This Stävie group lived in small, autonomous groups but still maintained old Funnel Beaker traditions.

The bearers of the Battle Axe culture thereby made a complete break with the old society and instead adopted an ideology and a symbolic language that took inspiration from the continent. In this society, power was structured not on the basis of kin relations but was acquired through social competence. The new individual ideology was emphasized and reproduced via flat-earth graves, long-distance contacts, status objects, and mobility in settlement. ∎

223

# A wider geographical perspective

*The geographical region, and the people who live there, functions like a living process in that places, regions, and identities are products of people acting within a historically constituted network of power relations and exchange of knowledge. Communication is expressed in the transfer of goods and people, of thoughts and ideas. Ceramic craft, house types, modes of production, and so on, were once innovations that were adopted and became part of the culture of the regions. In the following discussion I intend to place certain decisive events in the Neolithic of western Skåne in a broader Scanian and Danish perspective. The expression taken by different phenomena in different areas may give an understanding of the significance of the culture-historical background of particular regions for the spatial distribution of innovations.*

The Funnel Beaker culture and the Battle Axe culture are the designations given to Early and Middle Neolithic population groups in northern and central Europe with a partially shared material culture and a similar way of life. The Neolithic meant not only a new element in the economy but a whole new way to order both the social world and the natural environment (see chapter 5). The domestication of resources was part of the conceptual world that concerned social relations and the link between the community, the ancestors, and the landscape. The new ideology was about the mastery of time and place, and the domestication of plants and animals was a part of this control, with tillage and animal husbandry involving a transformation of the landscape. Later, monuments were constructed which further dominated the landscape and which created a lasting relationship between time and place. In my account of Neolithic societies in western Skåne, however, I have considered it important to proceed from the regional situation. The form of a society is dependent on the specific culture-historical background of each area, and despite shared supraregional structures, the way in which innovations arise, spread, are accepted and used can vary from one region to another.

In the Mesolithic we see relatively extensive settlement in the valley landscape of coastal western Skåne (Jennbert 1984a:103ff), and in the Early and Middle Neolithic it is clear that the area was a significant population region in Skåne. In my work I have found how similar structures were active, governing the form of organization of the societies that inhabited the west Scanian valleys. Geographically the region comprises the gently undulating areas around the two river valleys from the Öresund coast about twenty kilometres inland, and it is demarcated by the transition to more highland terrain to the north-east and south-west (figs.

1 and 3). The definition of this region is thus based on obvious geographical conditions, but it is of course chiefly the archaeological observations that determine the interpretation. A greater density of Neolithic settlements, votive finds, and graves was already documented in the area (Malmer 1962; Strömberg 1980; Karsten 1994; Tilley 1996), and my investigation has shed light on the special organization of Neolithic settlement and society in the region. Large, increasingly permanent settlements had already arisen in the Late Mesolithic along the bays at the estuaries of the Saxån and Lödde Å, at Tågerup and Löddesborg respectively, with continuity into the Early Neolithic. The places functioned as main settlements to which the society's various secular and sacred activities were attached. The number of similar main settlements seems to have increased in the Early Neolithic, and the link to the Late Mesolithic traditions and power structures was strong. The identity of the local community was thus bound in time and place to the settlement, but the landscape was open in so far as no demarcated settlement districts existed yet. Settlement gradually expanded inland and the landscape was socialized. It has been possible to follow how different landscape spaces or settlement districts were formed within the region, within which special places intended for different activities arose, and it was the relationship of these places to each other that defined the landscape spaces. The different landscape spaces, which were built up in a similar way with one or a few large dwelling sites (main settlements), grave monuments, and votive sites, functioned as the spaces within which a local community performed its different activities over the annual cycle. It should be emphasized, however, that prehistoric societies rarely had clearly defined borders, whether geographical or mental, although they can be associated with a specific area (Giddens 1984:163).

I have defined a society as consisting of a group of people who feel that they have a shared identity which differs from that of surrounding societies. The existence of the society is therefore based in part on the occurrence of external relations, in that an internal identity is partly created through contacts with other groups. The organization in time and place on and between sites in the valley landscape spaces thus shows the similar structural principles that prevailed, which meant that the area can be regarded as a united region in which different local communities interacted closely.

The geographical region, and the people who live there, functions like a living process in that places, regions, and identities are products of people acting within a historically constituted network of power relations and exchange of knowledge. Communication is expressed in the transfer of goods and people, of thoughts and ideas. Ceramic craft, house types, modes of production, and so on, were once innovations that were adopted and became part of the culture of the regions. In the following discussion I intend to place certain decisive events in the Neolithic of western Skåne in a broader Scanian and Danish perspective. The expression taken by different phenomena in different areas may give an understanding of the significance of the culture-historical background of particular regions for the spatial distribution of innovations.

Even before a Neolithic way of life was established in southern Scandinavia (see chapter 5), the Late Mesolithic groups were in contact with continental populations who had adopted cultivation and animal husbandry. The ceramic craft is clear evidence of these contacts. Finds of shaft-hole axes of rock, known as *Schuhleistenkeile*, are examples of direct imports reaching Scandinavia. Finds of bones from domesticated livestock in layers which can probably be dated to the Late Mesolithic at Löddesborg (Jennbert 1984a:90f) and impressions of cereal grains in Ertebølle pottery at Löddesborg and Vik (Jennbert 1999) are further signs of links with the south.

Although relations with continental farming groups were evidently significant, the hunter-gatherers of southern Scandinavia did not adopt many Neolithic elements in their economy until much later (Tilley 1996). Most scholars agree that agriculture in some form was not pursued in southern Scandinavia before about 5000 BP (3950 cal. bc) (Kristiansen 1988; Hodder 1990; Welinder 1998), although cultivation on a small scale may have occurred already in the Late Mesolithic. The first agriculture was probably only a small part of the total economic activity. Perhaps the cereals and livestock, as Jennbert has suggested, functioned as goods consumed at feasts or as "productive gifts" used to maintain diplomatic relations (Jennbert 1984a:141f).

The region of south Scandinavia which has seen the largest archaeological investigation in recent years is probably the Malmö area, in connection with large projects to construct housing, industry, roads, and railways in and around the city since the 1960s (Björhem 2000). A large number of the excavated remains have included Neolithic material.

Here too, several of the Neolithic settlements which can be dated to the start of the Early Neolithic were located on the coast and at places previously used by Late Mesolithic people, such as Soldattorpet, Gränsstigen, Kvarteret Nore, and Elinelund (Kjellmark 1903; Salomonsson 1960a, 1971; Larsson, M. 1984:211; Jennbert 1984a:64f). Soldattorpet was excavated by Knut Kjellmark in 1901–1904. He believed that the dwelling site may have extended over a long narrow area for about 450 m on the Järavallen ridge. It is uncertain whether Soldattorpet may have been connected with Gränsstigen, immediately north of the dwelling site, which was excavated in 1960 by Bengt Salomonsson. The stratigraphy of the two sites was very similar. On the two sites, bones of domesticated animals were found in the same layer as Early Neolithic pottery belonging to the Oxie group (EN I). At Kvarteret Nore and Elinelund, pottery was likewise identified in the upper layers which can be placed in the Oxie group. Occasional tooth fragments from cattle have been identified in features which can be dated to the transition from the Late Mesolithic to the Early Neolithic at Elinelund (Jonsson 2002). The four sites are evidence that settlement on the coast was probably still important at the start of the Neolithic. At the same time, as Mats Larsson has noted (1984), a move of settlement to the freshwater systems of the interior can be observed at places like Björkesåkra, Sturup, Oxie, Skabersjö, Värby, and Hässleberga. This movement probably does not mean that the coast was abandoned for settlement, but

226

that different parts of the landscape were claimed in a new way, earlier, and on a larger scale than further north in Skåne. Unlike the valley landscape in western Skåne, there are clearer indications that long barrows were constructed here already in the initial phase of the Neolithic. At Kristineberg there was an excavation in 1977 of the remains of settlements and two long barrows which have been dated by $^{14}$C analyses and pottery to EN I (Rudebeck & Ödman 2000). Elisabeth Rudebeck and Katarina Ödman say that it is hypothetically possible to imagine on the site three or four phases in EN I and at the transition to EN II. The oldest phase represents activities at the transition between the Late Mesolithic and the Early Neolithic. A piece of charcoal in a feature from this phase has been dated to 5320±120 BP (4327–3985 cal. bc, LuA–4538). If this value can also be used to date a potsherd with impressions of emmer or spelt wheat found in the feature, it is the earliest date of Funnel Beaker pottery with grain impressions in southern Scandinavia (Rudebeck & Ödman 2000:99; Gustavsson 2000). Probably belonging to the second phase are several periods of occupation and burial with brief intervals between them. During this phase, work began on the construction of the two long barrows. In the third phase, at the transition to EN II, a burial chamber was built in the southern long barrow (Rudebeck & Ödman 2000:99f; Rudebeck 2002: 104f). In connection with the archaeological excavations in 2002 preceding the construction of the City Tunnel in Malmö, four ploughed-out long barrows and two presumed dolmen sites were excavated at Almhov, just a few hundred metres from the coast as it was then. In all four long barrows it was possible to document stone-lined ditches or post-holes at the east façade, and a few metres west of the façade there were stone structures which probably represent the primary graves. One of the graves contained skeletal parts belonging to one individual; fragments of the top of the skull suggest that the skull was placed at the feet. Parts of the filling were preserved in one of the long barrows. A thin-butted axe was retrieved from here adjacent to the primary grave.

A charcoal sample taken from a façade post-hole has yielded a date in EN I, 4990±70 BP (3940–3700 cal. bc, Ua-17158). Early Neolithic pits have been found in the vicinity of the long barrows (Gidlöf & Johansson 2002:12; Gidlöf, K., Johansson, T. and Sarnäs, P., pers.com.). It is uncertain, however, whether these are connected to rituals held at the monument or are the remains of a settlement phase. Two more partly excavated long barrows in south-west Skåne are Örnakulla at Skabersjö and Jättegraven outside Trelleborg, both of which are assumed to have been built early in the Early Neolithic (Larsson, L. 2002). In relation to the situation in western Skåne, Neolithic elements seem to have been adopted earlier in the area around present-day Malmö.

The interdisciplinary Ystad Project has charted the prehistory of parts of south-east Skåne (Larsson, L. et al. 1992). In this area too, the earliest phase of the Early Neolithic saw continued settlement along the coast, at places like Mossby in Västra Nöbbelöv parish, Kabusa in Stora Köpinge parish, and Ystad Sandskog in Ystad parish. In the lagoon environment at Ystad Sandskog, site continuity can be followed from the Late Mesolithic, while the settlements at Mossby and Kabusa by river mouths seem not to have been established until the Early Neolithic. The distance between Mossby and Ystad Sandskog is just over 15 kilometres, and from there it is four more kilometres to the Kabusa site. It is reasonable to presume that these places were used by different populations. A settlement pattern similar to that in western Skåne can possibly be discerned, with different groups establishing themselves at estuaries or lagoons. Places which were already inhabited in the Late Mesolithic were chosen, but other areas were also claimed as time passed. The distribution of pointed-butted axes suggests that the inner hummocky landscape was also used (Hellerström 1988; Larsson, M. 1992; Larsson, L. 1998). A few kilometres north of Kabusa, a long barrow has been excavated. When a ploughed-out Bronze Age barrow was excavated at Skogsdala it was found that it had been preceded by both a long dolmen and a long

228

barrow. The pottery which can probably be associated with the long barrow suggests that it was built at the end of the Early Neolithic (Jacobsson 1986). The archaeological evidence shows that contacts between south-east Skåne and above all Bornholm were close in much of prehistoric time – a natural consequence of the fact that south-east Skåne is the nearest mainland for the people of Bornholm. In clear weather it is possible to see the Scanian coast from the cliffs at Hammeren in northern Bornholm. Since there is no primary supply of flint in Bornholm, this raw material had to be imported, which presupposes the maintenance of regular contacts with the mainland. Settlement in the earliest part of the Neolithic also seems to have been structured according to principles similar to those in south-east Skåne. There are several settlements and stray finds which can be placed in the first part of the Early Neolithic, both on the coast and inland (Nielsen, F. O. 1996). At Limensgård in southern Bornholm, remains of two two-aisled houses have been documented in an occupation layer with Early Neolithic pottery. The most complete of the two houses had gently rounded gables and an estimated length of 18 m and a width of almost 6 m. A cereal grain from one of the roof-bearing post-holes in one of the two houses has been $^{14}$C-dated to EN I. There are no datings of long barrows in Bornholm (Nielsen & Nielsen 1990; Nielsen, P. O. 1999; Nielsen, F. O. 2001).

Despite the size of the excavated areas, no certain Early Neolithic two-aisled houses have been documented in the Malmö region. The excavations of Fosie IV in Malmö yielded only small and highly uncertain evidence of houses from the Early and Middle Neolithic (Björhem & Säfvestad 1989:16ff). Two buildings, houses 14 and 82, have been considered as possible Early or Middle Neolithic structures, but their dating is uncertain. At Valdemarsro a house of trapezoidal form has been excavated. It was about 12 m long and 6 m wide. The length is uncertain, however, since the eastern part was right at the edge of a trench. The highly unsure dating of this house to the

Early Neolithic is based on a small amount of pottery found in one of the post-holes (Lindahl Jensen 1992). The lack of house remains may of course be due to the houses actually lying outside excavated areas in Malmö. Yet such large areas have been excavated that it cannot be ruled out that a slightly different settlement organization prevailed in the Early Neolithic in this part of the country. In the areas around the valleys of western Skåne we have seen that the Late Mesolithic tradition of large settlements where the majority of the society's activities were performed survived into the Early Neolithic. The main settlements were central places to which the identity of the group and the individual was attached and the significance of the place maintained and manifested through pit offerings and burial ceremonies. There are no large excavated dwelling sites which can be dated with certainty to EN I in south-east Skåne, but the Mossby site, just over 15 kilometres west of Ystad, with its two-aisled house, suggests that the southern and south-east parts of Skåne can also have had main settlements of the same character as in western Skåne. In Bornholm the houses at Limensgård, one of which was about 18 m long and may have functioned as a multi-family house, suggests a similar state of affairs. Perhaps the settlements in the Malmö region never attained this status during the Early Neolithic, which simultaneously meant that they are more difficult to identify in the archaeological record. The evidence at Late Mesolithic coastal sites, such as Kvarteret Nore, Gränsstigen, Elinelund, and Soldattorpet, shows that they were also used in the Early Neolithic, but it is hard to determine the character of the occupation. Since the excavations were concentrated on occupation layers and finds, it is impossible to judge the scope of remains of settlement on these coastal sites. We find a varied inventory of tools at some inland sites (Larsson, M. 1984), perhaps showing that they functioned as main settlements. It is uncertain, however, whether they were the scene of the different activities of the society. In an early phase of the Early Neolithic, large gatherings, where social and spiritual activities were performed, may perhaps have been located in places where long barrows were built – places which may of course previously have functioned as settlements. The dating of the Scanian long barrows is uncertain, but one can detect a tendency for the earliest of them to have been constructed in the Malmö area and south-west Skåne. The long barrow at Skogsdala was probably erected in a later phase of the Early Neolithic, while the dating of Krångeltofta is uncertain.

Perhaps it is reasonable to imagine that a Neolithic way of life gained a foothold first and more distinctly in the south-west of Skåne and gradually spread to the north and east. This idea is corroborated by the excavations at the Early Neolithic site of Nymölla III, by the Hanöbukten bay in north-eastern Skåne, which showed that the element of new Neolithic subsistence here was virtually non-existent (Wyszomirska 1988). The rich occurrence of flint and mining in the Malmö area probably meant that this region acquired special significance early on. The demand for high-quality flint, particularly necessary for axes, increased in the Early Neolithic. Proper flint mines were opened at different places in southern Scandinavia where flint was accessible (Rudebeck 1998).

In Denmark too, the population in the initial phase of the Early Neolithic chose largely to live along the coasts and the fjords (Nielsen, P. O. 1985; Skaarup 1985; Andersen 1993). Often these were places with an ancestry – earlier generations had lived there. Nielsen (1985) has shown that almost 30% of the settlements in Denmark and Skåne which can be associated with the Oxie group (ENA/EN I) were located in places also used by Late Mesolithic populations. The assumption that the coastal sites were used solely for short-term seasonally occupied fishing places, as suggested by Madsen (1982:203–205) and others, is contradicted by the excavations of Bjørnsholm on Limfjorden in northern Jutland. "*The presence of a habitation area and a rich grave behind the shell-mound (S. H. Andersen & E. Johansen 1992) indicates that this*

*site must have had a high economic and social importance in the Early Neolithic. Therefore, it could not have been a short term seasonal catching site*" (Andersen 1993). Apart from the settlements on the coast, special inland areas on lakes and rivers were gradually occupied. Unlike the situation in Skåne, a large number of Early Neolithic flat-earth graves are known in Denmark. Ebbesen (1994) has documented 86 graves from 71 sites. In several cases it was difficult to judge whether the graves were covered by a long barrow or not. What is clear, however, is that in the Early Neolithic there were graves both under flat earth and under long barrows. The majority of the flat-earth graves have been found in Jutland. In several cases the link between dwelling site and graves is not fully elucidated because of small excavation areas or insufficient documentation. There are nevertheless some sites where remains of Early Neolithic settlement are registered beside the graves, which could indicate there was an intimate connection after all. There are a number of examples of long barrows being built on earlier settlements (Liversage 1981, 1992). It is conceivable that some of the main settlements, which also had functions as places for social and ritual gatherings, later had grave monuments erected on them. The place was thus transformed from a settlement into a wholly ceremonial site. A plausible hypothesis is that flat-earth graves were dug on or beside special main settlements in the opening phase of the Early Neolithic. The graves were a part of the rituals to confirm the group's identity which was linked to the place through the ancestors, and in this way the prevailing social order was legitimized and reaffirmed. The construction of a barrow over the graves presumably only happened at certain places in special circumstances. In connection with the socialization of the whole landscape, when some of the activities formerly associated with the main settlement were relocated, material from a dwelling site was gathered in a mound which sealed the graves. The significance of the place was thereby marked physically and it was transformed into a venue for religious ceremonies. What then were the circumstances that led to grave monuments being built earlier in some regions than in others – and not at all in some places?

It is striking that Late Mesolithic society in southern Scandinavia was evidently characterized by tenacious structures. Neolithization came much later here than on the continent, and the transition seems to have been protracted and fairly undramatic. The majority of scholars believe that the economic conditions in southern Scandinavia in the fifth millennium BC were so favourable that a switch to a food-producing lifestyle was not necessary. It was only in connection with a minor change to a cooler, damper climate around 4000 cal. bc that Neolithization, according to this school, got under way. A reduction of the salt content in the sea impaired conditions for oysters and possibly for other marine resources as well (e.g. Rowley-Conwy 1983, 1984, 1985; Zvelebil & Conwy 1984). I have previously touched on the uncertainties in this line of thought. Since the Late Mesolithic population evidently used such a varied range of resources, small ecological changes probably did not affect their subsistence. Moreover, cultivation and animal husbandry never acquired any great economic significance in the initial phase of the Neolithic. To begin with the changes in the social and economic organization were probably limited. It is presumably also the case that Late Mesolithic society was in equilibrium, with harmony in the interaction of the social organization, the environment, and the cosmology (cf. Tilley 1996:68f). Although Late Mesolithic skeletons show that a large share of the population seem to have been victims of violence, this should perhaps be seen primarily as reflecting disputes between different groups (cf. Fischer 2002:372). In the material from graves and dwelling sites there are no clear signs of any serious tensions within the group – between different factions such as men–women, old–young etc. – which could lead to abrupt changes. The structural principles were maintained and reproduced in everyday pursuits and through the funeral rituals; the status is preserved through particularly active deeds. This state of affairs may have prevailed in the initial phase of the Early Neolithic.

Despite the tenacity of a society's structural principles, change nevertheless seems to be something that always exists, even though we do not always note it. We choose change in preference to absence of change to avoid saturation processes in our everyday life (Asplund 1967; Nilsson 2001:69f). The transformation of society at the transition from the Late Mesolithic to the Early Neolithic was a slow process whereby a new ideological concept gradually led to new perceptions of time and place and a change in the power structures of society. It was not a sudden event; the contact maintained between different groups, both within the Ertebølle culture and with the populations on the continent who had adopted agriculture, functioned as a catalyst whereby ideas were inevitably spread along with the traded commodities.

However, it was not a ready-made "Neolithic package" that was delivered to southern Scandinavia, but various expressions of the continental farming societies, the meaning of which was received and transformed in various ways in the different regions of southern Scandinavia. This probably explains why the Neolithization process went on at varying speeds and with varying expressions in different parts of Skåne and Denmark (cf. Tilley 1996:73). Receptiveness to different Neolithic elements was dependent on conditions in each specific society. For example, the need to construct megalithic tombs varied from one area to another.

In Denmark, as in the Malmö area, there are early datings of long-houses and they are concentrated in densely settled areas. One of the oldest known long barrows is from Bjørnsholm in northern Jutland, which has been dated to 5100±160 BP (3990–3650 cal. bc) (Andersen & Johansen 1992:52). Like Barkær, which is also dated to EN I (Liversage 1992), the two long barrows are adjacent to primary deposits of flint and not far from the flint mines in Thisted and Bleg-vad. At least two of the mines in Thisted were in use in the Early Neolithic (Madsen, B. 1993:127). Elisabeth Rudebeck suggests that flint mining in the opening phase of the Early Neolithic should perhaps be regarded as a rare and esoteric pursuit. An analysis of pointed-butted and thin-butted flint axes – made of Senonian flint probably deriving from the mines at Södra Sallerup – showed that the majority of the pointed-butted axes, unlike the thin-butted ones, had kept a small part of the cortex at the butt section. According to Rudebeck, this could be interpreted as showing that it was considered important to leave a "trademark" indicating the origin and quality of the flint. It also suggests, possibly, that the flint obtained by mining was in demand not just because of its physical properties as raw material but was also significant as a symbol of special events within the social sphere. Cortex was therefore not only a guarantee of quality and origin but also showed the importance of the actual flint mining as a social ritual (Rudebeck 1998).

In south-west Skåne and northern Jutland, then, there is evidence of flint mining in the Early Neolithic and, at least in south-west Skåne, at the very start of the Early Neolithic. I believe that the communities in these areas had yet another dimension in their organization. The flint circulated as raw material between different communities, and it is possible that these regions, by selling flint, established early long-distance contacts, which included the continental farming cultures to the south. The belief that flint taken from deep mineshafts possesses special qualities apart from purely physical ones gave the raw material a special exclusiveness. Skill in mining and flint technology therefore gave authority to local experts in these areas, which contributed to a more distinct social hierarchy here than in other regions. The exchange of goods is an important medium through which social obligations and debts are built up and a higher social position is attained. The growing social complexity together with the far-reaching contacts with groups on the continent led to "Neolithic power monuments" like the long barrow being established earlier in certain flint-rich areas in southern Scandinavia. These groups thus adopted the tradition of building grave monuments, partly as a way to assert the right to a particular territory and its resources. This took place in areas which were probably fairly densely populated already in the Late Mesolithic. The mining areas may have functioned as centres from which the innovations were passed on to other parts of southern Scandinavia.

The population in western Skåne, in contrast, adopted the custom of building megalithic tombs in connection with the occupation of new land (see chapter 5). Tensions between different groups arose when an older élite acquired social control which they legitimated at ceremonies. Some of the population sought freedom from this supremacy and settled new areas which had only been temporarily visited before this. Grave monuments were erected, probably not until the second half of the Early Neolithic, as a stage in the socialization of the "new" landscape and not, as in south-west Skåne or northern Jutland, to confirm and strengthen the "old" lands and resources. The basic power structures of society nevertheless persisted, and rituals at the megalithic tombs served to legitimize the new people in power.

In some places, then, it seems that monument building took place later, while other areas did not adopt the tradition at all. It is striking that the grave monuments in Skåne are concentrated in the most densely populated areas – where we have the most numerous and most distinct remains of Neolithic settlement. In the central and northern parts of the province there are few or no megalithic tombs. Randsborg (1975) has linked the occurrence of megalithic tombs to densely populated areas. It is probably the case that a relatively large population was a necessary condition for the social and ideological environment required for the construction of these monuments. Building megalithic tombs was a part of the ideological concept which involved a new perception and control of time and place. A Neolithic economy and ideology were interwoven, but not all population groups adopted all the elements. The building of the monuments presupposed the formation of established settlement districts or landscape spaces. Neolithic settlements, votive sites, megalithic tombs, and stray finds show a clear distribution in coastal areas and possibly in the area around Ringsjön as well (Malmer 1957; Sjöström 1992; Karsten 1994). Excavations in the interior of Skåne are limited in number, but it is reasonable to

231

imagine that there was never a need in these areas to socialize the landscape since settlement in the interior was perhaps of a more temporary kind and the transformation of the landscape was limited. The few votive sites and the megalithic tombs might suggest that these activities were still concentrated at the settlements.

At the end of the Early Neolithic, changes in the settlement pattern can be observed in many parts of southern Scandinavia. The changes vary from area to area, but generally speaking it may be said that the number of settlements increases and that they are concentrated in special areas.

In the south-west parts of Skåne, according to Mats Larsson, there was a shift of settlements from the hummocky interior to the rich clay soils on the coast at places like Bellevuegården, Stolpalösa, and Elisedal (Larsson, M. 1984). The coastal areas, as we have seen, were also inhabited during EN I at places like Soldattorpet, Gränsstigen, Kvarteret Nore, and Elinelund, sites already used during the Late Mesolithic. On the other hand, it seems as if settlement became denser on the coast in EN II. In addition, there are elements of pottery belonging to the Bellevuegården group (ENC/ EN II) at Soldattorpet and Gränsstigen which suggest site continuity. In south-east Skåne too, we see a concentration of settlements on the coast, and continuity from EN I can be discerned at some places, such as Kabusa. In both areas of southern Skåne there is distinct site continuity between the late Early Neolithic and the early Middle Neolithic (Larsson, M. 1984, 1985, 1992; Svensson 1986; Larsson, L. 1992a, 1998). It is thus also during this period that the first megalithic tombs are built and deposits in wetlands increase significantly (Karsten 1994). South-west and south-east Skåne are two of the areas in the province with the greatest density of megalithic tombs, and several excavations have demonstrated a link between settlement and megalithic tombs within these regions (Larsson, M. 1988a, 1988b, 1992; Larsson, L. 1992a, 1992c, 1998; Strömberg 1988b). In Bornholm too it is

striking how well the distribution of settlements from EN II–MNA II agrees with the distribution of megalithic tombs and votive deposits (Nielsen, F. O. 1996). In Denmark, Madsen (1982), Skaarup (1985, 1993), Andersen (1997), and others have pointed out the link between dwelling site, burial place, and votive site in the late Early Neolithic and the early Middle Neolithic in central Jutland, on the islands south of Fyn and in south-west Fyn. In these regions too, we can probably discern the rise of special landscape spaces. The number of long barrows, dolmens, and passage graves, however, is much larger in Denmark than in Skåne. Of the roughly 7,000 known megalithic tombs in Denmark, dolmens account for about 90%, which can be compared with the situation in Skåne, where we know of approximately 45 dolmens and 50 passage graves (Skaarup 1993; Bägerfeldt 1993; Burenhult 1999; Tilley 1999a). Above all, the megalithic tombs are concentrated in eastern Denmark and northern Jutland. A partial explanation for the large number of grave monuments in Denmark in relation to Skåne can be given if we also study other phenomena such as votive activity at the big central places.

It seems as if there are regional differences in Early and Middle Neolithic votive customs. In most areas of southern Scandinavia the frequency of deposits shows a considerable rise late in the Early Neolithic compared to the preceding period. On the other hand, dissimilarities can be discerned as regards the type of objects deposited. I have previously dealt with the aspects of source criticism associated with finds from votive sites, since the majority have been found by people working with the land and few sites have been excavated. With these considerations in mind, it may be observed that it was evidently much more common to deposit pots in wetlands in Denmark than in Skåne. Finds of deposited pots are rare in Skåne, with only a few known sites (Karsten 1994:61f). The pottery from the votive fen at Saxtorp 26 is highly fragmented. The sherds are estimated to represent at least 32 pots. However, only fragmented pots have been found in the

232

fen, which might suggest that whole vessels were not deposited, only parts or sherds (Nilsson & Nilsson 2003). At the Neolithic votive fen at Hindby outside Malmö, three Early Neolithic pots were deposited. They were placed at the northern edge of the fen (Svensson 1993). At Röekillorna, parts of Early Neolithic pots were placed in the spring (Stjernquist 1997). Single pots have been documented at four other places (Karsten 1994:61f). In Denmark deposits of pots are common alongside flint axes, amber and bones of animals and humans in the late Early Neolithic and the early Middle Neolithic. In the Danish wetlands the finds are often whole pots or large parts, although small sherds also occur (Becker 1947; Koch 1998).

I have previously discussed the possibility that the varying forms and decoration of the pots emphasized the differences between different groups in a way that axes did not. Dissimilarities in the combination of decorative patterns on the pottery could be an expression of group affiliation. In western Skåne the need to mark social control and group affiliation was not particularly strong at the end of the Early Neolithic. Some of the coastal population had broken up from their old kin groups and established themselves in the interior. In western Skåne – and many other parts of the province – we therefore see that private sacrifices seem to dominate at the end of the Early Neolithic, with deposits of axes. It is only when the inland settlement districts are established at the start of the Middle Neolithic that the demand once again grows for institutionalized rituals, where group identity is marked and the prevailing order confirmed. Pottery now acquires greater significance in the ritual, chiefly at collective activities held at the megalithic tombs, which now acquire a significant role as meeting places as well. In northern Jutland and eastern Denmark this period of "independence" never seems to occur. There are clear signs that the social groups were held together more firmly here, without the same opportunity for breakaway groups as in

western Skåne. In EN II–MNA I a number of enclosed places, known as Sarup enclosures, were established, chiefly in eastern Denmark and northern Jutland. Just over twenty of these are known to date. The design of the enclosure at Sarup, with sections of several smaller enclosures, according to Niels H. Andersen (1997, 2000), can be interpreted as a reflection of the social organization. He believes that the population was organized in a segmented tribal system with each tribe occupying an area of roughly the same size. The different tribes in a given area were politically and economically united, and one expression of this was their assemblies at the big central places – the Sarup sites. Each enclosed section at the central place would thus correspond to one family unit, settlement, or tribe. This regulated organization, in my opinion, could have counteracted the breaking away of certain groups which can be distinguished in western Skåne in the same period.

These structures can thus be viewed as testimony to how formalized the organization was in these parts of Denmark in the late Early Neolithic. For the individual, identity and belonging to the tribe or the local community were important, and it was also essential to mark one's distinctiveness *vis-à-vis* other societies. It is thus reasonable to assume that the role of pottery in the ritual both at the Sarup enclosures and at the megalithic tombs and votive sites had a powerful symbolic meaning in the late Early Neolithic and the early Middle Neolithic. This of course does not rule out the possibility that offerings of a private character could also have occurred in Denmark. The large number of dolmens was thus required to satisfy each society's need for an identity and to maintain the internal balance within the group. Perhaps each family strove to be represented by one dolmen. Like the situation in western Skåne, the dolmen was a guarantee of the prevailing conditions and tied the past together with the present and the future. In the strictly regulated organization in eastern Denmark and northern Jutland, on the other hand, the dolmens marked, in a more significant way than the case was in Skåne, the distinctive character of each local community within the larger union that regularly met at the assembly places. In contrast to the megalithic tombs, rather few Early Neolithic flat-earth graves are known in Sjælland. The majority have been found in Jutland, above all in the northern part of the peninsula (Ebbesen 1994). As in the areas in Skåne which lack megalithic tombs, this might be an expression of the existence of a slightly different social and economic environment. Burials took place adjacent to the dwellings in areas where lasting settlement districts were never established.

There is still no securely documented Sarup enclosure in Skåne in the period. I think that there is no evidence that the Stävie site was constructed in the period EN II–MNA II, although the system of ditches does resemble that of the Sarup-type sites. The material in the ditches at Stävie can be unambiguously dated to the late MNA. Another place which has been proposed as a conceivable Sarup enclosure is Kärragård in southern Halland. On a prehistoric promontory, remains of a ditch about 50 m long (within the excavated area) were excavated and found to contain pottery and flint which can be dated to EN II–MNA II (Wattman 1996). The excavated area was too small, however, to allow a secure assessment of the character of the place. It nevertheless seems likely that in Skåne it was usually the grave monuments and in certain cases the settlements that functioned as assembly sites or central places at the end of the Early Neolithic and the start of the Middle Neolithic.

Thanks to the large areas excavated in connection with the construction of the West Coast Line, it was possible to dig and document large parts of Early and Middle Neolithic settlements along the Saxån and Välabäcken valleys. This meant that a more varied and nuanced image of the organization of a Neolithic dwelling site emerged, and at some of the sites it was assumed that several households could have coexisted on the same site. Our image of Scanian Early and Middle Neolithic settlements has previously been that they

were small, with an area of 400–600 m², and consisted exclusively of single farms (e.g. Larsson, M. 1984, 1992; Edenmo et al. 1997). This view, however, is usually based on limited excavation areas, where perhaps only remains of a single house or parts of an occupation layer have been excavated. These digs have been able to give answers about matters such as the appearance of the material culture and sometimes of buildings, but scarcely about the organization of a dwelling site. Excavations along the West Coast Line showed a varied picture of Early and Middle Neolithic settlement, with both single farms and coexisting farms seemingly occurring. Saxtorp 23 and Dagstorp 19 demonstrated that already in EN I there are examples of several contemporary household units standing on the same spot. At Dagstorp 19, where at least four houses are supposed to have functioned simultaneously, it is reasonable to speculate about the existence of a conglomerate of different farm units in an early phase of the Middle Neolithic. The results from Dagstorp 19 agree with the knowledge we have about Danish dwelling sites from the early Middle Neolithic. The settlements in Langeland illustrate clearly the occurrence of dwelling sites covering large areas. Troldebjerg covered least 30,000 m² and Klintebakken has been estimated as at least 37,000 m² (Skaarup 1985:363). At Troldebjerg a number of horseshoe-shaped houses stood partly dug into the slope. Along the shore are the vestiges of two post-built structures which have been interpreted as long-houses but should perhaps rather be considered as remains of an enclosure or palisade. There have therefore been attempts at a reinterpretation. A small-scale excavation beside the suspected palisade was aimed to ascertain whether there was a pit system similar to that at the central place of Sarup. No such system could be observed at Troldebjerg, so it is still uncertain whether it is a dwelling site or some form of enclosed central place with a ritual function (Skaarup 1985:47). On the site of the big Sarup enclosure in south-west Fyn, a settlement was established in MNA II comprising roughly 40,000 m² (Andersen 1997:115). In Jutland too, there are excavations showing that Middle Neolithic settlements can cover areas of several hectares (Madsen 1982).

The general tendency of settlements varying in area in several parts of southern Scandinavia is probably connected with the general development towards an increasingly collective ideology in MNA. It is likely that several people were tied to one and the same place. This made it easier for the leading stratum to supervise social relations and maintain the prevailing structures. We see that this trend seems to culminate in some areas of Skåne in MNA III. The settlement at Dagstorp 19 probably had its largest population in this period. In Malmö it seems as if settlement was agglomerated on a larger site, namely, Hindby Mosse. Several smaller settlements were concentrated here in a larger unit, located in a naturally well-protected place. The settlement at Hindby was circular with a diameter of about 100 m, a central section virtually without finds, and a division into two demarcated areas (Svensson 1986). In Denmark several of the settlements from this period are likewise large in area with numerous finds, such as Bundsø (Mathiassen 1939), Trelleborg (Mathiassen 1944), Lindø (Winther 1926), Sarup IV (Andersen 1997), and Tøvelsø, which is estimated to have covered an area of 150,000 m² (Skaarup 1985:365). At Lindø remains of at least two houses were documented, one measuring roughly 8×5 m, the other 7×4 m (Winther 1926:24).

I am aware of the problem of determining whether different remains on a site are contemporary. It cannot be ruled out that the large dwelling sites may be the result of repeated visits over a long time. The available radiometric datings and finds, in the form of flint and pottery, do not allow the fine chronology required to decide whether different remains on a site functioned simultaneously. Moreover, the remains, in the form of fences and proper farm structures, are of such a character that the organization of the sites does not give any clear answers. I nevertheless think that the visible traces of settlement, in the form of site organization and patterns, together with theories about social relations, strengthen the hypothesis that the big sites are a result of settlement being concentrated in one place. While the number of settlements both in western Skåne and in areas around Malmö and Ystad was decreasing in MNA III, some of the remaining sites grew in area, which could be viewed as the result of a contraction of settlement (Svensson 1986; Larsson, L. 1998:441). Andersen makes the same reflection about the settlement pattern around Sarup in the period

MNA II–III (Andersen 1997:115–125). For Langeland, Skaarup describes a settlement situation in which the population was grouped in "village-like communities" (Skaarup 1985:365). In places where several buildings not overlapping each other have been documented, as at Dagstorp 19, Lindø (Winther 1926), and Troldebjerg (Winther 1935), or where a regulated site organization can be demonstrated, as at Hindby (Svensson 1986), I believe that there is reason to speak of an agglomerated and contemporary settlement unit.

The absolute zenith in the whole of southern Scandinavia as regards votive deposits – in the form of stone, pottery, and bone objects – in wetlands is reached in EN II. In Denmark, unlike Skåne, pottery is of great significance in the votive ritual, being important for showing group affiliation. This is manifested in the construction of Sarup sites which show the fixed organization that existed here. At the same time, the building of megalithic tombs began in the most densely populated areas. At the start of the Middle Neolithic the votive ritual was redirected to the megalithic tombs and pottery dominated at collective ceremonies. Private sacrifices continued to be made on a small scale, however. At the same time, we see a growth in the size of settlements as the people of a district are brought together in larger units. In Skåne it seems as if this process reached its climax in MNA III, with large settlements such as Dagstorp 19, Barsebäck 48, and the Hindby Mosse site.

Ebbesen has shown that depositions of pottery in grave chambers continued throughout MNA in Denmark, while the customs of offering pottery outside the megalithic tombs, with few exceptions, took place only in MNA I–II on the Danish islands and slightly longer, MNA I–III, in Jutland (Ebbesen 1975, 1978). Hårdh's chronological study of the pottery from the megalithic tombs of western Skåne showed that deposition continued outside these in MNA I–IV, culminating in MNA I–III (Hårdh 1986, 1990b). Deposits of pottery in wetlands likewise reached their zenith in the late Early Neolithic and the early Middle Neolithic in Denmark, after which they decreased sharply (Bennike et al. 1986; Koch 1998). Instead it is deposits of axes that now dominate both away from the megalithic tombs and in the wetlands (Ebbesen 1975; Andersen 2000). In Skåne axes were likewise deposited in front of megalithic tombs in the late Funnel Beaker culture (Strömberg 1968). The changes in the ceremonies at the grave monuments and in the votive practices around the wetlands are thus observed in both Skåne and Denmark in the middle part of MNA, albeit not exactly at the same time. In the period EN II–MNA II votive ceremonies were generally more varied and comprehensive than in later phases. Pottery was important throughout the whole phase in Denmark and the early Middle Neolithic at the passage graves in Skåne. At the end of MNA the flint axe stands out as the most important object to deposit throughout southern Scandinavia. How can the changes in votive activity in the latter part of the Funnel Beaker culture be linked to settlement in the different parts of southern Scandinavia?

In the closing phase of the Funnel Beaker culture and at the transition to the Battle Axe culture there was a change in the settlement pattern in Skåne. The large agglomerated settlements ceased to function, and instead the population lived in small groups. The society consisted of small, autonomous groups which were integrated on special occasions at major central places like those at Dösjebro and Stävie in western Skåne. In Malmö too, within a limited area at Hyllie, two palisaded enclosures have been documented – Hyllie beside Annetorpsleden (Svensson 1991; 2002) and Bunkeflo at Skjutbanorna (Jonsson 1995; Svensson 2002). The latter was on the coastline as it was then, while the other was located beside a wetland area about four kilometres inland. The two sites were located on small elevations in an otherwise flat landscape. The palisades presumably formed oval, completely closed enclosures with an area of between 30,000 and 50,000 m². They consisted of a complicated system of three to five rows of palisades. The finds in the enclosures are limited, but deposits of

axes in post-holes have been registered at both places. The large number of preforms for thick-butted and hollow-edged flint axes collected on the Järavallen ridge at Sibbarp close to Bunkeflo is interesting. These suggest contemporary axe manufacture on a significant scale at the enclosure. The two palisaded enclosures outside Malmö have been dated by means of finds and [14]C analyses to the first half of MNB, that is, the Battle Axe culture (Jonsson 1995; Svensson 1991, 2002). In south-east Skåne there is at least one site which could have functioned as a Middle Neolithic central place. In 1995 a palisade structure was excavated in Stora Herrestad outside Ystad, located on a slight rise which in the Neolithic was a promontory surrounded by wetlands. The structure, which consisted of closely placed post-holes, extended for 110 m over the whole excavation area. The dating of the structure is problematic since no deposited artefacts or charcoal remains of posts were observed (Andersson, T. 1999). The topographical situation of the palisade, however, suggests a Neolithic date (Svensson 2002). At none of these palisaded enclosures have remains of ordinary settlements been found, nor at Stävie. At Hyllie virtually the whole enclosed area was excavated without revealing traces of contemporary houses. It is clear that the sites in Skåne were not used as dwelling sites but functioned as special places of assembly.

In relation to Skåne, the situation in Bornholm seems to have been partly different in the late Funnel Beaker culture. The dwelling sites at Limensgård and Grødbygård in Bornholm have yielded a large amount of material with a great many house remains from the end of MNA and the start of MNB (Nielsen & Nielsen 1985, 1990; Nielsen, P. O. 1999:155). The dwelling sites were used for a long period, and in several cases the houses overlap each other, which makes it difficult to analyse the site organization. At Grødbygård 16 houses have been assigned to MNA V and the first part of MNB. The circumstances at Limensgård are similar, with 18 documented houses, several of which

236

overlap each other. The number of houses on the two sites from MNA V and the first half of MNB is so large that it is likely that some of the units which do not overlap may have been in use simultaneously. Alongside the big settlements, two palisaded enclosures from MNA V have been the subject of trial digs, one at Rispebjerg, the other at Vasagård Øst in southern Bornholm (Nielsen, F. O. 1996, 2000, 2001). The investigations have above all concerned Rispebjerg, where the enclosure and the quantity of finds are much larger than at Vasagård Øst. Systems of several different palisade ditches enclosed an area of about 60,000 m². Traces of settlement in the form of occupation layers with finds of habitation character and remains of houses have been documented inside the enclosures. Perhaps the palisaded enclosures here, unlike those in Skåne, also functioned as settlements. Buildings, in the form of round post-built structures, between seven and eight metres in diameter, also occur at the palisaded enclosures. Whereas the sites in Skåne were used as places for gathering people together from their scattered settlements, their function in Bornholm may also have included habitation. It is interesting that all four sites – Limensgård, Grødbygård, Vasagård Øst, and Rispebjerg – are in a zone stretching just ten kilometres. It is thus clear that settlement in southern Bornholm was concentrated during the late Funnel Beaker culture and the early Battle Axe culture. Bornholm is the only area in southern Scandinavia where clear house remains from MNA V and early MNB have been documented (Nielsen, F. O. 1989).

The pottery on the Bornholm sites from the late MNA and early MNB shows a partly separate development, although there are similarities in form and decoration between late Funnel Beaker pottery from Bornholm and pottery from the Hagestad area in south-east Skåne, which was previously designated Pitted Ware (Hulthén 1977:123ff). Vasagård and Grødbygård have been nominated as type sites for two phases of the late Funnel Beaker culture on the island (Nielsen & Nielsen 1991). In this connection it has been proposed that the Valby phase

should be divided into an early and a late part, represented by Vasagård and Karlsfält for the early phase and by Grødby and Stävie for the late phase (Nielsen and Nielsen 1991:63f). Vasagård and Karlsfält are dated by Nielsen and Nielsen (1991:64) to MNA and Stävie and Grødby to MNB. The differences in form and decoration between the material from Vasagård and Grødby are significant, however. It is therefore uncertain how the house remains and dwelling sites should be interpreted in terms of cultural history. Judging by the ¹⁴C datings, however, the Grødby phase is contemporary with the early Battle Axe culture in southern Sweden. The settlement concentration in southern Bornholm is thus evidence that the split-up of settlement that seems to have taken place in Skåne in the late MNA did not take place in Bornholm until the middle part of MNB (Nielsen, P. O. 1999:156). It seems as if the influences of the Battle Axe culture on the social organization reached Bornholm slightly later than the rest of southern Scandinavia. Only a small quantity of pottery which can be defined as belonging to the Pitted Ware culture has been found on the island (Nielsen & Nielsen 1991:64).

The special conditions prevailing on the island of Bornholm may have meant that the structural principles behind the social organization were more tenacious here than on the mainland. The social environment on the island favoured a reproduction of the dominating organization, and the traditional values prevailing in the Funnel Beaker culture could therefore survive longer. Since the groups lived closer together in a defined geographical area, it may have been easier to maintain the existing power structures. Although the people of Bornholm did not live in isolation from external contacts, new ideas may have reached the island with a slight lag. The leading stratum preserved their social control, so we see the big settlements at the same time as the adoption of the tradition of building large places of assembly, as the palisaded enclosures were, and their possible use as settlements as well.

Settlement development in Denmark, just as in Bornholm, has been considered to lead to increasingly

238

large sites, culminating in MNA V (Skaarup 1985). Rather few of the excavated Danish settlements have yielded information about the internal organization of the sites, however. It is probable that some of the "big settlements" also, or perhaps solely, had a function as places of assembly like the Scanian central places. At Sigersted I in central Sjælland a double palisade was documented in the 1970s. The site is at the confluence of three rivers beside an older Sarup site (Nielsen, P. O. 1985). Only a small part has been excavated, and the feature was initially interpreted as being part of a longhouse (Davidsen 1978) but has subsequently been interpreted by Andersen as a defensive structure (Andersen 1997). The date of the structure (MNA V), the occurrence of a palisade with axe offerings and pottery deposits, and small votive pits make it more likely that the site should be compared to the palisaded enclosure in Dösjebro. A fresh analysis by Henrik Pihl and Mac Svensson of the large amount of flakes from the postholes showed that a large share were flakes from axe manufacture. This means that the site can be compared with the palisaded enclosure in Dösjebro (Svensson 2002). At Spodsbjerg in Langeland, about fifty postholes from an enclosure system have been documented along the former shoreline. The place was at the foot of a hill that in the Neolithic was partly surrounded by the sea and a fjord. The enclosure, which measures 16 m within the investigation area, led down to a dam. The site, which is dated to MNA V, has extensive finds in the form of fragments of thick-butted axes and chisels, flake scrapers, transverse arrowheads, and so on. In addition, objects of bones and antler were found, such as chisels, pressure tools, shafts, and pointed weapons (Skaarup 1985:41f; Sørensen 1998). The function of the enclosure is uncertain, but theories about livestock pens have been put forward (Sørensen 1998:52). The topography of the site, the enclosure, and the dating indicate that the site can be compared with the Scanian palisaded enclosures. Troldebjerg, also in Langeland, is another site where a palisade-like enclosure has been documented. The place is on a promontory surrounded

by wetlands. The majority of the finds from the site can be dated to MNA I, but elements of MNA V have been observed (Davidsen 1978:21; Skaarup 1985:47f). The function of the palisade and the Neolithic dating are uncertain, but similarities to the sites mentioned above can be pointed out.

The above places indicate that the concept of dwelling site in Denmark, above all at the end of the Funnel Beaker culture, can be discussed, since the function of the big sites has not been sufficiently elucidated. The excavations of palisaded enclosures in Skåne and Bornholm give new perspectives on the big Danish settlements in MNA V. The lack of house remains at Spodsbjerg and Sigersted I may of course be ascribed to the limited excavation areas, but might also suggest that the sites, like Dösjebro, Hyllie, and Bunkeflo, did not function as traditional settlements but were places of assembly for scattered settlements. Evidence that palisaded enclosures really did occur in Denmark as well in MNA V and at the transition to MNB comes from two recently discovered structures. At Helgeshøj, between Copenhagen and Roskilde, two parallel palisades were documented in 1999 which may have enclosed about 40,000 m² of a hill beside a small watercourse. Finds from several phases of the Funnel Beaker culture have been registered, but remains from the closing phase of the Funnel Beaker culture predominate and are regarded as contemporary with the palisade structure. Pits have yielded, among other things, axe planks, some of them burnt, fragmentary axes, flakes from axe manufacture, and pottery. Pottery of Valby type from MNA V occurs together with butt sections of B-axes. Because of this combination of artefact types, the feature has been dated to the MNA/MNB transition (Giersing 2000). Only a kilometre from Helgeshøj, at Bakkegård, yet another palisade has been excavated; it could be followed for about 150 m. It probably surrounded a hill (Staal 1999). It has not been possible to date the feature, but the proximity to three megalithic tombs and the design of the palisade makes a Neolithic dating reasonable. It is also known that some of the big Middle Neolithic settlements were established on sites of Sarup type, for example, at Trelleborg in Sjælland, where a large number of pits were identified, with material belonging to MNA V (Becker 1957).

The picture above suggests that different variants of assembly places can be discerned in the late Funnel Beaker culture and early Battle Axe culture in southern Scandinavia. The ceremonies at the megalithic tombs did not occur as regularly as in the early Middle Neolithic, and they had a more private character, with individual status objects like the axe being deposited. Palisaded enclosures, and – depending on the social environment – perhaps also large settlements with extended functions, served as central places where the population of the district met on special occasions.

The transition to MNB and the introduction of the Battle Axe culture seem to have unfolded differently in different parts of southern Scandinavia. Several scholars have pointed out that Funnel Beaker society developed towards a system whereby power was concentrated with fewer persons and increasingly large resources were required to preserve the prevailing power structures (Tilley 1984; Damm 1991). The resource-demanding social system finally resulted in its own dissolution, and the emergence of new power structures was dependent on the culture-historical background of each region. On the island of Bornholm, as we have seen, the new continental influences caught on later than on the mainland.

In Denmark, as in Skåne, one can observe the existence of three different material cultures at the MNA/MNB transition. Apart from the encounter of the Funnel Beaker and Battle Axe cultures, material influenced by the Pitted Ware culture also appears, above all in the north-eastern and eastern parts of Denmark (Rasmussen 1993:114). In the 1980s the sites of Kainsbakke and Kirial Bro in Djursland, eastern Jutland, were excavated (Rasmussen 1984). This yielded important information about the Pitted Ware culture in this area. The finds from the two sites display similarities to the Pitted Ware

culture in south-west Sweden, but it is also clear that they represent a local tradition. Points of contact with the Funnel Beaker culture are noticeable, for instance, in the clay discs and the thick-butted axes of Valby type. A series of $^{14}$C datings indicate that the two sites were used at the same time as the early Single Grave culture and possibly also the latest phase of the Funnel Beaker culture (Tauber 1986; Rasmussen 1986, 1993).

The archaeological material, together with the datings from Kainsbakke and Kirial Bro, suggests that the rise of the Pitted Ware culture in Denmark has parallels with the way it emerged in Skåne. I believe that the Funnel Beaker society dissolved as part of the population assimilated a way of life which had been practised for a long time by groups living on the coasts of central and southern Sweden. The earliest Pitted Ware settlement in Denmark, like that in Skåne, is later than the coastal settlements of western and central Sweden (Tauber 1986; Edenmo et al. 1997). Most coastal MNA V settlements in Jutland are located on the east coast south of Århus (Davidsen 1978:11; Rasmussen 1986:168). The movement towards north-eastern and eastern Denmark may have been further propelled by the contemporary deterioration in climate and the transgression which is believed to have favoured an economy based on marine resources (Christensen 1993). The other part of the population who did not adopt this way of life accepted the continental ideas spread by the Corded Ware culture.

The distribution of the Single Grave culture in Jutland seems, by and large, to comprise the areas not inhabited by the bearers of the Pitted Ware culture. Charlotte Damm paints a picture of how the Funnel Beaker culture in Denmark in the later part of MNA was divided into two distinct groups – one in western and central Jutland and one in eastern Denmark – chiefly expressed in different mortuary customs (Damm 1993). The western group, which is associated with the stone packing graves, is contrasted with the eastern group, where burial in megalithic tombs continued. The approach to resolving the dissatisfaction with the increasing social

240

control varied between the two regions. In eastern Denmark the solution was to allow a larger share of the population to be buried in the megalithic tombs. The cult of the ancestors was thus continued here, and collectivism was strengthened at the expense of individualism. In western Denmark a tradition arose instead of individual burials in stone packing graves. The intention was probably to let part of the population have a formal burial in which status was marked by the grave goods placed in the adjacent mortuary houses. In this society the individual was asserted more than the collective, and a contrast was created *vis-à-vis* those who were buried in megalithic tombs. The focus on the individual was accompanied by a similar development in other spheres of society. Ox teeth have been noted at several places adjacent to the stone packing graves, which indicates that ox heads were placed here. Perhaps the ox was an important symbol in the ritual, reflecting the increased significance of animal husbandry. Damm believes that a situation may have arisen in which the power structure in eastern Danish society was based on control of esoteric and ritual knowledge while power in western Denmark was based on control of the material world, for instance livestock. Within the latter area a breach with the traditional Funnel Beaker society is noticed more clearly and perhaps earlier, and the symbolism of the continental Corded Ware culture was adopted on a large scale. Power was not structured on the basis of kin relations but acquired through social competence and control over material valuables. The pollen diagrams from here testify to a significant amount of forest clearance. Changes in mortuary practice and in material culture thus suggest radical changes in society. In eastern Jutland and the islands, these upheavals are not as noticeable. Analyses of the finds here suggests a relatively calm and continuous development from MNA to MNB (Skaarup 2001).

Conditions in western Skåne in the early MNB can be compared, in part, to the situation in eastern Denmark. Although the bearers of the Battle Axe culture broke away from the old society and adopted an ideol-

ogy and symbolism which derived inspiration from the continent, we see some continuity in settlement. The very earliest Battle Axe settlement in the valley landscape seems to have gained a foothold in the old core areas of the Funnel Beaker culture, and at least some of the megalithic tombs were still used. In southern Skåne, studies of distribution maps have shown a somewhat different picture. Larsson points out that the archaeological evidence here indicates that the early remains of the Battle Axe culture can be found in the hummocky landscape, outside the traditional Funnel Beaker districts, while the later remains are more concentrated on the coastal plain. The distribution of finds in the landscape, according to Larsson, reflects an initial situation of competition, with the bearers of the Battle Axe culture at first assigned to marginal areas and later expanded into the core areas of the Funnel Beaker culture. This thesis is based on $^{14}$C datings which indicate that the Funnel Beaker culture existed parallel to the earliest phase of the Battle Axe culture. In the later part of MNB the bearers of the Battle Axe culture took over the coastal plain from the declining Funnel Beaker culture. Larsson views the distribution of the Battle Axe culture as a kind of missionary movement, representing a new ideology with powerful religious overtones (Larsson, L. 1989b). It is possible that part of the population in southern Skåne in a transitional phase preserved the customs of the Funnel Beaker culture, while another group broke away from the traditional society, adopted continental ideas, and settled in the marginal areas.

In the last phase of MNA, in connection with the dissolution of the Funnel Beaker culture, we thus see that part of the population preserved the traditional values and a power structure in which the social control was based on ritual and spiritual knowledge, and they did so by becoming assimilated to the Pitted Ware way of life, as in western Skåne and north-eastern Denmark, or by sticking to the Funnel Beaker tradition, as in southern Skåne and Bornholm. Other population groups in western and central Jutland made an outright break with the old and adopted the continental way of life represented by the Corded Ware culture, in which social control was maintained through power over material objects and individual status. Although the new social organization in all regions can be derived in part from the existing Funnel Beaker society, this change in power structures took place in different ways in different areas. In central Jutland the structural principles behind power changed as early as the late MNA towards a focus on control of the material world. Here the breach with the old had a greater impact on material culture. In eastern Denmark and much of Skåne the coming of the Battle Axe culture is more influenced by the old traditions in that the old monuments were still used and continuity in settlement is noticeable. This does not mean that the power structures did not change radically; the new ideology adopted and partly re-evaluated the old symbols.

Apart from the houses in Bornholm, the lack of distinct house remains in southern Scandinavia in the early and middle Battle Axe culture is striking. This should be understood in the same way as the development of settlement in western Skåne at this time, namely, that a relatively brief occupation on each site, together with a different outlook on the landscape and an attitude to waste that differed from that in the Funnel Beaker culture, in other words, a different deposition tradition, influenced the occurrence of remains of the Battle Axe culture. Animal husbandry seems to have been an important element of the Battle Axe culture and may have been pursued in a way comparable with nomadism (cf. Larsson, L. 1989b:73). The available evidence from dwelling sites consequently indicates that people moved in fairly small groups of one or a few nuclear families and that there were no big sites where several households coexisted.

There are, on the other hand, a few dwelling sites with more or less sure houses from the later part of the Battle Axe culture and the Single Grave culture, such as the houses at Dagstorp described above. A partly sunken structure from Kabusa in southern Skåne sur-rounded by post-holes has been interpreted as a house. This interpretation is highly uncertain, but there are some similarities to structures from the late MNB and Late Neolithic from Denmark and Skåne. The presumed house at Kabusa has been [14]C dated to the late MNB, which agrees well with the typological dating of pottery from the site (Larsson, L. 1989b, 1992a: 103ff). A few houses have been documented in Jutland. One of the clearer buildings was excavated at Hemmed Kirke (Boas 1993). It has been dated on the basis of the finds to the MNB/LN transition. At Enderupskov in southern Jutland a house has been found with pottery which allows a probable dating in the Single Grave culture (Ethelberg et al. 2000:120ff). The houses at Myrhøj in northern Jutland, where the finds show influences from the Bell Beaker culture, have already been mentioned.

It is obvious that the building tradition that was developed in the Late Neolithic in southern Scandinavia had already started in the closing phase of the Battle Axe culture and the Single Grave culture. A more uniform and almost standardized building tradition emerged very quickly in much of southern and central Scandinavia (see e.g. Björhem & Säfvestad 1989; Artursson et al. 2003). In the late MNB the house and dwelling site probably grew in social and economic importance once again. The increased contact with people on the continent which can be suspected because of the appearance of material showing influences from the Bell Beaker culture, together with the growing number of metal finds, probably led to the rise of more complex social relations, as those who exerted control over the flow of goods between different regions acquired increasing influence. Their status was materialized in the houses, which functioned as power symbols. The significance of the megalithic tombs in the Middle Neolithic – defining the group's social identity and functioning as a stabilizing factor which symbolized the permanence of social identity – seems to have been partly transferred to the house and the dwelling site.

# The society and the landscape

*It may thus be concluded that people's use and perception of the landscape and the place varied through the Early and Middle Neolithic in a way that can be related to the form of the social organization. Changes in the organizational structure of society influenced the way in which people moved socially and physically in the landscape and made their impact on it. At the same time, the use of the environment involved its transformation, so that it took on a different, meaningful role which in turn affected the social sphere.*

In my study I have sought to understand the emergence, organization, and change of Neolithic societies in the river valleys of western Skåne: Saxån–Välabäcken and Lödde Å-Kävlingeån. Archaeological excavations and surveys of ancient monuments have shown that the area contains extensive remains of Neolithic settlement complexes – in the form of dwelling sites, cemeteries, megalithic tombs, deposits in wetlands, and central places – ranging from the earliest to the latest phase of the Funnel Beaker culture and the Battle Axe culture. The surroundings of the two valleys thus saw long-term use in the Neolithic. Recent years' excavations in connection with the expansion of the West Coast Line have given new and valuable insight into how Neolithic people organized themselves in social space, both within places and between places in the landscape space. In particular, the major excavations of dwelling sites from several different Early and Middle Neolithic phases have allowed us completely different insight into the organization of Funnel Beaker sites.

People's way of life, both in the Neolithic and today, varies through time and place. Although there are shared supraregional structures in the areas inhabited by the bearers of the Funnel Beaker culture and later the Battle Axe culture, regional differences in the spread and reception of innovations can be observed in the archaeological evidence. It is equally obvious that the identity of individual regions changed in the period of more than 1,500 years that the Early and the Middle Neolithic constituted. The human landscape has meaning in each specific culture-historical context and thus has a dynamic, meaning-bearing role in interaction with the people living in it. Alongside – and as a part of – the ecological conditions, the landscape is filled with social memories and meanings created by the work of previous generations. The historical landscape must therefore be read, interpreted, and perceived not only in terms of different patterns in space but also with a temporal perspective. Time and place are active forces in the formation of the structural principles that shape the social organization and hence the key to an understanding of societal development. My interpretation of the organization of society in the investigation area has therefore taken its point of departure in the region's Neolithic remains, and the manner in which the Neolithic way of life was adopted and developed here has been considered in terms of the distinctive regional conditions and the Late Mesolithic background.

Ethnographic sources have shown that spatial patterns on a dwelling site and in the landscape are often ordered according to rules which are in part a reflection of the social organization. Important traditions leave traces in the landscape and in the material culture because the preservation of the social order must be ensured through repeated social acts and rituals. The meaning of customs is passed on to subsequent generations through buildings, social relations, and rituals. In this way patterns arise at different places in the landscape which can be regarded as signs for the archaeologist to combine and read. Spatial patterns which repeat themselves in the archaeological evidence have therefore been investigated with the aim of distinguishing the society's underlying structures and achieving an understanding of the people's acts. The social organization, however, is not static and permanent; instead, there is constant interaction between actions and the underlying structures. My line of thought has been influenced by theories of action developed in sociology and anthropology in that I seek to give consideration equally to the diachronic, the subject, the structure, and its dualism. Structures act as a series of rules and resources which direct, initiate, or prevent action, but they are also in turn a product of the action: they are constantly shaped, reproduced, and reshaped through active actions. It may be debated to what extent individuals as single agents can affect the structural principles of a society, but I believe that, in the relationship to other individuals and to the surroundings, the dynamic is created that determines people's actions and can thereby change the underlying structures. The form of social relations and the power structure has therefore been studied here in relation to the development of society, and breaks in the spatial patterns have been considered just as important to consider as the regularities that we perceive. We may expect that tensions and antagonisms existed even in small social formations where unequal relations can occur, as between, say, men and women, children and parents, old and young, or between social groups such as kindreds etc. Generally speaking, the exercise of power can be divided into two forms: those aiming at control of the material world and those referring to control over the social and cultural world – and it is the ideology that is the foundation for the reproduction of the prevailing social and political order.

My study has found that the social and economic organization in western Skåne in the opening phase of the Early Neolithic largely followed the same lines as the closing phase of the Mesolithic. The transition was not a dramatic and sudden event but rather a long-drawn-out, continuous process. The society was one of tenacious structures, with changes coming slowly and gradually. Links with the farming societies of the continent nevertheless led to innovations, and ideas were inevitably spread along with trading commodities. It was thus not a complete "Neolithic concept" that arrived in southern Scandinavia but various expressions from the continent, the meaning of which was received and transformed in different ways in the different regions of southern Scandinavia.

In several cases it can be shown that Early Neolithic settlements were located in places which had previ-ously been used in the Late Mesolithic. Tradition was evidently important when dwelling sites were established. The coastal settlements were not abandoned at the transition to the Neolithic; several of the big Late Mesolithic sites were also occupied in EN I. In this way the ancestors' sense for and knowledge of the landscape were passed on and a social landmark was created, constituting a permanent place in a partly mobile way of life. This understanding was not just a matter of the physical landscape but also of the landscape as a social construction.

There is still no sure evidence that monuments were erected in the valleys of western Skåne in the opening phase of the Neolithic to mark the specific territory of a people. Perhaps there were no clear landscapes in this phase, in the sense that a population group was socially tied to a specific area of land in its activities. The wooded landscape was also an open landscape in that the populations could move freely in the area in their seasonal pursuits. The distribution of settlements indicates that five or six groups of dwelling sites were active synchronously in the investigation area. The four groups of dwelling sites along the Saxån and Välabäcken may have functioned as a local community while the groups at the Barsebäck foreland and the Saxån bay may have made up one community. The figure is intended to show how the populations probably moved over relatively large areas, with no distinct boundaries (fig. 103).

A long place-based tradition was nevertheless particularly important for the group's identity, intended to manifest and confirm its origin. In terms of cultural history, for people's identity it is probably just kinship than can be said to be as important as place. Even nomads attach memories, myths, and collective self-images to topography and landscape. In accordance with the prevailing structural principles in the Late Mesolithic and Early Neolithic, the settlement acquired a rich symbolic meaning, which was reproduced through people's actions. Some of the Early Neolithic main settlements were much larger in area than previous archaeologists had found for Skåne. Both large and small dwelling sites appear to have existed in parallel. At least Dagstorp 19 and Saxtorp 23 seem to have been big enough to be occupied by groups larger than a single family, perhaps a whole kin group. The size of dwelling sites shows that space was required for different activities and that there was successive expansion. The big settlements in EN I were not just places for dwelling; they were also the scene of burials and votive ceremonies which meant that larger areas were claimed.

244

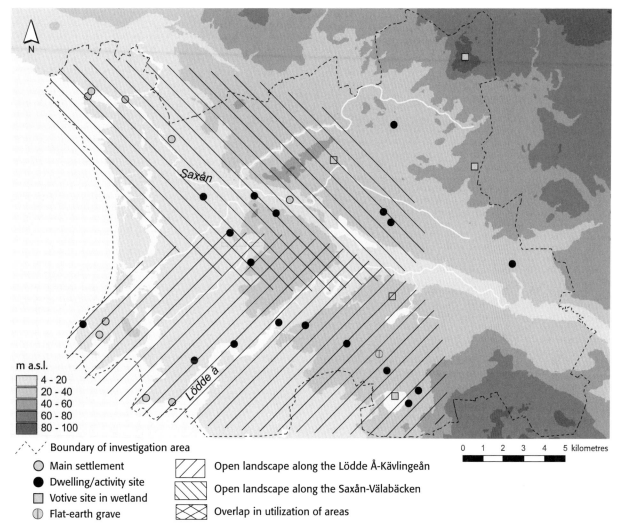

**m a.s.l.**
- 4 - 20
- 20 - 40
- 40 - 60
- 60 - 80
- 80 - 100

Boundary of investigation area

○ Main settlement
● Dwelling/activity site
▢ Votive site in wetland
◍ Flat-earth grave

▨ Open landscape along the Lödde Å-Kävlingeån
▨ Open landscape along the Saxån-Välabäcken
▨ Overlap in utilization of areas

0  1  2  3  4  5 kilometres

Fig. 103. The "open landscape" around the bays at the estuaries of the Saxån and Lödde Å in the opening phase of the Neolithic.

The distribution of settlement in the landscape and the organization of dwelling sites do not reveal anything to contradict the accepted opinion of Early Neolithic society as having been organized on the basis of kinship. The structural principles behind social relations were established and preserved through various bonds of kinship and friendship between individuals and groups. Studies of traditional societies have shown that it is usually the elders who possess the highest power. Because of their age they were considered to have close ties to the ancestors' spirits and the founders of the society. They were thus the intermediaries in the transfer of the ancestors' knowledge to the contemporary members of the society. Since the ancestors still had a role to play in everyday life, it was important to retain their benevolence through recurrent rituals. The organization of some Early Neolithic settlements in the investigation area illustrates this state of affairs and gives some, albeit vague, hints as to what the power structure might have been like. There was a

246

distinct and deliberate division of the site into different activity areas. Burials and associated rituals took place close to the habitation areas. The close link between dwelling site and burial place can be seen as a territorial marker, with the concrete remains of the ancestors justifying the society's claim of its right to the site. The ancestors did not just confirm the solidarity of the society, but also asserted its right to the resources. It is likely that the power of the dominant group in Early Neolithic society was legitimized and passed on through the rituals to do with burial. They maintained their social dominance by controlling the spiritual and social world. The collective activities, both profane and sacred, were performed on the dwelling site. The link between the group and the place, between the everyday activities and the social processes in the society as a whole, is clearly seen at the settlements.

Although it must have meant a sacrifice to abandon a coastal way of life, new settlements were also established further inland in the first part of the Early Neolithic, chiefly along the rivers. In the coastal region there was a long tradition and knowledge of how to organize the landscape. At lagoons and bays, people exploited the diversity of food resources in the sea and on land. The establishment of inland settlements has sometimes been explained in terms of a minor change in climate affecting the ecological and economic conditions for the coastal populations and forcing a transition to a cultivation economy and movements inland. The Late Mesolithic and Early Neolithic economy, however, was flexible, and a minor ecological change probably did not mean that people altered their way of life. Nor is there anything to suggest that cultivation became of any great importance for subsistence. The movements inland must have been propelled by other causes than purely economic ones.

I believe instead that it is necessary to explain the changes in terms of conditions within the society. Since there are always tensions of some kind in social relations, there is always a seedbed for the conflicts that can lead to changes in society. To a certain extent

the dominant class in the opening phase of the Early Neolithic could legitimize its supremacy through special rituals. At some point in time, however, the repressed people in western Skåne became aware of increasing social coercion. When settlement became more permanent in the Late Mesolithic and the Early Neolithic, the population grew and hence also the social unit. The increasingly stationary way of life together with a new Neolithic mentality gave the possibility for new production conditions so that the landscape was gradually transformed. Cleared areas were created for tillage and livestock, although on a limited scope. In this landscape there was a greater need to assert a sense of belonging to a place. The social traditions which highlighted the length of time and the social memory of a place were reinforced. The social power that was the result of acquiring the past and using it with reference to the present and the future was attached to the settlement. Ties to the place were therefore emphasized with increasing strength through rituals associated with the cult of the ancestors, in which the significance of the place and the social relations were confirmed. The result was a structure in which one-sided ties of dependency and obligations arose for the younger generation *vis-à-vis* the older generation. The power and social control vested in the elders, the leaders of the ritual, thus increased. Social relations became more complex and internal tensions became obvious. It is important in this context to bear in mind that people in prehistoric societies were probably much more tied to the past than we are in today's modern society. Those in power in the Funnel Beaker culture accentuated bygone times to legitimize and reproduce prevailing conditions. Those in possession of power – probably some of the elders – were those who had the knowledge about the past and the ancestors. This is a fundamental difference from today's society where power is instead associated with the ability to quickly create and assimilate new technology, to look forwards instead of gazing backwards.

Awareness of the growing social coercion made the social control more fragile. At the start of the Neolithic, however, there was scope for the younger generation to avoid subjection to the elders by migration and expansion to new, previously unoccupied areas. The coastal society was consequently split up and some of the population settled inland along the water systems. This meant that the bonds and obligations between the generations were weakened. The ancient norm system, the underlying structures, were thereby partly transformed. In reality, as we have seen, this did not mean that the power structures were changed, but that the inequalities in society were temporarily mitigated. The ancestors' role and influence remained important, and power was obtained through control of social and spiritual knowledge. On the other hand, the view of the landscape changed, As the familiar coastal areas were left behind, it became necessary to socialize the new and partly unknown landscapes. This could be done by taking some of the activities formerly tied to the main settlements and moving them out into the landscape. Votive activities outside the settlement increased greatly in the form of deposits in wetlands; in other words, the customs of depositing objects in pits acquired a wider meaning. The burial ritual was no longer automatically tied to the dwelling site; instead, the western European tradition of erecting burial monuments was now adopted by the communities in the valleys. The entire landscape space within which people moved can therefore be regarded as a kind of macro dwelling site.

It has been possible to distinguish in the archaeological evidence how Neolithic settlement districts or landscape spaces were gradually established along the Saxån and Välabäcken, and subsequently southwards to the Kävlingeån and Stångby Mosse, finally occupying the area around the Mare Bäck and Barsebäck. The spatial distribution of dwelling sites, burial places, and votive sites indicates that there may have been three or four different landscape spaces in the area in the early part of the Middle Neolithic. A landscape space corresponds to the geographical area in which a group of people, a local community, performed their seasonal and annual activities. However, it is possible to detect dissimilarities between different areas in the organization of dwelling sites. At the main settlement of Dagstorp in the Välabäcken valley, several house remains were documented which could correspond to more than one contemporary household unit. This organization lacks parallels in the other areas, where isolated farms seem to have been the prevailing form of settlement. In these latter landscape spaces it seems to

have been possible to make divisions into smaller spaces consisting of one or a few households around one of the megalithic tombs or groups of megalithic tombs. The landscape spaces that have been proposed are of course hypothetical constructions based on available evidence about the functions of the places, their mutual relations, their location in the landscape, and the nature of the terrain. Even more source material would perhaps change the picture somewhat, but the important thing in this context is that a picture has been sketched of how people perceived and moved in the landscape in different phases of the Early and Middle Neolithic (fig. 104).

The new landscape spaces were created, preserved, and reproduced through the rituals performed at settlements, wetlands, and grave monuments. Those who controlled the establishment of the new spaces thus also acquired power over social reproduction, that is, the maintenance of relations of power between individuals and groups. Whereas power had formerly been based on rituals at the dwelling site, these were now relocated in a larger space – the macro dwelling site or what I have called the landscape space. The megalithic tombs can be regarded as steering the social relationship between and above all within different local groups, rather than as territorial markers. They served to define the group's social identity and acted as a stabilizing factor symbolizing the survival of social identity. The lack of exceptional monumental locations lets us understand that it was not the intention that the graves should be visible from far away; they were instead exposed towards the settlements and the groups that built them. Death is of course an individual event but simultaneously a social happening. While death means that an individual is separated from the society to which he or she once belonged, the social order is recreated or reproduced in a lasting form through the funeral rituals. In the initial phase of the Early Neolithic these activities were carried out at the settlement itself, to which the identity of the group was linked. As new areas of land were established, the group marked

248

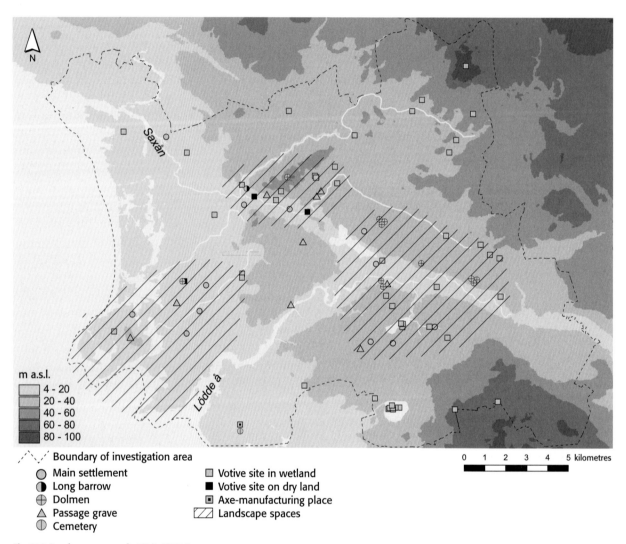

**m a.s.l.**
- 4 - 20
- 20 - 40
- 40 - 60
- 60 - 80
- 80 - 100

⌁ Boundary of investigation area
- ◯ Main settlement
- ◐ Long barrow
- ⊕ Dolmen
- △ Passage grave
- ◑ Cemetery
- ◻ Votive site in wetland
- ◼ Votive site on dry land
- ▣ Axe-manufacturing place
- ▨ Landscape spaces

0  1  2  3  4  5 kilometres

Fig. 104. Landscape spaces in EN II–MNA II.

a larger space through these places and rituals connected with them. The votive deposits in wetlands, at secluded locations away from the dwelling sites, were not as obviously meeting places for the whole collective, but could have been performed by individuals or small groups. It is clear from similarities in the composition of depositions that the different categories of place had a shared origin as different activities at the settlements and that they are parts of a cohesive whole. Fragments of human bones do not just occur at

the megalithic tombs but are also often found on the dwelling sites and votive sites of the Funnel Beaker culture. Perhaps the ancestors' bones were moved around between the sites precisely to emphasize that the places belonged together. There is reason to suspect that fragmented objects underwent the same treatment.

As the landscape spaces were established, there was a growing need to confirm the prevailing conditions. The significance of collective rituals thereby increased.

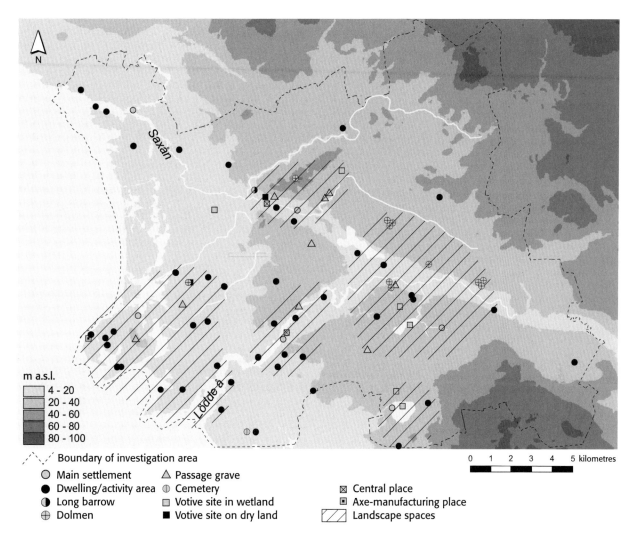

m a.s.l.
- 4 - 20
- 20 - 40
- 40 - 60
- 60 - 80
- 80 - 100

Boundary of investigation area
- ○ Main settlement    △ Passage grave
- ● Dwelling/activity area    ◐ Cemetery
- ◑ Long barrow    □ Votive site in wetland
- ⊕ Dolmen    ■ Votive site on dry land

- ⊠ Central place
- ▣ Axe-manufacturing place
- ▨ Landscape spaces

0  1  2  3  4  5 kilometres

Fig. 105. Landscape spaces in MNA III–V.

In the early Middle Neolithic there was an emphasis on rituals at passage graves, and richly decorated pottery – which probably marked group affiliation – was an important constituent element. At the same time, there was a decrease in votive deposits in wetlands, which were presumably of a more private character. The passage grave with its narrow passage suggests that access to the "holy of holies" was permitted only to a small, exclusive group. As yet another effect of the growing collective ideology, there is a tendency, at least in some of the landscape spaces, for the main settlements to expand. Dwelling sites become fewer in number and more concentrated around some big main settlements (fig. 105).

By gathering the population of the district at a main settlement, it was easier for the people in power to maintain their social control. Since more people occupied the same space, the complexity of social relations also increased. There is a tendency for deposits of both whole and fragmented objects in pits to become even more important in MNA III. The deposited artefacts were reflections of the activities pursued on the site, and the pits were therefore a metaphor for everyday chores. Through a manifestation of everyday work, the social community could be strengthened and inequalities could be masked.

The institutions of the traditional Funnel Beaker society may be said to culminate in MNA III. The consolidation of the settlement districts thus gave greater power to the leading stratum. In the reproduction of the social order, the ritual through which an élite made increasing claims to control over the sacred – and hence also to social and economic control – became more complex. Inequalities were concealed by an ideology which emphasized the collective and sought to strengthen the sense of solidarity. The Funnel Beaker society had developed a system in which great resources were channelled into rituals which confirmed the prevailing order. In the latter part of MNA this policy seems to have reached a point where it was impossible to produce the surplus required for the ceremonies. We see once again a situation where the aroused consciousness of the social coercion created an explosive situation which finally led to a break-up of society. In EN I the social pressure was relieved when certain groups moved to establish settlements in new areas. This possibility did not exist in the late MNA, when far-reaching changes in the society's underlying structures were necessary.

There are several indications in the archaeological evidence of a watershed in this phase of the Funnel Beaker culture. Settlement was split up and a movement towards the coast is gradually noticeable. The big main settlements in the interior were abandoned, and it seems as if the landscape spaces created in EN II were now broken up. Shared rituals at megalithic tombs also became less important. The flint inventory at the settlements along the coast begin to show clear Pitted Ware influences, and the pottery shows partly different vessel forms and decorative patterns. It is clear that the older social and economic organization broke up and was replaced with new forms and power relations. The internal tensions in the society had become too great, and consequently parts of the population left the kin groups to settle in other areas.

At the end of MNA the Funnel Beaker population no longer lived in an equally cohesive society. Variations in pottery styles between different places may indicate that more independent groups existed, marking their group identity in their pottery, among other things. There has also been speculation that there were several different "variants" of Funnel Beaker and/or Pitted Ware culture in Skåne and Denmark in this phase. In the investigation area there are places with material which can be regarded as belonging to both the Stävie group (Stävie 3 and Stävie 17) and the Karlsfält group (Barsebäck 48 and Västra Karaby 101). The unequal social relations that arose in the late MNA had the consequence that some of the Funnel Beaker population joined the groups living along the coasts of southern Scandinavia. These Pitted Ware groups probably continued to live in more egalitarian forms but shared a common origin with the Funnel Beaker culture. The cult of the ancestors occupied a major place in the ritual, and social relations were confirmed and maintained through ceremonies in which the ancestors were invoked. Élite rule, however, did not take on such extreme forms as in the Funnel Beaker culture. The coastal groups had never created landscape spaces confirmed by the construction of large grave monuments (fig. 106).

Even the part of the population that still continued the Funnel Beaker traditions for a time eventually abandoned the old customs. On the continent, different expressions of the Corded Ware culture had spread over much of northern and central Europe. The ideologies prevailing in these groups advocated a more individual way of thinking than the Funnel Beaker culture. For the people in the highly traditional Funnel Beaker society, the new ideology that spread through various trading links was probably enticing. The structural principles behind the organization of the society were fundamentally changed. The tensions in society facilitated the adoption of a new ideological system.

There are few traces of Battle Axe culture settlements in the province. A partial explanation for this is that the people simply did leave any distinct traces behind them. This is probably due to two circumstances. Firstly, they led a mobile way of life with short-term camps which did not leave any remains of post-built structures and which was probably based mainly on animal husbandry. Secondly, and

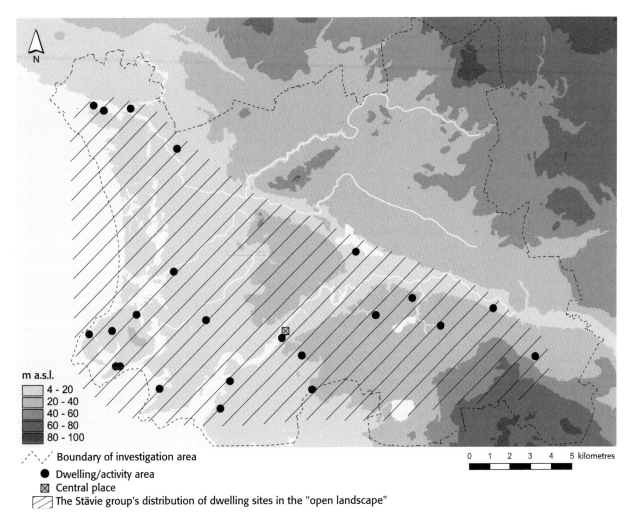

m a.s.l.
- 4 - 20
- 20 - 40
- 40 - 60
- 60 - 80
- 80 - 100

0  1  2  3  4  5 kilometres

Boundary of investigation area
● Dwelling/activity area
⊠ Central place
▨ The Stävie group's distribution of dwelling sites in the "open landscape"

Fig. 106. The distribution of Stävie group settlement sites in the landscape and the location of the central place in Stävie.

as a consequence of the first circumstance, a great deal of the stock of artefacts was carried on to the next place. It also seems as if the attitude to waste was different from what we saw in the Funnel Beaker/Pitted Ware culture. In the latter cultures waste was a part of the activities. By-products of the manufacture of tools, cooking, and other chores were a part of site life and did not need to be cleared away. Moreover, the waste marks a sense of belonging to the place. Place was also important for the Battle

Axe people, of course, but it was marked differently. Natural formations in the landscape or already existing monuments may have functioned as nodes. To begin with, their identity was attached to the big central places, the palisaded enclosures, like that in Dösjebro and those in Malmö. It was at these places that the scattered groups gathered at set times to carry out activities, probably with both an economic and a social content. The production, consumption, and distribution of axes was particularly im-

252

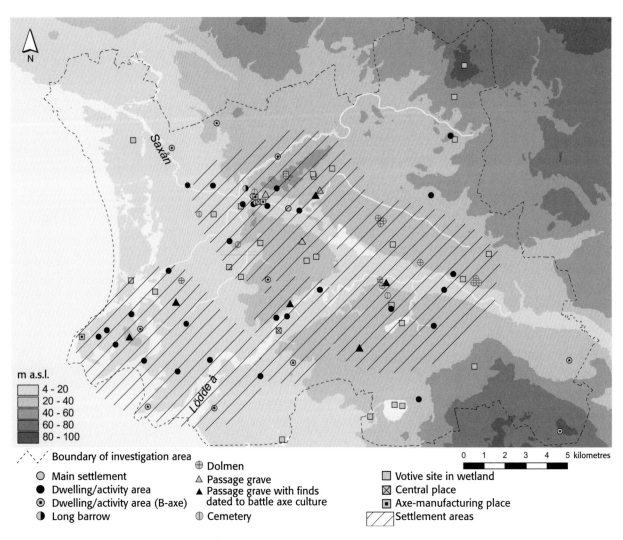

m a.s.l.

| | |
|---|---|
| | 4 - 20 |
| | 20 - 40 |
| | 40 - 60 |
| | 60 - 80 |
| | 80 - 100 |

⌐‸⌐‸ Boundary of investigation area

◯ Main settlement
● Dwelling/activity area
◉ Dwelling/activity area (B-axe)
◖ Long barrow

⊕ Dolmen
△ Passage grave
▲ Passage grave with finds
   dated to battle axe culture
⊖ Cemetery

☐ Votive site in wetland
⊠ Central place
⊡ Axe-manufacturing place
▧ Settlement areas

0  1  2  3  4  5 kilometres

Fig. 107. Settlement areas during the Battle Axe culture.

portant. These features also illustrate how the power structures in society had changed. Social status and power were no longer based on inherited control of the spiritual sphere but on individual ability and craft skills. Those who possessed these qualities and/or controlled the distribution of goods were the social élite. Perhaps the linear cemeteries, along ancient communication routes, should also be regarded as symbolizing a people in movement, with the emphasis on the individual.

At the end of MNA and the start of MNB both the view and the use of the landscape changed. The old landscape spaces were broken up and the people returned to a mentally more open landscape where they could move freely in small groups. There was no total breach because old sites continued to be used. It is probable that both the Stävie group and the bearers of the Battle Axe culture emerged within the old Funnel Beaker society, due to external influences. Continuity between the Funnel Beaker culture and the Battle Axe culture in the investigation area is noticed in the way that the megalithic tombs are still used, albeit to a limited extent. The new culture also arose right from the beginning in the core areas of the Funnel Beaker culture. My sketch of settlement in the Battle Axe culture should illustrate that virtually the same areas were used as during the Funnel Beaker culture, but that the spaces in the landscape were probably loosely tied together. There were not as clear relationships between different categories of place as in the late Early Neolithic and the first part of the Middle Neolithic (fig. 107).

Unlike the groups that assimilated a Pitted Ware way of life, what we call the Stävie group, however, the power structures changed, as we have seen.

This group was to retain the old power structures for a time, although they were much less rigid than in Funnel Beaker society. Because they lived in small groups, the social coercion never became too heavy to tolerate. Even the coastal Stävie group needed places of assembly, however. Since the underlying structures of the society were basically the same as in the Funnel Beaker culture, it was natural that their assembly place in Stävie should resemble the Sarup sites.

It is not until the closing phase of MNB that we find traces of structures on dwelling sites which once

again suggest increased permanence of settlement. Influences from continental Bell Beaker cultures can be detected in the material found at some of the houses in southern Scandinavia which can be dated to the MNB/LN transition. A growing import of metal strengthens the hypothesis of significant long-distance contacts. As a consequence, the complexity of social relations increased. An upper class emerged, marking its social status in the houses and later in the new form of grave, the stone cist.

It may thus be concluded that people's use and perception of the landscape and the place varied through the Early and Middle Neolithic in a way that can be related to the form of the social organization (Table III). Changes in the organizational structure of society influenced the way in which people moved socially and physically in the landscape and made their impact on it. At the same time, the use of the environment involved its transformation, so that it took on a different, meaningful role which in turn affected the social sphere. ▮

253

Table III. Model of social organization in relation to space and time.

| Period: | EN I (Funnel Beaker culture) | EN II–MNA II (Funnel Beaker culture) | MNA III–IV (Funnel Beaker culture) | MNA V/MNB (Funnel Beaker culture/ Stävie group) | MNB (Battle Axe culture) |
|---|---|---|---|---|---|
| Landscape organization: | Open landscape | Landscape spaces Establishment phase | Landscape spaces Consolidation phase | Landscape spaces open up | Landscape spaces open up |
| Place organization: | Main settlement | Main settlement Megalithic tomb Votive site | Main settlement Megalithic tomb Votive site | Settlement Central place | Settlement Central place Megalithic tomb |
| | Group identity attached to the site | Group identity attached to the landscape space | Group identity attached to the landscape space | Group identity attached to the central place | Group identity attached to the central place |
| Social organization and power structure: | Built on kinship relations | Built on kinship relations | Built on kinship relations | Built on kinship relations | Built on social ability |
| Degree of societal integration: High / Low | | | | | |

# References

## A

Adamsen, C. & Ebbesen, K. 1986. (eds.). *Stridsøksetid i Sydskandinavien. Beretning fra et symposium. 28.–30.X. 1985 i Vejle.* Arkeologiska skrifter 1. Copenhagen.

Åkerlund, A. 1996. *Human Responses to Shore Displacement. Living by the Sea in Eastern Middle Sweden during the Stone Age.* Riksantikvarieämbetet, Arkeologiska undersökningar, Skrifter 16. Stockholm.

Albrechtsen, E. 1954. Et Offerfund i Sludegårds Mose. *Fynske Minder* 1954. Odense.

Albrethsen, S. E. & Brinch Petersen, E. 1977. Excavation of a Mesolithic Cemetary at Vedbæk, Denmark. *Acta Archaeologica* 47. Copenhagen.

Allison, J. 1999. Self-Determination in Cultural Resource Management. Indigenous peoples' interpretation of history and of places and landscapes. In Ucko, P. J. & Layton, R. (eds.), *The Archaeology and Anthropology of Landscape. Shaping your landscape.* One World Archaeology, New York.

Almgren, O. 1914. De pågående undersökningarna om Sveriges första bebyggelse. *Fornvännen.* Stockholm.

– 1919. Några svensk-finska stenåldersproblem. *Antikvarisk tidskrift för Sverige* XX. Stockholm.

Almquist, U. & Svensson, M. 1990. Palissaderna från Annetorpsleden. En märklig fyndplats från strids-yxekulturen. *Limhamniana.* Malmö.

Althin, C. A. 1954. *The Chronology of the Stone Age Settlement of Scania, Sweden. 1. The Mesolithic Settlement.* Acta Archaeologica Lundensia, Series in 4°, No. 1. Lund.

Andersen, N. H. 1974. En befæstet, yngre stenalders-boplads i Sarup. *Fynske Minder* 1974. Odense.

– 1997. *The Sarup Enclosures. The Funnel Beaker Culture of the Sarup site including two causewayed camps compared to the contemporary settlements in the area and other European enclosures.* Sarup vol. 1. Jysk Arkæologisk Selskab, Moesgaard.

– 2000. Kult og ritualer i den ældre bondestenalder. *Kuml* 2000. Århus.

Andersen, N. H. & Madsen, T. 1978. Skåle og bægre med storvinkelbånd fra yngre stenalder. Overgangen mellem tidig- og mellemneolitikum. *Kuml* 1977. Århus.

Andersen, S. H. & Johansen, E. 1992. An Early Neolithic Grave at Bjørnsholm, North Jutland. *Journal of Danish Archaeology* 9. Odense.

Andersen. S. H. 1993. Bjørnsholm, A Stratified Køkken-mødding on the Central Limfjord, North Jutland. *Journal of Danish Archaeology* 10. Odense.

Andersson, A. 1997. Ett kulthus från tidigneolitikum? Skåne, Lackalänga sn, Lackalänga 19:2, Anslutnings-väg Lackalänga–Väg 108. Arkeologisk slutundersökn-ing 1995. RAÄ 36. *Riksantikvarieämbetet UV Syd Rapport* 1997:11. Lund.

Andersson, M. 1996. Delsträcka 3. In Svensson, M. et al. (eds.), Arkeologisk utredning. Skåne, Malmöhus Län, Järnvägen Västkustbanan, delen Helsingborg–Kävlinge. *Riksantikvarieämbetet UV Syd Rapport* 1996:25. Lund.

– 1999. Tidig- och mellanneolitiska boplatslämningar. Skåne, Saxtorp sn, Kvärlöv 8:4, fornlämning RAÄ 23, SU 10. *Riksantikvarieämbetet UV Syd Rapport* 1999:72. Lund.

– 2003. *Skapa plats i landskapet. Tidig- och mellanneolitiska samhällen utmed två västskånska dalgångar.* Acta Archaeologica Lundensia, Series in 8°, No. 42. Lund.

– 2004. Domestication and the first Neolithic concept 4800–3000 BC. In Andersson, M., Karsten, P., Knarrström, B. & Svensson, M. *Stone Age Scania. Significant places dug and read by contract archeology.* Riksantikvarieämbetet. Skrifter No 52. Lund.

Andersson, M., Grønnegaard, T. & Svensson, M. 1999. Mellanneolitisk palissadinhägnad och folkvandringstida boplats. Skåne, Västra Karaby sn, Västra Karaby 28:5, Dagstorp 17:12, VKB SU 19. *Riksantikvarieämbetet UV Syd Rapport* 1999:101. Lund.

Andersson, M. & Knarrström, B. 1999. *Senpaleolitikum i Skåne – en studie av materiell kultur och ekonomi hos Sveriges första fångstfolk.* Riksantikvarieämbetet, Avdelningen för arkeologiska undersökningar, Skrifter 26. Lund.

Andersson, M. & Pihl, H. 1997. Plats 7A:7 – Boplatslämningar från tidig- och mellanneolitikum samt ett eventuellt gravfält från tidigneolitikum. In Svensson, M. & Karsten, P. (eds.), Arkeologisk förundersökning. Skåne, Malmöhus län, Järnvägen Västkustbanan, Avsnittet Landskrona–Kävlinge. RAÄ. Avdelningen för arkeologiska undersökningar. *Riksantikvarieämbetet UV Syd Rapport* 1997:83. Lund.

Andersson, M. & Svensson, M. 1999. Palissadkomplexet i Dösjebro. In Burenhult, G. (ed.), *Arkeologi i Norden 1.* Stockholm.

Andersson, T. 1997. Neolitiskt hus med väggränna från St Herrestad. In Karsten, P. (ed.), *Carpe Scaniam. Axplock ur Skånes förflutna.* Riksantikvarieämbetet Arkeologiska Undersökningar, Skrifter 22. Lund.

– 1999. Boplatslämningar från stenålder–äldre järnålder. Skåne, St. Herrestads sn, Herrestad 68:88 m. fl. RAÄ 60. Arkeologisk slutundersökning 1995. *Riksantikvarieämbetet UV Syd Rapport* 1999:8. Lund.

Apel, J., Hadevik, C. & Sundström, L. 1997. Burning Down the House. The transformational use of fire and other aspects of an Early Neolithic TRB site in eastern central Sweden. *Tor* 29. Uppsala.

Apel, J. 2000. Kunskap, handlag och råmaterial – en diskussion kring produktionen och konsumtionen av senneolitiska flintdolkar i Skandinavien. *Tor* 30. Uppsala.

Artursson, M. (ed.). 1997. Tjugestatorp. En tidigneolitisk boplats i östra Mellansverige. Närke, Glanshammar sn, Raä 195. *Slutundersökningsrapport från Arkeologikonsult AB.* Upplands Väsby.

– 1999. Boplatslämningar från tidigneolitikum-mellanneolitikum och romersk järnålder-folkvandringstid. Skåne, Saxtorp sn, Tågerup 1:1 och 1:3. Västkustbanan SU 8, RAÄ 26. *Riksantikvarieämbetet UV Syd Rapport* 1999:79. Lund.

Artursson, M., Linderoth, T., Nilsson, M.-L. & Svensson, M. 2003. Byggnadskultur i södra och mellersta Skandinavien. In Svensson, M. (ed.), *Det neolitiska rummet. Skånska spår – arkeologi längs Västkustbanan.* Riksantikvarieämbetet, Lund.

Aspeborg, H. 1997. Fyra hus och en begravning. Lämningar från neolitikum och bronsålder. Arkeologisk förundersökning. Skåne, Västra Karaby socken, Ålstorp 2:1. *Riksantikvarieämbetet UV Syd Rapport* 1997:75. Lund.

Asplund, J. 1967. *Om mättnadsprocesser.* Uppsala.

Bägerfeldt, L. 1993. *Megalitgravarnas mysterium. Skuggor från Götalands forna historia.* Gamleby.

Bagge, A. 1951. Fagervik – Ein Rückgrat für die Periodeneinteilung der Ostschwedische Wohnplatz – und Bootaxtkultur aus dem Mittelneolitikum. Ein vorläufige Mitteilung. *Acta Archaeologica* XXII. Copenhagen.

Bagge, A. & Kaelas, L. 1950. *Die Funde aus Dolmen und Ganggräber in Schonen* I–II. Lund.

Bagge, A. & Kjellmark, K. 1939. *Stenåldersboplatserna vid Siretorp i Blekinge.* Kungl. Vitterhets, Historie och Antikvitets akademin, Stockholm.

Bakels, C. C. 1978. Four Linearbandkeramik Settlements and their Environment. A paleaecological study of Sittard, Stein, Elsloo and Hienheim. *Analecta Praehistorica Leidensia* 11. Leiden.

Barber, M. 1997. Landscape, the Neolithic, and Kent. In Topping, P. (ed.), *Neolithic Landscapes. Neolithic Studies Group Seminar Papers* 2. Oxbow Monograph 86. Oxford.

Barth, F. 1969a. Ecologic relationships of ethnic groups in Swat, North Pakistan. In Vayda, A. P. (ed.), *Environment & Cultural Behaviour. Ecological Studies in Cultural Anthropology.* University of Texas Press, Austin and London.

– 1969b. Introduction. In Barth, F. (ed.), *Ethnic Groups and Boundaries. The Social Organization of Culture Difference.* Universitetsforlaget, Oslo.

Becker, C. J. 1947. Mosefundne lerkar fra yngre stenalder. *Aarbøger for nordisk Oldkyndighed og Historie* 1947. Copenhagen.

– 1951. Den grubekeramiske kultur i Danmark. *Aarbøger for nordisk Oldkyndighed og Historie* 1950. Copenhagen.

257

# B–C

– 1954. Die mittelneolitichen Kulturen in Südskandinavien. *Acta Archaeologica* XXV. Copenhagen.
– 1955. Stenaldersbebyggelsen ved St. Valby i Vestsjælland. *Aarbøger for nordisk Oldkyndighed og Historie* 1954. Copenhagen.
– 1957. Den tyknakkede flintøkse. Studier over tragtbægerkulturens svære retøkser i mellem-neolitisk tid. *Aarbøger for nordisk Oldkyndighed og Historie*. 1957. Copenhagen.
– 1980. Om grubekeramisk kultur i Danmark. Korte bidrag till en lang diskussion (1950–1980). *Aarbøger for nordisk Oldkyndighed og Historie*. 1980. Copenhagen.
– 1993. Tragtbægerkulturens kulthuse. In Hvass, S. & Storgaard, B. (eds.), *Da klinger i muld ... 25 års arkæologi i Danmark*. Copenhagen.
– 1996. Tragtbægerkulturens mellemneolitiske kulthuse. In Fabricius, K. & Becker, C. J. *Stendyngegrave og Kulthuse. Studier over Tragtbægerkulturen i Nord- og Vestjylland*. Copenhagen.
Bell, C. 1992. *Ritual Theory, Ritual Practice*. Oxford.
Bender, B. 1999. Subverting the Western Gaze. Mapping altenative worlds. In Ucko, P. J. & Layton, R. (eds.), *The Archaeology and Anthropology of Landscape. Shaping your landscape*. One World Archaeology. New York.
Bennike, P., Ebbesen, K. & Bender Jørgensen, L. 1986. The Bog Find from Sigersdal. Human sacrifice in the Early Neolithic. *Journal of Danish Archaeology 5*. Odense.
Berg, H. 1951. *Klintebakken, en boplads fra yngre stenalder på Langeland. Tre langelandske megalitgrave.* Meddelelser fra Langelands Museum. Rudkøbing.
Berg, H. & Skaarup, J. 1979. Yngre Stenalder. In Rud, M. (ed.), *Jeg ser på oldsager*. Copenhagen.
Berggren, Å. 1999. Burlöv 20C – rumsutnyttjande på en höjdrygg under stenålder, bronsålder och järnålder. In *Bulletin för arkeologisk forskning i Sydsverige* 2. Arkeologiska institutionen, Lund.
Bergh, S. 1995. *Landscape of the Monuments. A study of the passage tombs in the Cúil Irra region, Co. Sligo, Ireland.* Studier från UV Stockholm. Riksantikvarieämbetet, Arkeologiska undersökningar, Skrifter 6. Stockholm.
Berglund, B. E. 1969. Vegetation and human influence in S. Scandinavia during prehistoric time. *Oikos 12*. Copenhagen.
– 1991. The Köping area. In Berglund, B. (ed), *The Cultural Landscape during 6000 years in Southern Sweden – the Ystad Project. Ecological Bulletins* 41. Copenhagen.
– 1999. Odlingslandskapets framväxt i Norden. In Burenhult, G. (ed.), *Arkeologi i Norden* 1. Stockholm.
Billberg, I. & Magnusson Staaf, B. 1999. *Rapport över arkeologiska förundersökningar. Öresundsförbindelsen* II. Stadsantikvariska Avdelningen, Kultur Malmö.

Björhem, N. 2000. *Föresundsförbindelsen på väg mot det förflutna*. Malmö Stadsantikvariska Avdelning, Kultur Malmö.
Björhem, N. & Säfvestad, U. 1989. *Fosie IV. Byggnadstradition och bosättningsmönster under senneolitikum*. Malmöfynd 5. Malmö.
Bjørn, C. 1988. (ed.). *Det danske landbrugets historie* I. *Oltid og middelalder*. Odense.
Blomquist, R. 1951. *Lunds Historia 1. Medeltiden*. Lund.
Blomqvist, L. 1989a. *Neolitikum. Typindelningar, tid, rum och social miljö. En studie med inriktning på västra Götaland*. Falköping.
Blomqvist, L. 1989b. *Megalitgravarna i Sverige. Typ, tid, rum och social miljö*. Theses and Papers in Archaeology 1. Stockholm.
Boas, N. A. 1993. Late Neolithic and Bronze Age Settlements at Hemmed Church and Hemmed Plantation, East Jutland. *Journal of Danish Archaeology 10* (1991). Odense.
Bourdieu, P. 1977. *Outline of a Theory of Practice*. Cambridge.
Bradley, R. 1990. *The Passage of Arms. An archaeological analysis of prehistoric hoards and votive deposits*. Cambridge.
– 1993. *Altering the Earth. The origins of monuments in Britain and continental Europe*. Society of Antiquaries of Scotland. Monograph series 8. Edinburgh.
– 1998. *The Significance of Monuments. On the shaping of human experience in Neolithic and Bronze Age Europe*. London.
– 2000. *An Archaeology of Natural Places*. London.
Brorsson, T. 1996. Analys av trattbägarkeramik från en boplats vid Nöbbelövs mosse. In Olson, T., Regnell, M., Nilsson, L., Erikson, M. & Brorsson, T., Boplatslämningar från neolitikum, bronsålder och äldre järnålder. Skåne, Väg 108, N Nöbbelövs, Stångby, Vallkärra och Lackalänga socknar, Lunds och Kävlinge kommuner. *Riksantikvarieämbetet. Arkeologiska undersökningar. UV Syd Rapport 1996:60*. Lund.
Bruzelius, N. G. 1880. *Antikvarisk Beskrifning om Torna Härad i Skåne: upprättad år 1880*. Dalby.
Burenhult, G. 1991. *Arkeologi i Sverige 1 – fångstfolk och herdar*. Höganäs.
– 1999. *Arkeologi i Norden* 1. Stockholm.

Cademar Nilsson, Å. & Ericson Lagerås, K. 2000. Gravfält från senneolitikum och bronsålder vid Häljarps mölla, Skåne, Tofta sn, Häljarp 1:6 och 2:5, VKB SU 2. *Riksantikvarieämbetet UV Syd Rapport 1999:96*. Lund.
Carlie, A. 1986. Om gropkeramisk kultur i Skåne, speciellt Jonstorp. In Adamsen, C. & Ebbesen, K. (eds.), *Stridsøksetid i Sydskandinavien. Beretning fra et symposium. 28.–30.X. 1985 i Vejle*. Arkeologiska skrifter 1. Copenhagen.

# C–E

Carmichael, D., Hubert, J., Reeves, B. & Schanche, A. (eds.). 1998. *Sacred Sites, Sacred Places*. London and New York.

Carsten, J. & Hugh-Jones, S. 1995. *About the House – Levi-Strauss and Beyond*. Cambridge.

Chapman, J. 2000. *Fragmentation in Archaeology. People, places and broken objects in the prehistory of South Eastern Europe*. London.

Chisholm, M. 1968. *Rural Settlement and Land Use*. London.

Christensen, C. 1982. Stenalderfjorden og Vedbæk-bopladserna. Havspejlets svingninger 5 500–2 500 f Kr. *Nationalmseets Arbejdsmark*. Copenhagen.

– 1993. Land og hav. In Hvass, S. & Storgaard, B. (eds.), *Da klinger i muld ... 25 års arkæologi i Danmark*. Århus.

Cooney, G. 1999. Social Landscapes in Irish Prehistory. In Ucko, P. J. & Layton, R. (eds.), *The Archaeology and Anthropology of Landscape. Shaping your landscape*. One World Archaeology. New York.

– 2000. *Landscapes of Neolithic Ireland*. London.

Cooney, G. & Grogan, E. 1999. People and Place During the Irish Neolithic: Exploring Social Change in Time and Space. In Edmonds, M. & Richards, C. (eds.), *Understanding the Neolithic of North-Western Europe*. Glasgow.

Cronberg, C. 2001. Husesyn. In Karsten, P. & Knarrström, B. (eds.), *Tågerup specialstudier. Skånska spår – arkeologi längs Västkustbanan*. Riksantikvarieämbetet, Lund.

Damm, C. 1991. Burying the Past. An Example of Social Transformation in the Danish Neolithic. In Garwood, P. (eds.), *Sacred and Profane. Proceedings of a conference on archaeology, ritual and religion, Oxford 1989*. Oxford.

– 1993. The Danish Single Grave Culture – Ethnic Migration or Social Construction? *Journal of Danish Archaeology* 10 (1991). Odense.

Darvill, T. 1997. Neolithic Landscapes: Identity and definition. In Topping, P. (ed.), *Neolithic Landscapes. Neolithic Studies Group Seminar Papers* 2. Oxbow Monograph 86. Oxford.

Davidsen, K. 1975. Neolitiske lerskiver belyst ved danske fund. *Aarbøger for nordisk Oldkyndighed og Historie*. 1973. Copenhagen.

– 1978. *The Final TRB Culture in Denmark. A Settlement Study*. Arkæologiske Studier V. Copenhagen.

Descola, P. 1994. *In the Society of Nature. A Native Ecology in Amazonia*. Cambridge.

Digerfeldt, G. 1975. Investigations of Littorina Transgressions in the Ancient Lagoon Barsebäcksmossen, Western Skåne. *Department of Quaternary Geology*. Report 7. Lund.

– 1982. The Holocene Development of Lake Sämbosjön 1. Regional Vegetation History. *University of Lund Department of Quaternary Geology* Report 23. Lund.

Dodgshon, R. A. 1987. *The European Past. Social Evolution and Spatial Order*. London.

Douglas, M. 1966. *Purity and Danger. An analysis of the concepts of pollution and taboo*. London.

– 1973. *Natural Symbols*. Harmondsworth.

Dybeck, R. 1840. (Unpublished report). Fornminnen IV från Skåne och Dalsland. Antikvarisk-Topografiska Arkivet. Stockholm.

Ebbesen, K. 1975. *Die jungere Trichtenbecherkultur auf den dänischen inseln*. Arkæologiska Studier II. Copenhagen.

– 1978. *Trattbægerkultur i Nordjylland. Studier over jættestuetiden*. Nordiske Fortidsminder Series B 5. Copenhagen.

– 1979. *Stordyssen i Vedsted. Studier over Tragtbægerkulturen i Sønderjylland*. Arkæologiske Studier VI. Copenhagen.

– 1983. Yngre stenalders depotfund som bebyggelse-historisk kildemateriale. In Thrane, H. (ed.), *Om Yngre Stenalders Bebyggelsehistorie*. Odense.

– 1984. Trattbægerkulturens grønstensøkser. *KUML* 1984. Copenhagen.

– 1986: Fred i enkeltgravstid. In Adamsen, C. & Ebbesen, K. (eds.), *Stridsøksetid i Sydskandinavien. Beretning fra et symposium. 28.–30.X. 1985 i Vejle*. Arkæologiska skrifter 1. Copenhagen.

– 1994. Simple, tidigneolitiske grave. *Aarbøger for Nordisk Oldkyndighed og Historie* 1992. Copenhagen.

Ebbesen, K. & Mahler, D. 1980. Virum. Et tidigneolitisk bopladsfund. *Aarbøger for nordisk Oldkyndighed og Historie* 1979. Copenhagen.

Edenmo, R., Larsson, M., Nordqvist, B. & Olsson, E. 1997. Gropkeramikerna – fanns de? Materiell kultur och ideologiska förändringar. In Larsson, M. & Olsson, E. (eds.), *Regionalt och interregionalt. Stenåldersundersökningar i Syd- och Mellansverige*. Riksantikvarieämbetet, Arkeologiska undersökningar, Skrifter 23. Stockholm.

Edmonds, M. 1999. *Ancestral Geographies of the Neolithic. Landscapes, monuments and memory*. London.

Ekström, A. 1999. Icke Megalitiska Tidig Neolitiska gravar (IMTNgravar) i Sydskandinavien. En strukturerad utredning. Photocopy. Arkeologiska institutionen, Lunds universitet.

Ellen, R. 1977. Anatomical Classification and the Semiotics of the Body. In Blacking, J. (ed.), *The Anthropology of the Body*. London.

Ericson Borggren, T. (Unpublished ms) Banverket, Dubbelspåret Lund–Kävlinge, 1994. Punkt 10. Riksantikvarieämbetet UV Syd.

259

# E–H

Ericson Lagerås, K. 1999. En långhög vid Krångeltofta. Skåne, Krångeltofta, Västkustbanan. *Riksantikvarie-ämbetet UV Syd Rapport* 1999:44. Lund.

Eriksen, P. & Madsen, T. 1984. Hanstegård. A settlement site from the Funnel Beaker culture. *Journal of Danish Archaeology* 3. Odense.

Eriksen, T. H. 1995. *Small Places, Large Issues.* London.

Eriksson, N., Rogius, K., Rosendahl, A. & Wennberg, T. 2000. Fyndrika TN-gropar i sydvästra Skåne. Photocopy. Arkeologiska institutionen, Lunds universitet.

Ethelberg, P., Jørgensen, E., Meier, D. & Robinson, D. 2000. *Det Sønderjyske Landbrugs Historie. Sten- og bronzealder.* Haderslev.

Fairclough, G. 1999. Protecting Time and Space. Understanding historic landscape for conservation in England. In Layton, R. & Ucko, P. J. (eds.), *The Archaeology and Anthropology of Landscape. Shaping your landscape.* One World Archaeology. New York.

Fischer, A. 2002. Food for Feasting? In Fischer, A. & Kristiansen, K. (eds.), *The Neolithisation of Denmark. 150 years of debate.* Sheffield.

Fleming, A. 1973. Tombs for the Living. *Man: the journal of the Royal Anthropological Institute.* N.S. 8. London.

Forssander, J-E. 1932. (Unpublished report). Antikvarisk-Topografiska Arkivet. Stockholm.

– 1933. *Die schwedische Bootaxtkultur und ihre kontinentaleuropäischen Voraussetzungen.* Lund.

– 1936. Skånsk megalitkeramik och kontinentaleuropeisk stenålder. *MLUHM 1936.* Lund.

– 1937. (Unpublished report). Västra Hoby. Antikvarisk-Topografiska Arkivet. Stockholm.

Frazer, J. G. 1890. *The Golden Bough.* London.

Friman, B. 1996. Neolithization and "Classical" Elm Decline. A Synthesis of Two Debates. *Lund Archaeological Review* 1996. Lund.

Gennep van, A. 1960. *The Rites of Passage.* London.

Giddens, A. 1979. *Central Problems in Social Theory.* London.

– 1981. *A Contemporary Critique of Historical Materialism.* London.

– 1984. *The Constitution of Society.* Cambridge.

Gidlöf, K. & Johansson, T. 2002. Almhov (delområde 1). In Lindhé, E., Sarnäs, P. & Steineke, M. (eds.), *Citytunnelprojektet. Rapport över arkeologiska förundersökningar. Rapport* 38. Malmö Kulturmiljö.

Giersing, T. 2000. *Arkæologiske Udgravninger i Danmark* 1999. Copenhagen.

Glob, P. V. 1944. Studier over den jyske Enkeltgravskultur. *Aarbøger for nordisk Oldkyndighed og Historie 1944.* Copenhagen.

Göransson, H. 1988. *Neolithic Man and the Forest Environment around Alvastra Pile Dwelling.* Theses and Papers in North European Archaeology 20. Stockholm.

– 1996. Om skottskogsbruk och utfodring med kvistar under mellanneolitisk tid och om skogsutnyttjandet under mesolitisk tid. *Kungl. Skogs- och Lantbruksakademin.* Solmed 17. Stockholm.

Göthberg, H., Kyhlberg, O. & Vinberg, A. 1995. *Hus och gård i det förurbana samhället. Rapport från ett sektorforskningsprojekt. Katalog.* Riksantikvarieämbetet, Arkeologiska undersökningar, Skrifter 13. Stockholm.

Gräslund, B. 1989. Gånggrifternas funktion i ljuset av primitiv själstro. In Larsson, L. & Wyszomirska, B., *Arkeologi och religion. Rapport från arkeologidagarna 16–18 januari 1989.* University of Lund, Institute of Archaeology, Report Series 34. Lund.

Gräslund, A.-S. 1991. Gravmaterialet som källa till kunskap om religiösa förhållanden. In Lagerlöf, A. (ed.), *Gravfältsundersökningar och Gravarkeologi. Rapport från riksantikvarieämbetets seminarium om "Gravmaterialet som källa för kunskap om människans livsvillkor, religiösa och sociala värderingar", 26–27 oktober 1988.* Stockholm.

Gustavsson, S. 2000. Arkeobotanisk rapport över analys av fröavtryck i keramik. Bilaga i Rudebeck, E. & Ödman, C. *Kristineberg. En gravplats under 4 500 år.* Malmöfynd 7. Stadsantikvariska avdelningen kultur Malmö.

Hansen, F. 1917. Några enmansgravar från stenåldern. *Fornvännen.* Uppsala.

– 1919a. (Unpublished report). Höjsmölla gånggriften. Höj sn, Harjagers hd, Sk. Antikvarisk-Topografiska Arkivet. Stockholm.

– 1919b. (Unpublished report). Redogörelse för undersökningen av en gånggrift i Södervidinge socken, Harjagers härad, Skåne. Antikvarisk-Topografiska Arkivet. Stockholm.

– 1920. (Unpublished report). Bilagda brev (5072/1920) från fil dr Folke Hansen, Lund. Inv nr 16438. Antikvarisk-Topografiska Arkivet. Stockholm.

– 1923. (Unpublished report). Undersökningar af gånggrift i Lackalänga. Antikvarisk-Topografiska Arkivet. Stockholm.

– 1926. (Unpublished report). Nr 32, Stora Harrie sn, Harjagers härad, Skåne. Antikvarisk-Topografiska Arkivet. Stockholm

– 1930. Gånggriften å Storegården i Barsebäck. *MLUHM 1930.* Lund.

– 1931. (Unpublished report). Undersökningar af gånggrift i Storegården. Antikvarisk-Topografiska Arkivet. Stockholm.

– 1932. Gånggriftsundersökningar i Harjagers härad. *Historisk Tidskrift för Skåneland.* Lund.

260

Hansen, M. & Rostholm, H. 1993. Grave fra enkelt-gravstid og senneolitikum. In Hvass, S. & Storgaard, B. (eds.), *Da Klinger i Muld ... 25 års arkæologi i Danmark*. Århus.

Hårdh, B. 1982. The Megalithic Grave Area around the Lödde-Kävlinge River. A research programme. *MLUHM* 1981–1982. Lund.

– 1986. *Ceramic Decoration and Social Organisation. Regional Variations seen in Material from South Swedish Passage-Graves*. Scripta Minora. Regiae Societatis Humaniorum Litterarum Lundensis. Studier utgivna av Kungl. Humanistiska Vetenskapssamfundet i Lund 1985–1986:1. Lund.

– 1990a. Annehill in Kävlinge. New studies of a double passage-grave in Scania. *MLUHM* 1989–1990. Lund.

– 1990b. *Patterns of Deposition and Settlement. Studies on the Maegalithic Tombs of West Scania*. Scripta Minora. Regia Societas Humaniorum Litterarum Lundensis. Studier utgivna av kungl. Humanistiska Vetenskapssamfundet i Lund. 1988–1989:2. Lund.

– 1993. Gånggriften Storegård, Barsebäck 11:1, Barsebäck sn, Skåne. Arkeologisk undersökning 1986–87. Photocopy. Institutionen för Arkeologi vid Lunds Universitet.

Hedeager, L. & Kristiansen, K. 1988. Oltiden O. 4000 f.Kr. – 1000 e.Kr. In Bjørn, C. 1988. (ed.), *Det danske landbrugets historie* I. Oldtid og middelalder. Odense.

Hellerström, S. 1988. Ystadbygden. En studie av lösfynd och bosättning under neolitikum. Photocopy. Arkeologiska institutionen, Lunds universitet.

– 1997. En trattbägarboplats vid Nöbbelövs mosse. In Karsten, P. (ed.), *Carpe Scaniam. Axplock ur Skånes förflutna*. Riksantikvarieämbetet, Arkeologiska Undersökningar, Skrifter 22. Lund.

Hernek, R. 1989. Den spetsnackiga yxan av flinta. *Fornvännen* 1988/4. Uppsala.

Hertz, R. 1960. *Death and the Right Hand*. Oxford.

Hill, J. D. 1995. *Ritual and Rubbish in the Iron Age of Wessex. A study on the formation of a specific archaeological record*. BAR British Series 242. Oxford

Hjelmqvist, H. 1955. Die älteste Geschichte der Kulturpflanzen in Schweden. *Opera Botanica* 1 (3). Stockholm.

– 1964. Kulturväxter från Skånes forntid. *Ale* 1964/1. Lund.

– 1975. Geitreidearten und andere Nutzpflanzen aus der frühneolitischen Zeit auf ein Langeländischer Wohnplatz mit Hausresten aus der frühneolithischen Zeit Langeland. In Skaarup, J., *Stengade. Ein langeländischer Wohnplatz mit Hausresten aus der frühneolithischen Zeit*. Meddelelser fra Langelands Museum. Rudkøbing.

– 1979. Beiträge zur Kenntnis der prähistorischen Nutzpflanzen in Schweden. *Opera Botanica* 47. Stockholm.

– 1982. Economic plants from a middle Neolithic site in Scania. Appendix in Larsson, L., A causewayed enclosure and a site with Valby pottery at Stävie, western Scania. *MLUHM* 1981–1982. Lund.

– 1985. Economic plants from two stone age settlements in southernmost Scania. Appendix in Larsson, L., Karlsfält, A settlement from the early and late funnel beaker culture in southern Scania, Sweden. *Acta Archaeologica* 54. Copenhagen.

Hodder, I. 1982. *Symbols in Action*. Cambridge.

– 1984. Beyond Processual Archaeology. *Perspective on Archaeological Theory and Method*. University of Lund, Institute of Archaeology, Report Series 20. Lund.

– 1986. *Reading the Past. Current approaches to interpretation in archaeology*. Cambridge.

– 1990. *The Domestication of Europe*. Oxford.

Högberg, A. 2002. Production Sites on the Beach Ridge of Järavallen. Aspects on Tool Preforms, Action, Technology, Ritual and the Continuity of Place. *Current Swedish Archaeology* 10. Stockholm.

Holmgren, P. & Tronde, B. 1990. Fornminnesinventering i Skåne 1985–87. *Arkeologi i Sverige* 1987. Riksantikvarieämbetet Rapport 1990:1. Lund.

Hulthén, B. 1977. *On Ceramic Technology during the Scanian Neolithic and Bronze Age*. Theses and Papers in North-European Archaeology 6. Stockholm.

Huntingdon, R. & Metcalf, P. 1979. *Celebrations of Death*. Cambridge.

Hviding, E. 1996. Nature, culture, magic, science: on meta-languages for comparison in cultural ecology. In Descola, P. & Pálsson, G. (eds.), *Nature and Society. Anthropological perspectives*. London.

Ingold, T. 1993. The Temporality of the Landscape. *World Archaeology* 5:2. London.

Iversen, J. 1949. The Influence of Prehistoric Man on Vegetation. *Danmarks Geologiske Undersøgelse* IV. Bd. 4, No. 3. Copenhagen.

Jacobsson, B. 1986. The Skogsdala Dolmen. *MLUHM* 1985–1986. Lund.

Jansson, P. 1999. Ängdalas gåta. – Vad yxade man till vid flintgruvorna? Photocopy. Arkeologiska institutionen, Lunds universitet.

Janzon, G. O. 1986. Stridsyxekultur med metallurgisk know-how. In Adamsen, C. & Ebbesen, K. (eds.), *Stridsøksetid i Sydskandinavien. Beretning fra et symposium. 28.–30.X. 1985 i Vejle*. Arkeologiska skrifter 1. Copenhagen.

Jennbert, K. 1984a. *Den produktiva gåvan. Tradition och innovation i Sydskandinavien för omkring 5 300 år sedan*. Acta Archaeologica Lundensia, Series in 4°, No. 16. Lund.

– 1984b. Unpublished report. LUHM m. rapp. fr. unders. av boplats och grav, Saxtorp 15:4, Saxtorp sn, Sk. Antikvarisk-Topografiska Arkivet. Stockholm.

261

# J–K

– 1999. Fångstfolk börjar odla i Skåne. In Burenhult, G. (ed.), *Arkeologi i Norden* 1. Stockholm.

Jensen, J. A. 1973. Bopladsen Myrhøj. 3 hustomter med klokkebægerkeramik. *Kuml* 1972. Århus.

Jeppsson, A. 1996a. Boplats, Stora Harrie socken, Eslöv P7. Arkeologisk slutundersökning. Sydgasprojektet, grenledning Eslöv P8. In Räf, E. (ed.), Skåne på längden. *Riksantikvarieämbetet UV Syd Rapport* 1996:58. Lund.

– 1996b. Boplats och gravar, Karaby 3:1, 4:1, Västra Karaby socken, RAÄ 39, Stamledning P36. Arkeologisk slutundersökning. Sydgasprojektet, grenledning Eslöv P8. In Räf, E. (ed.), Skåne på längden. *Riksantikvarieämbetet UV Syd Rapport* 1996:58. Lund.

Jonsson, E. 1995. Delområde 1. Skjutbanorna. In *Öresundsförbindelsen. Rapport över arkeologiska förundersökningar*. Malmö Museer.

– 2002. Nya undersökningar på Elinelund. En strandvallsboplats i övergången senmesolitikum/tidigneolitikum. Photocopy. Institutionen för arkeologi och antikens historia, Lunds universitet.

Jørgensen, E. 1977. *Hagebrogård – Vroue – Koldkur. Neolitische Gräberfelder aus Nordwest-Jütland*. Arkæologiske Studier IV. Copenhagen.

Kaelas, L. 1976. Pitted Ware Culture – the acculturation of a foodgathering group? In De Laet, S. J. (ed.), *Acculturation and Continuity in Atlantic Europe mainly during the Neolithic Period and the Bronze Age. Papers presented at the IV Atlantic colloquium, Ghent 1975*. Brugge.

Karlin, J. 1909. (Unpublished report). Berättelse öfver undersökning af fornlämning i Lilla Harrie by, Lilla Harrie socken, Harjagers hr, Skåne. Antikvarisk-Topografiska Arkivet, Stockholm.

Karsten, P. 1990. Aspects of the Survey of Ancient Monuments in the County of Malmöhus. *MLUHM* 1989–1990. Lund.

– 1994. *Att kasta yxan i sjön. En studie över rituell tradition och förändring utifrån skånska neolitiska offerfynd*. Acta Archaeologica Lundensia, Series in 8°, No. 23. Lund.

Karsten, P. & Knarrström, B. 1999. Tågerup. Skåne, Saxtorp socken, Tågerup 1:1, fornlämning RAÄ 3, SU 6. *Riksantikvarieämbetet UV Syd Rapport* 1999: 71. Lund.

– 2001. *Tågerup specialstudier. Skånska spår – arkeologi längs Västkustbanan*. Riksantikvarieämbetet, Lund.

– 2003. *The Tågerup Excavations*. Skånska spår. Arkeologi längs Västkustbanan. Riksantikvarieämbetet. Avdelningen för arkeologiska undersökningar UV Syd. Lund.

Kaul, F. 1988. Neolitiske gravanlæg på Onsved Mark, Horns Herred, Sjælland. *Aarbøger for nordisk Oldkyndighed og Historie* 1987. Copenhagen.

– 1992. Ritualer med menneskeknogler i yngre stenalder. *KUML* 1991–1992. Århus.

Kihlstedt, B., Larsson, M. & Nordqvist, B. 1997. Neolitiseringen i Syd- Väst- och Mellansverige – social och ideologisk förändring. In Larsson, M. & Olsson, E. (eds.), *Regionalt och interregionalt. Stenåldersundersökningar i Syd- och Mellansverige*. Riksantikvarieämbetet, Arkeologiska undersökningar, Skrifter 23. Stockholm.

Kjällquist, M. 2001. Gåvor eller avfall. In Karsten, P. & Knarrström, B. (eds.), *Tågerup specialstudier. Skånska spår – arkeologi längs Västkustbanan*. Riksantikvarieämbetet, Lund.

Kjellmark, K. 1903. *En stenåldersboplats i Järavallen vid Limhamn*. ATS 3. Stockholm.

Klassen, L. 2000. *Frühes Kupfer im Norden. Untersuchungen zu Chronologie, Herkunft und Bedeutung der Kupferfunde der Nordgruppe der Trichterbecherkultur*. Moesgård Museum. Jysk Arkæologisk Selskab. Århus.

Knarrström, B. 1995. Skåne, Stävie socken, Stävie 2:64, Egnahemsområdet. Arkeologisk utredning och slutundersökning. 1990. *Riksantikvarieämbetet UV Syd Rapport* 1995:64. Lund.

– 2000a. Tidigneolitisk social och rituell organisation. Analys av 95 skivskrapor i ett depåfynd. In Högberg, A. (ed.), *Artefakter och arkeologiska ting. En bok om föremål ur ett arkeologiskt perspektiv*. University of Lund, Institute of Archaeology, Report Series 71. Stadsantikvariska Avdelningen, Kultur Malmö.

– 2000b. *Flinta i sydvästra Skåne. En diakron studie av råmaterial, produktion och funktion med fokus på boplatsteknologi och metalltida flintutnyttjande*. Acta Archaeologica Lundensia, Series in 8°, No. 33. Lund.

– (Unpublished ms). Punkt 12 öst och väst. Banverket, Dubbelspåret Lund–Kävlinge, 1994. Riksantikvarieämbetet UV Syd.

Knarrström, B. & Wallin, L. 1999. Marbäcksgården verksamhetsområde i Löddeköpinge. Skåne, Löddeköpinge sn, Löddeköpinge 40 m. fl. *Riksantikvarieämbetet UV Syd Rapport* 1999:87. Lund.

Knutsson, H. 1995. *Slutvandrat? Aspekter på övergången från rörlig till bofast tillvaro*. AUN 20. Uppsala universitet. Uppsala.

Koch, E. 1998. *Neolithic Bog Pots from Zealand, Møn, Lolland and Falster*. Nordiske Forntidsminder Series B 16. Det Kongelige Nordiske Oldskriftselskab. Copenhagen.

Kopytoff, I. 1971. Ancestors as Elders in Africa. *Africa: Journal of the International African Institute* 41. London.

– 1986. The cultural biography of things: commoditisation as process. In Appadurai, A. (ed.), *The Social Life of Things*. Cambridge.

262

# K–L

Kriig, S. 1999. Från stenålder till medeltid i Särslöv. Skåne, Dagstorp sn, Dagstorp (SU 22), VKB SU 22. *Riksantikvarieämbetet UV Syd Rapport* 1999:106. Lund.

Kristiansen, K. 1988. De ældste bygder. In Bjørn, C. 1988. (ed.), *Det danske landbrugets historie I. Oldtid og middelalder*. Odense.

– 1991. Prehistoric Migrations – the Case of the Single Grave and Corded Ware Cultures. *Journal of Danish Archaeology* 8 (1989). Odense.

Lagergren-Olsson, A. 2003. En skånsk keramikhistoria. In Svensson, M. (ed.), *Det Neolitiska Rummet. Skånska spår – arkeologi längs Västkustbanan.* Riksantikvarieämbetet, Lund.

Lagergren-Olsson, A. & Linderoth, T. 2000. De neolitiska boplatslämningarna på plats SU 21. *Riksantikvarieämbetet UV Syd Rapport* 2000:22. Lund.

Larsson, L. 1982. A Causewayed Enclosure and a Site with Valby Pottery at Stävie, Western Scania. *MLUHM* 1981–1982. Lund.

– 1984. The Skateholm project – a late Mesolithic settlement and cemetery complex at a southern Swedish Bay. *MLUHM* 1983–1984. Lund.

– 1985. Karlsfält. A Settlement from the Early and Late Funnel Beaker Culture in Southern Scania, Sweden. *Acta Archaeologica* 54. Copenhagen.

– 1986. Skåne under sen trattbägarkultur. In Adamsen, C. & Ebbesen, K. (eds.), *Stridsøksetid i Sydskandinavien. Beretning fra et symposium. 28.–30.X. 1985 i Vejle.* Arkæologiska skrifter 1. Copenhagen.

– 1988a. Mortuary Building above Stone Age Grave. A Grave From the Battle Axe Culture at Ullstorp, Southern Scania, Sweden. *MLUHM* 1987–88. Lund.

– 1988b. *The Skateholm Project* I. *Man and Environment.* Acta Regiae Societatis Humaniorum Litterarum Lundensis LXXIX. Stockholm.

– 1989a. (ed.). *Stridsyxekultur i Sydskandinavien.* University of Lund, Institute of Archaeology, Report Series 36. Lund.

– 1989b. Boplatser, bebyggelse och bygder. Stridsyxekultur i södra Skåne. In Larsson, L. (ed.), *Stridsyxekultur i Sydskandinavien.* University of Lund, Institute of Archaeology, Report Series 36. Lund.

– 1992a. Settlement and Environment during the Middle Neolithic and Late Neolithic. In Larsson, L., Callmer, C. & Stjernquist, B. (eds), *The Archaeology of the Cultural Landscape. Field Work and Research in a South Swedish Rural Region.* Acta Archaeologica Lundensia, Series in 4°, No. 19. Lund.

– 1992b. Façade for the Dead. A preliminary report on the excavation of a long barrow in southern Scania. *MLUHM* 1991–92. Lund.

– 1992c. Neolithic Settlement in the Skateholm Area, Southern Scania. *MLUHM* 1991–1992. Lund.

– 1993. From MN A to MN B. A South Swedish Perspective. *Journal of Danish Archaeology* 10. Odense.

– 1995. Man and Sea in Southern Scandinavia during the Late Mesolithic. The role of cemeteries in the view of society. In Fischer, A. (ed.), *Man and Sea in the Mesolithic. Coastal settlement above and below present sea level.* Oxbow Monograph 53. Oxford.

– 1998. Neolithic Societies and their Environments in Southern Sweden. A case study. In Edmonds, M. & Richards, C. (eds.), *Understanding the Neolithic of North-Western Europe.* Glasgow.

– 2001. Det senaste kvartseklets stenåldersforskning i Skåne. In Bergenstråhle, I. & Hellerström, S. (eds.), *Stenåldersforskning i fokus. Inblickar och utblickar i sydskandinavisk stenåldersarkeologi.* Riksantikvarieämbetet, Arkeologiska undersökningar, Skrifter 39. University of Lund, Institute of Archaeology, Report Series 77. Lund.

– 2002. Långhögar i ett samhällsperspektiv. In Larsson, L. (ed.), *Monumentala gravformer i det äldsta bondesamhället.* University of Lund, Department of Archaeology and Ancient History, Report Series 83. Lund.

Larsson, L., Callmer, C., Stjernquist, B. (eds.). 1992. *The Archaeology of the Cultural Landscape. Field Work and Research in a South Swedish Rural Region.* Acta Archaeologica Lundensia, Series in 4°, No. 19. Lund.

Larsson, L. & Larsson, M. 1984. Flintyxor, Skoskav och massor av stolphål. *Ystadiana* 29. Ystad.

– 1986. Stenåldersundersökningar i Ystad-området. *Ystadiana* 31. Ystad.

Larsson, M. 1980. An Early Neolithic Grave from Malmö. *MLUHM* 1979–1980. Lund.

– 1984. *Tidigneolitikum i Sydvästskåne. Kronologi och bosättningsmönster.* Acta Archaeologica Lundensia, Series in 4°, No. 17. Lund.

– 1985. *The Early Neolithic Funnel-Beaker Culture in South-West Scania, Sweden.* British Archaeological Reports. BAR 264. Oxford.

– 1987. Människor vid en Havsvik. *Ystadiana* 32. Ystad.

– 1988a. Gravplats, boplats, åker. Ett exempel på kulturlandskapets utnyttjande kring Köpingebro i sydligaste Skåne. *Ale.* 1988:1. Lund.

– 1988b. Megaliths and Society. The Development of Social Territories in the South Scanian Funnel Beaker Culture. *MLUHM* 1987–1988. Lund.

– 1991. The Neolithic. The establishment of agriculture in the Köpinge area. In Berglund, B. E. (ed), *The Cultural Landscape during 6000 Years in Southern Sweden. Ecological Bulletins* 41. Lund.

263

# L–M

– 1992. The Early and Middle Neolithic Funnel Beaker Culture in the Ystad area (Southern Scania). Economic and social change, 3100–2300 BC. In Larsson, L., Callmer, J. & Stjernquist, B. (eds.), *The Archaeology of the Cultural Landscape. Field Work and Research in a south Swedish rural region*. Acta Archaeologica Lundensia, Series in 4°, No. 19. Lund.

Layton, R. & Ucko, P. J. 1999. Introduction. Gazing on the landscape and encountering the environment. In Layton, R. & Ucko, P. J.(eds.), *The Archaeology and Anthropology of Landscape. Shaping your landscape*. One World Archaeology, New York.

Lévi-Strauss, C. 1970. *The Raw and the Cooked*. London.

– 1977. *Structural Anthropology* 1. London.

– 1987. *Det vilda tänkandet*. 3rd ed. Malmö.

Liljegren, R. 1982. *Paleoekologi och strandförskjutning i en Littorinavik vid Spjälkö i mellersta Blekinge*. LUNDQUA Thesis 11. Lund.

Lindahl, A. 2000. The Idea of a Pot … Perception of Pottery. In Olausson, D. & Vandkilde, H. (eds.), *Form, Function and Context. Material culture studies in Scandinavian archaeology*. Acta Archaeologica Lundensia, Series in 8°, No. 31. Lund.

Lindahl Jensen, B. 1992. Valdemarsro från förundersökning till huvudundersökning. *Arkeologi i Malmö. Rapport* 4. Stadsantikvariska avdelningen. Malmö Museer.

Lindahl Jensen, B. & Nilsson, M-L. 1999. Ett källsprång i Saxtorp – med fynd från tidigneolitikum och yngre bronsålder. Skåne, Saxtorp sn, Kvärlöv 19:1, VKB SU 9. *Riksantikvarieämbetet UV Syd Rapport* 1999:92. Lund.

Lindblad, J. & Lund, K. 1997. Plats 6:3 – Förhistorisk gravplats och mesolitisk boplats. In Svensson, M. & Karsten, P. (eds.), Arkeologisk förundersökning. Skåne, Malmöhus län, Järnvägen Västkustbanan, Avsnittet Landskrona–Kävlinge. *Riksantikvarieämbetet UV Syd Rapport* 1997:83. Lund.

Lindsten, J. 1974. Stävie 4:1. En boplatslämning från stenåldern vid Lödde Å, Skåne. Photocopy. Arkeologiska institutionen, Lunds Universitet.

Liversage, D. 1981. Neolithic Monuments at Lindebjerg, Northwest Zealand. *Acta Archaeologica* 51 (1980). Copenhagen.

– 1982. An Early Neolithic Ritual Structure on Sejrø. *Journal of Danish Archaeology* 1. Odense.

– 1992. *Barkær. Long barrows and settlements*. Arkæologiske studier IX. Copenhagen.

Löfgren, A. 1993. *Skåne, S:t Ibb sn, Tuna by 13:22. 1989. RAÄ 65*. Arkeologisk för- och slutundersökning. Riksantikvarieämbetet, Byrån för arkeologiska undersökningar, Lund.

Löfstrand, L. 1974. *Yngre stenålderns kustboplatser. Undersökningarna vid Äs och studier i den gropkeramiska kulturens kronologi och ekologi*. Archaeo-logical Studies Uppsala Univerity. Institute of North European Archaeology. Aun I. Uppsala.

Löfwall, U. 1977. En Trattbägarboplats i Dösjebro, Västra Karaby socken. Photocopy. Arkeologiska institutionen, Lunds universitet.

Madsen, B. 1993. Flint – udvinding, forarbejdning og distribution. In Hvass, S. & Storgaard, B. (eds.), *Da klinger i muld … 25 års arkæologi i Danmark*. Århus.

Madsen, T. 1982. Settlement Systems of Early Agricultural Societies in East Jutland, Denmark. A regional study of change. *Journal of Anthropological Archaeology* 1. New York.

– 1988. Causewayed Enclosures in South Scandinavia. In Burgess, C., Topping, P., Mordant, C. & Maddison, M. (eds.), *Enclosures and Defences in the Neolithic of Western Europe*. BAR International Series 403 (i). Oxford.

– 1993. Høje med træbyggede grave. In Hvass, S. & Storgaard, B. (eds.), *Da klinger i muld … 25 års arkæologi i Danmark*. Århus.

Madsen, T. & Jensen, H. 1982. Setllement and land use in early Neolithic Denmark. *Analecta Praehistorica Leidensia* 15. Leiden.

Madsen, T. & Petersen, J. E. 1984. Tidlig-neolitiske anlæg ved Mosegården. Regionale og kronologiske forskelle i tidigneolitikum. *Kuml* 1982–83. Årbog for Jysk Arkæologi Selskap. Århus.

Magnusson Staaf, B. 1996. *An Essay on Copper Flat Axes*. Acta Archaeologica Lundensia, Series in 4°. Stockholm.

Malinowski, B. 1922. *Argonauts of the Western Pacific*. London.

– 1929. *The Sexual Life of Savages in North-West Melanesia*. New York.

Malmer, M. P. 1957. Pleionbegreppets betydelse för studiet av förhistoriska innovationsförlopp. *Finska fornminnesföreningens tidskrift* 58. Helsinki.

– 1962. *Jungneolitische Studien*. Acta Archaeologica Lundensia, Series in 8°, No. 2. Lund.

– 1969. Gropkeramikboplatsen Jonstorp RÄ. *Antikvarisk Arkiv* 36. Stockholm.

– 1973. Om den gropkeramiska kulturens väsen. In Simonsen, P. & Sramsø Munch, G. (eds.), *Bondeveidemann bofast-ikke bofast i nordisk forhistorie*. Tromsø Museums Skrifter XIV. Tromsø.

– 1975. *Stridsyxekultur i Sverige och Norge*. Lund.

– 2002. *The Neolithic of South Sweden TRB, GRK, and STR*. The Royal Swedish Academy of Letters History and Antiquities. Stockholm.

Malmros, C. & Tauber, H. 1977. Kolstof-14 dateringer af dansk enkeltgravkultur. *Aarbøger for nordisk Oldkyndighed og Historie* 1975. Copenhagen.

Malmros, C. 1980. Den tidlige enkeltgravkultur og stridsøksekultur. *Aarbøger for nordisk Oldkyndighed og Historie* 1979. Copenhagen.

Månsson, S. & Pihl, H. 1999. Gravar, yxtillverkning och hus från mellanneolitikum. Skåne, Dagstorp sn, Särslöv 3:6 m fl, VKB SU 17. *Riksantikvarieämbetet UV Syd Rapport* 1999:98. Lund.

Mathiassen, T. 1939. Bundsø, en yngre stenalders boplads på Als. *Aarbøger for nordisk Oldkyndighed og Historie 1939*. Copenhagen.

– 1944. The Stone-Age Settlement at Trelleborg. *Acta Archaeologica* XV. Copenhagen.

Mauss, M. 1925. *Gåvan*. Uppsala.

– 1950. *The Gift: Forms and Functions of Exchange in Archaic Societies*. London.

– 1973. Techniques of the body. *Economy and Society* 2. London.

Meillassoux, C. 1972. From reproduction to production. *Economy and Society* 1. London.

– 1981. *Maidens, Meal and Money. Capitalism and the Domestic Economy*. Cambridge.

Midgley, M. S. 1992. *TRB Culture. The First Farmers of the European Plain*. Edinburgh.

Miller, D. & Tilley, C. 1984. Ideology, power and long term social change. In Miller, D. & Tilley, C. (eds.), *Ideology, Power and Prehistory*. Cambridge.

Mohs, G. 1998. Sto:lo sacred ground. In Carmichael, D., Hubert, J., Reeves, B. & Schanche, A. (eds.), *Sacred Sites, Sacred Places*. London and New York.

Montelius, O. 1905. *Orienten och Europa*. Antiqvarisk tidskrift för Sverige. Stockholm.

Müller, S. 1898. De jydske Enkeltgrave fra Stenalderen. *Aarbøger for nordisk Oldkyndighed og Historie 1898*. Copenhagen.

– 1904. Vei og Bygd i Sten- og Bronzealdern. *Aarbøger for nordisk Oldkyndighed og Historie 1904*. Copenhagen.

Munkenberg, B-A. 1996. En boplats vid Kävlingeån från senare delen av mellanneolitikum. Arkeologisk undersökning för väg 934. *Riksantikvarieämbetet UV Väst Rapport*. Kungsbacka.

Munn, N. 1986. *Walbiri Iconography*. Chicago.

– 1918. *Oldtidens kunst* I. Copenhagen.

Nagmér, R. B. 1976. Arkeologisk undersökning 1972. Fornlämning 7. Bronsåldershög, Karaby. V. Karaby sn. *RAÄ Rapport: B 41*. Stockholm.

– 1979. Gravfält från äldre järnålder–vikingatid samt boplats från gropkeramisk tid, bronsålder och äldre järnålder, Stävie 4:1, Stävie socken, Skåne. Arkeologisk undersökning 1973–1975, 1977, 1978. *Riksantikvarieämbetet och Statens Historiska Museer Rapport* 1979:47. Lund.

– 1990. *Stävie 4:1, Stävie sn, Skåne*. Rapport. Riksantikvarieämbetet, Byrån för arkeologiska undersökningar, Lund.

– 1991. *St Harrie 28:4 m fl, St Harrie sn, Skåne*, 1988–1989. Delar av fornlämning 35. Undersökning av boplatslämningar. Riksantikvarieämbetet, Byrån för arkeologiska undersökningar, Lund.

Nagmér, R. B. & Räf, E. 1996. Boplats och grav. Stävie 4:1. Stävie socken. RAÄ 5. Stamledning P 30. In Räf, E. (ed.), Skåne på längden. *Riksantikvarieämbetet UV Syd Rapport* 1996:58. Lund.

Nash, G. 1997. *Semiotics of Landscape. Archaeology of mind*. BAR International Series 661. Oxford.

Needham, R. (ed.). 1973. *Right and Left. Essays on dual symbolic classification*. Chicago.

Nielsen, F. O. 1989. Nye fund fra stridsøksetiden på Bornholm. In Larsson, L. (ed.), *Stridsyxekultur i Syd-skandinavien*. University of Lund, Institute of Archae-ology, Report Series 36. Lund.

– 1996. *Forhistoriske interesser*. Bornholms Amtsråd. Rønne.

– 2000. Bornholms museums antikvariske arbejde. *Bornholms Museum, Bornholms Kunstmuseum* 1998–1999. Rønne.

– 2001. Evaluering af et regionalt stenalderprojekt. In Bergenstråhle, I. & Hellerström, S. (eds.), *Stenålders-forskning i fokus. Inblickar och utblickar i sydskandi-navisk stenåldersarkeologi*. Riksantikvarieämbetet, Arkeologiska undersökningar, Skrifter 39. University of Lund, Institute of Archaeology, Report Series 77. Lund.

Nielsen, F. O. & Nielsen, P. O. 1985. Middle and late Neolithic Houses at Limensgård, Bornholm. *Journal of Danish Archaeology* 4. Odense.

– 1990. The Funnel Beaker Culture on Bornholm – Some Results from Recent Excavations. In Jankowska, D. (ed.), *Die Trichterbecherkultur. Neue Forschungen und Hypotesen. Material des Internationalen Symposiums Dymaczewo, 20–24 September 1988*. Teil I. Poznan.

– 1991. The Middle Neolithic Settlement at Grødbygård, Bornholm. A local society in times of change. In Jennbert, K., Larsson, L., Petré, R. & Wyszomirska-Webart, B. (ed.), *Regions and Reflections. In Honour of Märta Strömberg*. Acta Archaeologica Lundensia 8°, No. 20. Lund.

Nielsen, P. O. 1977. Die Flintbeile der frühen Trichter-becherkultur in Dänemark. *Acta Archaeologica* 48. Copenhagen.

– 1979. De tyknakkede flintøkser kronologi. *Aarbøger for nordisk Oldkyndighed og Historie 1977*. Copenhagen.

– 1984. Flint axes and megaliths – the time and context of the early dolmens in Denmark. In Burenhult, G. (ed.), *The Archaeology of Carrowmore*. Theses and Papers in North European Archaeology 14. Stockholm.

– 1985. De første bønder. Nye fund fra den tidligaste Tragtbægerkultur ved Sigersted. *Aarbøger for nordisk Oldkyndighed og Historie 1984*. Copenhagen.

265

# N–P

– 1993. Bosættelsen. In Hvass, S. & Storgaard, B. (eds.), *Da klinger i muld ... 25 års arkæologi i Danmark*. Copenhagen.

– 1999. Limensgård och Grødbygård. Settlements with house remains from the Early, Middle and Late Neolithic on Bornholm. In Fabech, C. & Ringtved, J., *Settlement and Landscape. Proceedings of a conference in Århus, Denmark, May 4–7 1998*. Jutland Archaeological Society. Mosegård.

Nielsen, S. 1979. Den Grubkeramiske kultur i Norden samt nogle bemerkninger om flekkepilspidsene fra Hesselø. *Antikvariske Studier* 3. Copenhagen.

Nilsson, B. 2001. I fortgången av möten mellan det som består. Lösa arkeologiska tankar kring förändringsförnimmelse och förändringsmonument. *Tidskrift. Arkeologi i sydöstra Sverige* 1. Kalmar.

Nilsson, L. 1996. Osteologisk rapport. In Olson, T., Regnell, M., Nilsson, L., Erikson, M. & Brorsson, T., Boplatslämningar från neolitikum, bronsålder och äldre järnålder. Skåne, Väg 108, N Nöbbelövs, Stångby, Vallkärra och Lackalänga socknar, Lunds och Kävlinge kommuner. *Riksantikvarieämbetet UV Syd Rapport* 1996:60. Lund.

Nilsson, M.-L. 2000. Den U-formade rännan – ett mellanneolitiskt kulthus? In Kriig, S. (ed.), Från stenålder till medeltid i Särslöv. Skåne, Dagstorp sn, Dagstorp (SU 22), VKB SU 22. *Riksantikvarieämbetet UV Syd Rapport* 1999: 106. Lund.

Nilsson, M-L. & Nilsson, L. 2003. Ett källsprång i Saxtorp. In Svensson, M. (ed.), *Det neolitiska rummet. Skånska spår – arkeologi längs Västkustbanan*. Riksantikvarieämbetet, Lund.

Nilsson, T. 1948. *On the Application of the Scanian Post-Glacial Zone System to Danish Pollen-Diagrams*. Kgl. Danske Vidensk. Biol. Skr. 5. Copenhagen.

– 1964. Standardpollendiagramme und C14 Datierungen aus den Ageröds mosse im mittleren Schonen. *Lunds Universitets Årsskrift* (NF) 2, 59:7. Lund.

Nordquist, P. 2001. *Hierarkiseringsprocesser. Om konstruktionen av social ojämlikhet i Skåne, 5500–1100 f.Kr*. Studia Archaeologica Universitatis Umensis 13. Umeå.

Nyegaard, G. 1985. Faunalevn fra yngre stenalder på øerna syd for Fyn. In Skaarup, J., *Yngre Stenalder på Øerne Syd for Fyn*. Rudkøbing.

Olausson, D. 1983. Lithic technological analysis of the thin-butted flint axe. *Acta Archaeologica* 52. Copenhagen.

– 1997. Craft specialisation as an agent of social power in the south Scandinavian Neolithic. In Schild, R. & Sulgostowska, Z. (eds.), *Man and Flint*. Warsaw.

Oldeberg, A.1952. *Studien über die schwedische Bootaxtkultur*. Kungl. Vitterhets Historie och Antikvitets Akademin, Stockholm.

– 1974. *Die ältere Metallzeit in Schweden*. Monografier utgivna av Kungl. Vitterhets Historie och Antikvitets Akademin I. Stockholm.

Olson, T., Regnell, M., Nilsson, L., Erikson, M. & Brorsson, T. 1996. Boplatslämningar från neolitikum, bronsålder och äldre järnålder. Skåne, Väg 108, N Nöbbelövs, Stångby, Vallkärra och Lackalänga socknar, Lunds och Kävlinge kommuner. *Riksantikvarieämbetet UV Syd Rapport* 1996:60. Lund.

Olsson, M. 1991. Inventering och fornlämningsregister. Registrerade bronsåldershögar i Malmöhus län – en källkritisk studie. Photocopy. Arkeologiska institutionen, Lunds universitet.

Olsson, M. 2000. Det historiska källmaterialet. Kronobetet i källorna. In Thomasson, J., Cardell, A. & Olsson, M., " ... en kronan tillhörig ödegrund". Ett härläger eller en krog från slutet av 1500-talet intill bron vid Dysiæ. *Riksantikvarieämbetet UV Syd Rapport* 1999:91 Arkeologisk Undersökning. Lund.

Olsson, M. & Thomasson, J. 2001. Vad är en by och varför? Om den medeltida byns uppkomst och rationalitet. *Scandia* 2001:1. Lund.

Olsson, T. 1971. Rapport från Västra Karaby. *Ale* 1971:2. Lund.

Paludan-Møller, C. 1978. High Atlantic food gathering in northwest Zealand, ecological condition and spatial representation. In Kristiansen, K. & Paludan- Møller, C. (eds.), *New Directions in Archaeology*. The National Museum of Denmark. Copenhagen.

Parker-Pearson, M. & Richards, C. 1994. *Architecture and Order*. London.

Persson, L.-E. 1988. En mellanneolitisk boplats i Tostarp, St Harrie. Photocopy. Arkeologiska institutionen, Lund universitet.

Persson, O. 1982. An Osteological Analysis of Some Bones from a Settlement at Stävie 4:1. Appendix in Larsson, L., A Causewayed Enclosure and a Site with Valby Pottery at Stävie, Western Scania. *MLUHM* 1981–1982. Lund.

Persson, P. & Sjögren, K.-G. 1996. Radiocarbon and the Chronology of Scandinavian Megalithic Graves. *Journal of European Archaeology* 3:2. Avebury.

Petersson, B. & Hägerman, B.-M. 1997. Fornlämningar från neolitikum, bronsålder och järnålder vid Braån. Skåne, Örtofta sn, Örtofta 21:1. Arkeologisk slutundersökning, Etapp I–III 1993 och 1996. *Riksantikvarieämbetet UV Syd Rapport* 1997:12. Lund.

Petersson, H. 1999. *Några anmärkningar kring nittioåtta år av tidigneolitisk forskning. Källkritiska resonemang och teoretiska analyser*. Uppsats för Fil. Lic. examen, Institutionen för arkeologi, Göteborgs universitet. http://www.hum.gu.se/ark/. Accessed 20 Dec. 2000.

Petersson, M. & Nilsson, L. 1999. Hantverksspecialisering och (L)yxtillverkning under Neolitikum? En komparativ

# P–S

analys av boplats- och depåyxor från TN till MNB. Photocopy. Arkeologiska institutionen, Lunds universitet.

Petré, R. & Salomonsson, B. 1967. Gånggriften i Hög. *Ale* 1967:3. Lund.

Pettersson, C. B. 2000. I skuggan av Karaby backar. Boplatslämningar från senneolitikum till folkvandringstid. Skåne, Västra Karaby sn, RAÄ 35, Västra Karaby 2:21. Arkeologisk för- och slutundersökning. *Riksantikvarieämbetet UV Syd Rapport* 2000:103. Lund.

Pihl, H. & Runcis, J. 2001. Ett mellanneolitiskt flatmarksgravfält och flintverkstad i Borgeby. Skåne, Borgeby och Flädie socknar, RAÄ 7 m.fl. Riksantikvarieämbetet. *UV Syd, Dokumentation av fältarbetsfasen* 2001:3. Arkeologisk slutundersökning. Lund.

Prahl, G. & Streijffert, M. 1994. Stenbocksvallar. Studie av en senatlantisk kustboplats. Photocopy. Arkeologiska institutionen, Lunds universitet.

Prown, D. 1993. The truth of material culture: history or fiction? In Lubar, S. & Kingery, W. D. (eds.), *History from Things. Essays on material culture*. Washington.

Randsborg, K. 1975. Social Dimension of Early Neolithic Denmark. *Proceedings of the Prehistoric Society* 41. Cambridge.

Rappaport, R. A. 1999. *Ritual and Religion in the Making of Humanity*. Cambridge.

Rasmussen, L. W. & Boas, N. A. 1982. Kainsbakke og Kirial Bro. To bopladser fra den grubekeramiske kultur ved Grenå. In Kristiansen, K. & Tönnesen, A., *Antikvariske studier 5. Fortidsminder og bygningsbevaring*. Copenhagen.

Rasmussen, L. W. 1984. Kainsbakke A 47: A Settlement from the Pitted Ware Culture. *Journal of Danish Archaeology* 3. Odense.

– 1986. Forholdet mellem grubekeramisk kultur og enkeltgravskulturen i Danmark. In Adamsen, C. & Ebbesen, K. (eds.), *Stridsøksetid i Sydskandinavien. Beretning fra et symposium. 28.–30.X. 1985 i Vejle.* Arkæologiske skrifter 1. Copenhagen.

– 1993. Grubekeramiske bopladser. In Hvass, S. & Storgaard, B. (eds.), *Da klinger i muld ... 25 års arkæologi i Danmark*. Århus.

Regnell, M. 1996. Makrofossilanalys. In Olson, T., Regnell, M., Nilsson, L., Erikson, M. & Brorsson, T., Boplatslämningar från neolitikum, bronsålder och äldre järnålder. Skåne, Väg 108, N Nöbbelövs, Stångby, Vallkärra och Lackalänga socknar, Lunds och Kävlinge kommuner. *Riksantikvarieämbetet UV Syd Rapport* 1996:60. Lund.

Renfrew, C. 1973. *Before Civilisation. The Radiocarbon Revolution and Prehistoric Europe*. London.

– 1976. Megaliths, territories and populations. In De Laet, S. J. (ed.), *Acculturation and Continuity in Atlantic Europe mainly during the Neolithic period and the Bronze Age. Papers presented at the IV Atlantic colloquium, Ghent 1975*. Brugge.

Rey, P. P. 1979. Class Contradiction in Lineage Societies. *Critique of Anthropology* 4.

Ringgren, H. 1968. *Religionens form och funktion*. Stockholm.

Rønne, P. 1979. Høj over høj. *Skalk* 1979:5. Århus.

Rowley, C. D. 1986. *Recovery. The politics of Aboriginal reform*. Victoria.

Rowley-Conwy, P. 1983. Sedentary hunters: the Ertebølle example. In Bailey, G. N. (ed.), *Hunter-Gatherer Economy in Prehistory*. Cambridge.

– 1984. The Laziness of the Short-Distance Hunter. The origins of agriculture in western Denmark. *Journal of Anthropological Archaeology* 3. New York.

– 1985. The Origins of Agriculture in Denmark. A review of some theories. *Journal of Danish Archaeology* 4. Odense.

Rudebeck, E. 1994. Ängdala och meningen med arkeologin. *Arkeologi i Sverige* 3. Riksantikvarieämbetet, Stockholm.

– 1998. Flint Extraction, Axe Offering, and the Value of Cortex. In Edmonds, M. & Richards, C. (eds.), *Understanding the Neolithic of North-Western Europe*. Glasgow.

– 2002. En tidigneolitisk långhög i Kristineberg. In Larsson, L. (ed.), *Monumentala gravformer i det äldsta bondesamhället*. University of Lund, Department of Archaeology and Ancient History, Report Series 83. Lund.

Rudebeck, E. & Ödman, C. 2000. *Kristineberg. En gravplats under 4 500 år*. Malmöfynd 7. Stadsantikvariska avdelningen kultur Malmö.

Runcis, J. 2002. *Bärnstensbarnen. Bilder, berättelser och betraktelser*. Riksantikvarieämbetet, Arkeologiska undersökningar, Skrifter 41. Stockholm.

Rydbeck, O. 1930. Nordens äldsta bebyggelse. En sammanfattning och ett genmäle. *Fornvännen*. Stockholm.

Säfvestad, U. & Ersgård, L. 1999. Inledning. Vetenskapligt program för UV Syd 1999–2002. *Riksantikvarieämbetet Rapport UV Syd* 1999:35. Lund.

Sahlins, M. D. 1968. *Tribesmen. Foundation of Modern Anthropology Series*. New Jersey.

– 1972. *Stone Age Economics*. London.

Salomonsson, B. 1960a. En nyupptäckt stenåldersboplats i Järavallen. *Limhamniana*. Malmö.

– 1960b. (Unpublished report). Undersökning av stensättning och kulturlager. Hofterup nr 12, Hofterup sn. Antikvarisk-Topografiska Arkivet. Stockholm.

– 1971. Malmötraktens förhistoria. In Bjurling, O. (ed.), *Malmö Stads Historia*. Malmö.

Sandén, U. 1995. Bevare oss väl. En studie av megalitgravarnas bevaringsgrad på Söderslätt. Photocopy. Arkeologiska institutionen, Lunds universitet.

## S

Sarnäs, P. & Nord Paulsson, J. 2001. *Öresundsförbindelsen. Skjutbanorna 1B & Elinelund 2A–B*. Rapport över arkeologisk slutundersökning. Malmö Kulturmiljö.

Saunders, T. 1991. *Marxism and Archaeology. The Origins of Feudalism in Early Medieval England*. University of York, Department of Archaeology.

Service, R. E. 1958. *Profiles in Ethnology*. New York.

– 1962. *Primitive Social Organization*. New York.

Shanks, M. & Tilley, C. 1982. Ideology, symbolic power and ritual communication. A reinterpretation of Neolithic mortuary practices. In Hodder, I. (ed.), *Symbolic and Structural Archaeology*. Cambridge.

Siech, S. 2002. En plats på jorden. Ritual, ideologi och social förändring vid Långvägsmossens källsprång, Södra Sallerup. En kritisk studie av platsens betydelse ur ett socialantropologiskt perspektiv. Photocopy. Institutionen för arkeologi och antikens historia, Lunds universitet.

Simonsen, J. 1983. A Late Neolithic House Site at Tastum, North-Western Jutland. *Journal of Danish Archaeology* 2. Odense.

Sjöborg, N. H. 1815. *Försök till en nomenklatur för nordiska fornlemningar*. Stockholm.

– 1824. *Samling för Nordens fornälskare*. Stockholm.

Sjöström, A. 1992. Landskapsutnyttjande under neolitikum i Skåne. En jämförande studie av arkeologiska och pollenanalytiska parametrar. Photocopy. Arkeologiska institutionen, Lunds universitet.

Skaarup, J. 1985. *Yngre Stenalder på Øerne syd for Fyn*. Meddelelser fra Langelands museum. Rudkøbing.

– 1993. Megalitgrave. In Hvass, S. & Storgaard, B. (eds.), *Da klinger i muld... 25 års arkæologi i Danmark*. Århus.

– 2001. Status over de seneste årtiers stenaldersarkæologi i Danmark. In Bergenstråhle, I. & Hellerström, S. (eds.), *Stenåldersforskning i fokus. Inblickar och utblickar i sydskandinavisk stenåldersarkeologi*. Riksantikvarieämbetet, Arkeologiska undersökningar, Skrifter 39. University of Lund, Institute of Archaeology, Report Series 77. Lund.

Skov, T. 1982. A Late Neolithic House Site with Bell Beaker Pottery at Stendis, Northwestern Jutland. *Journal of Danish Archaeology* 1. Odense.

Smith, C. 1999. Ancestors, Place and People. Social landscapes in Aboriginal Australia. In Ucko, P. J. & Layton, R. (eds.), *The Archaeology and Anthropology of Landscape. Shaping your landscape*. One World Archaeology, New York.

Sørensen, H. H. 1998. *Spodsbjerg – en yngre stenalders boplads på Langeland*. Rudkøbing.

Staal, B. 1999. *Arkæologiske Udgravninger i Danmark 1998*. Copenhagen.

Stafford, M. 1999. *From Forager to Farmer in Flint. A Lithic Analysis of the Prehistoric Transition to Agriculture in Southern Scandinavia*. Aarhus.

Stenholm, L. 1986. *Ränderna går aldrig ur – en bebyggelsehistorisk studie av Blekinges dansktid*. Lund Studies in Medieval Archaeology 2. Lund.

Stilborg, O. 2003. Keramikhantverk i Välabäcksdalen. In Svensson, M. (ed.), *Det neolitiska rummet. Skånska spår – arkeologi längs Västkustbanan*. Riksantikvarieämbetet, Lund

Stjernquist, B. 1963. Präliminarien zu einer Untersuchung von Opferfunden. *MLUHM 1962–1963*. Lund.

– 1997. *The Röekillorna Spring. Spring-cults in Scandinavian prehistory*. Acta Regiae Societatis Litterarum Lundensis. Skrifter utgivna av Kungl. Humanistiska Vetenskapssamfundet i Lund. LXXXII. Lund.

Strassburg, J. 2000. *Shamanic Shadows. One Hundred Generations of Undead Subversion in Southern Scandinavia, 7000–4000 BC*. Stockholm Studies in Archaeology 20. Stockholm.

Strömberg, M. 1968. *Der Dolmen Trollasten in St. Köpinge, Schonen*. Acta Archaeologica Lundensia, Series in 8°, No. 7. Lund.

– 1971. *Die Megalithgräber von Hagestad. Zur Problematik von Grabbauten und Grabriten*. Acta Archaeologica Lundensia, Series in 8°, No. 9. Lund.

– 1978. Three Neolithic Sites. A Local Seriation? *MLUHM 1977–1978*. Lund.

– 1980. Siedlungssysteme in südschwedischen Megalithgräbergebieten. *Fundberichte aus Hessen 19/20, 1979/80*. Festschrift U. Fischer. Bonn.

– 1982a. *Ingelstorp. Zur Siedlingsentwicklung eines südswedischen Dorfes*. Acta Archaeologica Lundensia, Series in 4°, No. 14. Lund.

– 1982b. Specialized Neolithic Flint Production with a Hoard of Scrapers at Hagestad as an Example. *MLUHM 1981–1982*. Lund.

– 1988a. *Från bågskytt till medeltidsbonde*. Ystad.

– 1988b. A Complex Hunting and Production Area. Problems associated with a group of Neolithic Sites to the South of Hagestad. *MLUHM 1987–88*. Lund.

– 1988c. Exchange and Trade between Battle-Axe Groups? Some reflections concearning certain finds from southeast Scania. In Hårdh, B., Larsson, L., Olausson, D. & Petré, R. (eds.), *Trade and Exchange in Prehistory. Studies in honour of Berta Stjernquist*. Archaeologica Lundensia, Series in 8°, No. 16. Lund.

– 1989. Stridsyxekulturens representation i Hagestadsprojektets arbetsområde. In Larsson, L. (ed.), *Stridsyxekulturen i Sydskandinavien*. University of Lund, Institute of Archaeology, Report Series 36. Lund.

– 1990. Problems Concerning the Funnel Beaker Settlement in South-East Scania. In Jankowska, D. (ed.), *Die Trichterbecherkultur. Neue Forschungen und Hypotesen. Material des Internationalen Symposiums Dymaczewo, 20–24 September 1988*. Teil I. Poznan.

# S-W

Svensson, M. 1986. Trattbägarboplatsen "Hindby mosse" – aspekter på dess struktur och funktion. *Elbogen* 16:3. Malmö.
– 1991. A Palisade Enclosure in South-West Scania – a Site from the Battle-Axe Culture. In Jennbert, K., Larsson, L., Petré, R. & Wyszomirska-Webart, B. (ed.), *Regions and Reflections. In Honour of Märta Strömberg.* Acta Archaeologica Lundensia 8°, No. 20. Lund.
– 1993. Hindby offerkärr – en ovanlig och komplicerad fyndplats. *Fynd* 1993:1. Göteborg.
– 1998. Det neolitiska rummet. In Karsten, P. & Svensson, M., Projektprogram. I Stenåldersdalen. Det mesolitiska och neolitiska rummet. Projektprogram inför arkeologiska slutundersökningar av Järnvägen, delen Helsingborg–Kävlinge. Avsnittet Landskrona–Kävlinge. Riksantikvarieämbetet UV Syd Arbetshandling.
– 2002. Palisade Enclosures – The Second Generation of Enclosed Sites in the Neolithic of Northern Europe. In Gibson, A. (ed.), *Behind Wooden Walls: Neolithic Palisaded Enclosures in Europe.* BAR International Series 1013. Oxford.
– 2003. I det neolitiska rummet. *Skånska spår – arkeologi längs Västkustbanan.* Riksantikvarieämbetet, Lund.
Svensson, M., Pihl, H. & Andersson, M. 2001. Palissadkomplexet i Dösjebro. Seminariegrävning vårterminen 2000. Riksantikvarieämbetet Avdelningen för arkeologiska undersökningar. *Riksantikvarieämbetet UV Syd Rapport* 2001:8. Lund.

Tauber, H. 1986. C-14 dateringer af enkeltgravskultur i Danmark. In Adamsen, C. & Ebbesen, K. (eds.), *Stridsøksetid i Sydskandinavien. Beretning fra et symposium. 28.–30.X. 1985 i Vejle.* Arkæologiska skrifter 1. Copenhagen.
Terray, E. 1975. Classes and class consciousness in the Abron kingdom of Gyaman. In Bloch, M. (ed.), *Marxist Analyses and Social Anthropology.* London.
– 1979. On Exploitation. Elements of an autocritique. *Critique of Anthropology* 4.
Thomas, J. 1991. *Rethinking the Neolithic.* Cambridge.
– 1996. *Time, Culture and Identity. An interpretive archaeology.* London.
– 1999a. Towards a Regional Geography of the Neolithic. In Edmonds, M. & Richards, C. (eds.), *Understanding the Neolithic of North-Western Europe.* Glasgow.
– 1999b. *Understanding the Neolithic.* London.
Tilley, C. 1982a. *An Assessment of the Scanian Battle-Axe Tradition. Towards a social perspective.* Scripta Minora, Regiae Societatis Humaniorum Litterarum Lundensis. Studier utgivna av Kungl. Humanistiska Vetenskapssamfundet i Lund. 1981–1982:2. Lund.
– 1982b. Social Formation, Social Structures and Social Change. In Hodder, I. (ed.), *Symbolic and Structural Archaeology.* Cambridge.

– 1984. Ideology and the legitimation of power in the middle neolithic of southern Sweden. In Miller, D. & Tilley, C. (eds.), *Ideology, Power and Prehistory.* Cambridge.
– 1994. *A Phenomenology of Landscape. Place, paths and monuments.* Oxford.
– 1996. *An Ethnography of the Neolithic. Early prehistoric societies in southern Scandinavia.* Cambridge.
– 1999a. *The Dolmens and Passage Graves of Sweden. An introduction and guide.* Institute of Archaeology, University College London.
– 1999b. *Metaphor and the constitution of the world.* Oxford.
Troels-Smith, J. 1954. Ertebøllekultur-Bondekultur. Resultater af de sidste 10 aars undersøggelser i Aamosen. *Aarbøger for nordisk Oldkyndighed og Historie* 1953. Copenhagen.
– 1960. Ivy, Mistletoe and Elm. Climate Indicators – Fodder Plants. *Danmarks Geologiske Undersøgelse* IV, Bd. 4, No. 4. Copenhagen.
Tuan, Y-F. 1979. Thought and Landscape. The eye and the mind's eye. In Meinig, D. W. (ed.), *The Interpretation of Ordinary Landscapes.* Oxford.

Vang Petersen, P. 1982. Jægerfolket på Vedbækbopladserne. Kulturudviklingen i Kongemose- og Ertebølletid. *Nationalmuseets Arbejdsmark.* Copenhagen.
– 1993. *Flint fra Danmarks Oldtid.* Copenhagen.
Vemming Hansen, P. & Madsen, B. 1983. Flint Axe Manufacture in the Neolithic. An Experimental Investigation of a Flint Axe Manufacture Site at Hastrup Vænget, East Zealand. *Journal of Danish Archaeology* 2. Odense.

Wagner, R. 1975. *The Invention of Culture.* Englewood Cliffs.
Waterson, R. 1995. Houses and Hierarchies in Island Southeast Asia. In Carsten, J. & Hugh-Jones, S. (eds.), *About the House. Lévi-Strauss and beyond.* Cambridge.
Wattman, N. 1996. Kärragård en boplats och centralplats från trattbägarkultur till medeltid. *Arkeologiska Rapporter från Hallands länsmuseer* 1996:4. RAÄ 164. Kärragård 3:7, Laholm lfs, Halland.
Weiner, A. 1976. *Women of Value, Men of Renown.* Austin.
– 1985. Inalienable wealth. *American Ethnologist* 12. Washington.
Welinder, S. 1971. Överåda. A Pitted Ware Site in Eastern Sweden. *MLUHM* 1969–70. Lund.
– 1973. Den gropkeramiska kulturen. In Simonsen, P. & Sramsø Munch, G. (eds.), *Bonde-veidemann bofast-ikke bofast i nordisk forhistorie.* Tromsø Museums Skrifter XIV. Tromsø.
– 1976. The economy of the Pitted Ware Culture in Eastern Middle Sweden. *MLUHM* 1975–76. Lund.
– 1978. The Acculturation of the Pitted Ware Culture in Eastern Sweden. *MLUHM* 1977–78. Lund.

269

# W–Z

– 1998. Del 1. Neoliticum-Bronsålder, 3900–500 f.Kr.
In Myrdal, J. (ed.), *Det svenska jordbrukets historia.
Jordbrukets första femtusen år. 4000 f. Kr.–1000 e. Kr.*
Stockholm.

Werbart, B. 1999. De mänskliga kontakterna i Östersjö-
området. Yngre stenålderns fångstsamhällen. In
Burenhult, G. (ed.), *Arkeologi i Norden* 1. Stockholm.

Whittle, A. 1988. *Problems in Neolithic Archaeology.
New Studies in Archaeology.* Cambridge.

– 1996. *Europe in the Neolithic. The creation of new
worlds.* Cambridge.

Wihlborg, A. 1976. Arkeologisk undersökning 1971.
Mellanneolitisk boplats. Löddeköpinge, Löddeköpinge
sn, Skåne. Riksantikvarieämbetet. Arkeologiska undersökningar. *UV Syd Rapport* 1976 B:34. Lund.

Winther, J. 1926. *Lindø. En boplads fra Danmarks
Yngre Stenalder.* Første del. Rudkøbing.

– 1935. *Troldebjerg.* Rudkøbing.

Wolf, P. 1956. *Utdikad civilisation.* Lund.

Wyszomirska, B. 1975. Radiocarbon datings of a pitted/
comb ware complex from North-East Europe.
*MLUHM* 1973–1974. Lund.

– 1984. *Figurplastik och gravskick hos nord- och nord-
östeuropas neolitiska fångstkulturer.* Acta Archaeologica Lundensia, Series in 4°, No. 17. Lund.

– 1988. *Ekonomisk stabilitet vid kusten. Nymölla III.
En tidigneolitisk bosättning med fångstekonomi i
Nordöstra Skåne.* Acta Archaeologica Lundensia,
Series in 8°, No. 17. Lund.

Zvelebil, M. & Rowley-Conwy, P. 1984. Transition to
Farming in Northern Europe. A hunter-gatherer
perspective. *Norwegian Archaeological Review* 17.
Oslo.

## Personal communications

Gidlöf, Kristina. Malmö kulturmiljö.

Hulthén, Birgitta. Keramiska
forskningslaboratoriet, Lund.

Johansson, Tobias. Malmö kulturmiljö.

Larsson, Lars. Institutionen för arkeologi
och antikens historia, Lunds universitet.

Regnell, Mats. Riksantikvarieämbetet
UV Syd, Lund.

Sarnäs, Per. Malmö kulturmiljö.

Svensson, Mac. Riksantikvarieämbetet
UV Syd, Lund.